PETER NORTON'S

5TH EDITION

INSIDE the PC

PETER NORTON'S

5TH EDITION

INSIDE the PC

by *Peter Norton*

/////Brady

New York   London   Toronto   Sydney   Tokyo   Singapore

Copyright © 1993 by Peter Norton

Brady Publishing
A Division of Prentice Hall Computer Publishing
15 Columbus Circle
New York, NY 10023

ISBN: 1-56686-097-0

Library of Congress Catalog No.: 93-30681

Printing Code: The rightmost double-digit number is the year of the book's printing; the rightmost single-digit number is the number of the book's printing. For example, 93-1 shows that the first printing of the book occurred in 1993.

96 95 94 93   4 3 2 1

Manufactured in the United States of America

Acknowledgments

My thanks to Tom Badgett and Corey Sandler whose efforts and assistance have brought this revised edition to fruition.

I would also like to thank Scott Clark and Kevin Goldstein, of Book Line, and my agent Bill Gladstone, of Waterside Productions, for their efforts on my behalf.

Finally, I would like to thank Jono Hardjowirogo and Kristin Juba of Brady who helped put this book into its final form.

Credits

Michael Violano
Publisher

Jono Hardjowirogo
Acquisitions Director

Kelly D. Dobbs
Managing Editor

Kristin Juba
Production Editor

Joanna Arnott
Copy Editor

Lisa Rose
Editorial Assistant

Scott Cook
Imprint Manager

MaryBeth Wakefield
Production Analyst

Kevin Spear
Book Designer

Tim Amrhein
Cover Designer

Craig Small
Indexer

*Diana Bigham, Katy Bodenmiller, Brad Chinn, Tim Cox, Meshell Dinn,
Mark Enochs, Howard Jones, Beth Rago, Carrie Roth, Marc Shecter, Greg Simsic*
Production Team

Contents at a Glance

Contents

Introduction

This is the beginning of a marvelous voyage of discovery. With this book, you can look at the secrets, wonders, and mysteries inside your personal computer. If you already are familiar with earlier versions of this book, notice the change in the title. The personal computer world is much broader now than when I first started writing about the IBM PC. Although IBM remains a strong and important force in this industry, there now are many different designs produced by many different companies. These other designs also are a part of what makes up the personal computer family of hardware so common on—and under—today's desktops.

From the day it first appeared, the IBM PC stirred excitement and fascination: The PC marked the coming of age of "personal" computing, a drastic change from the days when all computers were managed by other people who doled out computer power to users on an as-needed, as-available basis. Today, the PC is solidly established as the power tool without equal for helping business and professional people improve their performance and the quality of their work. And, increasingly, students and home users are expanding personal computing to an ever-growing range of applications from homework to recipes, games, instruction, and research.

The original IBM PC also spawned a great many other computers—some from IBM, but most from the makers of IBM-compatible computers—that make up the PC family. (In this book, when I say "PC," I mean all computers in this family. This includes IBM's versions as well as the many enhanced and redesigned versions available from the hundreds of other companies that also produce powerful and popular personal computers.)

I am excited and enthusiastic about the PC family; I want to lead you into understanding the workings of this marvelous machine and to share with you the excitement of knowing what it is, how it works, and what it can do.

About This Book

This isn't a book for people who are having trouble finding the on/off switch on their computers. Instead, it's for people who have enough experience and curiosity to beginning examining in greater depth this wonderful family of machines. My goal is to make understanding the PC easy as well as fun.

This is, more than anything else, a book written to help you learn what you really need to know about the PC. You can very successfully use a PC without really understanding it. However, the better you understand your PC, the better equipped you are to realize the potential in the machine and—don't forget this—to deal with emergencies that can arise when working with a PC. After all, when something goes wrong, the better you understand the machine, the more likely you are to make the right moves to fix the problem and reduce its impact on you and your business.

There are many reasons you might want to understand the inner workings of your PC. One reason, a really good one, is simply for the intellectual satisfaction and sense of mastery that comes with understanding the tools with which you work. Another is to open up new realms for yourself. After all, there is plenty of demand these days for people who have PC savvy. But, perhaps the most practical reason is the one that I suggested above. By analogy, think back to the early days of the automobile when you had to be an amateur mechanic to safely set out on a journey by car. It doesn't take the skills of a mechanic to drive a car today because cars have been tamed for everyday use. I'd like it to be that way with computers, but, frankly, computing hasn't progressed that far. Today, to safely and successfully use a personal computer, you need some degree of expertise, and the more expertise you have, the better you can deal with the crises that sometimes arise.

If you know anything about me or the first edition of this book, you know that I made my reputation by explaining the technical wizardry of the PC. In the early days of the PC, that was what PC users needed most—an inside technical explanation of how the PC worked. The world of the PC has matured and changed since then, and so have the needs of mainstream PC users. Today, people still need to understand how their machines work and what it takes to make them sing, but the focus of people's needs has changed, so this new edition of *Inside the PC* has changed as well.

If you're looking for interesting and useful technical information about the PC from the inside out, you won't be disappointed. I am dedicated to making this book a guide to what makes the PC tick. But, just as the hardware has changed drastically over the past couple of years, so has the focus of the user. And, I address both the technology's and the users' changes.

To that end, I divide the material covered in this book into two types: first, the basic principals of theory and operation that I feel PC users want and need to know; and, second, the more detailed technical information for readers who really want to dig deeper into the underlying engineering that gets things done inside the PC.

It is easy for you to differentiate between these areas in this book. The sections that contain the heavier, technical stuff are introduced with a "Technical Notes" icon.

The advanced sections are for anyone who wants more than a practical understanding of the PC. When you see this symbol, you either can explore the technical details or skip those sections.

And, while this is primarily a book about PC hardware, you really can't separate the machine from the software that makes it do what it does. Thus, you also find some sample programs that you can use to show off some of the PC's capabilities, illustrate and exercise features of the machine, or just have some fun. Most of these programs are written in the BASIC programming language, so it should be relatively easy for you to try out what they have to show you by simply keying them in from the listings that appear.

I also talk a little about the operating systems that perform the housekeeping functions of running the machine and talking to the application software (spreadsheets, word processors, database managers, and so on). I show you some of the most important features of the various shells or user interface programs, such as Microsoft Windows, that help isolate you from the nuts-and-bolts of hardware operation.

You also find, at the end of most chapters, some exercises that you can use to test your understanding or to develop your PC skills. You can try these exercises as you read each chapter or use them for review after you have finished major sections. Simply read through them for additional information or step through them for some hands-on experience or enlightenment.

Some of these exercises involve BASIC programming, but don't let the concept of writing computer programs intimidate you. Everyone who has a PC can use BASIC: it comes free as part of DOS (the Disk Operating System). In the early days of PCs, users relied heavily on BASIC to make their computers perform because there weren't many commercial programs available. And, in the beginning, many of the programs used for business and personal applications were written in BASIC. By writing some of your own simple programs, you can develop a deeper understanding of how the hardware does what it does and can gain an appreciation for the complex, user-friendly, and capable software applications that are so much a part of today's PC.

The standard version of BASIC is called either BASICA (if you have IBM's DOS) or GW BASIC (if you have Microsoft's DOS). The languages are virtually identical. Starting with DOS version 5.0, a new form of BASIC, called QBasic, was included with DOS. Within this book, I use both versions. It is easy to tell which is which: the older BASICA/GW BASIC programs have line numbers; the more modern QBasic programs do not.

A Maze To Think About

For the fun of it, I wrote a little program in BASIC that illustrates what a lot of life is like, including learning about PCs. (You can find the listing for this program, called MAZE, in Appendix C, along with all of the longer programming examples.) Figure I.1 shows the program in progress. This program draws two boxes, START and FINISH, and works a path from one to the other. The program doesn't know where it's going, so it winds a random path until it stumbles onto the goal; however, when it gets there, it rewards you with some fanfare (as you can see if you run the full program).

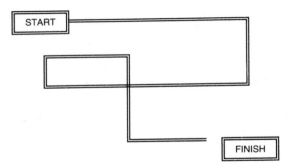

Figure I.1.   *The start-to-finish maze in progress.*

Fortunately, this book isn't like that. I help you work your way in a purposeful fashion toward the goal of understanding the PC. Sometimes, though, it can feel like the path from start to finish is as aimless as the operation of this program.

I offer this toy program for two reasons. The first is that you actually may find a use for it—for example, if you ever have to convince someone just how circuitous the path to success can be. The second reason is to provide a little food for thought.

One of the most important and valuable things to learn about your computer is just how complex a task it is to add polish and refinement to the programs it uses. If you understand that, then you're better prepared to understand the realities of the programs with which you work (or any programs you may want to design and build).

Some Things To Try

Here are some questions to ponder about the maze program before you plunge into Chapter 1 and explore the basic ideas of computers.

1. If you haven't already taken a peek at the maze program listing in Appendix C, ask yourself how complex a task it is to write a program that draws a random path from a box called START to one called FINISH and recognizes when it gets there. Write an outline—in English or in any programming language with which you're familiar—of a program to do this. How can you make sure that the lines don't run off the edge of the screen? How can you know when the program reaches its goal?

2. Take a look at the maze program listing. Is it longer and more complex (or shorter and simpler) than you thought it would be? If you know how to read a BASIC program, or if you can puzzle your way through it, check to see if this version includes any important details that yours didn't and vice versa.

3. As the maze program draws its path, it writes over any lines that already have been drawn. What if you want to recognize when you cross an old line or avoid retracing an existing line? Without getting into the programming specifics, try to work out the logical details that have to be added to the program. What details are most important? Which details might be called icing on the cake? Does adding a feature like this make the program much more complex? What does that suggest to you about the overall character of computer programs?

4. Remember that the basic PC hardware can't do anything by itself. Aside from checking itself for proper operation and loading the first information from a disk during the start-up process, the hardware—even though it is extremely powerful—can't do very much without sophisticated

instructions. These instructions must be excruciatingly detailed, must account for every conceivable contingency, and must be flexible enough to accommodate a wide variety of end-user needs.

The maze program can become rather complex, as evidenced by the questions I posed above. However, it is functioning at a very high level. The actual instructions that control your PC function at a much lower level.

Suppose that a person whom you do not know is sitting in a chair in the middle of the room. That is all you know about the situation. Now, think about what kind of instructions at the lowest possible level are required to instruct that person to stand, walk across the room, open the door, and exit.

You may be tempted to say something like "Stand up." But wait. I said at the lowest possible level, so you have to go behind the English language (or whatever language this unknown person may speak) to provide more basic instructions.

For example, you need to specify how much electrical energy must be sent along the thousands of nerve paths from the brain to all parts of the body to cause a specified amount of force to be applied at specific angles to specific muscles to cause the body to stand up. That's one level of instruction. Also going on in the background, however, are many layers of simultaneous instructions, including:

- Interpreting impulses from the semicircular canals to feedback information to the original muscle instructions to maintain balance

- Processing visual information from the eyes to help with balance and direction and to provide modifying instructions to the original muscle movement orders

- Noting and interpreting aural data to turn your spoken instructions into movement data

- Heart rate, breathing, and other basic life process instructions

You get the idea. While your PC is in no way as complex as your body, many of the same programming functions are required. There are low-level, background instructions that keep the machine functioning, there are environmental sampling functions that help it know what is happening (e.g., has a key been pressed, is the mouse moving), output processing (e.g., updating the display screen, sending information to a printer), and more.

Thankfully, most of people don't have to interact with the machine at this level (although designers and programmers do). But, by understanding at least part of what is going on inside the PC, you can have a better understanding of how it works, what it is capable of, what is wrong when it malfunctions, and what to do about it.

Ready to look at basic PC components and hardware types? If so, move on to Chapter 1.

Inside the PC

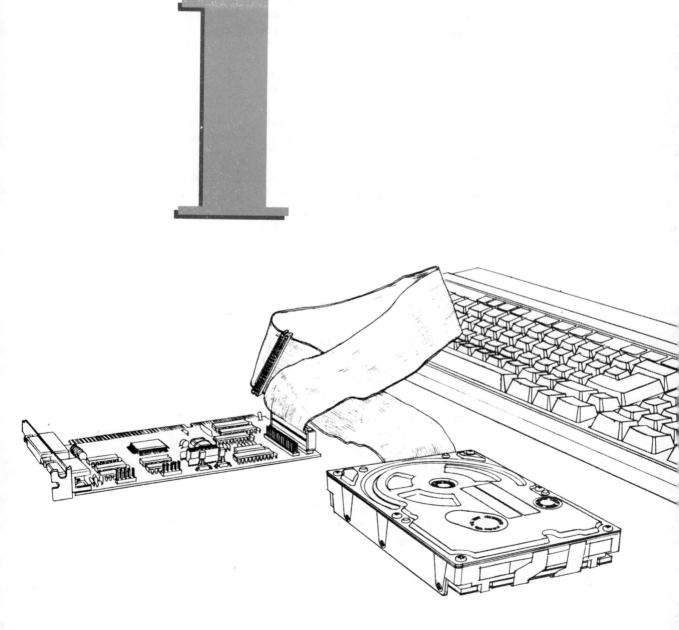

W hen I first started using computers, they weren't all that common. A few intrepid types had them in their workshops or studies and a few really adventurous people were using them for business applications. For the most part, however, people, if they were aware of computers at all, viewed them as something that somebody else needed. Moreover, the people who were computer savvy, who really understood the power and functionality computers offered, usually didn't believe the PC or anything like it was up to the job. The experienced believed that only minicomputers or even mainframes from giants such as Digital Equipment Corporation, Hewlett-Packard, Wang, IBM, and others could be trusted with real work.

That's not true today, of course. Computers are nearly everywhere and are capably handling jobs of all types. Even the most inflexible holdout has had to accept the ubiquitous nature of powerful desktop computers, which are many times more powerful than the megabuck marvels of a few years ago and easy enough for anybody to use.

Still, it's not always obvious just what is inside the box you're using or how these components work together. In this chapter, I show you how the basic personal computer is designed, introduce you to its major components, and help you find some specifics about the machine you're using. In Chapter 2, I revisit some of these components to offer additional detail on what they are and how they function.

Computer Components

There are five key parts to a computer. These include the processor (sometimes called the central processing unit, or CPU), the memory (of which there are several types), the input/output circuitry (I/O, as it usually is called), disk storage, and programs. There also are other components that form part of the packaging and support for these basics, such as the power supply, the motherboard, the bus (really part of the I/O interface), and the card cage. Figure 1.1 shows these basic components and how they fit together.

I take a quick look at each of these key parts here. Later in this chapter, I provide an overview of the basic computer types in common use today. The rest of the book is devoted to delving into the fascinating details of these topics and more.

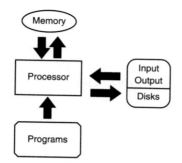

Figure 1.1. *The major components of a PC.*

System Board (Motherboard)

The motherboard concept was a new one when personal computers started gaining popularity. Before the miniaturization brought on by highly integrated circuits, individual portions of computers were housed on separate boards or even in separate sections made up of many boards. Today, however, the majority of the components that make up the computer proper are housed on a single printed circuit board called the system board or motherboard.

The usual components housed on the motherboard include the CPU and its support circuits, memory, I/O interface (serial port, parallel port, keyboard interface, disk interface, and so on), and bus (which enables the CPU to talk to other components that are not integrated with the motherboard). Figure 1.2 shows a typical motherboard with the major components labeled. Next I discuss each of the major components to give you an overview of their function.

The processor is the brain of the computer. It is the engine, the working heart, of this marvelous machine. The processor carries out the instructions to the computer at a very low level (see the discussion of computer function later in this chapter). In other words, the processor runs (executes) programs. The processor is the part that knows how to add and subtract and carry out simple logical operations. In a mainframe computer, the processor often is called a central processing unit, or CPU. In a microcomputer, like a PC, the processor is sometimes called a microprocessor, or just processor. These are the terms I use almost exclusively in this book. Although early PCs used a single, common type of processor, today's collection of hardware uses a wide variety of processors. Nevertheless, all IBM-compatible PC processors are based on the same basic family of processors, the Intel 86 family. In Chapter 3, I cover the different types of PC processors and some specifics of what they can do.

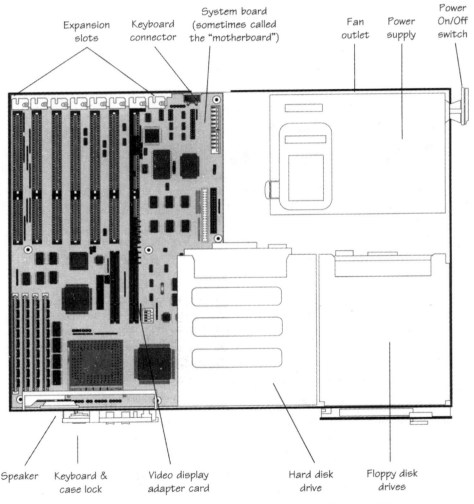

Figure 1.2.   *A typical PC motherboard. (Drawing courtesy of Gateway 2000.)*

A computer's memory is nothing like a person's memory, so the term can be misleading until you understand what a computer's memory is and what it's used for. The memory is the computer's workplace. It's analogous to the desktop of an office worker, the workbench of a carpenter, or the playing field of a sports team. The computer's memory is where all activity takes place. The analogy to a workbench is particularly good because it helps you understand when the amount of memory is important and when it's not.

Like the size of a workbench, the size of a computer's memory sets a practical limit on the kinds of work that the computer can undertake. A handyman's skills and other factors are really the most important things in determining what the handyman can and cannot do. The size of the workplace matters as well. The same is true with computers. That's why you often see computers rated by the amount of memory they have, usually in megabytes (MB)—millions of bytes—and sometimes in kilobytes (KB)—thousands of bytes. (You learn more about measuring memory and other data factors in Chapter 16.) For example, when the IBM PS/2 model 75 computer was announced, it came with a minimum of 8MB of memory, which today is about the minimum reasonable configuration. When I first started working with computers, on the other hand, the basic models had as little as 256KB of memory. Things have certainly changed!

Input/output, or I/O, is how the computer takes in and sends out data. It includes what you type on the keyboard and what the computer shows on the video display screen or prints on the printer. Every time the computer is taking in or sending out data, it is doing I/O using I/O devices, which also are called peripheral devices. Among the many kinds of I/O devices is one that's so important to the operation of the computer that I single it out as the next of the five key parts of a computer, disk storage.

Disk storage is a very important kind of I/O. It's the computer's reference library, filing cabinet, and toolbox all rolled into one. Disk storage is where the computer keeps data when it's not in use in the computer's memory. Data can be stored in other ways, but disks are the most practical and important medium for storing data.

Programs are the last of the five key parts of a computer. They are what bring the computer to life, make it go, and turn it from a heap of fancy parts into a powerful working tool. Programs are the instructions that tell the computer what to do.

With that simple summary out of the way, I give you a slightly more detailed look at each of these key parts. Bear in mind that the real details come in the following chapters.

The Processor

The processor is the part of the computer designed to carry out or execute programs. The whole point of the computer is to carry out a series of steps called a program. Thus, both the purpose and the internal organization of the computer come together in this key component. To perform this miracle, the processor must have particular capabilities. The first is the capability to read and write information in the computer's memory. This is critical because both the program instructions that the processor carries out and the data on which the processor works are stored temporarily in that memory. The next capability is to recognize and execute a series of commands or instructions provided by the programs. The last is the capability to tell the other parts of the computer what to do so that the processor can orchestrate the operation of the computer.

As you might imagine, the way the processor carries out its assigned tasks and the way it acquires these varied skills are complex matters. Chapters 3 and 4 tell you how the processor performs its magic.

Throughout this book, I talk about programs and data. To the processor, the distinction between programs and data is vital. The program tells the processor what to do, and the data is what the program acts on. Not every part of the computer makes this distinction, as you see shortly.

Memory

Memory is where the computer's processor finds programs and data when it is doing its assigned task. As I have mentioned, the memory is the activity center, the place where everything is kept when it's being worked on. For you to understand your computer, you must understand that the computer's memory is just a temporary space (like a scratch pad or chalkboard) where the computer scribbles while work is being done. Unlike our memories, the computer's memory is not a permanent repository. Instead, the computer's memory simply provides a place where computing can happen. It is the playing field where the game of computing is played. After each game, the memory playing field is relinquished to the next team and the next game.

While the computer's processor makes a vital distinction between programs and data, the computer's memory does not. To the computer's memory (and to many other parts of the computer) there is no difference between programs and data—both are information to be recorded temporarily. A piece of paper neither knows nor cares what you write on it—a love poem, your bank balance, or instructions to a friend. It is the same with the computer's memory. Only the processor recognizes the difference between programs and data. To the computer's memory and also to the I/O devices and disk storage, a program is just more data, more information that can be stored, moved, or manipulated.

The computer's memory is more like a chalkboard than a piece of paper in that nothing is permanently recorded on it. Anything can be written on any part of the memory, and the writing can be changed in a wink by writing over it. Unlike a chalkboard, the computer's memory doesn't have to be erased before something new can be written to it; the mere act of writing information to the computer's memory automatically erases what was there before. Reading information from the memory is as simple and as straightforward as reading anything written on paper or a chalkboard. Both the processor and the I/O devices have the capability to read (and write) data from and to the memory.

The processor and the memory by themselves make up a closed world. I/O devices open that world and enable it to communicate with us. An I/O device is anything, other than memory, with which the computer communicates. As I've mentioned, these devices include the keyboard, the display screen, the mouse, the printer, a telephone line connected to the computer, and any other channel of communication into or out of the computer. Taken together, I/O is the computer's window on the world—the thing that keeps the processor and memory from being a closed and useless circle. The later chapters help you understand I/O devices.

I/O Devices

In general, I can say that the I/O devices with which the computer works have the user as their real target. I/O devices are an interface between the user and the computer. The computer sees what the user types on the keyboard; the user sees what the computer writes on the printer or displays on the screen.

However, there is one special category of I/O that is intended only for the computer's private use: the disk storage devices. Information on disk can't be read or written by users and is not for users; it can be read and written only by the computer. Disk storage is the computer's library, toolbox, and lumberyard. It's where the computer keeps its instruction manuals (programs), raw materials (data), and any other information it needs to have on tap.

Programs

Finally, you have to consider programs. Programs tell the computer what to do. As it turns out, there are two very different kinds of programs, and you need to know the difference. The two kinds of programs are systems and applications programs. All programs accomplish some kind of work. Systems programs help operate the computer; in fact, the inner workings of a computer are so complex that you cannot get them to work without the help of systems programs. An applications program carries out the task that you want done, whether it's adding up a column of numbers or checking the spelling of something you've written. In summary, applications programs get our work done, and systems programs help the computer manage itself (and carry out the work).

Some of the systems programs that the IBM PC needs to manage its operations are permanently built into it. These are called the ROM programs because they are permanently stored in read-only memory (unlike the rewritable main memory that I've been discussing). These kinds of systems programs do the most fundamental kind of supervisory and support work, such as providing essential services that all the application programs use. These service programs are called the Basic Input/Output Services, often referred to as the BIOS or ROM-BIOS.

Other systems programs build on the foundation created by the ROM-BIOS program and provide a higher level of support services. Operating systems, such as the PC's familiar DOS, are examples of these higher-level systems programs that aren't built into the computer (although there are a few computers that do come with the operating system stored in ROM). Systems programs are among the major topics discussed in the rest of this book. Although applications programs are very important and discussed later, systems programs are a more important topic right now. That's because the goal of this book is to help you understand the workings and the potential of the PC, both of which are tied closely to the PC's systems programs.

This outline of the computer gives you a good starting point. However, there are some additional components that also are important. These are discussed in the next sections. At the end of this chapter, I explain what it is that the computer—particularly the computer's processor—can and can't do for you.

Power Supply

The computer is an electrical device. It needs power for all of its components to function properly. And, while you plug the computer into the wall to connect it to 110-volt alternating current, this is not the kind of power the machine uses. Instead, the chord from the wall plug attaches to a power supply, an electronic device that converts the standard household current that runs your vacuum cleaner and microwave oven into a form the computer can use.

This power supply takes in a nominal 110-volt alternating current and puts out 5- and 12-volt direct current. Direct current does not change directions from negative to positive like alternating current; instead, it provides a constant voltage at a fixed polarity. Direct current is the type of current supplied by your car battery and is the type of power your computer needs.

Power supplies are rated in several ways. However, as a consumer of computers, you probably will deal with the power rating of the supply, expressed in watts. A watt is a measure of the capacity of a power device and is the product of the voltage and the current supplied by the device. Even though today's devices offer more features and capabilities than ever before, a 200-watt power supply can operate almost any personal computer today because of large-scale integration and low-power designs.

Card Cage

As I mentioned earlier in this chapter, the majority of the components that make up the computer proper are located on a single printed circuit board called the motherboard. However, there are times when you need to attach other devices to the motherboard so that they can work with the processor and other computer components. This frequently is done by plugging an expansion card into one of the bus (I/O) connectors on the motherboard.

When you add an expansion card, it plugs into a slot on the motherboard and rests perpendicular to the motherboard. A card (or cards) attached to the main computer in this way resides in a card cage that helps protect it, provides physical stability, and helps provide air circulation to keep it cool. Early computer designs contained elaborate card cages; today, the card cage may consist of merely a card guide on one end and a screw terminal on the other to hold the card in place. When you install the cover on the computer case, the top of the cover and the bottom of the case together form a cage of sorts to cradle any expansion cards you may have installed.

Computer Types

Desktop and deskside computers come in a wide variety of designs. All of them, strictly speaking, are "personal" computers in that they are small, relatively inexpensive, and designed primarily for use by one person, or at least one person at a time. These computers include designs from Apple, Commodore, and other companies. However, the computers these companies produce generally are not referred to as PCs because they use microprocessors that aren't part of the conventional IBM-compatible PC design.

The PC moniker generally applies only to computers based on the Intel 86 family of microprocessors and compatibles. This started with IBM's original Personal Computer, which was based on the Intel 8088 processor and quickly labeled PC when it reached the market in the early 1980s. (For more information on IBM's early machines and some general PC history, see Appendixes A and B.)

Even with this limitation, there are many PC designs. In this section, I provide an overview of these basic designs to set the stage for conventions and terms used in the rest of this book.

IBM PCs, PS/1s, and PS/2s

IBM is the company that started it all. There were many other personal computers on the market before IBM released its version, but these computers lacked the backing of a big company, suffered from shaky or nonexisting standards, and failed to develop a dedicated business following. All of this changed when IBM released its machine with open architecture.

For a while, only IBM manufactured and sold the PC design. Before long, however, a number of other companies released compatible designs of their own. Today the tables have practically turned; instead of assessing a non-IBM computer on the basis of its compatibility with the original IBM design, many users are concerned with how well these machines match one or more of the industry-wide standards. The questions asked today to judge PC compatibility include the following:

- Which bus does it use?

- Which processor does it use?

- What operating system does it use?

- What type of display adapter and monitor does it use?

A few years ago users might have asked simply, "Is it PC compatible?" meaning will it accept expansion cards designed for IBM personal computers and run software written for IBM personal computers.

Now, it is IBM with its PS/1 and PS/2 designs that has stepped slightly away from the original design to produce a machine uniquely its own. The new IBM machines run software designed for other PCs, but there are some hardware issues—such as display adapter compatibility or bus structure—that tend to set off the current IBM offerings from other designs generally available in the computer marketplace.

For example, by far the majority of PCs sold today use the ISA (Industry Standard Architecture) expansion and I/O bus. This is sometimes referred to as the AT bus because it is the bus around which the original IBM PC/AT was built. Nearly all of IBM's current machines, on the other hand, now use the MCA (Micro Channel Architecture) bus, which is not compatible with the more common ISA bus.

PC Clones

The fact is that most of the personal computers sold today don't come from IBM. Most are designed, built, and sold by one of the dozens of high-profile manufacturers who offer a wide range of PCs for business, education, and home use. These machines used to be called "clones" because they were made to look, feel, and work like an IBM PC although they weren't built by IBM. As I've said, these manufacturers aren't really copying anybody now because they have gone off in their own direction, and IBM has changed its design. However, the clone name seems destined to stay with these machines, at least for the time being.

This section takes a broad overview of these clones. More detail is available in later chapters.

ATs, 386s, and 486s

While IBM's machines are given names reminiscent of minicomputer designations of a few years ago (for example, PS-2 M57 or PS/2 model 90), most clone manufacturers base their machine names on the type of processor inside. Thus, a Gateway 2000 (the company name) machine designated as a 4DX2-66V is interpreted easily: it's an 80486 processor using a DX2 speed doubling design, running at 66MHz, and using local bus video.

Another manufacturer might offer a model called simply a 386-33 to show that the machine uses an 80386 processor rated at 33MHz. You don't know what other design features it may have, but you know, at least, what processor it uses.

In fact, the majority of today's PCs are AT-type machines (there are fewer and fewer of these), 386-based machines, or 486-based machines. The AT-type machines use an 80286 processor, while the 386 and 486 designs use 80386 or 80486 processors, respectively. I give you a lot more information on these processors later in this book, so don't worry if all these numbers are rattling around inside your head. The point is to show you general conventions within the industry so that you can begin to interpret the advertising you read, understand a little better the specifications of your machine, and have some common ground for discussion in the rest of this book.

Servers and Disk Arrays

Servers and disk arrays are network configurations of personal computers. Networks enable multiple computers and their users to share processing power, disk storage, printers, and other peripheral devices.

Most of the computers already discussed also can function as a server or as the controller for a disk array. In fact, personal computers increasingly are evolving peer-to-peer relationships where the differentiation between clients or workstations and servers that operate as a network repository is becoming less. A server is usually a high-end PC (one with a lot of memory and one or more large disks for storage) dedicated to managing network traffic, storing common programs or data used by many people across the network, or directing communications data via telephone lines or dedicated links outside of the local network.

The server concept evolved because traditional networking required considerable processor power and above average storage to manage the many requests for processing and data from attached users. Many popular networks today require less computer resources than before and, at the same time, individual users' machines have gotten more powerful. The result is that, for many network installations, one machine is pretty much like another, each functioning as a server when it is handling requests from other network machines and acting as a client when it asks another machine for information or processing.

A disk array is a special kind of server that uses a large portion of its processor power simply to manage I/O for a large collection of disk drives. Whereas a regular PC may contain one or two hard drives with a total of 500–1,000MB of storage, a disk array may contain many times this much room for programs and data.

But How Does It Work?

Computers are based on the simple idea of modeling, or imitation. Radios and compact disc players work that way too, and if you pause to think about them, you can understand your computers more easily.

When you play a compact disc, you hear music even though there are no musicians inside the CD player. Instead, the disc contains an electronic model or imitation of the sound. Radios and CD players exist because someone discovered a way to capture a mechanical or electronic imitation of sound and build machines that can reproduce the sounds. The same sort of thing goes on with the visual images provided by television and motion pictures.

Computers do essentially the same thing, but they do it with numbers and arithmetic. The most fundamental thing that goes on within a computer is that the computer imitates and creates an electronic working model of numbers and arithmetic.

If you set out to invent a machine that can do arithmetic, you must find a way to match what machines can do with whatever the essence of arithmetic is. Needless to say, accomplishing this calls for a great deal of intellectual creativity and some heavy-duty mathematical theory. Essentially, a meeting ground had to be found where math and machines could merge. This meeting ground is binary arithmetic.

The numbers that you and I work with are based on the number 10. The decimal number system works with 10 symbols—0, 1, 2, ... 9—and builds numbers using these 10 symbols. However, there is nothing fundamental about the decimal system; you can base numbers on any quantity of symbols. Math theory and some simple exercises demonstrate that you can write the same numbers and do the same arithmetic operations in any number system. However, you cannot use a number system smaller than 2; the binary, or base 2, number system captures the smallest essence of what information is.

This is important for hardware designers. It is very easy to make a machine, particularly an electronic machine, that models binary numbers. A binary number is written with two symbols, 0 and 1 (just as decimal numbers are written with 10 symbols). Electric parts, such as switches, naturally have two states: on or off. It's easy to see that an on/off switch can represent a binary 0 or 1. In fact, it's such a natural connection that you see the power switches on many appliances and machines, including computers, labeled 0 and 1 for off and on, respectively.

Of course, it's a giant step between seeing that a switch or an electric currentcan represent a 1 or a 0 and having a computer that can perform complex calculations. However, it shouldn't be too hard to see how this electronic model of a simple binary number can be elaborated upon or built into something much larger. It's like knowing that, after children have learned to write simple sentences, they can grow up to write essays, term papers, and books. A lot of work is required, and many complicated steps are involved, but the basic idea is clear enough.

That's the foundation on which computers are built. Information, including numbers and arithmetic, can be represented in a binary form; electronic parts, such as switches that are turned on and off, are binary at heart. Using switches and other parts, an electronic machine can model numbers and all other forms of information.

At this level, a computer would be very difficult to use. In fact, this is how early microcomputer users interacted with their machines. They flipped switches on the front panel to set the on and off state of specific memory locations that in turn had to be specified by setting another series of switches in binary format.

Today, using a computer is much easier because the hardware and firmware are more sophisticated and because you have the benefit of high-level software that enables you to interact with the hardware at a very different level.

For more information on the software aspects of your computer system, see Chapters 20–24.

Your Computer

What kind of computer do you have? Now may be a good time to conduct a little inventory of your system. If you already know about your computer—if you know what kind of processor, how much memory, the type of display, and so on, that it has—you can skip this section. If, on the other hand, you are interested in the things I have discussed so far, but don't have a clue about how your computer fits into it all, read this section to know more than the average user.

First, it might be useful to make this little inventory exercise somewhat more formal. If you like, use a piece of paper to design a simple chart, such as the one in figure 1.3 to help you record various features of your machine. The sample I have shown here includes more detail than I cover in this section, but you can fill in the other blanks as you read through other sections of this book.

Personal Computer Inventory

Manufacturer	
Model	
Case Design	
CPU	
System Speed	
BIOS	
Base Memory	
Upper Memory	
Floppy A:	
Floppy B:	
Hard Disk	
Network	
Mouse	
Display Adapter	
Monitor	
Other adapters	
Operating System Version	

Figure 1.3.   *A sample personal computer inventory sheet.*

Start by issuing a few DOS commands to see what you can learn about your system. Turn on the computer and wait until the DOS prompt is displayed. This should be something like:

```
C:\>
```

If your computer is configured to start Windows or another user interface automatically, use the appropriate command to return to DOS. In Microsoft Windows you must click on File, choose Exit, and then press Enter when Windows asks for confirmation that you want to leave Windows.

Type the following:

```
VER
```

(When you type a command in DOS, you need to press Enter or Return after typing the command. That tells DOS you have entered all of the letters that make up the command. When you press Enter, DOS starts processing the command.)

You should see a display similar to this:

```
MS-DOS Version 6.0
```

Your version number may be different from this, but this command tells DOS to display its version number. Write down the results in the appropriate column of your computer inventory chart. This gives you some insight to the machine you are using. If your DOS is earlier than 5.0, it probably has been a long time since your system was updated. Your computer may contain a lot of relatively old software, and it is time for a general housecleaning and updating.

If the version is 5.0 or later, your system has been updated fairly recently (particularly if it says 6.0). This means the rest of the software you are running probably is current as well. DOS 6.0 is the latest version of DOS available as this book goes to press.

What else can you learn about your system? Do you know how large a hard drive you are using or how much memory you have? Use the CHKDSK command at the DOS prompt to find out. You should get a display similar to this:

```
Volume GATEWAY2000 created 05-05-1993 12:08p
Volume Serial Number is 2950-15EB

340746240 bytes total disk space
 48758784 bytes in 8 hidden files
  1409024 bytes in 170 directories
281346048 bytes in 3330 user files
  9232384 bytes available on disk

     8192 bytes in each allocation unit
    41595 total allocation units on disk
     1127 available allocation units on disk
   655360 total bytes memory
   615264 bytes free
```

(If you receive an error message, such as Bad Command or File Name, when you issue a DOS command it means one of two things. Either these files are not on your system or (more likely) they reside in a subdirectory for which there is no path. Locate the directory that contains your DOS files (normally C:\DOS) and make that directory the default. Then try the command again.)

The CHKDSK (Check Disk) command, a part of DOS, examines your hard drive for error conditions (although it is no substitute for a really thorough disk utility) and reports the total size of the disk, how many files are stored there, and the space remaining. Additionally, CHKDSK reports on the total amount of conventional memory in your system and tells you how much is still available. In the example, a total of 655,360 bytes of conventional memory exists and 614,264 of it is available for use. This test machine also contains another 16MB of extended RAM, but CHKDSK doesn't report that.

You can find out something about the way your system is using upper memory, however, with the MEM command, which also is a part of DOS. In its simplest form, MEM reports on available conventional and upper memory. Type the following:

```
MEM
```

You should get a display similar to the one below:

Memory Type	Total	=	Used	+	Free
— — — — — — —	— —		— —		— —
Conventional	640K		39K		601K
Upper	167K		167K		0K
Adapter RAM/ROM	0K		0K		0K
Extended (XMS)	14937K		13913K		1024K
— — — — — — —	— —		— —		— —
Total memory	15744K		14119K		1625K
Total under 1 MB	807K		206K		601K

```
Largest executable program size         601K   (614976 bytes)
Largest free upper memory block          0K       (0 bytes)
MS-DOS is resident in the high memory area.
```

Now you know a little more about the internal workings of this particular machine. You know the largest executable program size, for one thing. Notice that when CHKDSK was run a larger amount of available RAM was reported. This is probably because the available RAM is broken up into more than one segment and programs need contiguous memory to execute. In this case, 614,976 bytes is the largest program you can run.

With MEM you also get a report on memory above 640KB. This machine has a total memory of 16MB, as you can see from the MEM report. Some of the conventional memory (between 0 and 640KB) is in use, but there is some available memory in this area. However, all of the memory above 640KB is in use on this machine. That's because this report was generated inside a DOS partition within Microsoft Windows. When you start Windows, all available memory is taken over so that Windows can manage it for you.

Your MEM report may not look exactly like this, but it should be similar. This sample report was done in DOS 6.0; if you are using an earlier version the format is different. The report varies with the amount of memory in your machine, what software is running, and so on.

The MEM command has a number of switches you can use to get different information. For example, to find out what programs are running where, use this version of the command:

```
MEM /C
```

Try it on your machine and see what happens. It is an interesting way to look into your computer's memory and find out what is running there. Notice that you have discovered a fair amount of information about your computer without really looking at the physical computer. You have used built-in features of the machine to tell you what you want to know. Isn't that what computers are supposed to do anyway, relieve you of redundant, menial tasks?

Now go a step further. If you are running Windows 3.1 or DOS 6.0, you have another built-in utility that can tell you a lot more about your machine. Type the following command at the DOS prompt and see what happens:

MSD

This is the Microsoft System Diagnostics, a utility that scans your system hardware and software and displays a summary screen like the one in figure 1.4.

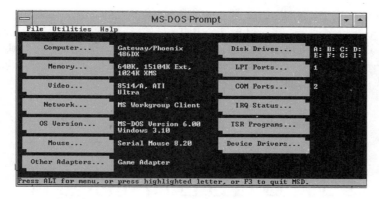

Figure 1.4. *An MSD screen.*

This is an extremely valuable report, and you can click on any of the topic buttons to open windows with additional information. You can see from figure 1.4 that the computer is a Gateway 2000 with an 80486 processor. You also can see the amount of memory, the type of video display, the operating system version, and more. Again, if you are running a version of Windows before 3.1 and DOS prior to 6.0, you do not have access to MSD. If you have it, it is an easy way to learn some interesting information about your computer; if you don't have it, you still can get a lot of this information in other ways. I show you how a little later.

What else do you need to know about your system? You might be interested in the type of keyboard you have. There are two basic types with an almost unlimited number of variations on each. The original PCs used a keyboard with about 84 keys, similar to the one in figure 1.5.

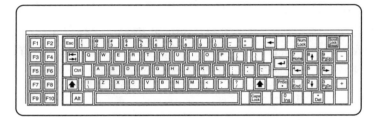

Figure 1.5.   *An 84-key PC keyboard.*

Many keyboard manufacturers still produce a keyboard similar to this one for people who have became accustomed to the small footprint of this keyboard or for users who simply don't want to take up a lot of desktop space. The enhanced keyboard (see fig. 1.6) is the most common design on newer machines. This keyboard is larger and has about 101 keys.

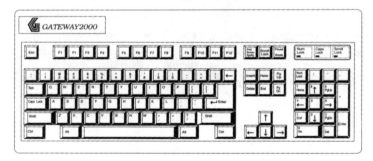

Figure 1.6.   *An enhanced 101-key PC keyboard. (Drawing courtesy of Gateway 2000.)*

What type does your computer have? How does it differ from the samples shown here? Write down a description or model number in the space available on your computer inventory sheet.

Later in this book, I ask you to take the covers off of your machine for some real "inside" information. For now, settle for what you can learn from the outside.

When you look at your PC, you see three main physical parts. First, there is the box, called the system unit, which holds most of the computer. Next is the keyboard. Finally, there's the display. All PCs are small, but the smallest ones sit right on the desktop, with the display on top. (The portables, including notebooks and laptops, of course, have the displays built into the system unit.) Larger computers stand up-right on the floor. Take a look at the system unit case of your PC. There are three general types: compact desktop, standard desktop, and tower (assuming you don't count the portables).

If your machine is designed to sit on the floor, like the one in figure 1.7, it is a tower.

Figure 1.7. *A deskside tower PC. (Photo courtesy of IBM.)*

Notice that a lot of users place desktop machines on the floor instead of on top of the desk. If you are using a tower, the disk drives are oriented so that the floppies are inserted horizontally, parallel to the floor. If yours is really a desktop machine sit-ting on its side on the floor, it's a good bet that the floppies are inserted vertically, perpendicular to the floor. What kind do you have?

The advantage to the tower design is obvious if you want to place the system unit on the floor. The tower is oriented so that the disk drives are easy to access. And, when you place the main system unit on the floor, you clear up a lot of desktop space. Tower designs usually have more room for internal disk drives, both those you can access from the front panel and those that are hidden inside the case. Tower power sup-plies sometimes supply more power than desktop designs.

The disadvantages to the tower case include its size, if you have limited room around your desk or if you sometimes move your office computer from desk to desk, and its cost. Most manufacturers extract an additional fee to package the computer components in a tower instead of one of the desktop designs. This is minor, however, and usually ranges from $100 to $150.

A full-sized desktop machine looks like the one in figure 1.8. It has room for three or four disk drives that you can access from the front panel and one or two internal bays to hold a hard drive. There also probably is room for eight expansion cards.

Figure 1.8.   *A full-sized desktop computer. (Photo courtesy of IBM.)*

This is more or less the "standard" PC case and it can take on several styles, depending on the manufacturer. The advantage to this case design is it is big enough to hold a reasonable number of expansion cards and disk drives, yet small enough to sit on your desk with the monitor on top and the keyboard in front. As the standard PC case, the full-sized desktop enclosure usually is included in the price of the basic machine; you don't usually pay extra for this case design.

The disadvantage to this design is also its size. For many users, it is too thick (tall) to sit on the desk with the monitor on top. For many people, the size of this case places the monitor too high for comfortable viewing. And, because it is designed to sit on the desk, it isn't always that easy to put it on the floor. You can do it, and there are third-party add-ons to hold your desktop case in a firm, deskside position. Still, the disk drives are oriented the wrong way when you do this. And, when you purchase a complete system designed around the standard, full-size case, monitor and power cables frequently are too short to reach the system case if you place it on the floor.

There also is a compact desktop case that is popular today. These look similar to the one in figure 1.9.

Figure 1.9. *A compact desktop computer. (Photo courtesy of IBM.)*

The advantage to this design is that the computer takes up a minimal amount of desk space. It also isn't very tall, so it is easy to sit a monitor on top without having to stretch your neck to view it. The disadvantage is that there may be only one drive bay accessible from the front. There probably is only one drive slot inside, and you may have room for only two or three expansion cards. However, motherboards designed for these compact cases frequently have more built into them, so you may not miss the additional expansion slots available in the bigger cases.

That's enough for now. If you've stepped through this series of investigations, you probably know a lot more about your computer than you did when you started. Keep your personal inventory sheet handy. You use it later to refer to what you already know and add to it in future hardware discussions.

Following are a few additional exercises for you to try if you want to play some mental games and test your understanding of computer theory. In the next chapter, I delve a little deeper into computer hardware theory and help you take a closer look at your machine.

Some Things To Try

1. I've said that computers model arithmetic just as radios and compact disc systems model sound. Are there other machines that work by modeling? You could say that television models both sight and sound. Do our computers model more than numbers?

2. Suppose that electrical switches were somehow completely different than they are. Instead of having two settings or states (on and off) they always had three states. Would it still be possible to make a calculating machine out of them? Would anything be fundamentally different or would the details just change while the principles stayed the same?

3. List any computer programs with which you're familiar. Which ones would you categorize as systems programs and which as applications programs? Is there a strict dividing line between the two groups? Are there programs that have characteristics of both?

2 Hardware: The Parts of the PC

I t's time to look at the insides of the PC—the hardware parts that make up the computer. In this chapter, I look at the PC's hardware from three angles. First, I provide a basic breakdown of how the PC is organized into mechanical and electrical modules, each a major PC component. Next, I examine some of those components and the options they offer for assembling different kinds of PCs. Finally, on a more technical level, I describe specific circuit chips that make the PC work.

The Breakdown

Remember from the discussion of computer components in Chapter 1 that the basic personal computer consists of three components: the system unit, the display, and the keyboard. Your particular PC may have some other things attached to it, but what you need for basic functionality is contained in these three components.

At the same time, you should understand that it makes more sense to talk about a computer system than about a simple, single computer. The system includes the system unit and all it contains, the display, the keyboard, the printer, and other optional parts, including a mouse, a modem, extra disk drives, tape drives, a scanner, and so on. In fact, as you see shortly, the PC is designed so that all kinds of devices can be attached easily. Thus, although you always have a system unit, keyboard, and display, you should think of the computer as a system of parts all working together.

The best way to understand the system unit is to think of it as a box that contains the most common and important parts of the physical computer system.

The System Unit

When you look inside the PC system unit, you see that it's built around a modular design that breaks the computer down into electrical components. You can see a logical diagram of these components in figure 2.1.

The dotted line in figure 2.1 represents the case that encloses the system unit, and you see just about everything is inside it. For portable members of the PC family, the system unit also embraces the display screen; this changes the way the computer is built, but it doesn't change anything fundamental in the design. In fact, with smaller portables—laptops and hand-held computers—the keyboard, display, and system unit are all in one unit.

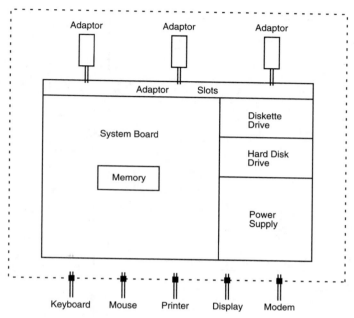

Figure 2.1. *A logical PC diagram.*

Although the physical layout may vary from one computer to another, the logical organization and the function of each of the components is the same for every member of the PC family. You also can match the parts discussed with the insides of the PCs shown in figure 2.2. Better yet, if you take the cover off your PC's system unit, you can follow along by matching what is discussed with your computer's parts.

The Power Supply

Start by looking at the power supply. From the outside of the system unit, you can't actually see the power supply, but you can locate where it is and see some obvious evidence of it. Look at the rear of your computer system case. (If you have to crawl under your desk to get to the back of the case, don't do that now. However, to get the most out of this discussion, you might want to shut your computer down and pull it out so you can get to it. Better yet, is there a computer nearby that you can see easily?) Somewhere toward one end of the case you should see a small circular opening about three inches across. Beside it should be two connectors for power input and output.

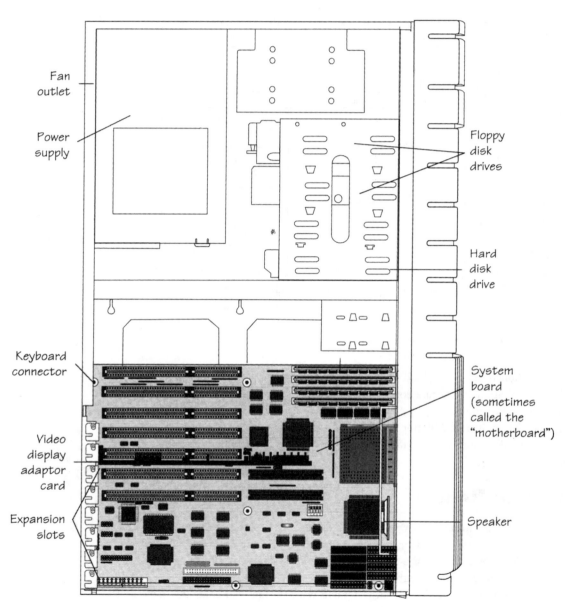

Figure 2.2. *The inside of a PC case. (Drawing courtesy of Gateway 2000.)*

The circular opening is for the cooling fan that is part of most power supply designs. The fan blows warm air out of this hole after sucking cool air across the system board and card cage inside the computer. If you don't see a fan opening on the back of your computer case, it probably means you are using a newer, compact case design that does not require a fan. Most computers, however, do have a fan for cooling.

These visible power supply components appear to be attached to the rear of the computer case; however, they actually are part of the power supply enclosure. You are viewing these components through a cutout in the rear of the computer case.

One of these polarized connectors takes power from the wall into the power supply. This is the one that already has a power cable attached to it (if your computer is plugged in). If there are no cables coming into the power supply, the input connector is the one with the visible metal contacts (a male connector). It is designed to accept the matching plug at the end of your power cable.

Why are the metal contacts visible on the power supply case? When you remove the power cord there shouldn't be any voltage at the power supply side of the connection. There may be voltage at the power cord, however, so the contacts on the power cord are recessed to make it a lot harder to get an accidental shock.

Look at the other power connector on the back of the power supply, if there is one. It looks more like the end of your power cord, with the metal contacts hidden inside (a female connector). It is designed this way because this connector is an output connector. And, if there is no cable attached, you don't want bare metal hanging out with potentially dangerous voltage on it. This connector is designed to power external equipment such as a monitor. The original PCs frequently included monitors with a power cord that matched this reverse connector. Today, the majority of monitors are designed to plug directly into the wall.

You still can attach your monitor to the power supply at this connector if you purchase a separate "gender bender" pigtail that has a three-way connector for the monitor's power cord on one end and a concave connector for the power supply on the other. However, if you do this, make sure that the power supply can output enough power for the monitor. Some of today's monitors require more power than this external connector on some power supplies can deliver. There should be a label beside this connector that tells you the maximum output it can deliver. Compare this with the power requirements printed on the rear panel of your monitor to see if you can power your monitor from this power supply connector.

From inside the case, the power supply is easy to find. It's a heavy box screwed to one end of the case and has several colored wires coming out of it. The power supply uses alternating current (AC) and converts it into the direct current (DC) voltages that the computer parts need. The power unit supplies three DC voltages: +12 volts, -12 volts, and +5 volts. Besides converting the electricity from high-voltage alternating current to low-voltage direct current, the power supply also grooms the power, smoothing out unevenness in the flow of electricity.

In fact, the good news is that today's PC power supplies are so good that they work just about anywhere under any reasonable condition. The bad news is that there still is some variation in quality among different brands and designs. I have a number of PCs clustered around my desk right now, for example, and I notice some real differences in power supply capability. For example, if you work in an area with frequent summer thunder storms and the associated power fluctuations and microsecond interruptions, some of your machines will sit through one of these storms, even when a power interrupt causes lights to flash off momentarily, and keep on working fine. Other machines (and not necessarily the older or cheaper ones, either) may shut down and reboot at even a hint of power problems. If constant up time is important to your application, ask plenty of questions before you buy, find someone else who has the same brand and model, if possible, and add an uninterruptable power supply (UPS) for ultimate protection.

The capacity of the power supply sets a limit on how much optional equipment can be installed. With older PCs this can sometimes be a problem. For example, the original PC model supplies about 65 watts of power—not a generous amount. Later models supply more. The PC XT, for example, provides about 130 watts, and the PC AT provides 200 watts of power. People sometimes get into trouble when they try to add components that require more power than the computer can provide. For example, people who add hard disks to an original PC often find that they have to replace the power supply with a more powerful one. In fact, you may want to think of a PC XT as an original PC with a larger power supply and a hard disk. (There aren't very many PC XTs around in serious business use today, of course, unless they are left over from much earlier installations. Thousands of these machines were sold, but they now are relegated mostly to the spare parts closet or for such dedicated tasks as label printing or terminal emulation.)

These days, computers generally offer an ample supply of power. Moreover, hardware components now require less power. Thus, the computer you buy today may use less power than an older computer, even though the newer computer offers far more computing and disk resources. For example, the power supply of the PS/2 model 55 SX supplies 90 watts of power, while the older PC AT supplies 195 watts. On the other hand, the large floorstanding PS/2 model 95 XP provides 329 watts of power. This reflects the model 95's capability to support up to 1.6GB of disk storage. Disk drives and other electromechanical accessories require the most power of any of the components in your PC.

If you pick up a PC system unit, you find that it's heaviest on the side that holds the power supply. That's because the power supply includes filters and coils that are part of the power smoothing circuitry. And, the metal case (a primary structural component as well as an electronic barrier to help prevent spurious radiation from the power supply to the computer components), fan, and other components in the power supply are just plain heavier than circuit boards or even disk drives. Older power supply designs may include a transformer to reduce the voltage, but this task is conducted with electronic circuitry on newer computers.

The System Board (Motherboard)

The most important part of a PC is the system board. This is a large printed circuit board that holds the silicon chips that make the PC work. These chips include the processor and optional math coprocessor as well as the supporting chips that the processor needs to help it perform its tasks, such as the clock chip, which sets the work pace for the whole computer. A typical PC motherboard is shown in figure 2.3. Yours may be larger or smaller than this one, the components may be arranged on the board differently, and your board may contain more or fewer components than this one. However, the general layout and design of your system board should be very similar to this one.

Also on the system board is the computer's basic complement of working memory and the special read-only memory (ROM) chips that hold built-in programs. Because the system board is clearly the most important part of the computer, it sometimes is called the motherboard. Another term you might encounter, especially if you read IBM literature, is planar board.

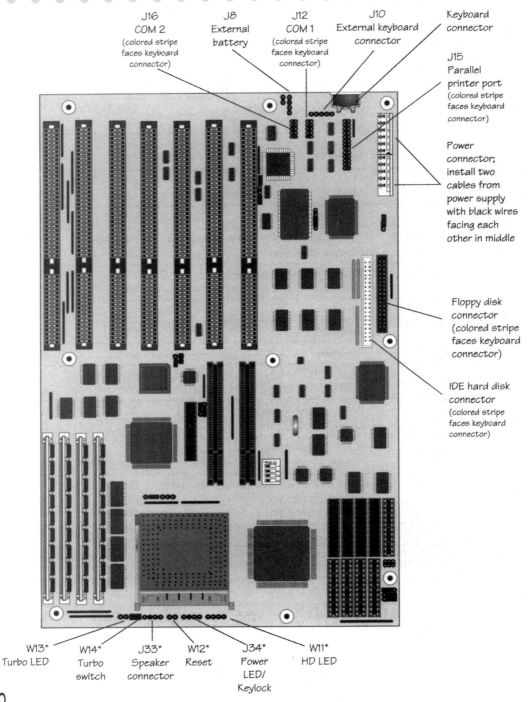

J16
COM 2
(colored stripe
faces keyboard
connector)

J8
External
battery

J12
COM 1
(colored stripe
faces keyboard
connector)

J10
External keyboard
connector

Keyboard
connector

J15
Parallel
printer
port
(colored stripe
faces keyboard
connector)

Power
connector;
install two
cables from
power supply
with black wires
facing each
other in middle

Floppy disk
connector
(colored stripe
faces keyboard
connector)

IDE hard disk
connector
(colored stripe
faces keyboard
connector)

W13*
Turbo LED

W14*
Turbo
switch

J33*
Speaker
connector

W12*
Reset

J34*
Power
LED/
Keylock

W11*
HD LED

32

Figure 2.3. A typical PC motherboard. (Drawing courtesy of Gateway 2000.)

The system board is the largest single electronic component of the computer and, by far, the largest of all the printed circuit boards in the machine. It fills practically the whole bottom of the system unit box. The space above the system board is where all the other components in the system unit are placed.

At the front of the system unit are the disk drives and, possibly, a tape drive. Different members of the PC family feature different sizes and types of disk storage devices. The disk and tape drives are the only mechanical parts in the system unit. They use more power than most of the electronic parts so they connect directly to the power supply. In PS/2s, disk and tape drives plug into a connector that has direct access to the power supply. In computers that follow the older design (still used by most IBM-compatible clones), the drives are connected to the power supply by cables.

The drives and power supply occupy most of the space above the system board. Most of the remaining space is set aside for optional parts called adapters, or options. These are cards that plug into a row of sockets called expansion slots that are built into the system board. The expansion slots represent one of the most important features of the PC: open architecture.

The Bus

An open architecture is extremely important to users and to manufacturers who must design adapters to fit into any IBM-compatible computer. What makes it possible is an engineering concept known as a bus.

The various electronic chips and other parts of the computer have to be connected to one another so that they can pass signals back and forth, or "talk" to one another. If the connections were made with individual wires, stretching from part to part as needed, only those parts that were wired to each other could communicate. The bus concept, on the other hand, establishes a common set of wires (on the circuit board, these sets are called lands) with a series of connectors that attach to each of the wires. A simplified drawing of a computer bus is shown in figure 2.4.

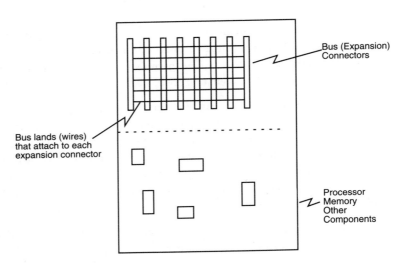

Figure 2.4. *A simplified drawing of a computer bus.*

This system of common connections provides a way to connect things so that any part—particularly new parts—can talk to any other part. These new parts attach to the bus through adapter slots that are connected to the bus. Thus, anything you plug into a slot can talk to every part of the PC that uses the bus, including the memory and the processor. These adapter slots—which you can think of as bus connectors—give you an easy way to plug in optional equipment. This enables you to use practically any combination of equipment that you want.

Figure 2.5 shows a typical bus adapter card. The metal-plated fingers at the bottom of the card insert into the bus adapter socket, connecting to the common wires that form the bus. As soon as the card plugs into the slot and you turn on the power, the new card has access to the common signals and information inside the computer, and the computer (as well as any other adapter cards) can access the newly installed card.

In theory, each slot is an equally good connection to the bus. However, for certain technical reasons, certain adapter boards must be plugged into particular slots. If this is the case, it is mentioned in the documentation that comes with the adapter. For more technical information, see the technical sections on individual buses later in this chapter.

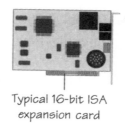

Typical 16-bit ISA
expansion card

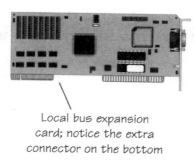

Local bus expansion
card; notice the extra
connector on the bottom

Figure 2.5. *A typical bus expansion card showing connectors. (Drawing courtesy of Gateway 2000.)*

What Does the Bus Do?

The designers of the original PC had to provide a way to connect various optional devices such as printers and telephone modems. They could have made a special-purpose connection for each option, but that would have reduced the flexibility of the PC and restricted the variety of options that could be added, making the PC a closed system with only predefined possibilities.

Instead, the designers created general-purpose expansion slots whose uses were not defined. What was defined is the type of connection that should be made to each of the pins of the expansion slot. One set of pins is designated for power, for example, another for data I/O, another for addressing, and so on. A series of these slots, all connected together with proper electrical isolation, forms a bus that enables the system board components and any attached peripherals to share common connections and information.

This type of open architecture contributed enormously to the success of the original IBM PC family and the later clones built on the IBM design because it enabled third-party manufacturers to sell adapters. Within a few years of the introduction of the original PC, a large number of adapters for the PC family appeared in the market.

Bus Standards

In the beginning there was only one bus design, IBM's. Later, other manufacturers and IBM introduced new computer designs with different bus configurations. By far the most popular of these remains the ISA (Industry Standard Architecture), which is based on the original IBM AT design. However, there are other designs that also are gathering a following, and I discuss the major ones in the following sections.

ISA: Industry Standard Architecture

The Industry Standard Architecture (ISA) bus, sometimes called the "AT bus," today remains the most popular and most common of the PC bus designs. It is a 16-bit data bus based on a 98-pin expansion connector design. As with most bus designs, the ISA bus uses double-sided connectors with pins arranged in rows. When you plug in an expansion card, each connector position actually is two connections, one on the A side of the board and one on the B side. Figure 2.6 shows a drawing of the connector end of an expansion board.

The component side of the expansion board carries connections for pins A1–A31 (the main socket and part of the original PC bus) and C1–C18 (the extended socket was added with the PC AT model). The back side of the board has connections for pins B1–B31 and D1–D18. Pins A2–A9 are the first eight data lines, and pins C11–C18 are the second set of eight data lines. As you can see, the original PC bus with its 64 connectors had only eight data lines, pins A2–A8. With the PC AT, an additional eight lines were added on the second row of connectors.

The side B and D connectors carry more mundane signals, such as the 12- and 5-volt lines for power, interrupt lines, and the like. This design, as you can see, separates the all-important signal lines and address lines from the lines that supply power and other data to the system, reducing the chance of interference.

These expansion cards plug into the system board I/O channel connectors, or bus slots, to receive power, to attach to the address lines and data lines, and to make use of whatever other signals they require. If you examine a few expansion cards, you see that no card (well, virtually no card) ever uses all 98 pins. If a particular card doesn't need all of the signals available on the bus, the manufacturer saves money by eliminating the gold-plated land for that connector position.

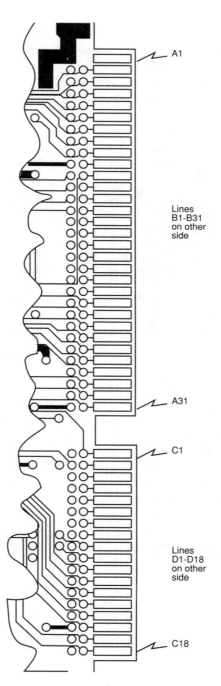

Lines
B1-B31
on other
side

Lines
D1-D18
on other
side

A1

A31

C1

C18

Figure 2.6.   *An ISA expansion board showing A connections.*

In addition, you may see two basic types of expansion boards designed for the ISA bus: 16- and 8-bit boards. Notice the system board drawing in figure 2.7. This shows the double-row arrangement of bus attachments. Most 8-bit boards are relatively short and have connectors only for the first row of pins; a 16-bit board, on the other hand, has protrusions and pins that plug into a double-row connector position.

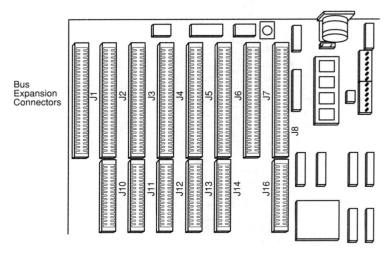

Figure 2.7. *A typical ISA bus motherboard.*

Likewise, the original PC bus had only 20 address lines, enough to reach 1MB (2^{20} = 1,048,576 bytes). Seven additional lines were added to the extended AT connector (four of those new lines are actually memory address lines), providing support for up to 16MB (2^{24} = 16,777,216 bytes). That's right, 16MB. So how do ISA machines that advertise 64MB on the system board do it? They do it through page swapping, a kind of phantom memory. The memory exists physically but it can't be addressed except in 16MB blocks. So, to use memory above 16MB on an ISA machine, the system software must readdress memory on the fly, positioning different blocks of memory within a range the CPU can reach, given the limited address lines available.

MCA: The Micro Channel Architecture

The Micro Channel Architecture (MCA), an IBM design, introduced a completely different bus. Strictly speaking, a bus consists of a collection of signal lines. The definition of a bus specifies the purpose of each line and the timing relationship of the electrical signals. Channel refers to a specific bus along with the protocols that govern the transfer of data over that bus. Thus, MCA is a set of highly technical specifications upon which various buses are based. Informally, the new PS/2 bus is referred to as the Micro Channel, and the old-style bus is referred to as the AT bus (or ISA bus).

The standard MCA bus comes in two versions. The first passes 16 bits of data at a time; the second passes 32 bits at a time. These buses are described as 16- and 32-bit, respectively. (To compare, the original PC bus was 8 bit, and the PC AT bus was 16 bit.)

The 16-bit MCA bus is designed to accept adapters that have 58 pins. Each pin connects on both sides for a total of 116 connections, which are assigned as follows: 77 signal lines, 12 power lines, 17 ground lines, 1 audio ground line, 5 reserved lines, and 4 keyed positions.

Each power line provides one of three DC voltages: +5, +12, or -12 volts. The ground lines are spread evenly along the length of the connector to minimize noise interference and enhance data integrity. (This is an important improvement over the old bus, which had much more rudimentary grounding.)

Of the remaining connections, the signal lines are the most interesting. Of the 77 lines, 24 are address lines and 16 are data lines.

The 24 address lines are named A0, A1, and so on, through A23. They pass signals that indicate what part of the computer is being talked to. Each line carries a signal that can be interpreted as one bit. Thus, you can send addresses of up to 24 bits. This provides up to 2^{24} possible addresses, which enables you to access up to 16MB (16,777,216 bytes) of memory. This is the maximum memory capacity of the 286 processor.

The address lines also can be used to specify an address for an input/output adapter called an I/O slave. In this case, only the first 16 lines (A0–A15) are used. The 16 data lines are referred to as D0–D15. They are used to pass 16 bits of data. Thus, the 16-bit MCA bus can transfer 2 bytes of data at a time.

The rest of the signal lines are used for a variety of control purposes, most of which are highly technical. Some of the more interesting are the following: one line indicates whether the address lines are carrying a memory or I/O address; a set of lines is used to signal interrupt requests (hardware signals indicating that some part of the computer needs attention); and one line carries a high-speed clock signal with a frequency of 14.318MHz.

There is a variation of the 16-bit bus that provides an auxiliary video extension. This extension contains an extra 10 connections (20 signal lines) used as follows: five are grounds; eight (P0–P7) carry digital video information; one is reserved; and six carry control signals.

Most people do not need a special video connector because, unlike the older PCs, PS/2s come with a built-in plug for the display. However, if you use a special video board, you must make sure that it plugs into an adapter slot that contains the video extension. Most MCA machines have such a slot.

What I have described so far is the standard 16-bit MCA bus. This is suitable for the 286 and 386SX processors, which can transfer data 16 bits at a time and can address up to 16MB. However, the 386 and later processors can transfer up to 32 bits at a time and can address up to 4GB. To take advantage of this, you need a 32-bit bus.

The 32-bit MCA bus accepts adapters with 93 connections, for a total of 186 signal lines. In general, the 32-bit MCA bus can be thought of as a 16-bit bus with extra signal lines. First, there are 32 address lines (A0–A31). These provide up to 2^{32} different addresses, which means the processor can address up to 4GB of memory (4,294,967,296 bytes). There are also 32 data lines (D0–D31), which enable the simultaneous transfer of up to 32 bits (4 bytes). Thus, the 32-bit bus can harness the full capabilities of the 386 and 496 processors.

The MCA bus is an important improvement over the AT bus. Although comparing the details of the two buses may not be something you are interested in doing, it is a good idea to be aware of a few of the advantages of MCA.

First, MCA uses adapters that generate less electrical interference than the old adapters, thereby providing enhanced data integrity. Second, MCA can respond better to hardware requests for attention (interrupts), which increases reliability and minimizes loss of data.

Third, the MCA provides special adapters called bus masters. Bus masters have their own processors and can carry on their work independent of the main processor by sharing control of the bus. For example, a computer might contain a bus master adapter that connects to a network. The bus master can handle most of the work involved in sending data to and from the network, while the main processor continues with its work. With a regular network adapter, the main processor would have to control most of the work itself.

Fourth, within a network, MCA enables you to identify each adapter in each computer without having to open the cover. Thus, MCA was designed to enable a network manager to take inventory without leaving his or her desk.

Finally, MCA provides a facility for turning off a particular malfunctioning adapter from a remote point. For example, a program might regularly test all the adapters in a network and, after alerting the network manager, turn off those that are broken.

MCA was first introduced by IBM with the PS/2 computers. However, IBM's strategy includes using the MCA in a broad range of computing platforms—from personal computers to scientific workstations to powerful mainframes.

Not long after IBM announced MCA, a group of companies who made IBM-compatible computers decided to create an alternative. This alternative was called EISA (Extended Industry Standard Architecture) and is explained below.

EISA: The Extended Industry Standard Architecture

IBM announced MCA, along with the PS/2 line of PCs, on April 7, 1987. At first, only IBM manufactured MCA computers; most of the makers of IBM-compatible machines initially resisted the change to MCA.

On September 13, 1988, a consortium of nine such companies, led by Compaq, announced that it was developing an alternative to MCA. This consortium vowed to keep selling the old-style computers, which were based on what it decided to call the Industry Standard Architecture (ISA)—that is, the original IBM PC/XT/AT architecture. The alternative to MCA was called the Extended Industry Standard Architecture (EISA).

From the beginning, it was clear that the development of EISA was based on marketing, not engineering, needs. From the day of announcement, it took about two and a half years for the first EISA adapters to hit the market. And to this day, there are very few EISA machines around.

However, the EISA consortium was successful in one regard: it delayed wholesale acceptance of MCA. This meant that non-MCA clone makers were able to sell ISA machines long after MCA alternatives were available. People began to choose sides, and most of the arguments had more to do with peoples' feelings toward IBM as a company than with the actual worth of MCA.

However, let me make a few comments and dispel a few myths. As I mentioned, the decision to develop EISA was based on marketing, not engineering. The principle advantage of EISA was that it enables users to use all their old PC/XT/AT boards in new computers, which they cannot do with MCA computers. This type of marketing approach appealed greatly to users with an established base of older PCs and an investment in a range of adapter cards. Whether it really works, from a technical standpoint, depends on the type of boards you are trying to use and how technically advanced they are.

For example, you certainly don't want to pull an 8-bit adapter out of your old PC and plug it into your new PC, whatever the bus design on the new machine. And, if the boards you're trying to use are more than a year old, you probably don't want to incorporate them in a new machine because a comparable board of a new design would cost less than you paid for the original, include a new warranty, and almost certainly offer more functionality.

So, while EISA engineers, almost incredibly, succeeded in designing a system that could compete with MCA while accommodating the old boards, the reality of the situation is that EISA only was intended for the very high-end, non-IBM PCs. The vast majority of clone buyers ended up with ISA, the architecture of the old PC AT. For a while that seemed almost like a giant step backward or at least an exercise in standing still.

However, as local bus designs evolved, the question of how the main I/O bus was configured became somewhat less important. Here's why. Remember that originally the main system bus was used for all I/O between the system board and peripheral devices, including memory, disks, and the display. However, one of the main reasons for new I/O bus designs in the first place was to speed up display response, enhance processor interaction with main memory, and improve disk performance. Expanding the original 16 data lines to 32 on the main bus obviously speeds things up, but data transfer still is limited to the speed of the bus.

The memory communication problem took care of itself when manufacturers started putting main system RAM on the system board and hooking it up to the processor via a direct connection, or local bus. This left other peripherals to use the main system bus, but memory had its own, private path to the CPU.

Then the VESA and PCI local bus designs came along and opened up local bus communication to display devices and to hard disks. With these standards, the processor and system RAM can talk directly with display adapters and disk controllers at high speed using the bandwidth of the main system design (usually 25 or 33MHz), instead of at the limiting 8MHz of the main bus.

Today, direct (or local) bus video adapters communicate 32 bits at a time with memory and the screen, bypassing the slow general bus. Likewise, IDE and SCSI controllers designed to plug into the local bus can carry information from main memory and the processor along a 32-bit highway at main system speed without waiting for the slower main bus.

Note that "main system speed" in this case means the actual I/O speed, not the published speed of the processor. So, for example, if you have a machine that is using a 66MHz 486DX2 chip, you still are communicating with main memory and other peripherals at 33MHz (half the DX2 speed). The 66MHz processing takes place inside the processor, not along the I/O channel.

So what's left on the main bus? You find sound cards, mouse interfaces, modems, and other I/O devices that are a whole lot slower than the main bus. There essentially is no degradation in speed for these devices when they are on the main bus. Now, for the vast majority of PC users, which bus you choose is a matter of personal preference and what your vendor of choice offers rather than perceived technical advantages or disadvantages. Assuming you select a modern display adapter design with local bus access, and your disk controller sits on the local bus instead of the main bus, actual I/O performance should be quick, regardless of the design of the main bus.

The Local Bus

Ever try to run two or three graphics-oriented applications simultaneously in a Microsoft Windows environment on a 20MHz 386SX with 2MB of RAM? It is not a pretty sight. And, even if you eliminate many of the unrealistic restrictions I described in that scenario, running Windows can be a frustrating experience. Now, when you try adding full-motion video, your display response can be grindingly slow.

One solution to this display problem, and to the more general problem of sending and receiving data from the processor to any high bandwidth device, is a local bus design. With conventional designs, everything that comes and goes from the processor (well, almost everything) is sent along the main system bus. Because it must maintain backward compatibility with previous designs and because it has to work with a broad range of peripheral devices, this is a relatively slow bus with limited bandwidth. Even newer bus designs that can carry 32 bits of data generally run at slow speeds compared with the capability of the processor.

Local bus systems, on the other hand, communicate at system speed—33MHz or better—and always carry data in 32- or 64-bit chunks. Local bus designs are taking today's computers a step further down the road toward high performance without changing very much about the basic engineering of the machine. As mentioned in the previous section, local bus machines remove from the main bus those interfaces that need quick response: memory, display, and disk drives. As I/O requirements become more important, it is likely that networking, audio, and perhaps other functions will be added to the local bus environment.

Local bus designs have been around for a while, but they mostly have been proprietary to a particular vendor's hardware. There still is no single, agreed-upon standard, but there are a couple of contenders that are gaining a lot of attention among manufacturers and users. In this section, I show you a little about these emerging standards, VESA and PCI.

Designers who work with the VESA VL bus and PCI bus definitions are working at a low level, dealing with finely detailed specifications such as the rise time in milliseconds of a trigger voltage on a specific pin. Don't worry. I don't talk about anything like that. However, if you want to consider designing to one of these specifications, knowing the pinouts and understanding the overall concept isn't enough. Contact the appropriate association for a copy of its standard.

VESA VL Bus

Of today's two local bus standards, the VESA VL bus, from the Video Electronics Standards Association, the folks who have coordinated video display standards and other things, seems to be the most popular among manufacturers. However, there is a real push for PCI (see below). Frankly, I can't foresee which of these will win out—maybe neither. Perhaps you'll see parallel development of these standards for a while until there is the engineering or the marketing strength to break away from ISA, MCA, and EISA.

It doesn't matter for this discussion which path the industry might take. For now, there are three main bus designs and two local bus designs. The VL is one of the local bus designs. (For more information, contact the Video Electronics Standards Association at 2150 North First Street, Suite 440, San Jose, CA 95131-2029, (408) 435-0333 or (408) 435-8225 fax.)

The VL bus standard is the result of work by the VESA local bus committee, organized in December 1991. The VL bus 1.0 standard received VESA ratification in August 1992. Industry acceptance followed quickly, with over 100 companies producing VL-compatible products. The VL bus 2.0 standard was written within a few months of 1.0 approval and was adopted about a year after the first standard.

The VESA VL local bus standard consists of detailed specifications for electrical, mechanical, timing, and connector designs. As with other current bus specifications, the VL bus is an open design, which means any vendor willing to build products that adhere to the specification is free to do so, and many already are. The VESA organization has more than 60 companies; presumably, most of them are backing the VL bus specification.

The VL bus 1.0 standard supports a 32-bit data path but also can use devices that transfer data 16 bits at a time. The later standard, 2.0, is a 64-bit bus in keeping with the newest PC processors. The bus is implemented through an MCA-style connector with 112 pins. It is a 16-bit connector with the pins redefined to support a 32-bit data path. The VL connectors are placed in line with existing ISA, EISA, or MCA connectors on the system board (see fig. 2.8).

VL supports speeds from 16 to 66MHz, enough bandwidth to work with any of today's current PC designs. However, the 1.0 specification is limited to 40MHz signals on any expansion slot (as opposed to motherboard-based components), and the 2.0 specification is limited to 50MHz. A VL bus can have up to ten devices (under revision 2; revision 1 supports only three slots) at any time, whether the devices are plugged into an expansion slot or are part of the system board. Sustained data transfer rates of 106MB per second are supported, with a projected rate of 260MB per second for the 64-bit bus. And, while the VL bus design is optimized for CPUs of the 86 family, it also works with other processors, making VL a potential candidate for cross-platform designs.

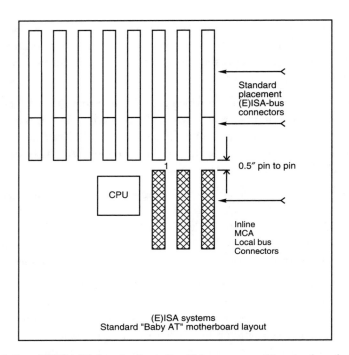

Figure 2.8. *A VESA VL bus showing in-line ISA connectors. (Drawing from the VESA specification.)*

Another interesting and useful design feature of the VL bus is that a 64-bit device operates in a 32-bit VL slot as a 32-bit device and that a 32-bit device can work in a 64-bit slot but, of course, only supports 32-bit data transfer. The VL bus also supports 16-bit peripherals and CPUs such as the 386SX with a 16-bit I/O.

Two main types of VL bus devices are recognized in the specification: target devices (local bus targets, or LBTs) and bus master devices (local bus masters, or LBMs). A bus master device can initiate data transfers along the bus and may include its own processor. A target, on the other hand, answers requests initiated by an LBM elsewhere in the system. A bus master device also can function as a target for other LBM devices.

Among the desirable features of the VL bus is its capability to operate with a broad range of system and application software designs. Configuration of VL bus devices is handled entirely in hardware, which means that application and system software don't have to understand the VL bus to operate properly with it.

The VL bus uses a 5-volt DC standard, and each connector can draw up to 10 watts (2 amps) from the slot. The VL specification also includes 3.3-volt devices, so the newer, low-voltage CPUs and support devices can be used with the VESA bus.

As I mentioned earlier, VL bus connectors are located in line with the existing I/O bus, whether it is an ISA, EISA, or MCA device. Revision 2.0 specifications should not change the basic physical arrangement of the connectors. When the standard moves into the 64-bit world, it is expected that the existing 32-bit connector will carry multiplexed signals, enabling the present connector design to do double duty.

PCI Local Bus

As I have said already, local bus or direct bus is the way today's computers are increasing performance without any real engineering breakthroughs. Today, there are two local bus standards: VESA, which I described in the previous section, and PCI, which I talk about here.

The PCI standard is designed and maintained by the Peripheral Component Interconnect Special Interest Group, or PCI SIG, an unincorporated association of microcomputer industry representatives. As I write this, the latest PCI specification is revision 2.0. (The PCI SIG can be contacted at Mail Stop HF3-15A, 5200 NE Elam Young Parkway, Hillsboro, OR 97124-6497, (503) 696-2000 or (503) 693-0920 fax.)

The PCI local bus can be a 32- or 64-bit pathway for high-speed data transfer. It supports both 5- and 3.3-volt signaling environments, so PCI can fit into today's 5-volt desktop environment as well as into the emerging, low-power, 3.3-volt world. The focus of the PCI SIG is to maintain a standard that can grow with hardware design and also be functional across multiple platforms. Ideally, at least, PCI can work with PCs as well as with other computer designs. Because the design is not dependent on the 86 family of processors, according to the PCI SIG, it can work with current PCs and with future designs, regardless of the processor used.

Specifically, PCI is targeted at desktop PC hardware with an eye toward including it in notebook and laptop computers as well. There already are a few laptop designs that include local bus video and disk I/O, so the industry is recognizing the need for high-performance computing on and off the desktop.

And, while the major need for local bus attachments currently is to speed up computer graphics displays and improve disk I/O performance, the not-too-distant future holds a local bus world that includes full-motion video, sound, and network inter-faces (including the FDDI high-speed fiber Ethernet) among others.

Think of the PCI bus as a parallel data highway that runs alongside an ISA, EISA, or MCA bus. The system processor and memory attach directly to the PCI bus, and there is a separate attachment, through a PCI bridge, to the standard (ISA, EISA, or MCA) bus. Other devices such as graphics display adapters, disk controllers, sound cards, and so on, also can attach directly to the PCI bus. A conceptual drawing of one possible PCI bus arrangement is shown in figure 2.9.

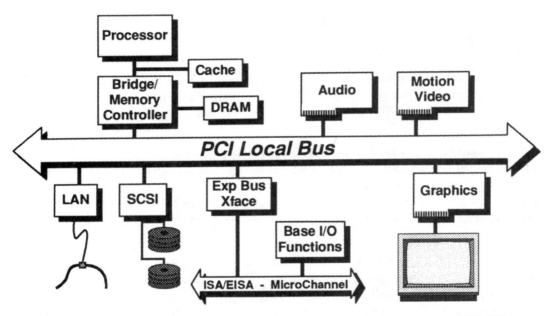

Figure 2.9. A PCI bus showing PCI attachments. (Drawing courtesy of PCI SIG.)

As presently defined, typical PCI local bus designs support up to three add-in board connectors. So, if you have a system board that includes the PCI local bus, you would have four or six main bus slots to hold ISA, EISA, or MCA expansion cards. You then would have another one or three slots for PCI expansion devices. These are MCA-style (not MCA-compliant) connectors. However, because the connectors are separate from the main bus, they can be used in machines with any main bus design.

Among the design features promoted by the PCI SIG is the PCI local bus transparent upgrade path from a 32-bit data path to a 64-bit data path. The 32-bit design is capable of transferring data at up to 132MB per second, while the 64-bit design can transfer information at up to 264MB per second. This is really fast compared with some of the conventional data transfer facilities used in PCs. Standard Ethernet, for example, transfers data at 10MB per second, while the much touted FDDI fiber Ethernet transfers data at 100MB per second. A standard SCSI-1 disk drive, if it is functioning at top efficiency (which it can't for various technical reasons), can move data at only 5MB per second, and state-of-the-art, 32-bit SCSI-2 is good for only 40MB per second.

In addition, the specification calls for automatic configuration of PCI add-in cards. This is accomplished by storing information about the PCI peripheral right on the expansion card. The processor uses this information to automatically find out what type of device it is talking to without requiring the user to run a configuration program or throw any switches.

Two types of PCI device are defined: a target and a master. A target is a device that accepts commands and responds to requests of the master. The master, or bus master, is a more intelligent device that can conduct processing independent of the bus or other devices. A bus master device shares the bus with the main processor and targets. A master device also can serve as a target for other masters.

Hardware and Software Details

The PCI definition requires a minimum of 47 pins for a target-only device and 49 pins for a master. That's pretty incredible when you consider the potential for this bus and the fact that this includes data handling and addressing, interface control, arbitration, and system function. However, the rest of the story is that the specification provides for up to 120 connections for a standard 32-bit card and 184 for 64-bit cards, most of which are used for a full implementation of the standard. This is a multiplexed design, where multiple signal types are carried on the same pins. Figure 2.10 shows a functional pin diagram of a PCI connector for a combination master/target device. You can see from the arrows in this drawing the direction of data flow.

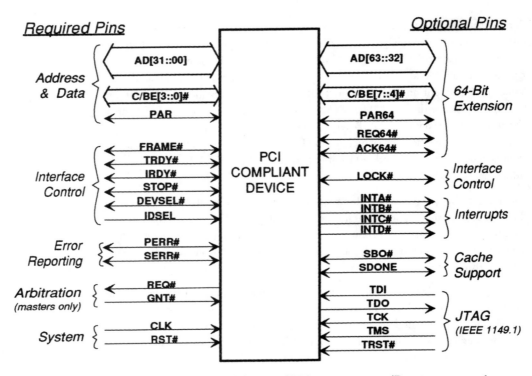

Figure 2.10. *A functional diagram of PCI pin connections. (Drawing courtesy of PCI SIG.)*

In fact, addresses and data are multiplexed on the same pins. Thus, a single PCI bus transaction consists of two phases: an address phase followed by one or more data phases. The master device sends out an address along a set of pins that effectively taps a specific bus-resident device on the shoulder and says "Wake up, I'm about to talk to you." The signaled device goes into the proper mode to receive data or instructions, and then the master sends along a burst of data on the same pins used for the wake up call. After the address is established, the master can keep sending data without the need for repeating the address because the target device already is listening. Also, after the address has been established, the data bursts can include both read and write information.

Three physical address spaces are defined for PCI: memory, I/O, and configuration. Memory and I/O addressing are pretty common and are used by all bus designs. The PCI configuration address space is used for the automatic hardware configuration feature that is part of the definition. Remember, this enables each attached device to configure itself or to be configured by the system through the use of information stored on the expansion card.

Another design feature that simplifies the basic bus is distributed address decoding. That means each device attached to the PCI local bus conducts its own address decoding. So, with the PCI standard, there is no need for additional central decode logic or for device selection signals beyond the one used for configuration.

What about the physical arrangement of PCI components? Next, I take a brief look at some of those issues. Obviously, anything as complex as the PCI local bus has some pretty stringent hardware requirements to go along with the electrical specifications. As a user, you need not be overly concerned with the specifics of hardware design. However, it is useful to be aware of how such devices are structured so that, if for no other reason, you can look at an expansion board and understand where to plug it in.

Physical Characteristics

Two physical cards are defined under the PCI specification—a full-length card and a short card—just as is the case in a conventional bus expansion card. The standard 32-bit cards have 120 connections active, with four pin locations used for card keying, making a total of 124 pin locations. A 64-bit extension to the basic card is built into the same connection and adds another 60 pins for a total of 184. Figure 2.11 shows a 32-bit connector diagram; figure 2.12 shows a 64-bit connector diagram. You can see from these illustrations how the standard is designed to accommodate both 32- and 64-bit products simply by extending the length of the basic connector.

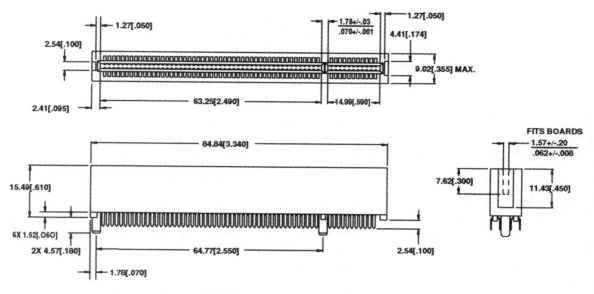

Figure 2.11. *A PCI 32-bit connector diagram. (Drawing courtesy of PCI SIG.)*

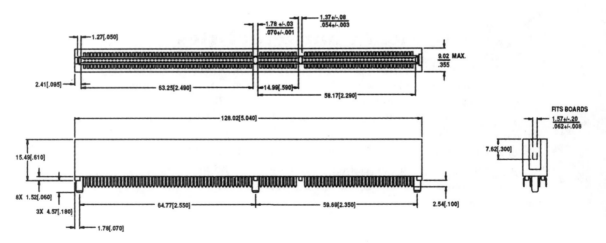

Figure 2.12. *A PCI 64-bit connector diagram. (Drawing courtesy of PCI SIG.)*

As an example of PCI's self-configuration features, each board stores information on the maximum power it requires and presents this information at specific pin locations. System software can then read this information and determine, for example, whether adequate power and cooling are available for reliable operation at system start-up.

The components on a PCI card are located on the opposite side from cards designed for ISA, EISA, and MCA busses. The idea is to leave room for PCI cards even in systems with a limited number of card slots so that the PCI slot can coexist within a single slot with a standard bus connector. Such shared slots enable you to install a PCI board, or a conventional bus board, in the same slot. Remember, only one board at a time. And, of course, only two types of cards can be shared: a PCI card and an ISA card, for example, a PCI card and an EISA card, and so on. Figure 2.13 shows a piece of an ISA motherboard that contains shared connectors along with ISA- and PCI-only slots.

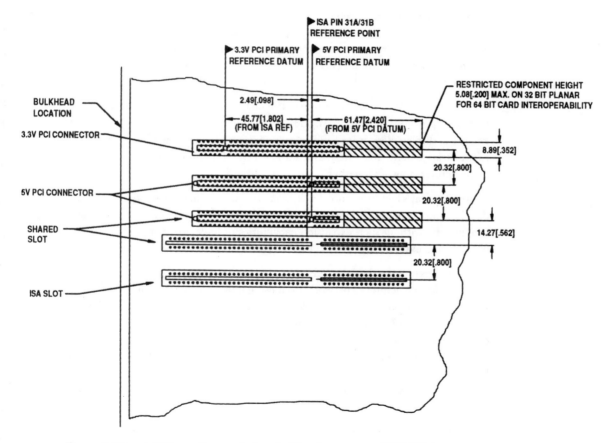

Figure 2.13. A PCI-compliant motherboard. (Drawing courtesy of PCI SIG.)

Well, those are the basics of PCI. Obviously, this is a complex specification that goes way beyond what is covered here. From this information, you should have a fairly good idea of how PCI is implemented. If you're into engineering-level work with PCI or if you are a designer, get a copy of the specification; it is more than pinouts and connectors.

PCMCIA: Laptop Expansion Standard

Computer designers and users are never happy. Not only do they want more and more functionality, they want ever smaller and cheaper computers. Well, as incongruous as these requirements seem, that's precisely what's happening. And the rising acceptance of the PCMCIA (Personal Computer Memory Card International Association) expansion cards is evidence of that.

Remember from our earlier discussion in this chapter that the computer's main components—processor, RAM, ROM, and so on—talk with external components—the keyboard, display, disk drives, and so on—through the main bus. This is a convenient arrangement that provides a standard way for the products from various manufacturers to work together.

However, today's laptop and notebook computers are too small to incorporate a standard bus and the relatively large expansion cards that go with it. For years, users have simply done without such expansion capabilities or have used peripherals such as modems and external disk drives provided by the computer manufacturer.

Doing without meant that all kinds of strange methods were used to exchange data with a desktop machine or network, from using null modem cables and third-party software to sitting down beside the desktop machine, hooking up the laptop to the telephone line, and calling a second number to access the desktop data. Some people carried "pocket" Ethernet adapters (which weren't all that small compared with the size of the computer and the other stuff they had to carry) to attach the laptop to a local area network (LAN) to share data. Whatever the method, many people ended up carrying a lot of extra equipment and doing a lot of wiring, rewiring, and software installation.

Using the manufacturer's proprietary expansion slot for memory expansion or modems meant the computers weren't compatible with other computers and, because vendors held people captive to their products, users paid through the nose for everything. A 2,400-bps modem that could be purchased on the street for a standard bus expansion slot for about $70 cost around $300 for the proprietary laptop expansion slot.

That's why there was such a push for standards in laptop peripheral connections. PCMCIA, for now, is the standard. It specifies a credit card-sized peripheral attachment. These "smart cards" are actually very compact circuit boards with connectors on one or both ends. One end of the card attaches inside the laptop via a small hole in the case, and the other end connects to the external device (if any) that the card is designed to support. Figure 2.14 shows a typical PCMCIA expansion card.

Figure 2.14. *A typical PCMCIA expansion card. (Photo courtesy of Intel.)*

Because this card sits outside the conventional bus, it is compatible with all existing bus designs for the PC and even can be used on Macintosh computers, Amigas, and other computers. Acceptance is broadening quickly, and I believe this standard will start showing up on just about all computers before long. By using the standard 68-pin bus (two rows of 34 pins each) and by building into the card some intelligence about what it is supposed to do and how it functions with any attached devices, there should be no need for half a dozen software drivers for different, even exotic, peripherals. All the attached computer needs do is be able to talk to the PCMCIA slot in a standard way, sending data and requests out and accepting data and instructions back.

The push for card-sized computer expansion has been around since 1984 or so, primarily as a memory addition. Small computer manufacturers wanted to provide users with a way to store and remove information without having to include the large, power-hungry disk drives of the day. That worked for some, but the lack of standards slowed things down because designers were afraid of investing heavily in a plan that might be replaced by another design.

With the establishment of PCMCIA in 1988, the market began to heat up, but it wasn't until near the end of 1990 that the first, formal PCMCIA standard was introduced. There are three levels, or versions, of PCMCIA expansion slot: types I, II, and III (also called versions 1.0, 2.0, and 3.0 as well as releases 1, 2, and 3). Each has its special uses and came about in answer to end-user and manufacturer needs.

Proposed in September 1990, type I PCMCIA was the first standard. It specifies a card that is 3.3 millimeters thick, big enough for memory expansion but little else. A card this thin can't include the I/O circuitry and connectors required of, say, a modem.

Type II PCMCIA was published a year later to address the needs for I/O support as well as memory support. At 10.5 millimeters thick, type III is over twice as thick as type II. This is enough room to include a removable hard drive right on the card.

As this book is written, the majority of devices use type II, and this is the standard I focus on in this section. At 5 millimeters thick, type II cards are a little thicker than type I. That's not much difference, but it is enough to provide a lot more functionality. For one thing, type II cards draw their power from inside the laptop via the standard 68-pin socket, whereas type I cards generally use internal batteries. Type II also was designed to maintain backward compatibility with type I, so earlier cards should work in a slot designed for the type II standard. Going the other way—plugging a type II card in a type I slot—also is theoretically possible. However, this may or may not work, depending on the particular features implemented in the newer card.

Type II offers many enhancements over the earlier standard, including the capability to run programs inside the card without having to download them to conventional computer memory. This is a significant step that enables manufacturers to distribute their applications, such as spreadsheet programs or database applications, right on the card. This approach eliminates the need for installation and enables you to move the software from machine to machine without violating copyright regulations.

Other features included in the type II standard include the following:

- Specified file formats and data structures
- A method for a card to tell its host about its configuration and capabilities
- A device-independent means of accessing card hardware
- The capability to operate independent software links

PCMCIA is a 16-bit device interface that supports only one interrupt request (IRQ) line. However, the sophisticated underlying architecture of this design makes room for future improvements and expansion, which is what is going on right now and probably will continue. PCMCIA is working on a 32-bit implementation that probably will involve multiplexing the existing 16 hardware data lines to manage 32 bits of information. The card's 26 address lines mean it can use up to 64MB of memory.

There are a number of other strengths in this bus design. For example, hardware that supports PCMCIA can have up to 255 PCMCIA adapters, the hardware components that match the signals of these cards to the computer. And, each adapter can hold up to 16 separate card sockets, for a theoretical maximum of 255×16 = 4,080 individual cards connected at any one time.

PCMCIA devices use a software interface called Socket Services to link expansion cards to Intel-architecture machines. A set of function calls under interrupt 1A— the CMOS clock—enables system or applications software to access these cards without having to understand the specifics of the underlying hardware. This Socket Services software can be built into the computer's ROM-BIOS or added to existing machines through a software driver.

In addition to Socket Services, PCMCIA has approved a Card Services standard that specifies how programs interact with Socket Services. With this additional interface software installed in the operating system or the computer's ROM-BIOS, a greater level of access across different computer hardware platforms is achieved.

Remember that PCMCIA cards have to be able to tell their host computer about themselves, sharing such information as how much storage they have, what kind of device they are (memory, I/O, hard disk, and so on), the format of the data, the speed of the card, and more. This is done with still another PCMCIA standard, the Card

Identification Structure (CIS) or "metaformat." By specifying strategic information about each card in the same way every time, computer-based applications can grab as much or as little of this data as they need as soon as a card is plugged in.

The CIS is a layered specification not unlike network protocols that start out with general information and get increasingly specific as you get closer and closer to the core of the data. With CIS, top layer information is general, and information in the innermost layers is machine or environment specific. This data, stored in a specific location on each card and called Attribute Memory, can tell a querying system such things as the format of the logical data stored on the card, the physical configuration of any disk drive (or how a drive is emulated), the operating environment for which the peripheral was designed, and so on.

By searching this Attribute Memory area, an operating system, BIOS, or application can find out what it needs to know about how to interact with the PCMCIA device without requiring the user to configure the card, install special software drivers, or perform any of the other extra chores people are so accustomed to doing with today's systems.

Although a 68-pin interface is the standard across all card types, pin assignments can vary under software control to accommodate the needs of different expansion devices. Table 2.2 shows the pin assignments for a memory-only PCMCIA card. (Note that pins marked with asterisks may have different functions on I/O cards.)

Table 2.1. *Memory-Only Card Interface*

Function	*Pin*
Address bit 25	56
Address bit 24	55
Address bit 23	54
Address bit 22	53
Address bit 21	50
Address bit 20	49
Address bit 19	48
Address bit 18	47

Function	Pin
Address bit 17	46
Address bit 16	19
Address bit 15	20
Address bit 14	14
Address bit 13	13
Address bit 12	21
Address bit 11	10
Address bit 10	8
Address bit 9	11
Address bit 8	12
Address bit 7	22
Address bit 6	23
Address bit 5	24
Address bit 4	25
Address bit 3	26
Address bit 2	27
Address bit 1	28
Address bit 0	29
Battery voltage detect 2	62*
Battery voltage detect 1	63*
Card detect	7
Card detect	36
Card enable	42
Card enable	67
Card reset	58

continues

Table 2.1. *continued*

Function	Pin
Data bit 0	30
Data bit 1	31
Data bit 2	32
Data bit 3	2
Data bit 4	3
Data bit 5	4
Data bit 6	5
Data bit 7	6
Data bit 8	64
Data bit 9	65
Data bit 10	66
Data bit 11	37
Data bit 12	38
Data bit 13	39
Data bit 14	40
Data bit 15	41
Extend bus cycle	59
Ground	1
Ground	34
Ground	35
Ground	68
Output enable	9
Programming supply voltage 1	18*
Programming supply voltage 2	52*

Function	Pin
Ready/busy	16*
Refresh	43
Register select	61*
Reserved	44*
Reserved	45*
Reserved	57
Reserved	60*
Voltage	17
Voltage	51
Write enable	15
Write protect	33*

All three PCMCIA standards are in use currently. Unfortunately, however, they don't always work as well as people have come to expect from older expansion standards. The technology and the level of cooperation among vendors is still evolving. And, because there are relatively few manufacturers of PCMCIA products and the market is smaller than for full-sized PC peripherals, the cost of PCMCIA devices remains considerably higher than conventional products. Still, this is the best of the current possibilities for expanding laptop and notebook computers.

Considering the size of these cards, the amount of functionality manufacturers are getting inside is truly amazing. For example, there are modems that include wireless circuitry to enable you to use RAM Mobile Data's wireless Mobitex network. Coupled with radio transceivers from companies such as Diablo Research and Gandalf Systems, a Mobitex modem can send wireless E-mail anywhere via Internet.

Wireless is actually a good way to go (although potentially expensive and not for everyone) because of the size of these expansion cards. Because type II cards are only 5 millimeters thick, there simply isn't room for a standard RJ-type telephone jack. You have to use another connection scheme. This is the data access arrangement (DAA) cable, which is not particularly large, but simply adds a level of complication and size to what should be a compact computer package.

Another attempt to solve the problem of size conflict between the adapter and the peripherals it has to work with comes from Megahertz Corporation. This company offers modem products that keep a telephone jack neatly tucked away in a small drawer within the external portion of the PCMCIA card. When you push on it, the drawer pops out, enabling you to plug the phone cord in from the top. The downside of this system, of course, is that the portion of the interface card that remains external to the computer is larger, creating some potential physical damage as you move the machine around.

Remember, however, that as this book is written, this standard is still very much evolutionary. There have been reported problems of compatibility among PCMCIA devices from various manufacturers, of connecting to the outside world, and that not every machine includes the PCMCIA expansion bus.

However, I believe that this bus—or something like it—will soon become the standard for notebook and laptop expansion. As this occurs, look for credit card-sized peripheral attachments to appear on the desktop as well. It makes sense. Here is a way to insert a modem, a disk drive, a SCSI port, or any number of peripherals and I/O cards without removing the cover from your computer.

And, because you can plug and unplug these cards so easily, you can buy only a single modem, for example, for use at the desktop and on the road. You would plug it into the desktop machine when at work in the office and unplug it and stick it in the side of the notebook computer as you walk out the door. The design includes the capability to insert and remove the card from a live system, so you don't have to switch off the power before you make the swap. So, even if prices remain a little high compared with conventional expansion devices, if you cut in half the number of modems and SCSI ports or sound cards you have to buy, perhaps the overall result is a savings of money and an improvement in convenience.

In addition, if this standard really finds broad acceptance and if the current bugs are ironed out, PCMCIA may become the long-awaited link between the computer and other consumer electronics devices. Can you imagine attaching your computer to your camera, for example, or to your VCR to download programming information (the clock no longer needs to blink 12:00 forever)?

Peripheral Devices

Considering the system board as the heart of your computer, notice that there are a number of devices attached to it. These are called peripheral devices, or simply peripherals. Every computer comes with at least three peripherals: a display, a floppy disk drive, and a keyboard. Most computers also have a hard disk drive and a printer. Other common devices are a mouse (sometimes called a pointing device), a modem (to connect the computer to a phone line), an extra disk drive, and a tape drive (for backups). Because all of these devices involve input and output, they also are known as I/O devices.

Each I/O device requires a controller to act as its supervisor and interface with the processor. Some controllers have their own special-purpose processors, and some even have their own memory. The controller can be either built into the system board or the device or can be on a separate adapter that must be plugged into the bus.

The old PCs (the original PC, PC XT, PC AT, and their clones) required an adapter for every device except the keyboard. (The keyboard plugged directly into a special outlet on the system board.) Usually, one adapter served both the floppy and hard disk drives, and sometimes another served both the display and printer. This meant that each computer had to have at least two adapters. In fact, most people needed more than the minimum, and it was common to see computers with five, six, or seven adapters.

As discussed earlier, the idea behind having a bus is that you can add adapters and customize your system to your needs. In fact, because the PC family can accept all kinds of adapters, many were developed that had not been dreamed of at the time the bus was designed. Without an adaptable open architecture, there would have been very little innovation, and the IBM PC would not be the standard it is today.

However, having so many adapters created problems. Each adapter had to be installed and configured, which could be time consuming. Inserting the old-style (pre-MCA) adapters and wading through technical manuals to figure out how to set the switches was not fun when you were in a hurry. Moreover, having to add adapters increased the complexity of the system, and it was not unusual to spend long hours trying to figure out why one adapter was conflicting with another.

The solution was to keep an open architecture with slots for adapters and to build into the system board controllers for all of the common peripherals. This meant that most people did not have to use adapters at all and that system units could be smaller and cheaper because they needed fewer expansion slots.

Whereas newer PC designs do away with the need for separate disk controllers and other common I/O ports (see the next section), there still are some common peripheral adapters that you either have in your PC or may want to consider adding. One of these is the display adapter. Some PCs have the display circuitry built into the system board, but the more common design is to use a bus slot to hold a display adapter (I give you more information on display adapters a little later in this chapter).

Remember that a peripheral interface is just a way to connect the internal parts of your PC to something in the outside world. Here "outside" doesn't necessarily mean outside the computer case; instead, it means outside the confines of the system board, processor, and memory. That's what the bus is designed to do.

As mentioned earlier, modern computer buses are designed to carry wider and wider paths of information, from 8 to 32 bits at a time. However, by far the most common type of peripheral interface today is the 16-bit device. Some peripheral boards still are designed for only an 8-bit data path. This probably is fine because, especially with mechanical devices, the peripheral you are using probably can't even come close to the speed of the PC, so sending data back and forth along an 8-lane highway is fast enough.

For other peripherals, however, you need 16 lanes. Also, a 16-bit board may provide some additional features made possible by the wider data path. So, if you have a choice between 8- and 16-bit peripheral adapters, the general rule is choose the 16-bit adapter.

You can tell whether you are installing a 16- or an 8-bit peripheral adapter by inspecting the connector side of the board where it plugs into the computer bus. If there is only one set of pins to plug into the bus, you have an 8-bit board; if there are two sets of pins separated by a small space, yours is a 16-bit board.

Among the popular adapters that aren't always installed in new PCs but which you are likely to need are SCSI (Small Computer System Interface), sound, network, and video adapters. Each of these provides your PC with an additional port designed to accept information of one kind or another from the outside world and to supply data from inside your computer to an outside destination.

SCSI Interface

SCSI (pronounced "skuzzy") is a peripheral interface that has been around for a number of years but which has gained popularity in the PC world only relatively recently. Although SCSI interfaces can drive printers, hard disks, tape drives, and other peripherals, the two most common uses for a SCSI adapter in today's PC market are for large hard disk drives and CD-ROM readers.

SCSI is an excellent choice whenever you need high-speed data transfer, when you need to share peripherals across multiple platforms (such as moving a CD-ROM reader from a PC to a Macintosh), or when you need to attach multiple peripherals to a single PC port. The SCSI interface operates as a serial bus to enable you to daisy chain up to seven devices from a single adapter board inside your PC. A cable attaches between your PC and the first peripheral device, then another cable runs from the first SCSI device to the second one, and so on. The last peripheral in the chain has a terminator plug attached to its second SCSI connector instead of a cable to another device. You can operate one device or several with this arrangement.

Traditionally, SCSI disk drives have cost a little more than the more common IDE or ST-series devices, but that price penalty is eroding as more SCSI drives appear. Another slight disadvantage is that DOS doesn't know how to handle a SCSI adapter, so you have to install a custom software driver to operate a SCSI device. This software should be supplied as part of your interface (board) package or should come with your SCSI peripheral. CD-ROM readers, for example, frequently come with software that enables you to access them through common SCSI boards, and the board manufacturers are supplying driver software that supports most CD-ROM readers and other devices.

Sound Cards

Sound cards also are becoming popular with the rise in multimedia applications. PC-based multimedia enables you to incorporate sound, motion video, and a variety of graphics images into presentations or even word processor documents. Although some multimedia software can use the PC's built-in speaker for sound output, you probably won't be happy with that. A better choice is a 16-bit sound adapter that plugs into your PC bus and attaches to a set of stereo speakers or to a stereo amplifier and speaker combination.

This arrangement often provides spectacular sound output from a variety of applications, including Microsoft Windows. For example, you can set up your system to give spoken reminders for calendar events, to play custom sounds or music when certain system events occur, or to record your own voice to use within memos and other documents. This may sound a little futuristic if your main experience is with conventional DOS-based applications, such as database management, spreadsheets, or word processing software. But, as I just mentioned, even these baseline products now support sound input and output to change the way you interact with your PC.

If you don't already have a sound card, you should consider getting one as part of a general modernizing of your PC system. They're not especially expensive, they are easy to install and configure, and more of today's new software offerings either require a sound card or can make use of one if you have one.

Network Adapters

Just as sound input and output is becoming more popular, so is networking, the connecting of multiple PCs through a series of wires so that they can share disk drives, printers, and other peripherals as well as information such as database and calendar data. In addition, when you have several PCs connected over a network, you can send and receive electronic mail to and from the other users on the network. Today, that mail can include not only text, but sound, photographs, and even full-motion video.

Obviously, if you work alone with only one machine, there is little need to consider a network interface card and the associated software. If you have at least two machines in your office or home, however, you are an excellent candidate for networking. The cost is reasonable, and the benefits are worth it. In fact, with even two machines sitting in the same room, networking can save enough time and frustration to pay for the modest cost. Figure 2.15 shows a typical, small office network diagram.

For one thing, networked machines can share a printer. So, if you have from two to a dozen users who need laser printing, a single printer is all you need, unless each user's printing requirements are so heavy that a single printer gets bogged down or worn out quickly. In addition, you can store important data that all users share in one place. The data then can be accessed over the network.

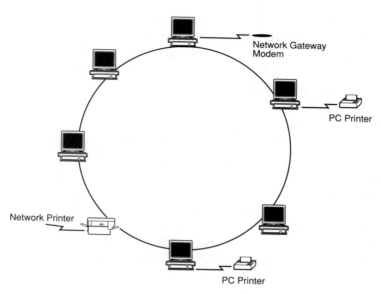

Figure 2.15. *A typical small office network configuration.*

The network interface is really another type of port, like a printer port or communications port. It is a way for data on your computer's bus to leave the confines of the system board and travel across a wire to another computer. As with a SCSI interface, you need additional software for the network adapter to function, and this software usually operates at two levels. You need low-level software to help the computer access the interface hardware and to send and receive information through this port. And, you need user interface software to help you use the facilities of the network such as sharing disk drives or a printer.

However, after the board and software are installed, and the system is configured, most networks become almost transparent. To access information from a remote disk drive, for example, you simply specify that drive's logical letter. If you have two floppies and a hard disk on your machine they are designated drives A, B, and C, respectively. The first drive on the network could then be drive D, the second drive on the network could be E, and so on. And, most networking software enables you to assign another level of names to computers and the drives they have attached. This helps you track what computer and which drives on that computer you are using.

Different installations use different naming schemes. For example, you may have a network configuration that names each computer by the user's name and the drives on each machine with a name and number: for example, JOHNB is used for John Brock's computer, JOHNB01 is John's first shared hard disk, and so on. Other companies get more creative and select a theme based on the interests of the group or on what the company does. Computers and drives are named after animals, fictional characters, medical terms, or whatever.

There are a number of different kinds of networking protocols, and each requires a board (interface) designed for it. By far the most popular network adapter, however, is Ethernet. You may not even be aware of what underlying protocol is being used to handle your network traffic because as a user you probably approach networking from the perspective of the software not the hardware. For example, you may be using a Novell network but not be aware of whether the hardware interface is Ethernet or something else. This doesn't matter in the long run because your network adapter provides the same basic functions whether you are using Ethernet or one of the other protocols.

If you are using Ethernet, the adapter board may have one of three connections or it may have all three Ethernet interfaces built in. Ethernet comes in ThickWire, ThinWire, and Twisted Pair configurations. You also can attach one of these to a fiber interface to use optical signals to carry network traffic. These names refer to the type of wire that is used to connect the network components. Figure 2.16 shows ThinWire Ethernet network connections; figure 2.17 shows a ThickWire Ethernet connection.

As with other peripheral adapters, you can find Ethernet boards in 8- and 16-bit formats. However, the newest adapters are 16-bit boards, and you should consider a 16-bit adapter to get the best possible performance from your network. A few years ago, 8-bit adapter cards were the most common, but today 16-bit cards are pretty much the standard. As technology progresses, of course, look for 32-bit peripheral adapters for some specialty applications.

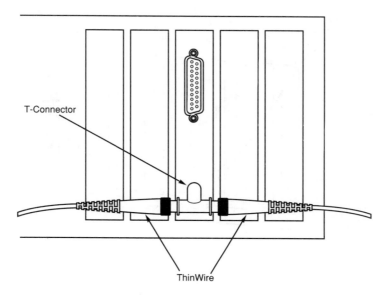

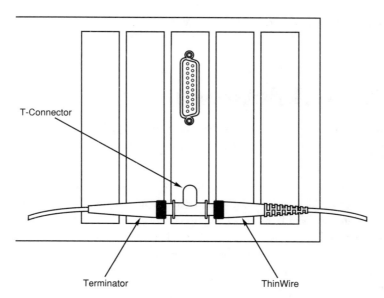

Figure 2.16. *A mid-cable ThinWire Ethernet connection (top); an end-of-network ThinWire Ethernet connection (bottom).*

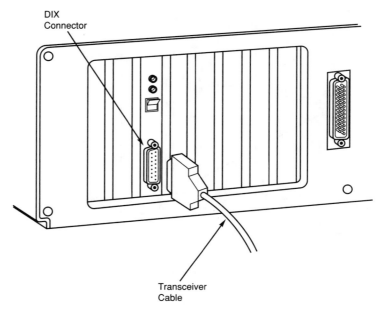

Figure 2.17. *A ThickWire Ethernet connection.*

Video Adapters

Although computer-based video is a relatively minor application—compared with word processing, spreadsheets, and other mainstream software—it is definitely on the rise.

You can load video segments off a CD-ROM reader or from a hard disk, but to capture your own video, you need a video adapter card (see fig. 2.18). This is simply another interface board that attaches to the bus of your PC. On the back are a series of connectors that enable you to attach a video camera, VCR, or other video device. Coupled with software installed on your computer, that adapter enables you to capture single video frames or full-motion video from an external source and store it on your hard disk.

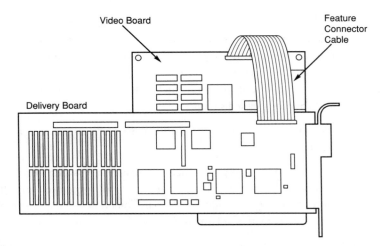

Figure 2.18. *A video interface board.*

Most interface boards, such as the ActionMedia II from Intel, include data compression with the data capture capabilities. This is required because video information requires a tremendous amount of storage space. Without some serious compression, even the largest hard disk would be full with a few seconds of captured video.

What else is on the card depends on the design and on the software that the card is designed to support. There may be stereo audio connections, for example, to enable you to play CD audio or camera/VCR audio through the board, and some boards include a separate audio output section that replaces a sound card for video and other multimedia applications.

Ports

Every device that is external to the system unit must be attached by a cable to the bus. This point of attachment is called a port, or a connector. I like to think of an airport or shipping port, where planes and ships connect to enable cargo and passengers to pass in and out of a city. Similarly, a port on a computer is the place at which a peripheral attaches so that data can move in and out of the system unit.

71

You can think of a port as a place in the system unit into which you can plug a cable. If the port is built in, you are plugging the peripheral directly into the system board. If the port is on an adapter, you are plugging the device into the bus. Either way, the data coming out of the computer is managed by the processor, and everything coming into the computer from outside is touched by the processor on its way into memory, to the display, or to the disk drive.

There are five common types of ports. The first three are a keyboard port, a video port (for the display), and a mouse port.

The next port is for a printer. This port, which is designed to pass data in groups of eight bits, is called a parallel port. Parallel ports are used only for printers and often are referred to as printer ports. In addition, they are sometimes called Centronics interfaces, after the company that originally developed the specification.

The last of the common ports is designed as a multipurpose facility into which you can plug a variety of devices. This port passes one bit of data at a time and, hence, is called a serial port. Sometimes this port also is called an RS-232 port, after the reference number of the technical specification that first defined serial interfaces. A wide variety of peripherals is designed to plug into serial ports, the most common being modems and certain printers. Before there were built-in mouse ports, many mice also plugged into the serial port.

While early PC users had to specify whether to install some of these ports and pay extra for the privilege, nearly all PCs today come with at least five built-in ports: keyboard, video, mouse, parallel, and serial ports. This means that most purchasers of new PCs don't need additional adapters for the majority of applications.

Disks

There are several categories of disks, the most important being floppy disks and hard disks. I discuss floppy disks first and then give you some information about the hard disks you're likely to encounter with most PCs.

Floppy Disks

The floppy disk was the first viable storage medium for practical personal computing. Early PCs used cassette tape to load and save programs, a technology that beat having nothing, but just barely. The first PC floppy drives accepted 5.25-inch diskettes that held 160,000 characters of information. This sounds extremely limited by today's standards, but it was a real boon back then.

Today, the majority of PC floppy drives use 3.5-inch diskettes, although many machines still are configured with 5.25-inch drives so you can read and write this older format. The need for the larger drive is becoming less and less. But, because floppy drives usually cost less than $100, it's a good idea to include a larger drive to give you the option of reading both popular floppy formats.

The original 160KB format for 5.25-inch drives is gone, but you still see software and data written in 360KB format. Most 5.25-inch disks store 1.2MB of data on a single floppy. A single drive can use either style diskette automatically after the data is written (in fact, you even can use the very old 160KB format, which you may need to do to read an old floppy). When you prepare a diskette for 360KB format, you have to tell the format utility what type of medium you are using

The 5.25-inch floppy is encased in a soft base that protects the data to some extent, but that remains flexible. When you insert the diskette into the drive, a rotating spindle in the center hole of the diskette spins the medium inside the case so information can be read like a phonograph record.

The floppy disks for the 3.5-inch drives are encased in a rigid plastic cover that helps protect the floppy magnetic media inside. Although the case is hard, if you open it up you will see that the disk surface is a flexible piece of thin plastic with a brown coating. This coating contains the magnetic particles that store the data.

There are currently three 3.5-inch storage standards: 720KB (the original format), 1.44MB, and 2.88MB. The majority of 3.5-inch drives read and write the first two formats, and an increasing number of drives also support the 2.88MB format.

Hard Disks

The hard disk is the workhorse. The name comes from the fact that the actual disk is rigid. In fact, hard disks usually contain more than one such disk (sometimes called a platter) enclosed in a hermetically sealed container. Hard disks also are called fixed disks because they are permanently mounted in the system unit. Another name that you might see is hard file. This name is used only by IBM, and you probably only will see it in IBM literature.

Hard disks hold much more data than floppy disks. The smallest hard disks hold several tens of megabytes, while the largest hold hundreds of megabytes. In fact, today's large capacity hard disk systems can hold several gigabytes of data.

Other Types of Disks

There is a hybrid disk that is a cross between a hard disk and a floppy disk: the removable hard disk. As the name implies, these disks, sometimes called cartridges, are removable like floppy disks, but hold a large amount of data like hard disks.

The last type of disk is the optical disk. These disks store and retrieve data using laser technology, like the compact audio disks, and require special disk drives.

Optical disks can hold hundreds of megabytes of data, and some computer systems make heavy use of them. The PC family still treats them as options, however, and they are far less common than regular magnetic hard disks.

One variation on the optical disk is the CD-ROM, which stands for compact disk, read-only memory. These disks, like audio disks, are manufactured with the data on them. They can be read, but not changed. CD-ROMs are useful for distributing large amounts of data, such as library catalogs, graphics images, photographs, video, large databases, applications software, and computer books. And, because they cannot be changed, you virtually are guaranteed that the data will not be corrupted.

Displays

There are different types of displays, each of which works with its own video controller. It used to be that video controllers always were manufactured as adapters called display adapters. Nowadays, many computer systems are designed with video controllers built into the system board. You can, however, still buy display adapters that plug into the bus. This is necessary when you want to use a high-performance type of display that requires a special controller. You must buy the appropriate adapter with the display.

Generally speaking, the video capabilities of a PC are referred to in terms of particular standards. The most common standard for newer PCs is called VGA, which stands for Video Graphics Array. All PCs today are supplied with at least a VGA-compatible interface, whether it is built into the system board or plugged into the bus. VGA is, by far, the most common and most important of today's display standards.

However, VGA is not necessarily VGA, if you know what I mean. There are various implementations of VGA, and most of them include enhanced performance with onboard or RAM-based software drivers. By far the most advanced display adapters use a local bus interface (see the previous discussions of local bus technology) and perhaps dedicated display accelerators or processors. Today's graphics-oriented interfaces and applications that require rapid manipulation of graphics, photos, and even motion video mean that standard VGA is seldom good enough.

IBM's low-end PS/2s (models 25 and 30) use a somewhat less powerful video system called MCGA, which stands for Multi-Color Graphics Array or Memory Controller Gate Array. MCGA apparently was an attempt to provide near-VGA performance at a lower cost for low-end PC platforms. Except for IBM, however, there isn't a ground swell of support for it and, with the new structure in IBM's personal computer line, it is doubtful whether MCGA will continue.

Among the most powerful of the video standards is IBM's XGA and XGA-2, which stands for Extended Graphics Array. If you are using software that requires high-performance graphics, such as computer-aided design, with an IBM machine, you probably will want to use an XGA display. The XGA controller is a bus master, which makes for fast, enhanced performance.

The most powerful PS/2s come with XGA. Some models have the XGA bus master built into the system board, while others enable XGA with an XGA bus master adapter. With other 386- and 486-based models, you can add an optional XGA bus master adapter if you want to upgrade from VGA.

While XGA was born in the IBM world, the Video Electronics Standards Association (VESA) has published an XGA extensions standard in an attempt to standardize a software interface to XGA-compatible video devices. This move recognizes that

XGA devices for non-IBM computers are becoming available. And, when there are several available bus designs, the need for standards can be acute.

An older, somewhat less powerful standard is named 8514 (the name comes from the model number of IBM's high-resolution 8514 display). Both 8514 and XGA offer more video performance than VGA. For the most part, however, 8514 has been replaced by XGA. Because XGA uses a bus master, it provides higher performance.

The XGA, VGA, MCGA, and 8514 standards came out with the PS/2s. Several older standards are used with the earlier PCs.

The original PC and the PC XT were built at a time when it was economical to offer two types of displays: one for text (characters) and one for graphics (pictures). These days, of course, all displays work with both text and graphics. In those days, however, there were two standards: one for text, MDA, which stands for Monochrome Display Adapter (the first text display was monochrome, that is, one color), and one for graphics, CGA, which stands for Color Graphics Adapter. CGA provided text as well as graphics but it was of lower resolution than MDA. In other words, with the PC and XT, you had a choice of either high-quality text and no graphics (MDA) or graphics and low-quality text (CGA).

(As an aside, let me mention that the Hercules Corporation devised and made popular a hybrid standard. This standard filled a gap by providing graphics along with high-quality text on monochrome displays. Today, however, this type of hybrid is all but unnecessary because of the reduced prices for full color, graphics adapters. And, the cost for color displays, at one time terribly high, is now at a much more reasonable level, meaning that relatively few users purchase monochrome displays or adapters that support only monochrome.)

At the time the PC AT was announced, it had become economical for IBM to sell color displays that offered both high-quality text and graphics. These displays used a standard called EGA, which stands for Enhanced Graphics Adapter. EGA, which offered more than MDA and CGA combined, was the prevailing standard until the PS/2 and VGA came along.

Table 2.2 shows each graphics standard along with its full name. Note that the A in MDA, CGA, and EGA stands for adapter. In other words, these standards were named after the adapter that plugged into the bus. With MCGA, VGA, and XGA, the A stands for array.

Table 2.2. *PC Family Video Standards*

Name	Stands For	Introduced In
MDA	Monochrome Display Adapter	1981
CGA	Color Graphics Adapter	1981
HGC	Hercules Graphics Card	1982
EGA	Enhanced Graphics Adapter	1984
PGA	Professional Graphics Adapter	1984
VGA	Video Graphics Array	1987
MCGA	Memory Controller Gate Array (or Multi-Color Graphics Array)	1987
8514/A	(Named for IBM 8514 display)	1987
Super VGA	(VESA specification)	1989
XGA	Extended Graphics Array	1990

Some Things To Try

You already know a lot about your particular computer from the exercises I suggested in Chapter 1. But you still can learn a lot about where things are and how they work. This time, however, you need to roll up your sleeves, pick up a screw driver, and play technician. In this section, I show you how to take the covers off of your machine and help you spot the major components.

1. Place your computer where you can get to the rear panel and where you have room to slide the case off of the chassis. This means you should disconnect all cables that are attached to the rear of the machine, including the power cable, keyboard, display cable, mouse, telephone wires, and so on. Remove all connections and place the computer system unit on a desk or table where you can access it.

2. All case designs are slightly different, especially if you are using a tower or a compact case, however, the principal is the same. The outside cover to your machine is a relatively thin piece of metal that flips up or slides off, leaving visible the bottom chassis and all of the computer components. On the rear apron, you should find a series of small screws, five on a conventional desktop enclosure. Use a medium-sized phillips-head screw driver or a 1/4-inch nut driver to remove these screws. Now the computer cover should slide forward or pull straight up. Remove the cover and set it aside where it will be out of the way. Figure 2.19 shows you how a conventional case looks and how to remove it.

If you have a compact computer, there may be only four screws holding the case on. These may be located on the left and right side of the case instead of on the rear apron. Some tower designs have a plastic outer covering on the back that covers up the real case. Use a flat blade screw driver to pry this cover off so you can get to the screws that hold the metal case in place.

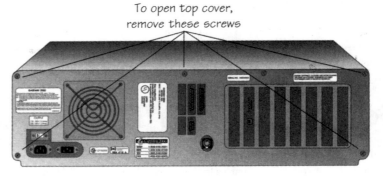

To open top cover, remove these screws

Figure 2.19. *A conventional case and removal. (Drawing courtesy of Gateway 2000.)*

3. With the cover off you should be able to spot most of the major components discussed in Chapters 1 and 2. See the power supply at one corner of the case? Notice how it attaches to the rear panel so that you can plug in the power cable. You should be able to see a bundle of colored wires that carry the converted power from the power supply to the computer. One set of wires goes to the system board to power the main computer components and any plug-in adapters you may have installed. Another set of wires goes directly to the disk drives.

4. Locate your hard disk. It probably is positioned near the middle of the computer case inside a rack or cage of its own. The hard drive is the device that is covered from the outside so you can't see it with the case on. There should be two sets of wires going to it: one is the power cord from the power supply, and the other probably is a broad, flat, gray cable that attaches the drive to the system board or to an adapter board. This is the data and control cable that carries signals in and out of the drive to the computer. If you have more than one hard drive, this cable attaches to both drives so they can share this path to the CPU. If you are using two types of hard drive—an IDE drive and a SCSI drive, for example—then you have two controllers and two separate cables attaching to the drives.

5. Locate your floppy drives. They are mounted so that the front of the drive protrudes through the front panel of the computer to enable you to insert and remove disks. These drives also have power cables attached and should have a signal cable similar to the one on your hard drive. If you have more than one floppy drive, notice how the signal cable attaches to both drives. These are programmable devices that share the signal cable, one at a time, as required.

6. Notice the board that attaches to the display. This is the board (or the portion of the system board) that has the small D-shell connector. Can you tell how many pins this board has? Notice the bus connectors in your machine. They can be of at least three types. You may have one or two connectors that have only one row of connectors. This type of connector is for any 8-bit expansion cards you may need to install. Then you should have six or seven connectors that have at least two rows of connectors. This type of connector is for 16-bit adapters. And, if yours is a newer machine, you may have one or more bus slots that have three rows of connectors. This type of slot is probably a local bus machine. If your hard disk controller and your video adapter are plugged into one of these three-row slots, they are using the local bus for high-speed communications directly with the CPU and memory. Some machines may use a single three-row slot as a memory expansion card. Does your machine have a separate card with no connections to the rear panel plugged into a three-row slot? This could be a memory card.

7. Can you find the main processor (CPU)? This is a large, square chip mounted directly on the system board. It is surrounded by several other

chips of a similar shape, but smaller. If you can see this chip (it may be on a section of the system board covered by your hard disk cage or by the floppy drives), you should be able to read the chip type printed on the surface. If it says i486, you are using an Intel 80486 processor. If it says i386, yours is an Intel 80386 CPU, and so on. You may be using a processor manufactured by another company. In which case the exact markings may be different, but you should be able to find 486, 386, or some numbers to indicate the type of CPU.

8. Locate the I/O section. This may be on the system board or part of a plug-in adapter. There should be two to four cables going to the rear of the computer (or direct connections if these ports are on the system board). This is for your printer and serial port connections. You can identify these ports by the number of pins they contain and the configuration of each one. On most newer machines the first serial port is a 9-pin, D-shell, male connector (the pins stick out of the connector on your computer). The parallel (printer) port also is a D-shell connector, but it has 25 pins and is a female connector (the pins are recessed). Your second serial connector, if you have one, should be a 25-pin male connector.

9. What other connectors do you have on the rear panel? There may be a dedicated mouse port (a small, round connector, most likely), a place for a scanner to attach, a telephone jack if you have an internal modem installed, speaker ports if you have a sound card, and so on. If you are not familiar with these components of your system, spend a few minutes trying to match up what you see inside with what you know about what attaches to these places from the outside.

Obviously, you don't have to understand the physical territory inside your computer to be an experienced and capable user. However, I believe that, the more you understand about the internal workings of a complex device such as a PC, the more capable you are to get the most out of it. In addition, when you are comfortable with the internal territory of your machine, it is easier to install new devices, and you can spot problems more quickly because you understand how things should be.

The next chapter takes a closer look at the processor, including processor types, how they work, and so on. You can leave the cover off of your machine as you read through this material if you want. Otherwise, carefully slide the cover back in place, replace the screws, and then make sure you properly reattach all the cables you removed.

Brains: The Processors

3

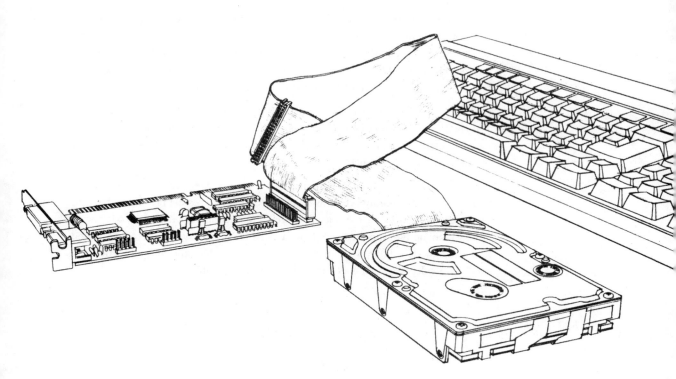

Because the processor is the key working part of a personal computer, if you want to understand the PC, you need to understand the capabilities of the processor that powers it. The PC family is based on the Intel 86 family of processors. The members of this family that are used in PCs are the 8086, 8088, 80286, 80386, 80386SX, 80386SL, 80486, 80486SX, 80486SL, and the Pentium (sometimes previously referred to as the 80586).

The 8086 and 8088 work in only one way. The 286 can work in one of two ways, called real mode or protected mode. In real mode, the processor acts like an 8086. In protected mode, the processor comes into its own, exhibiting all of its advanced features.

The 386 and 486 families also operate in both real mode and protected mode. Moreover, in protected mode, these processors can operate in a special way called virtual 86 mode. This enables the processor to work like an 8086 but adds some of the important features of protected mode.

The Pentium is the natural successor to the 80486. It offers the same features as the 486 and adds features that go beyond the 486.

But why did the Intel designers go to such trouble to enable the advanced processors to act like the older 8086? To provide compatibility. As newer chips were introduced, there simply was too much software already being used every day to throw it out in favor of a new processor design. So, while designers wanted to modernize the processor and improve it, they also knew that to turn too sharply off of the course they already had set would mean a large market backlash, perhaps causing users and system designers to choose another chip architecture for their machines.

In this chapter, I talk a little about the history of this popular chip family and show you the differences among the various members. I discuss current and ancestral models, describing how they differ and how they are alike, and also walk around some of the more technical issues.

But do you really need to know about your PC at this level? The answer is a qualified yes. In the beginning, there were only a couple of possible processors for your PC, and it was fairly easy to understand the differences between them. Today, with at least eight active chips being included in new PC designs, you need to understand how these models differ, what makes one chip better than another, and when you should consider purchasing a PC based on one chip or another.

Microprocessor Types

Actually, contemporary computers have a number of processors, each of them dedicated to a specialized job. There are processors in many display adapters, for example, and dedicated hard disk processors help speed the I/O process. However, there is always one main processor, the one referred to as the processor or central processing unit (or CPU).

With PCs, the processor is always a member of the Intel 86 family. Some PCs also have an auxiliary brain, called a coprocessor. Such coprocessors perform special-purpose mathematical operations and are members of the Intel 87 family—first cousins to the main processors.

Note that there also are third-party companies making processors and coprocessors today. Vendors such as Texas Instruments and Cyrix build their own versions of the Intel processors, and you find these in an increasing number of PC designs. Functionally, non-Intel processor-based PCs should be the same as Intel-based machines, but some non-Intel chips offer enhancements over the original. Nevertheless, as a user you aren't likely to notice which brand of processor you are using unless you pull the covers off of your machine and read the stamps on the top of your chip set.

As the name implies, the PC processors and coprocessors were designed by Intel. Table 3.1 shows the members of the 86 family along with the dates each member was introduced. In a moment, I discuss the various processors and how they are important to PCs. But, first, take a look at table 3.1 and straighten out the names.

Table 3.1. *A Chronological Summary of the Intel 86 Family of Processors*

Date of Announcement	Processor
Jun 1978	8086
Jun 1979	8088
Feb 1982	80286
Mar 1982	80186

continues

83

Table 3.1. *continued*

Date of Announcement	Processor
Mar 1982	80188
Oct 1985	80386DX
Jun 1988	80386SX
Apr 1989	80486DX
Oct 1990	80386SL
Apr 1991	80486SX
Mar 1992	80486DX2
Nov 1992	80486SL
Mar 1993	Pentium

At first, all the members of this family had names that started with 80. In fact, there were several ancestors of the 86 family, and all but one had names that began with 80. They were, from oldest to newest: 4004, 8008, 8080, 8080A, and 8085A.

Carrying on this tradition, the original names of the members of the 86 family were 8086, 8088, 80186, 80188, 80286, 80386, and 80486. By convention, these names were pronounced as two or three distinct numbers. For example, the 80386 was called the "eighty, three, eighty-six." In recent years, the 80 has been dropped from all but the 8088 and 8086, resulting in the following: 8086, 8088, 186, 188, 286, 386, and 486. For example, the 80386 became the 386, pronounced "three, eighty-six."

The newest member of the Intel processor family, the Pentium, broke the naming tradition. While this chip was under development, it frequently was referred to in the computer press as the 586. This would have been the next name in line if the previous conventions had been followed, but Intel obviously was looking for a way to set off its new processor and imply that it is new breed of processor. In some ways it is, but it also is backward compatible with previous members of the Intel chip family. The Pentium is a large step up in processor power, and I talk about some of the Pentium features a little later in this chapter.

There's another naming convention of which you should be aware. Notice that there are two versions of the 386 and 486 chips: the DX and SX versions. At first, there was one 386. When Intel came out with a second version (which I discuss later), the new version was called the 386SX, and the old one was rechristened the 386DX. However, most people still call the 386DX the plain vanilla 386. Later, the same thing happened with the 486. So, if you see a chip reference to 80386 or 386, it is the 80386DX processor. Similarly, a reference to a 486 or 80486 means an 80486DX chip.

Now consider the history of these processors and how they were used in PCs. The first important point to note is that there is no direct correspondence between the history of the PC and the history of the processors. There are two processors—the 80188 and 80186—that were never used to power PCs, at least not mainstream PCs. There were a few proprietary boxes that used these chips, but not in large commercial quantities. The 8086 was used in only two IBM computers. On the other hand, the 8088, 286, 386, and 486 all have been used in a number of different PCs.

The reason is that, although the 8086, 80188, and 80186 would have worked well, they were never available in large enough quantities at the right time to safely design a best-selling computer around them. Their role was usurped by the newer, more powerful 286. They fell, so to speak, through the cracks. (This does not mean, however, that these processors were not used at all. Companies other than IBM used the 8086 to power a variety of 8088 clones and laptops, and the 80186 was used in some option boards, such as theIBM ARTIC card, a special-purpose, real-time processor.)

To understand the history of PCs and how it depends on the processors, go back to 1980 when the original PC was being developed by IBM. The designers had to choose between the 8086 and 8088. The processors are identical except for the amount of data they can send or receive at one time.

As you may know (and as I discuss in more detail later), computers store and manipulate information as bits. You can characterize a processor by saying how many bits it can work with at a time and how many bits it can send or receive at a time. Both the 8086 and 8088 work with 16 bits at a time inside the chip and are described as 16-bit processors. However, where the 8086 can send or receive 16 bits at a time, the 8088 communicates only 8 bits at a time.

Another way to put this is that both processors work with 16 bits internally, but communicate with 16 bits (the 8086) or 8 bits (the 8088) externally. This means that an 8086-based computer uses devices, such as disk drives, and electronic chips that communicate 16 bits at a time.

However, most of the devices and chips available at the time the original PC was being built were 8 bit, having been designed for earlier and slower computers. To cater to this market, Intel designed the 8088 processor to be functionally equivalent to the 8086, except that it communicated 8 bits at a time. This meant that 8088-based computers could take advantage of the 8086's features but still use the older 8-bit components which, at the time, were more readily available and cost less. This means that the 8088 processor, which is newer than the 8086, actually is less powerful than the 8086.

In retrospect, it seems that the 8086 would have been a better choice for the original PC. However, at the time, the IBM designers had no idea that the PC was going to be so popular or that it would soon set international standards. In fact, the PC was not looked upon as an especially important computer. All IBM wanted was a small computer to act as an entry-level machine for its customers.

So, to take advantage of the existing collection of economical 8-bit devices, the PC was introduced with the 8088 processor. The 8088 was the heart of not only the PC but many other computers, including the PC XT, PC Convertible, PCjr, and a large number of the early clones. This is not to say that the 8086 was forsaken. IBM used it for the two low-end PS/2s, the models 25 and 30.

As I have mentioned, there are non-Intel alternatives to some of the chips popular in PCs. Two chips directly interchangeable with the 8088 and 8086 were Nippon Electric Company's (NEC) V20 and V30. Although the NEC chips used the same command set as the Intel devices, they were not strictly identical. Much of the microcode was different and more efficient because the NEC chips were designed with the benefit of hindsight. Replacing an 8088 with a V20 or an 8086 with a V30 improved overall microprocessor throughput as much as 30 percent.

Not long after the introduction of the 8086 and 8088, Intel began working on improvements. Until this time, all processors, including these two, relied on the support of other electronic chips. However, the Intel designers realized that there were important disadvantages to having these support functions performed by separate chips. By incorporating many of these functions into one chip, as a more powerful processor, the computer could work faster. Moreover, using fewer chips would decrease the overall cost.

The results of these improvements were the 186 and 188 processors. Their main feature was that they integrated several support functions into the processor itself. There were also a few other new capabilities, but these were less important. As you have probably guessed from the model numbers, both processors worked with 16 bits internally, but the 186, like the 8086, communicated 16 bits at a time, while the 188, like the 8088, sent and received 8 bits at a time.

The 80286

While the 186 and 188 were an important (if little-used) extension of the 86 family, they didn't make any dramatic improvements on the earlier processors. To do that, Intel labored mightily and came up with what was, at the time, its proudest achievement—the 286.

IBM used this chip as the processor for its Advanced Technology computer, the PC AT. This machine, perhaps more than any other in the IBM line, received the rapt attention of the user community and created excitement and expectation for months before and after it shipped.

The 286 was an enormous improvement over its predecessors in four important ways. First, it could make use of much more memory. Where the 8086, 8088, 188, and 186 could use up to 1MB of memory, the 286 could use up to 16MB.

The second advantage of the 286 is that it could make use of an important feature known as virtual memory. This enabled the processor to use external memory (such as disk memory) to simulate a large amount of real, internal memory. Although the 286 was capable of using up to 16MB of real memory, it could take advantage of external storage and simulate up to 1 gigabyte (GB) of virtual memory.

These improvements in memory usage—the increased real memory and a large amount of virtual memory—greatly expanded the scale of work that the 286 could undertake.

The third important new feature of the 286 added functionality in another way. It enabled the computer to work on more than one chore at a time. This facility is called hardware multitasking. Multitasking works by making it quick and easy for the processor to switch back and forth between tasks.

For example, you may have several windows on your screen, each of which contains a program. Although it looks as if your programs all are executing at the same time, the processor really is switching from one application to another at blinding speed. The older processors could attempt multitasking, but without hardware support, it was not completely reliable and was subject to breakdowns.

The fourth advantage was the chip's processor operating speed. The original PC operated at 4MHz, and the first PC AT, based on the 286, ran at 6MHz. However, this quickly was increased to 8MHz and became the standard. Clone manufacturers introduced speed enhancements of their own, with 286 chips running at 10, 12.5, 16, and even 20MHz. Faster processor clocks mean faster computing, so the capability to run this better chip at five times the clock speed of the original PC meant significantly improved performance.

IBM introduced the 286 processor to the PC family with the PC AT in August 1984. Since then, other companies have produced many AT clones. IBM ultimately used the 286 processor in seven different computers: the PC AT, five PS/2s, and the PS/1. In fact, until fairly recently, many of the IBM compatible computers were basically updated versions of the PC AT. Today there are few 286-based computers being sold, and for good reason. Newer chips offer a lot more functionality and, because prices have fallen drastically, it doesn't make much sense to accept fewer features by purchasing a 286 machine.

Unfortunately, although the 286 had advanced features, few users could take advantage of them. This was because most people used DOS as their operating system, and DOS was based on the old 8088 architecture. This meant that, for most practical purposes, 286-based computers behaved like fast versions of the old machines, almost as if they had been designed around the older 186 processor.

Unlike the earlier processors, which more or less acted the same way all the time, the 286 could affect either of two separate personalities: real mode or protected mode.

In real mode, the 286 acted like an 8086, which made it completely compatible with DOS and the vast body of existing software. However, it was in protected mode that the 286 came into its own, offering virtual memory, hardware multitasking, and a larger memory space. This mode was called protected because, as the processor was multitasking, each program ran in its own world, insulated from all the other programs. In real mode, a runaway program could crash the system; in protected mode, the worst a program could do was damage itself.

Unfortunately, DOS could run only in real mode. However, other operating systems, including OS/2 (an IBM alternative to DOS) and the UNIX systems (XENIX and AIX) could make use of protected mode and the advanced features of the 286.

80386, 80386SX, and 80386SL

The next member of the 86 family developed was the 386. Like the 286, it retained backward compatibility with the older processors by offering a real mode that emulated the 8086. And, its protected mode expanded on the features of the 286. The 386 was a significant advancement, bringing 32-bit power to the desktop—32-bit data I/O and 32-bit addressing. This doubling of internal addressing capability means the 386 can handle up to 4GB of real memory (2^{32} = 4,294,967,296 bytes) and up to 64 terabytes (TB) of virtual memory. (To put this in perspective, 64TB is enough to hold a name and identification number for every man, woman, and child in the world!)

Perhaps even more important, however, is that the 386 added a new mode of operation, called virtual 86 mode. This enabled the processor to multitask more than one DOS program, each of which thinks it is running in its own 8086 machine. And, in fact, there are special control programs, such as Microsoft Windows, that enable you to run multiple DOS programs that are protected from one another simultaneously. This was difficult to do with the 286 because DOS could not run in protected mode.

The 386 processes 32 bits at a time internally (twice as many as the 286, 8086, and 8088) and communicates 32 bits at a time externally (twice as many as the 286 and 8086 and four times as many as the 8088). However, most of the devices and chips available at the time this chip was introduced used 16 bits and were unable to take advantage of the capabilities of the 386.

Intel recognized this fact by bringing out a version of the 386 that communicated using 16 bits at a time. The advantages of this processor were that it was smaller and cheaper than the full 386. Thus, 386SX computers are less expensive than comparable 386 machines. The 386SX chip is virtually identical to the 386 inside. The main differences are that it uses 16- instead of 32-bit data lines and that it costs less. However, with the advent of 486 and Pentium chips, full-blown 386 chips are cheaper than ever, so there is little if any advantage to the 386SX today. In fact, given the very slight price differential between the 386SX and the 386DX, I wouldn't purchase a 386SX system today.

To distinguish between the two types of 386, the new one was called the 386SX, while the old one was renamed the 386DX (think of "single" and "double"). To make an analogy, you could say that the 386DX corresponds to the 186 and 8086, while the 386SX corresponds to the 188 and 8088. However, old habits die hard, and the 386DX still is called simply the 386 by most people.

Just as the 286 chips were designed to run with a faster clock speed than earlier processors, the 386 chip was designed to run at the high end of the 286 clock standard. The first 386 processors ran at 12.5 and 16MHz. However, compared with the number of machines in the field, not many of these chips actually were placed in service. Chips running at 20 and 25MHz followed fairly quickly, and the 33MHz clock standard finally was established. Although a few manufacturers produce special 386 chips that run at 40 and 50MHz, this isn't a popular alternative because 33MHz turns out to be about the upper limit of reliable performance with a 386 chip. Besides, the 486 models offer faster operation, even at 33MHz, so this is the natural upgrade path for speed-hungry 386 users.

Another 386 enhancement over previous chips includes 16 bytes of prefetch cache memory. This on-board memory stores the next few program instructions before they actually are needed. This helps the 386 run more smoothly, with less waiting to retrieve code from system memory.

Another variation of the 386 processor is the 386SL. Intel developed the SL for very small computers, especially those that run on batteries, such as laptop computers. This processor is small and was designed to conserve battery power whenever possible. Moreover, it performs many of the functions that, on regular PCs, must be provided by separate chips.

The 386SL chip series is based on an 80386DX-compatible microprocessor. Some models of the 386SL can operate on either 5 or 3 volts because of a dual, internal power plane. That means the chip can be used in laptop, battery-powered machines or conventional desktop units. Although the original intent was to conserve battery life in portable machines, manufacturers are turning to the SL chips for desktop machines to comply with the Environmental Protection Agency's Energy Star program. Not only do SL chips require less power than conventional chips while they are running, special power management circuitry can shut down the processor when it isn't being used. To comply with the EPA's guidelines (60 watts maximum power drain when the machine isn't being used), more than the processor must power back. However, a computer designed around the SL chips is a good start, and the SL CPU includes special control circuitry to power down other parts of the computer. (Intel calls this feature the System Management Interrupt [SMI], a nonmaskable interrupt that is used in conjunction with a complementary Resume [RSM] instruction to turn things back on.)

As this is written, Intel offers four 386SL chips:

- A 5-volt, 20/25MHz chip with cache

- A 5-volt, 16/20/25MHz cacheless chip

- A 3.3-volt, 20MHz chip with cache

- A 3.3-volt, 16/20MHz cacheless chip

In addition to low power and power management features, the SL chips can use an optional flash memory disk (Intel's term for nonvolatile, read/write RAM). Although flash memory is slower than conventional RAM and requires special interfacing, the SL chip can establish up to 16MB of flash disk memory as a standard ISA data bus drive.

Another way designers can reduce power requirements with SL chips is to slow down the system clock speed during operations that can't be helped by a faster clock speed. The faster a chip operates, the more power it consumes, so slowing the chip down saves power. Thus, when you are typing information on the keyboard, for example, the system could be designed to divide the system clock speed by 2, 4, or 8. When calculations or I/O operations need more speed, the SL can return to normal operation.

The SL series also has battery warning inputs that can be used to shut down a system if the battery gets too low. These inputs also can be used to send warning beeps to a speaker so the user knows a system shutdown due to low battery power is about to occur.

An interesting addition to the 386 line comes from IBM. The 386SLC is the result of an IBM study of existing 80386 chips and the programs that run on them. The 80386SLC is pin compatible with the Intel 80386SX CPU, was designed by IBM, and is manufactured by Intel. IBM claims the special features of its chip can mean a performance improvement of up to 88 percent in some applications over conventional 386 chips.

The 386SLC chip basically is a low-power 386SX with 8KB of onboard cache, similar to the cache that is standard with the 80486 chip (see below). In addition, the full, 80486SX instruction set is included in this chip. The SLC design also optimizes the most common processor instructions called by today's top applications, executing them in fewer clock cycles than conventional 386 machines.

The 80486 Processor

The Intel 486 is the next step up from the 386. Functionally, it incorporates into one chip the circuitry of the 386 plus two other important components: the math coprocessor and the cache controller, which directs special high-speed memory. It also is faster than the 386. Most important, because it is completely compatible with the 386, all the old programs run unchanged, only much more quickly.

As with the 386, there is a 486SX. However, the difference between the 486SX and the regular 486 (which Intel calls the 486DX) is not analogous to the difference between the 386SX and the 386. The difference for the 486 is simply that the 486SX does not have a math coprocessor.

Although the features of the 486 chip aren't a giant leap above the 386, design considerations that are built into it are significant. For one thing, the 486 chip uses a streamlined hardware design. This improved internal design means the 486 trims the number of clock cycles needed for most instructions. Many of the most common 486 instructions can be carried out in a single clock tick.

The 486 chip is highly integrated, one of the new ultra large-scale integration (ULSI) products with 1.2 million transistors. This is a lot of stuff to place on a single chip, and it is this level of integration that contributes to the 486's advanced design and processor speed.

One feature that improves 486 performance is the smaller size of the circuit elements themselves. Standard 486 chips use elements only 1 micron thick; the 50MHz 486 uses an 0.8 micron design, small enough to extend clock speeds to 100MHz.

The 486 math coprocessor is functionally equivalent to the 80387 separate chip used with 386 processors. But, because the coprocessor components are an internal part of the chip, everything is closer together, and the 486 math coprocessor works about twice as fast as an 80387.

And, the internal cache reduces the amount of time the processor must wait on slow DRAM (dynamic random-access memory). As the processor operates on an application, the cache memory fills up with current data and the information around the most recently used memory locations. When the processor needs information from main memory, it first checks the cache. Chances are good that the processor will find what it needs in cache. And, because the cache memory is onboard the chip, it operates a lot faster than system RAM.

The 486 processor runs at various speeds, depending on the model you choose. The top end today is 50MHz (66MHz with a DX2 chip), but the chip design could support 100MHz operation, or more. The faster the chip is operated, the faster it performs in direct proportion to its clock speed. You can expect a 50MHz 486 to be twice as fast as a 25MHz 486, for example, and the newest 66MHz chips runs 30 percent faster than the 50MHz chips. The newest 486 chips—50MHz 486DX2 and 66MHz 486DX2—are designed to plug directly into many existing 33MHz 486DX sockets for performance enhancement. These upgrade chips double the standard speed of internal chip processing, but talk to the outside world at the standard 33MHz clock speed, making them compatible with existing circuitry.

And, as I mentioned at the beginning of this section, the 486 chip is available in an SX model, but the only difference between the 486DX and the 486SX is that the SX lacks the onboard math coprocessor. In addition, the 486SX isn't available at the same clock speeds as the DX model, which further degrades the SX chip in comparison with the DX. You can purchase 25 and 33MHz models of the SX, but you can't get high-speed models (at least not from Intel; see the discussion of clone chips later in this chapter).

For this reason, most users consider the 486SX a logical, cost-effective replacement for the 386DX chip. It costs only slightly more, but, according to Intel, can run twice as fast as the 386DX, assuming both processors are operating at the same system speed. That makes the 486SX a better choice for relatively low-end machines than the 386DX for most applications. And, if you install a machine based on the 486SX and later decide you really do need the power of a coprocessor after all, you can install an Intel 487SX to do the job.

The 486 chip also is available in an SL model, designed initially for laptop and other portable applications. Like the 386SL, this chip uses 3.3 volts instead of 5 volts and includes internal shutdown circuitry to put itself and other selected system components to sleep when they aren't being used. The 486SL also slows itself down when tasks that require little processing power, such as keyboard entry, are being conducted.

IBM has its own version of the 486 as well, the SLC2 model. The following are among the significant features of the IBM version:

- It's 0.7 microns thick.

- It includes clock-doubling circuitry (like Intel's DX2 chips).

- It uses a 3.3-volt, low-power supply (like Intel's 486SL).

- It doubles the 386SLC's onboard cache to 16KB.

IBM promises enhanced SLC chips in the future that will provide improved performance through increased speed, a wider bus, and a larger cache. The company also is planning even lower-voltage and lower-power designs and is working on a better processor upgrade strategy that will include SLC technology.

Meanwhile, Intel has announced an integrated, low-power chip of its own that combines the features of the SL processor into a standard 486. This move, in essence, does away with the two separate chips, making the standard 486 line a low-power offering. The company did the same thing with the new Pentium chip (discussed later in this chapter), so it is a logical move to simplify the product line, add some continuity to the products, and reduce power needs.

No new product names or numbers are involved in this move. The power management circuitry (System Management Mode, or SMM, as Intel calls it) simply is being added to existing 486DX, 486SX, and 486DX2 chips. One new chip was added to the mix with this announcement, a 486DX2 that operates at 40MHz inside and 20MHz outside. The real significance of this new chip, however, is its voltage requirements, a mere 3.3 volts, which reduces overall power requirements. This chip probably will be used as a replacement for the existing 486SL chips in laptops and other portable machines.

I already have mentioned in passing a significant member of the 486 line, the clock-doubling chips or DX2s. This is a significant step for Intel and for the thousands of users who started out with low-end 486 machines and now want to upgrade. I suspect that, as chip technology develops over the next few years, people will look back and say, "Remember those awful DX2 designs?" and "Why did we have to do that?" For now, however, the DX2 offers an elegant and technologically sound way to upgrade your computer without having to throw everything away.

There are two ways to use the DX2 chips to double the speed of your existing 486-based machine, assuming your computer is designed for this upgrade path. You simply can remove the existing 486 CPU and plug in the DX2 model or, if your machine includes an overdrive socket, you can plug an overdrive chip into this socket. The DX2 chip takes over, running at twice system clock speed inside, but talking with the outside world (the rest of your computer) at the original clock speed.

So, if you install a 50MHz DX2 chip into a 25MHz machine, the CPU operates at 50MHz and conducts I/O with your machine at 25MHz. A 66MHz DX2 plugs into a 33MHz machine, functions inside at 66MHz, and talks with the rest of your computer at the original 33MHz speed.

SX Chips: A Closer Look

As mentioned earlier, Intel produced two versions of several processors—a full-powered processor and a similar processor, differing only in the number of bits used for external data communication. For example, the 8088 works like an 8086, except that it communicates using 8, rather than 16, bits at a time. The same goes for the 188 and the 186. Similarly, the 386SX communicates 16 bits at a time, while the regular 386 uses 32 bits. To make this distinction clear, Intel renamed the 386, calling it the 386DX.

The economic importance of the 386SX is that it is cheaper than the 386DX, making for a lower cost to manufacturers and, ultimately, lower-cost computers. (Of course, as higher-powered chips, such as the 486 and Pentium, have reached the market, the need for SX versions of the 386 line has declined with the overall price of this line.)

After the 486 had been selling for a year, Intel announced a 486SX. Like the 386SX, the new processor is cheaper than its big brother, making for lower-cost computers. However, unlike the 386SX (and the 8088 and 188), the 486SX communicates with the same number of bits (32) as the 486. The only difference is that the 486SX lacks a math coprocessor.

So, you might think that the 486SX would be smaller than the 486. After all, the math coprocessing part of the 486 must take up a large percentage of the chip. Actually, the 486SX is the same size as the 486. What is not generally known is that the 486SX really is a 486—the exact same chip—with its math coprocessing facilities deactivated.

What then is the 487SX, the math coprocessor that matches the 486SX? It is a regular 486, one that offers the full math capabilities. When you install a 487 in a computer, you really are inserting a full-function 486. At the same time, the existing 486—the 486SX—is deactivated.

You might ask, "Why bother to sell partially disabled processors in the first place?" There are two reasons. First, Intel tests all processors extensively as part of the manufacturing process. Any chips that are found to be defective must be discarded. With the 486, chips that are defective within the math coprocessor area but are otherwise functional can be sold as 486SX processors.

The second reason has to do with marketing. PC manufacturers want to be able to offer a variety of computers to different markets. By selling a 486SX processor, Intel enables manufacturers to sell two types of 486 computers—one for those who want the most power (the 486) and one for those for whom economy is a prime consideration (the 486SX).

Be forewarned: if you buy a 486SX computer and you later decide that you want a regular 486, you may find the upgrade expensive. After all, the 487 that you have to buy is actually a fully functional 486.

Pentium

I already have hinted at the immense popularity of the Intel 86 line of microprocessors. Before I talk about the newest member of this line, I help you bring things into perspective. If you're reading any of the computer press, the *Wall Street Journal*, or watching popular television programs such as ABC's "Night Line," then you know that the new Pentium processor has generated a lot of interest among users, vendors, developers, and even the news media. It's almost hard to believe the little package shown in figure 3.1 could create so much interest from so many different areas, isn't it?

Figure 3.1. The Pentium processor packaging. (Photo courtesy of Intel.)

But the Pentium is popular. It is popular partly because people have been told it is important and partly because it is important.

Pentium Popularity

There are a number of reasons why this new chip is so important and why you, as a user and someone interested in the inner workings of your PC, also should be interested in it. For one thing, because Intel introduced the 86 line of processors (the 286, 386, and 486), there have been more than 100 million of them built and installed. Nearly half of these—40 million or so—are based on full, 32-bit versions of the 386 or 486 processors.

High-end computing is popular. For years users have waited for the technology to catch up with their expectations and, with each new generation of chips to power their desktop machines, they have anticipated the many more marvelous things they could do. Most of these wild expectations have come to pass. Face it, people now are doing things with PCs that would have been almost beyond imagination only three or four years ago.

Now, the Pentium, with its backward compatibility coupled with almost futuristic power, has the potential for taking desktop and mobile computing even further. In fact, I expect the changes brought about in personal computers by the Pentium will be much more drastic and broader than the difference between the early Intel chips and the 386/486, 32-bit line.

Remember that the 32-bit architecture made windowing environments with multitasking feasible, which is one of the major changes in microcomputer development. The 32-bit machines also brought faster performance and larger memory to support graphics-intensive functions such as CAD, desktop publishing, and multimedia applications.

Expect the Pentium and the innovative, high-end computer systems it prompts to move affordable, desktop computing to a significantly higher level. At 100 million instructions per second (MIPS), the Pentium is powerful enough to assume duties that only minicomputers could do before. And, I expect Pentium-based workstations for graphics, video editing, network servers, disk servers, and other high-end applications to develop quickly. In fact, I expect that video and sound editing and production will be among the Pentium's strongest positions.

Alone or in multiprocessing environments, I expect the Pentium will take on other computer-intensive roles in engineering and business. And, because it can run DOS, UNIX, Windows, and the new Windows NT, the Pentium will form the foundation of a broad-based computer architecture that will be available to users at nearly every level. This will improve cost-performance ratios and help enhance industry standard computing.

All of this won't happen over night. The price of initial Pentium systems will limit them to high-end applications, but the concurrent reduction in prices for 486-based systems will help raise the overall power level of desktop computing. And, as applications are written to catch up with the Pentium's power, more systems will be sold, and the price will come down.

So what is it about this processor that enables it to do all this? That's part of what I discuss in the next section.

Pentium Technology

Like its 32-bit predecessors, Pentium operates in protected and real modes. In addition, this 64-bit chip includes System Management Mode (SMM), first introduced in the SL series 386 chips. This is basically power management with some extras. By using signals at appropriate Pentium pens (external chip connections), programmers can use SMM to control the operation of other parts of the system. For example, SMM can enable power management features of a hard disk drive, spinning it down during extended periods of inactivity and turning it back on again when a request for data is received.

The Pentium processor is housed in the same type of ceramic package as the 486, but it's bigger. You could spot the Pentium in a side-by-side comparison with the 386 and 486 chips easily. The 486 is slightly bigger than the 386, and the Pentium is noticeably larger than the 486. However, when you consider that this chip has the equivalent of 3.1 million transistors in a space only about an inch square, this chip is an engineering marvel. The line width of each internal component is only 0.8 microns, or about 1/100 the thickness of the hair on your head.

As I mentioned, the "business" part of the Pentium, the 3.1 million switches that make up the CPU, are housed in a space about an inch square. The chip is bigger than that, of course, because you have to plug it into a system board and access the 273 connections on the chip. The chip connections are shown in figure 3.2.

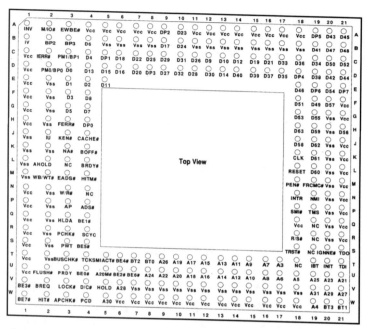

Figure 3.2. *A Pentium processor pinout. (Illustration courtesy of Intel.)*

Because the Pentium application instruction set includes the complete Intel 486 instruction set, with extensions to accommodate the additional features of the Pentium, any software written for the 486 or 386 chips should run on the Pentium chip. Pentium is available in two speeds, 60 and 66MHz. Intel says the 66MHz version runs about 10 percent faster than the slower version.

As a 64-bit chip, Pentium should be a lot faster than its predecessors, assuming the applications it is running are written to take advantage of the chip's features. And, with hardware designed for the Pentium, you should see things moving really quickly even with today's 486-based software.

However, the Pentium is more than a wide data path. It includes some additional features that also should help improve performance. For one thing, a dual pipeline arrangement enables the processor to execute two instructions simultaneously. This is done by partially decoding one instruction in the pipe and then looking at the next instruction in line to determine whether it could be executed in parallel. If it can, both instructions are sent down the pipeline for execution at the same time. This is implemented through a small cache (the branch target buffer) that predicts which way an execution will branch. According to Intel, the prediction is correct over 90 percent of the time, and when it is, the branch is executed without delay. This is done with a pair of prefetch buffers that take in code before it is needed for execution.

Like the 486, the Pentium includes its own, internal math coprocessor. However, the floating-point unit inside the Pentium has been completely redesigned to provide a tenfold speed improvement over the 486 when conducting common operations such as add, multiply, and load.

On-chip caching is one way to improve overall processor throughput, and modern chips have been using it for a while. Now, with the Pentium, there are two 8KB cache memories, one for program code and one for data. Separating the cache in this way reduces cache conflicts, and can improve performance. Obviously, if the processor knows where to go to look for data, it should find it faster than if it has to separate data and code on the fly. In fact, with the dual cache system enabled, Intel says that the data and code required by any given program is in the cache 95 percent of the time. This is one more reason to expect excellent performance from the Pentium.

The precise function of each of these components is beyond the scope of this book, but you may find it interesting to scan the block diagram in figure 3.3 to see how these various modules interface with each other.

You can see from this illustration how the code and data cache units are functionally separate, for instance. Notice the modules for the two separate pipelines, the U pipe and the V pipe. These, too, are parallel but separate functional units, with the U pipe dedicated to all integer and floating-point instructions, and the V pipe dedicated to executing simple integer instructions as well as the FXCH (exchange register contents) floating-point instructions.

This also is a good illustration of how the address and data buses operate separately. As you can see, the Pentium uses a 32-bit address bus, like its predecessors, enabling it to address up to 4GB (2^{32} = 4,294,967,296) of memory. Obviously, that's more than you're likely to cram onto today's motherboard, but wait until true multiprocessing and distributed processing are available—multiple gigabytes of memory may not be that much of a stretch any more.

One other issue worth mentioning is that Intel has planned from the beginning to be able to upgrade many existing 486-based systems to the Pentium processor. There were some initial problems with heat generation when the Pentium was added to a 486 box, but the newest overdrive chips placed in systems designed with the Pentium upgrade in mind should work fine. This is a way to avoid having systems become obsolete as technology advances.

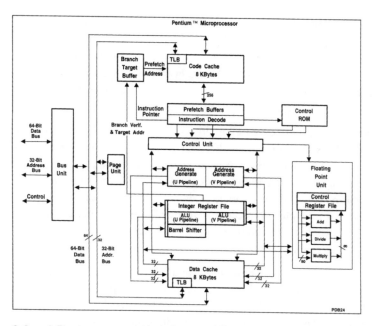

Figure 3.3. *A Pentium processor block diagram. (Illustration courtesy of Intel.)*

That's the basic Pentium—a big, bad, fast, and mean CPU that's capable of powering today's and tomorrow's PCs and still staying ahead of the majority of software development. For those who are interested, I take a closer look at a few of the most significant features of this chip.

Pentium: A Closer Look

Pipelining is an important feature of current chips. This is the capability of the chip to fetch one instruction while operating on the previous instruction. Pipelining has been around since the early days of such processors as the 6502, a very popular, high-speed, 8-bit chip that predated the IBM PC design. The Intel 486 uses pipelining as well.

The Pentium has pipelining, too, but it is a more efficient design that provides better throughput. Part of this efficiency is because of the superscaler design of the chip. It can execute two parallel instructions simultaneously, so two pipelines are needed to fetch the instructions. This parallel execution, or pairing, can handle integer instructions in each pipeline in a single clock cycle.

This instruction pairing would double the speed of the processor, except for the fact that the two pipes are not created equal. The U pipe can execute any instruction in the 86 instruction set, but the V pipe is capable only of "simple" instructions, ones that have been established as instructions capable of being paired with other instructions. Each pipeline consists of five stages executed in order: prefetch, instruction decode, address generate, execute, and write back.

For two instructions to execute simultaneously, both instructions must be classified as simple. These are instructions that are entirely hardwired into the processor and, therefore, don't require any microcode control. These simple instructions also are generally capable of executing in a single clock cycle. As a programmer interested in optimizing your code, you should study carefully Intel's list of paired instructions and design your application to put as many of these together as possible. For the majority of people, it is interesting to know that parallel execution can be done and that it isn't as simple as it sounds.

Branch prediction is another interesting and forward-looking feature of the Pentium processor. Although every branch can't be correctly predicted by the Pentium's branch target buffer (BTB), most of them are. This enables most branches to execute within a single clock and in parallel with other integer instructions.

This can mean a significant speed improvement for some operations. For example, a program loop (such as one that computes prime numbers) that includes a move, a compare, an add, and a jump, might take six clock cycles to execute on the 486. On the Pentium, however, the move and add instructions are paired and the compare and jump instructions are paired and then, with branch prediction, the look executes in two clock cycles. In actual time that's not very much, but within an application that requires hundreds or thousands of such loops over time, overall throughput can be significantly improved.

Consider again the 16KB of internal cache included with the Pentium. This memory is divided into two 8KB modules, one dedicated to data and the other to program code. Remember that a cache is designed to hold data or instructions that haven't yet been called for, but which the cache control logic believes will be wanted soon.

That's what this cache does for programs running on the Pentium. And, according to Intel, the control logic is right about 95 percent of the time on what data or program code should be held in the cache memory. Both cache memories can be addressed at the same time, and the calling program can pull in 32 bytes of raw code and two data references in a single clock cycle.

Finally, consider a standard chip feature that is new with the Pentium, but which Intel is retrofitting to standard 486 CPUs as well. This is System Management Mode (SMM). SMM enables system designers to implement very high-level systems functions, including power management or security transparent to the operating system and to running applications.

SMM ranks right up there with protected mode as a major feature of the Pentium. SMM is one of the chip's operating modes, just as protected mode is. However, SMM is not designed for applications access. Instead, the features of this mode are controlled only through firmware (ROM containing system-level program code) that is built into the hardware design.

Take a look at figure 3.4. This shows the core nature of SMM. Under proper firmware control, the Pentium can enter SMM from any other mode, do whatever it is supposed to do there, and return to the original mode.

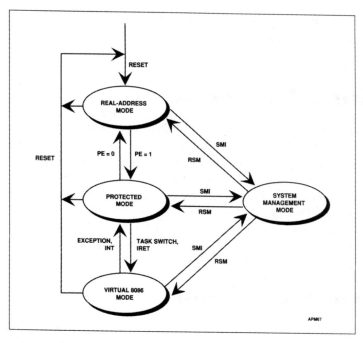

Figure 3.4. *A diagram showing SMM access from any mode. (Illustration courtesy of Intel.)*

This type of two-way transition is possible because the Pentium has a special memory location, called SMRAM (System Management Random-Access Memory) that is used to store SMM program instructions and also to save the register state of the interrupted program. At the same time, all interrupts normally handled by the operating system or by applications software are disabled, giving the SMM program complete control of the system.

After SMM code executes, everything is put back to where it was when the SMM interrupt occurred. The application or system software can pick up where it left off without realizing it has been suspended for a time.

The most obvious application for this facility is power management. An SMM program can put the processor and system peripherals to sleep after a defined period of inactivity and then wake them up and pick up where it left off as soon as a key is pressed or the mouse is moved. SMM is not limited to this feature, however. SMM code has full control of the system, including conducting I/O and the capability to address the full 4GB of RAM. Thus, a computer vendor could use SMM to implement product-specific features, if desired.

Clone Processors

I talk about Intel-based computers and Intel processors and the Intel 86 family because Intel is the company that got it all started. However, there are a number of alternative processor offerings today. I already have mentioned that NEC had a popular replacement (an upgrade, actually) to the original 8088 processor. That is no longer a viable chip, but 486 CPUs from companies such as Texas Instruments and Cyrix are. I discuss very briefly some of these alternative chips so you will be aware of them and understand that, while Intel is the mainstream supplier of processors for personal computers today, there are other sources.

Texas Instruments

Texas Instruments has been a big name in electronics for a long time and now is offering its own line of 486 processor chips. Because the company already supplied personal computer products, portable terminals, and so on, that use 86 family CPUs, this was a logical move. If TI can provide chips for its machines, the cost should be lower, and TI should have more control over the design.

At the same time, however, TI is promoting its TI486 line as a reasonable alternative to the Intel processors. The company offers two basic processors, the TI486DLC and the TI486SLC. They both are 486 code compatible, but they have some interesting design features. (See fig. 3.5 for a side-by-side view of these two chips.)

Figure 3.5. *TI 486DLC and 486SLC chips side by side. (Photo courtesy of Texas Instruments.)*

The SLC model, for example, is backward compatible with the 386SX pinout and is supposed to be nearly 2.5 times faster than the 386SL and 386SX running at the same clock frequency. (That's not so surprising because this is a 486 chip.) The SLC model also includes a suspend mode that shuts nearly all of the on-chip logic down for a resting current draw of only 0.4 mA, according to TI. In addition, there is a version of this chip for 3-volt operation. The SLC is housed in a 100-pin plastic package and addresses only up to 16MB of memory.

The DLC model, on the other hand, is a full, 32-bit implementation of 486 logic that is backward compatible with the 386DX pinout and runs twice as fast as the 386DX. This chip, too, has a sleep mode that requires only 0.4 mA at rest. There also is a 3-volt version. The DLC chip is packaged in a 132-pin ceramic package and includes a full, 4GB physical address range.

While these chips are marketed by TI under the TI name, the chips actually are manufactured for TI by Cyrix.

Cyrix

Cyrix Corporation has had a name for producing "alternative" CPUs for some while. Among the newest chips from Cyrix are the members of the Cx486S line, which include six 486 processors and four companion coprocessors. These chips are 486SX-compatible designs that include power management features and higher operating speeds than comparable Intel offerings. As I mentioned earlier in this chapter, Intel's 486SX chips are available only in 25 and 33MHz versions. Cyrix's answer is to offer SX-compatible chips that operate at 40 and 50MHz.

Cyrix targets the 486S chips, particularly the 40MHz model, at budget-priced or laptop VESA-based systems because that clock speed is a good match for the VESA bus and because the energy savings features of the chips make them appealing to portable system designers. In addition, Cyrix claims that the 40MHz version out-performs all standard 486SX models as well as the 33MHz 486DX.

Comparing the Power of Processors

We live in a competitive world and are used to comparing. One of the questions that comes up over and over is, "How fast is this computer compared with that one?"

Sometimes, the total work that is done by a computer is called throughput. There are different ways to measure throughput, and it depends on a number of factors, including the size and speed of the disks, whether or not there is a coprocessor, and the speed of the memory chips. However, the most important factor, and the one that is compared the most, is the power of the processor.

Before you get started, make sure that you keep things in perspective. As a general rule, newer processors are faster than older ones. For example, a 386 or 486 is faster than an 8086. Also, 386s and 486s are preferable for more than just speed. It is the advanced features of these processors (which were discussed in the previous sections) that are most important. Many people forget that it's not only how fast a processor works but what it can do that is of consequence.

Each member of the processor family comes in more than one model. The only difference among these models is that they run at different speeds. Here is how it works:

each processor depends on an electrical impulse that occurs many times a second. This signal acts as the pulse of the processor, and the time it takes to perform a particular operation is measured in pulse beats (often called cycles). For instance, it takes more cycles to multiply two numbers than to add two numbers.

The number of cycles per second is in the millions, even for the slower processors, and is expressed in megahertz (MHz). (Hertz is simply the scientific term for cycles per second. Thus, 10MHz is 10 million cycles per second.)

All other things being equal, a computer with a fast processor runs quicker than a computer with the same processor running at a slower speed. For example, when the PC AT made its debut, it had a 286 processor that ran at 6MHz. Eventually, IBM came out with a faster PC AT; it used the same 286, but ran at 8MHz.

One last point: when you compare processor speeds remember that newer processors run more efficiently than older processors. Thus, a 486 running at 25MHz is faster than a 386 running at 25MHz. When in doubt, choose the fastest computer you can afford. You won't be sorry.

Computer companies use these different chips to build variations of specific models. For example, the PS/2 model 70, based on a 386, was sold as a 16, 20, or 25MHz machine. Moreover, certain model 70s can be upgraded to 486 machines.

Take a look at table 3.2. It lists each member of the 86 family of processors, from the least to the most powerful. Notice that each processor is available with different speeds. I have listed all the speeds that have been available at one time or another. However, for some of the processors, the slower speeds have been discontinued. Also note that Intel has licensed the design of the 286 and some of the older processors to companies that have offered them at other speeds. The speeds listed in table 3.2 are only those that were officially offered by Intel.

Table 3.2. *Members of the Intel 86 Family of Processors*

Processor	Speeds (in Megahertz)
8088	4.77, 8
8086	4.77, 8, 10
188	8, 10, 12.5, 16

continues

Table 3.2. *continued*

Processor	Speeds (in Megahertz)
186	8, 10, 12.5, 16
286	8, 10, 12.5
386SX	16, 20
386SL	20, 25
386DX	16, 20, 25, 33
486SX	16, 20, 25, 33
486DX	25, 33, 50
486DX2	50, 66
486SL	20, 25
Pentium	60, 66

Note that you will see computers advertised with 486 processors running at 66MHz. These are DX2 machines that run at 66MHz inside the chip, but which still communicate with the rest of the computer at 33MHz. The fastest 486 chip—and the fastest computer bus—is 50MHz. However, this is not a particularly popular arrangement because designers have found that conventional PC buses don't work well at that speed. The most reliable systems still use a 33MHz bus and, besides, tests show that the 66MHz DX2 systems can, under some conditions, outperform the 50MHz models.

The Math Coprocessors

Although the processor acts as the main brain of the computer, special processors—coprocessors—can be used to extend the power of the main processor. These coprocessors are devoted to mathematical operations. In fact, they often are referred to as math coprocessors.

Your computer does not automatically come with a coprocessor (unless you're using a 486DX CPU); it is an option. If you don't have one, the main processor does all the work, including the math. If you do have one, it can handle most of the computational demands of your programs.

You might say to yourself, "I don't do a lot of math, so I don't need a coprocessor." However, your programs may be doing a lot more math than you think. Clearly, if you are using large spreadsheets, a coprocessor can make a difference. What is less obvious is that any program that manipulates geometric shapes, circles, rectangles, wavy lines, and so on, often is doing a lot of computation.

Thus, a coprocessor is really not the luxury most people think it is. In fact, this has been acknowledged by Intel; the 486 comes with the coprocessor built in.

The important thing about coprocessors is that they must be matched correctly to the main processor. This means that, when you buy a coprocessor for your computer, you must choose the one that matches your processor. It must be the correct type and run at the correct speed. (Processor speed is discussed earlier in this chapter.)

Thus, there is a family of coprocessors, the Intel 87 family, that complements the 86 family of processors. Take a look at table 3.3, which shows each processor, along with its corresponding coprocessor.

Table 3.3. *The Intel 87 Family of Coprocessors*

Processor	Math Coprocessor
8088	8087
8086	8087
188	8087
186	8087
286	287
386SX	387SX
386SL	387SX
386	387

continues

Table 3.3. *continued*

Processor	Math Coprocessor
486SX	487SX
486	Coprocessor built in
Pentium	Coprocessor built in

And, just as with main processors, math coprocessors are available from vendors other than Intel. Cyrix, for example, produces a line of coprocessors to complement its CPUs. Again, you don't have to worry about who made the chips unless you're designing computers. And, if your computer is using a Cyrix (or another company's) processor, then the coprocessor probably is from the same vendor. It makes sense to pair up a main processor and a coprocessor from the same company because, while all 86 and 87 family chips are compatible, the offerings of one company or another may have certain features designed to tweak one or more functions. Chips from the same vendor should work together better than mixed chips from various vendors.

When people speak of coprocessors, they normally mean math coprocessors, but there are other types of coprocessors. For example, there are special graphics coprocessors that speed up complex video operations. And, there are bus master adapters that contain their own processors, which can operate independently of the main processor. However, when most people speak of a coprocessor, they mean one of the Intel 87 family of math coprocessors.

The coprocessor chips enable the main processor to offload appropriate number crunching onto the coprocessor's specialty circuits. However, this only can happen when a coprocessor is installed in the PC, when you're using software that knows how to take advantage of the coprocessor, and when there is suitable work for the coprocessor to do.

Nearly all members of the PC family are designed to accommodate a coprocessor, but not many PCs have them installed. Usually they're installed only when there is a particular need for them—when there's a combination of heavy computational work to be done and computer software that can take advantage of the coprocessor.

On the subject of programs that know how to use the coprocessor, it's worth knowing that there are two general categories of software that use the coprocessor. One is programs, such as IBM's version of the APL programming language, that require the coprocessor. Generally, programs that require the coprocessor are oriented toward engineering and scientific work. The other is programs that can take advantage of a coprocessor if one is installed, such as computer-aided design (CAD) systems. Many spreadsheet programs are like this. And, because compilers for programming languages have the capability to detect and use a coprocessor without requiring any special effort from the programmer, you're seeing an increase in the number of programs that benefit from a coprocessor.

You should not expect, though, that installing a coprocessor in your computer will automatically accelerate the speed of the programs you use. First, many programs, such as word processors, simply have no use for a coprocessor. Second, even programs that you think would use the coprocessor heavily don't. For example, some spreadsheet programs that know how to use a coprocessor, do so only for exotic calculations like exponentiation, not for routine arithmetic.

What can a coprocessor do for you? Basically, it can add both speed and accuracy to calculations. The speed comes from the fact that the coprocessors produce their results roughly 50–100 times faster than software subroutines can build the same calculation with the main processor's conventional arithmetic commands. (That spectacular speed improvement is for the calculation alone. When you combine it with a program's routine operations and the overhead that comes with using the coprocessor, the advantage drops to something in the 5–20 times range—less, but still very impressive.)

The added accuracy comes from the fact that coprocessors do all their calculations with the 10-byte format (see Chapter 16). The main processor can present data to the coprocessor in a variety of formats—long and short integer format, three sizes of floating-point number formats, and even a decimal format. The coprocessors actually do all their work in the longest 10-byte, floating-point format (called temporary real), which means that any calculations done with the coprocessors are performed in the highest possible precision. Often, that doesn't matter in the least. But, in lengthy calculations with demanding requirements for high precision, coprocessors can add a great deal of accuracy to the results.

Coprocessors have one curious benefit in addition to those already mentioned. They offer some special features that go beyond the ordinary bounds of floating-point arithmetic in two ways. One is that the coprocessor has seven special constant values built into it, values such as pi that are commonly used in scientific calculations. Those built-in values are a convenience for programmers and provide a way to make sure that a standard, highly accurate value is used to represent those seven mathematical quantities. The other special feature is that, in addition to the four standard arithmetic operations, coprocessors have so-called transcendental operations, which are essential for performing trigonometric and logarithmic calculations. For scientific and engineering calculations, these special instructions reduce the burden of programming and ensure that the calculations are performed in a standard way.

A coprocessor works as an auxiliary to the main processor. It's interesting to know how this is done. The coprocessor acts as a subsidiary of the main processor and springs into action only when the processor generates a special signal for it. A special instruction, called ESCAPE, is used by the main processor to pass a command to the coprocessor. (Don't confuse this special ESCAPE command with the Escape character, decimal code 27, that is part of the PC's character set.) The main processor's ESCAPE instruction includes the instruction code for whichever coprocessor instruction is to be performed. When the coprocessor receives its instruction, it begins performing independently of the main processor, which is then free to either wait for the result from the coprocessor or go on performing other tasks. The sequence of steps involves a little dance of cooperation between the two chips:

- The processor sets the coprocessor into action with an ESCAPE instruction.

- The coprocessor swings into action leaving the main processor free.

- The processor proceeds with other work (for example, preparing data for the next coprocessor instruction) if it has anything useful to do; otherwise, it proceeds to the next step.

- When the processor is ready for the results from the coprocessor, it performs an FWAIT instruction, which waits for the completion of the coprocessor's instruction (in case it's not yet done).

- After the FWAIT, the processor safely can use the results of the coprocessor's calculation.

This sequence seems cumbersome, but it's simpler than it looks. The only thing special about writing assembly language programs like this is that ESCAPE instructions are used instead of regular arithmetic instructions, and FWAIT instructions are added before using the results of the calculations. Of course, only assembly language programmers have to bother with these details. For those who use programs that take advantage of the coprocessor, all the fuss and bother is taken care of—you just enjoy the benefits the coprocessor provides.

The Coprocessor's Constants and Special Ops

As mentioned, coprocessors have built into them something more than just high-powered, floating-point arithmetic. They also have a set of special constant values and transcendental operations that are especially useful for mathematics and engineering.

There are seven special constants. Two—0 and 1—are quite ordinary. They save you the trouble (and space) of storing these values in the program's data. Another, which is familiar to everyone is pi, the ratio of the diameter of a circle to its circumference. The other four provide the basic values needed to work with logarithms, either in base 10 or the natural base mathematicians call e. These four are $\log_2 10$ (the logarithm to the base 2 of 10), $\log_2 e$, $\log_{10} 2$, and $\log_e 2$.

The coprocessor's transcendental operations are needed to calculate functions that can't be built from ordinary, four-function arithmetic. Transcendental functions usually are calculated by approximate formulas, but these five built-in functions provide the basis for performing many different transcendental functions without having to grind through an approximation formula (the standard approximations are built into the coprocessors). These are the functions (the first three functions are available only with the 387 and 487):

- Sine

- Cosine

- Both sine and cosine

- Partial tangent

- Partial arctangent

- $2^x - 1$

- $Y \times \log_2 X$

- $Y \times \log_2 (X + 1)$

These functions may seem obscure—even if you have a vivid memory of mathematics classes—but rest assured that they do indeed provide the core of what is needed to calculate the most common transcendental functions.

113

The Future of PC Processors

It is fascinating to speculate on the future of PCs. The technology has matured so rapidly that constant improvement seems to be the norm. Because each PC is designed around its processor, I take a look at what the future has in store for the 86 family.

Before starting, let me remind you that all speculation in the PC world has to be taken with a grain of salt. In fact, the predictions that I am about to make are based on technology that, in large part, has yet to be developed.

Having qualified my remarks, I start with the Pentium—by far, the most remarkable processor ever developed by Intel. It is highly integrated and includes new features such as a 64-bit bus, branch prediction, dual code, and data cache. The Pentium runs at least twice as fast as a 66MHz 486DX2, giving the Pentium a 100 MIPS (million instructions per second) rating or more at a clock speed of 60MHz. Compare this with the 4.77MHz speed of the 8088 used in the original IBM PC. Moreover, the Pentium is more efficient than the 8088; the actual throughput is several times what you would expect if you simply compared speeds in megahertz.

According to Intel, however, even faster processors are just around the corner. By the middle of the 1990s, expect the 686 (or whatever Intel decides to call it); by the turn of the century, expect the 786.

If current industry scuttlebutt is correct (and it probably is), the 786 will run at 250MHz and contain four separate processor units as well as two vector processors for manipulating lists of numbers. Additionally, large parts of the chip will be devoted to self-testing and to providing a very high-resolution graphical interface, including real-time, full-motion video. And, the 786 will remain compatible with all of today's software! Within Intel, this futuristic processor is known as the Micro 2000 (although it may have another name by the time you see it).

At this time, the fastest available Intel processor is the 66MHz version of the Pentium. In February 1991, Intel demonstrated an extremely fast 100MHz version of the 486, but it never became a commercial product because the Pentium offers higher performance at a lower speed. You may, however, see 100MHz Pentium processors before the advent of the 686.

In addition to faster processors, you should see new processor facilities. An interesting example is the performance improvement, or overdrive, socket that is built into some machines today. Early on, people weren't sure what this socket was for. Now they know it can hold a math coprocessor or an overdrive chip (as described earlier in this chapter). With the Pentium design, I expect to see multiprocessor PC designs before long that will rival high-end minicomputers in performance at a fraction of the cost.

To close this chapter, take a look at table 3.4, which shows each processor and its approximate number of transistors. Because it is difficult to explain exactly what one transistor does, just use the table to furnish yourself with a rough idea of the complexity of each processor. To illustrate the enormous progress of computer technology, I have included entries for the ancestors of the 86 family.

Table 3.4. *The Ancestors, Members, and Future Members of the Intel 86 Family of Processors*

Processor	Approximate Number of Transistors	Year of Introduction
4004	2,300	1971
8008	3,500	1972
8080	6,000	1974
8080A	6,000	1976
8085	6,500	1976
8085A	6,500	1978
8086	29,000	1978
8088	29,000	1979
188	100,000	1982
186	100,000	1982
286	134,000	1982
386	275,000	1985

continues

Table 3.4. *continued*

Processor	Approximate Number of Transistors	Year of Introduction
386SX	275,000	1988
386SL	855,000	1990
486SX	1,185,000	1991
486	1,200,000	1989
Pentium	3,100,000	1993
686	22,000,000	1994–1996
786	100,000,000	1999–2001

Notice the capability of the 786 compared with the early processors. What is almost unbelievable is the prediction that the 786, with its enormous number of transistors, will be packaged as a small chip, measuring only 1 square inch!

Looking at these numbers, it doesn't take much imagination to conceive of a world in the not too distant future in which people will carry around small, portable computers of unbelievable power.

This chapter gives you a pretty good overview of processor types, what the processor can do, and some background and history of the CPUs that are most popular today. For additional details on the inner workings of these fascinating components, read Chapter 4. If you've had enough of processors for now, skip to Chapter 5 to start learning about the world of mechanical storage, disks.

Microprocessor Traffic Control

I've talked about the history of the 86 family processors and coprocessors you can find installed in PCs. I've talked about performance, operating speed, and voltage requirements. I've shown you how the processors use the main and local buses to talk to the rest of the world and transfer information.

In this chapter, I delve a little deeper into how the processor functions and where it stores data, even looking at some simple program code to demonstrate some features. Don't worry! Although this is not an engineering-level discussion, it may go beyond what you want if you are a savvy user but couldn't care less about this level of internal operation. If that's you, turn to Chapter 5.

In this chapter (you still here?), I try to give you an understanding of and an appreciation for the internal workings of today's processors by looking closely at the Intel 8086. Remember from our earlier discussion in Chapter 3 that this older processor is really the processor on which today's modern CPUs are based.

Remember that the 8086 is quite similar to the 8088. Both work with 16 bits at a time and follow the same instructions. The major difference is that the 8086 sends and receives 16 bits at a time, while the 8088 sends and receives 8 bits at a time. The 8086 architecture is the foundation of the original PC. More important, it is also the foundation of DOS.

When studying the Intel family of processors, it is important to get a firm grasp of how the 8086 works. First, I discuss the inner workings of the Intel family of processors, based on the 8086. Then I explain how the newer processors have improved things. In fact, for the purposes of this book, most of what you learn about the 8086 processor applies to the entire processor family. Regardless of how fancy the Intel family of processors becomes, the first key to understanding your PC is understanding the 8086 at a relatively low level.

There's another factor that makes this a logical approach to learning about your PC and its inner workings. That is, when today's chips—an 80386 and later chip—are placed in virtual 86 mode to multitask multiple DOS programs, they are set up to emulate the 8086. So, even if you have a new processor, there may be times when it is running like an 8086. Besides, as I have said, the basic theory of how work gets done at the processor level remains the same whether you are talking about the relatively ancient 8086 or the newest Pentium.

If you want a little more background on how the processor does what it does, stick with me for the next few pages.

What the Processor Can Do

The best place to start is with the fundamental instruction set of the processor. Again, for this technical level of discussion, I concentrate on the 8086. This keeps things relatively simple and, as I mentioned, if you understand the basics of this chip, understanding the Pentium isn't a giant step.

Anything you ask the computer to do is a complex task from the computer's viewpoint. The computer must perform a series of steps built out of the computer's own instruction set. These basic instructions are called machine language, or assembly language. (When it's in the form that programmers write, it's called assembly language; when it's in the form that the computer works with, it's called machine language.) One of the best ways to grasp the power of a computer is to see what its basic machine language instructions can do and how quickly they can do it.

If you tried to look at them in depth, you'd get bogged down in lots of tedious details, the details with which assembly language programmers have to work. That isn't the purpose of this discussion; here, you get a good working idea of what the computer's skills are. I start with simple arithmetic because arithmetic forms the basis for a great deal of what the computer does.

A PC processor can perform the four basic operations of arithmetic: addition, subtraction, multiplication, and division. Addition and subtraction are the simplest and by far the most common operations. Because the 8086 and 8088 are 16-bit processors, you know that they can do their adding and subtracting on 16-bit numbers, but they also can perform arithmetic on individual 8-bit bytes. You might wonder why computers need to do both 8- and 16-bit operations. If 16-bit operations are inherently more powerful, why bother with 8-bit numbers?

There are at least three good reasons for using 8- instead of 16-bit arithmetic. First, if you are working with numbers that can be accommodated in an 8-bit byte, why use twice as much storage as is really needed? When working with lots and lots of numbers that could be stored in 8-bit bytes, the added efficiency of using only single bytes can be very worthwhile. The second reason for using 8-bit arithmetic appears when you want to work on individual bytes.

Here's an example. Sometimes (more often than you might think) you need to convert alphabetic character data to all uppercase. If you look at the numeric equivalents of letters, you find that the lowercase letters fall 32 places above the corresponding uppercase letters in the ASCII coding scheme. (For more information on the PC character set, see Chapter 14.) A program can convert a lowercase letter into uppercase simply by subtracting 32 from the byte that holds the lowercase letter, and that's done with an 8-bit subtraction command. You can demonstrate this by trying this simple command in BASIC:

```
PRINT "a", ASC("a"), ASC("a") - 32, CHR$( ASC("a") - 32 )
```

Finally, the third good reason for using 8- in addition to 16-bit arithmetic is that 8-bit arithmetic easily can be used as the building blocks of more powerful operations. For example, suppose you want to add and subtract numbers that are larger than 16 bits can handle. You may need to work with numbers that are as large as 24 bits, or 3 bytes. You can see how the computer can do this by looking at how you add numbers together. For example, when adding 123 and 456, you do it digit by digit, starting on the right side. You add 3 and 6, getting 9, and then move left to the next place. If any pair of digits gives you a sum over 10, you carry 1 to the next place. Computers can do the same thing using 8-bit arithmetic. With 8-bit addition and subtraction operations, processors can work byte by byte with numbers of any size. Carries from one byte position to the next are handled by a special feature called a carry flag. (For more on flags, see "The PC's Flags" section later in this chapter.)

Note that 8- and 16-bit numbers can be treated as signed or unsigned. The signed formats enable the computer to use negative numbers, and the unsigned formats enable computer to use larger numbers. Processors have variations on the basic addition and subtraction operations that enable programs to choose between 8- and 16-bit size, signed or unsigned values, and using or ignoring carries from previous operations. All of these operations concern the computer's basic binary (base 2) number system. There also are some auxiliary instructions that make it practical for the computer to work with decimal (base 10) numbers.

While processors handle just about every possible variation on addition and subtraction, they take a slightly less complicated approach to multiplication and division. Computers can multiply 8- or 16-bit (byte or word) numbers and treat them as signed or unsigned. For division, computers always divide a 32-bit (or double-word) dividend by an 8- or 16-bit dividend, signed or unsigned.

That's the basic arithmetic that the 8086 processor can do. If you need anything richer, such as larger numbers or floating-point format, the arithmetic usually is handled by a math coprocessor or by special-purpose subroutines (small programs) that can build a larger operation from simple arithmetic building blocks. Interestingly, the 8086 was the first processor family to partition the processing unit to support high-performance number crunching. The companion 8087 coprocessor for this family handled these duties when required. (You can find more information on coprocessors in Chapter 3.)

The 486, 486SX, 386, 386SX, and 386SL can be programmed to work directly with 32-bits, which enables you to use larger numbers (although most DOS programs do not do so). Remember that the 486 was the first 86 family processor with a built-in math coprocessor. PCs based on a 486 always have a coprocessor available and never have to resort to the special-purpose arithmetic subroutines mentioned above.

Snooping at Code

If you want to learn more about the power and features of the PC's instruction set, there are several ways you can do so without taking on the often difficult and tedious task of learning assembly language. This requires some cleverness on your part in deciphering some of the cryptic codes used in assembly language, but the effort can be rewarding in the satisfaction of knowing some of the most intimate details of how the PC works.

The trick is to get your hands on some assembly language programs that you can read and inspect to see just how things are done directly with the PC's instruction set. The best of all is to see some assembly language programming complete with the programmer's comments, which explain a great deal of what is going on.

One source is the IBM *Technical Reference Manual* for a pre-PS/2 computer. These manuals contain fully annotated listings for the ROM-BIOS programs that are built into all PCs. Unfortunately, with the introduction of the PS/2s, IBM stopped publishing the BIOS listings. (Figure 4.1 shows a page from one of these manuals.)

```
                        TITLE TEST1 11/28/83 ROM POST
    ;-------------------------------------------------------------------
    ;
    ; BIOS I/O INTERFACE
    ;
    ;          THESES INTERFACE LISTINGS, PROVIDE ACCESS TO BIOS ROUTINES
    ;          THESE BIOS ROUTINES ARE MEANT TO BE ACCESSED THROUGH
    ;          SOFTWARE INTERRUPTS ONLY.  ANY ADDRESSES PRESENT IN
    ;          THE LISTINGS ARE INCLUDED ONLY FOR COMPLETENESS,
    ;          NOT FOR REFERENCE.  APPLICATIONS WHICH REFERENCE
    ;          ABSOLUTE  ADDRESSES  WITHIN  THE  CODE  SEGMENT
    ;          VIOLATE THE STRUCTURE AND DESIGN OF BIOS.
    ;
    ;-------------------------------------------------------------------
    PAGE
    ;-------------------------------------------------------------------
    ; MODULES REQUIRED
    ;          DATA.SRC        -->     DATA AREA
    ;          TEST1.SRC       -->     TEST.01 THRU TEST.16
    ;          TEST2.SRC       -->     TEST.17 THRU TEST.22
    ;          TEST3.SRC       -->     PROCEDURES
    ;                                  ROS_CHECKSUM
    ;                                  BLINK_INT
    ;                                  ROM_CHECK
    ;                                  XPC_BYTE
    ;                                  PRT_HEX
    ;                                  PROT_PRT_HEX
    ;                                  PROC_SHUTDOWN
    ;          TEST4.SRC       -->     E_MSG
    ;                                  P_MSG
    ;                                  BEEP
    ;                                  ERR_BEEP
    ;                                  KBD_RESET
    ;                                  D11 DUMMY INT HANDLER
    ;                                  INT13 - X287 HANDLER
    ;                                  PRT_SEG
    ;                                  DDS
    ;                                  HARDWARE INT 9 HANDLER (TYPE 71)
    ;          TEST5.SRC       -->     EXCEPTION INTERRUPTS
    ;          TEST6.SRC       -->     STGTST_CNT
    ;                                  ROM_ERR
    ;                                  XMIT_8042
    ;                                  BOOT_STRAP
    ;          TEST7.SRC       -->     PROTECTED MODE TEST
    ;          SYSINIT1.SRC    -->     BUILD PROTECTED MODE DESCRIPTORS
    ;          GDT_BLD.SRC
    ;          SIDT_BLD.SRC
    ;          DSKETTE.SRC     -->     DISKETTE BIOS
    ;          DISK.SRC        -->     HARD FILE BIOS
    ;          KYBD.SRC        -->     KEYBOARD BIOS
    ;          PRT.SRC         -->     PRINTER BIOS
    ;          RS232.SRC       -->     RS232 BIOS
    ;          VIDEO1.SRC      -->     VIDEO BIOS
    ;          BIOS.SRC        -->     MEM_SIZE
    ;                                  EQUIP_DET
    ;                                  NMI
    ;                                  SET_TOD
    ;          BIOS1.SRC       -->     DUMMY CASSETTE (INT 15)
    ;                                  DEVICE OPEN
    ;                                  DEVICE CLOSE
    ;                                  PROGRAM TERMINATION
    ;                                  EVENT WAIT
    ;                                  JOYSTICK SUPPORT
    ;                                  SYSTEM REQUEST KEY
    ;                                  WAIT
    ;                                  MOVE BLOCK
    ;                                  EXTENDED MEMORY SIZE DETERMINE
    ;                                  PROCESSOR TO VIRTUAL MODE
    ;          BIOS2.SRC       -->     TIME OF DAY
    ;                                  TIMER1 INT
    ;                                  PRINT_SCREEN
    ;          ORGS.SRC        -->     PC COMPATABILITY AND TABLES
    ;                                  POST ERROR MESSAGES
    ;-------------------------------------------------------------------
C   INCLUDE POSTEQU.SRC
C   ;-------------------------------------------------------------------
C   ;                      EQUATES
C   ;-------------------------------------------------------------------
= 0000  C   TEST            EQU     0               ; CONDITIONAL ASM (TEST2.SRC)
= 0000  C   KY_LOCK         EQU     0               ; CONDITIONAL ASM (TEST2.SRC)
= 0000  C   KEY_NUMS        EQU     0               ; CONDITIONAL ASM (KYBD.SRC)
        C   ;-------------------------------------------------------------------
= 00F0  C   X287            EQU     0F0H            ; MATH PROCESSOR
        C   ;-------------------------------------------------------------------
= 0020  C   LOOP_POST       EQU     020H            ; MFG LOOP POST JUMPER
        C   ;-------------------------------------------------------------------
= 0010  C   REFRESH_BIT     EQU     010H            ; REFRESH TEST BIT
        C   ;-------------------------------------------------------------------
= 0000  C   POST_SS         EQU     0H              ; POST STACK SEGMENT
= 8000  C   POST_SP         EQU     8000H           ; POST STACK POINTER
= FFFF  C   TEMP_STACK_LO   EQU     0FFFFH          ; SET PROTECTED MODE TEMP_SS
= 0000  C   TEMP_STACK_HI   EQU     0               ; 0:FFFFH
        C   ;-------------------------------------------------------------------
= 0060  C   PORT_A          EQU     60H             ; 8042 KEYBOARD SCAN/DIAG OUTPUTS
= 0061  C   PORT_B          EQU     61H             ; 8042 READ WRITE REGISTER
= 00C0  C   PARITY_ERR      EQU     0C0H            ; RAM/IO CHANNEL PARITY ERROR
= 00F3  C   RAM_PAR_ON      EQU     11110011B       ; AND THIS VALUE
= 000C  C   RAM_PAR_OFF     EQU     00001100B       ; OR THIS VALUE
= 0040  C   IO_CHK          EQU     01000000B       ; IO CHECK?
= 0080  C   PRTY_CHK        EQU     10000000B       ; PARITY CHECK?
        C   ;-------------------------------------------------------------------
= 0064  C   STATUS_PORT     EQU     64H             ;8042 STATUS PORT
= 0001  C   OUT_BUF_FULL    EQU     01H             ; 0 = +OUTPUT BUFFER FULL
= 0002  C   INPT_BUF_FULL   EQU     02H             ; 1 = +INPUT BUFFER FULL
= 0004  C   SYS_FLAG        EQU     04H             ; 2 = +SYSTEM FLAG -POR/-SELF TEST
= 0008  C   CMD_DATA        EQU     08H             ; 3 = -COMMAND/+DATA
= 0010  C   KYBD_INH        EQU     10H             ; 4 = +KEYBOARD INHIBITED
= 0020  C   TRANS_TMOUT     EQU     20H             ; 5 = +TRANSMIT TIMEOUT
= 0040  C   RCV_TMOUT       EQU     40H             ; 6 = +RECEIVE TIME OUT
= 0080  C   PARITY_EVEN     EQU     80H             ; 7 = +PARITY IS EVEN
= 00FE  C   SHUT_CMD        EQU     0FEH            ; CAUSE A SHUTDOWN COMMAND
= 00AB  C   INTR_FACE_CK    EQU     0ABH            ; CHECK 8042 INTERFACE CMD
= 00E0  C   KYBD_CLK_DATA   EQU     0E0H            ; GET KYBD CLOCK AND DATA CMD
= 0001  C   KYBD_CLK        EQU     001H            ; KEYBOARD CLOCK BIT 0
        C   ;-----------------------MANUFACTURING PORT--------------------------
= 0080  C   MFG_PORT        EQU     80H             ; MANUFACTURING CHECKPOINT PORT
        C   ;-----------------MANUFACTURING BIT DEFINITION FOR MFG_ERR_FLAG+1-----
= 0001  C   MEM_FAIL        EQU     00000001B       ; STORAGE TEST FAILED (ERROR 20X)
= 0002  C   PRO_FAIL        EQU     00000010B       ; VIRTUAL MODE TEST FAILED (ERROR 104)
= 0004  C   LMCS_FAIL       EQU     00000100B       ; LOW MEG CHIP SELECT FAILED (ERROR 109)
= 0008  C   KYCLK_FAIL      EQU     00001000B       ; KEYBOARD CLOCK TEST FAILED (ERROR 304)
= 0010  C   KY_SYS_FAIL     EQU     00010000B       ; KEYBOARD OR SYSTEM FAILED (ERROR 303)
= 0020  C   KYBD_FAIL       EQU     00100000B       ; KEYBOARD FAILED (ERROR 301)
= 0040  C   DSK_FAIL        EQU     01000000B       ; DISKETTE TEST FAILED (ERROR 601)
```

Figure 4.1.   ROM-BIOS *code from the* IBM PC AT *Technical Reference Manual.*

If you can't get your hands on an *IBM Technical Reference Manual*, you can try decoding (unassembling) some code (from unintelligible machine language into the slightly more readable assembly language) using an unassembler. One crude but usable unassembler is available as a part of DOS. It's included in the DEBUG program.

You can use DEBUG to unassemble any programs to which you have access, including the PC's built-in ROM programs. You can find an example of how to do this later in this chapter in the "Looking at an Interrupt Handler" section. However, it is important to remember that computer programs are proprietary. You can look, but don't even consider using the routine you find in your own programs.

Although arithmetic forms a large part of the important core of the computer's operations, the computer's processors can do more than arithmetic. If all the computer could do was arithmetic (and other straightforward manipulation of data, such as just moving it around), they would be nothing more than glorified adding machines. What makes computers much more powerful than simple calculators is a variety of instructions known as computer logic.

The computer's logic operations enable it to adjust what's being done to the situation at hand. There are three main kinds of logic operations that computers have in their repertoire: tests, conditional branches, and repeats. As an example, let the computer play the role of a parking lot attendant.

If a parking lot charges, say, $1 an hour with a $5 maximum, the parking lot attendant has to calculate your hourly charge and then check to see if it's over the maximum. The attendant multiplies $1 times the number of hours you were parked and then compares the amount with $5. In computer logic, that comparison is the test, and the result of the test is noted in some special-purpose flags, like the carry flag already mentioned. Generally, the test is some form of arithmetic (such as comparing two numbers, which is the equivalent of subtracting one from the other to see if one is bigger or if they are equal). The flags that are used have an arithmetic meaning. The zero flag means the result of an arithmetic operation was zero or that a comparison of two numbers found them equal. Similarly, the sign flag means the result was negative. These flags, which are the result of any general arithmetic operation or any test comparison operation, set the stage for the second part of computer logic—conditional branches.

Conditional branches enable the computer to adjust its operation to the situation. A branch is a change in the sequence of steps the computer is carrying out. A conditional branch skips from one set of commands to another based on a condition, such as how the flags are set. The parking lot attendant computer, after comparing your total hourly parking charge with the $5 maximum, charges you only $5 if the total hourly charge were higher.

Conditional branches are used in computer programs in two quite different ways. The instruction, the conditional branch, can be the same, but the use to which it's put is quite different. One use, which you already have seen, simply is to select between two courses of action, such as charging the hourly rate or the maximum limit. The other way to use a conditional branch instruction is to use control looping, repeating a series of instructions. The parking lot attendant computer, for example, repeatedly performs the operation of parking a car as long as there are parking spaces available and customers waiting to leave their cars. The parking attendant loops through, or repeats, the process of parking a car, as long as the test and conditional branch instructions show that there are cars to park and places in which to put them.

A regular conditional branch instruction can be used for either purpose—selecting between two courses or controlling a loop—in a computer program. But, because loops are so important to computer work, there are also special-purpose instructions that are customized for the needs of looping. These are the repeat instructions. Some of them are designed to repeat a series of instructions, and some repeat a single instruction—a tightly coupled operation that can be executed with amazing speed and efficiency.

What you've seen so far of the instructions that the computer's processors can perform is really just a sampling of their full repertoire of commands. However, it is a summary of the most important things that the computer can do and should give you some feeling for the basic building blocks out of which programs are constructed.

Whether you are looking at a fast or a slow PC, you should be aware that the processor executes instructions with blinding speed—hundreds of thousands or millions of instructions every second. And, as you may expect, newer processors are continually faster than their predecessors.

And, one reason performance at the instruction level is so important to consider is the fact that even the simplest thing you ask a computer to do involves hundreds and thousands of individual detailed instructions. Moreover, most of the programming done with a processor is conducted at a relatively high level. If you issue a JUMP instruction through an assembler, for example, there is a lot of complicated underlying code required to carry out that seemingly low-level instruction.

Tools at Hand: Memory, Ports, Registers, and Stacks

So far, I've talked about the kinds of operations processors can perform by themselves and with the help of coprocessors. Now, it's time to take a look at the tools that the processor has at its disposal to help it carry out these instructions. I look at how the processor uses memory, ports, registers, and stacks.

The computer's processor has only three ways of talking to the world of circuitry outside of itself. One of the three is the special communication that it has with the 87 coprocessors through the ESCAPE command mentioned in Chapter 3. The other two are much more ordinary and play a key role in the core of the computer's operation. These are the computer's memory and the use of ports.

Remember that memory acts as the computer's desktop, playing field, and workplace. The memory is the place where the processor finds its program instructions and data. Both data and instructions are stored in memory, and the processor picks them up from there. The memory is internal to the computer, and its essential function is to provide a work space for the processor. I take a closer look at memory in Chapter 17.

If memory is essential for the processor's internal use, there has to be a way for the processor's memory to communicate with the world outside. This is what ports are for. A port is something like a telephone line. Any part of the computer's circuitry with which the processor needs to talk is given a port number, and the processor uses that number like a telephone number to call up the particular circuit or part. For example, one port number is used to talk to the keyboard, and another is used for the programmable timer. Controlling the disk drives and transferring data back and forth also is done through ports. The display screen, too, is controlled by using ports. However, the data that appears on the display screen is handled through memory rather than ports, as you see in Chapter 11.

Note that I'm using the word "port" here in a slightly different way than I did in Chapter 2 when I discussed the parts of the computer. In Chapter 2, I used the word to refer to a connection where the cable from a peripheral plugs into the system unit.

The two meanings are related, however. A port is an interface through which data passes—either to and from the processor (as in this section) or to and from the system unit (as in Chapter 2).

The 8086 processor has 65,536 port "telephone numbers" available to it. Not all of them are connected. The designers of any microcomputer decide which port numbers to use for various purposes, and the circuit elements of the computer are wired to respond to those port numbers. The computer's bus (covered in Chapter 2) is something like a telephone party line, which is used in common by every part of the computer that is assigned a port number. When the processor needs to talk to one circuit part or another, it signals the port number on the bus, and the appropriate part responds.

The processor has a number of special assembly language commands that are used to communicate with ports. The OUT command sends one byte or one word of data to a port number; the OUTS and REP OUTS commands send multiple bytes or words of data. Similarly, the IN, INS, and REP INS commands request data from a port number. (Note: The 8086 and 8088 processors support only the simpler OUT and IN commands.)

You usually have no way to experiment with assembly language instructions, such as IN and OUT commands, unless you work directly with assembly language. But, in the case of these two instructions, BASIC provides two commands, called INP and OUT, that do exactly what the assembly language instructions do. You can use them to experiment with the computer's ports, although it's very tricky to do. To give you a quick example, here is a short program that turns the PC's sound on and off simply by using the ports:

```
10  SOUND 500,1
20  X = (INP (97) MOD 4) * 4
30  PRINT "Press any key to stop this infernal noise!"
40  OUT 97, X + 3 ' turn sound on
50  FOR I = 1 TO 250 : NEXT I ' kill time
60  OUT 97, X ' turn sound off
70  FOR I = 1 TO 250 : NEXT I ' kill time
80  IF INKEY$ = "" THEN GOTO 40
```

Here is the same program in QBasic:

```
SOUND 500, 1
X = (INP(97) MOD 4) * 4
PRINT "Press any key to stop this infernal noise!"
DO
   OUT 97, X + 3 ' turn sound on
   FOR I = 1 TO 250: NEXT I  ' kill time
   OUT 97, X ' turn sound off
   FOR I = 1 TO 250: NEXT I  ' kill time
LOOP WHILE INKEY$ = ""
```

To get some firsthand experience in toying with the PC's ports, give this program a try.

Unless you're doing some very special and unusual kinds of programming, you never have any reason to do anything directly with ports. Ports are almost exclusively reserved for use by the BIOS. The purpose of this discussion is so that you understand that ports are the mechanism the processor uses to talk with other parts of the computer's circuitry.

Next, I discuss registers and stacks, the tools available to the computer's processor to carry out its work. As you read, remember that I am describing the architecture of the 8086 and 8088—the architecture that is used in real mode by the 286, 386, 486, and Pentium series processors and in virtual 8086 mode by the 386, 486, and Pentium series processors, respectively. This architecture describes how PCs work most of the time when you are using DOS. I also try to differentiate these early processors from the 386 and later CPUs. Later in the chapter, I discuss a few of the special features that these processors offer in protected mode.

A register is basically a small special-purpose kind of memory that the processor has available for some particular uses. There are several groups of registers in each processor. One group of registers is designed for programmer control. The number of this type of register ranges from 14 in the pre-386 units to 16 in the later processors. In addition, there are many more registers that really aren't designed for programmer control, but that the CPU uses during some of its operations. There are 32 registers total in 386 and later CPUs.

Registers are similar to main memory in one way. They are a set of places where data can be stored while the processor is working on it. However, the computer's main memory is large and is located outside the processor. It can be used for just about anything and is referred to through memory addresses; the registers are different in each of these respects. Figure 4.2 shows the registers used by early PC processors.

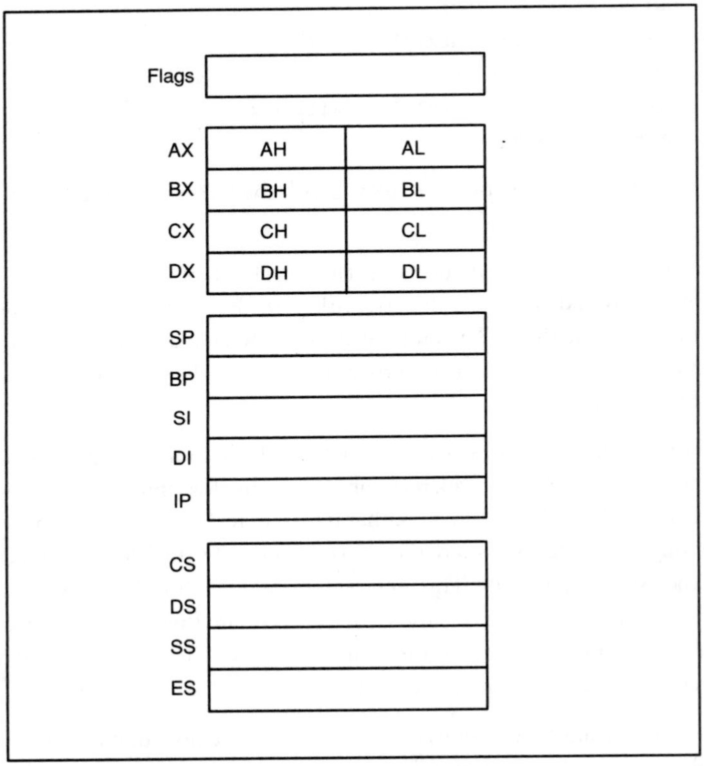

Figure 4.2. *Registers used by the 8088, 8086, 188, 186, and 286 processors.*

The registers are 14 16-bit places where numbers can be stored. Each is an integral, internal part of the processor. Later processors, from the 386 through the Pentium, have a couple more registers, some of which are designed to hold 32 instead of 16 bits of information. Figure 4.3 shows the 16 Pentium processor registers.

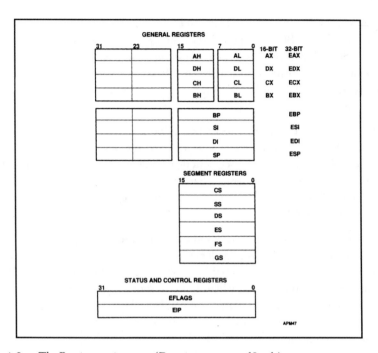

Figure 4.3. *The Pentium register set. (Drawing courtesy of Intel.)*

In effect, each register is a small scratchpad that the processor uses for calculations and record keeping. Some registers are dedicated to one special use, while others have a broad, general use. I take a quick look at each of them. Their actual use, however, really matters only to assembly language programmers.

The first group of registers is the general-purpose registers, which truly are used as scratchpads for calculations. There are four of them (in the pre-386 processors), and they are known as AX, BX, CX, and DX. The 386 and later processors, on the other hand, have eight general-purpose registers. All of these general-purpose registers are 32-bit registers and are called EAX, EBX, ECX, EDX, ESI, EDI, EBP, and ESP.

Programmers can use each general-purpose register as a temporary storage area and scratchpad for calculations. Each register is either 16 or 32 bits in size, depending on the processor. If you want to work with just half of any register, you easily can do so because they are divided into high- and low-order halves (8-bit slices), called AH and AL, BH and BL, and so on. These same subsets are available in all processors. Plus, 386 and later processors can access 16-bit subsets of the 32-bit registers not available on earlier processors. They are labeled BP, SI, DI, and SP. A great deal of the work that goes on inside computers takes place in these general-purpose registers.

The next group of four registers (six on 386 and later processors, including the Pentium) is used to assist the processor in finding its way through the computer's memory. These are called the segment registers. Each one is used to help gain access to a section, or segment, of memory. Earlier processors access memory in 64KB blocks, but later CPUs use segments of varying length. A segment can be as little as 1 byte or as much as 4 gigabytes.

The code segment, or CS, register indicates where in memory a program is located. The data segment, or DS, register locates data that a program is using; the extra segment, or ES, register supplements the data segment. The stack segment, or SS, register locates the computer's stack, which I discuss shortly. There are two more registers on 386 and later processors. These are the FS and GS registers, two more segment designations for memory. These segment registers store information about memory locations, giving programmers the flexibility to choose from several possible memory organizations. You get a clearer idea how registers are used in Chapter 17, when I take a closer look at memory.

While the segment registers are used to gain general access to large chunks of memory, the last group of registers is used in conjunction with a segment register to help find specific bytes in memory. There are five of these registers, each used for a particular purpose. The instruction pointer, IP, register retains the processor's place in the program being executed. The stack pointer, SP, and base pointer, BP, registers are used to help keep track of work in progress that is stored on the stack (a holding area that records information about what the computer currently is doing). The source index, SI, and destination index, DI, registers are used to help programs move large amounts of data from one place to another.

Finally, there is the flag register, which is used to hold the condition flags that I talked about earlier. The various flags tell the programs the state of the computer—the results of arithmetic operations, whether interruptions are allowed, and similar status conditions.

The PC's Flags

The PC's processor is controlled largely through a series of 1-bit flags, each of which signals or sets a particular state in the computer. The flags operate independently of each other, but they are, for convenience, gathered together in the flag register, or EFLAGS register in later chips. Individual flags can be tested and set with special-purpose instructions, and the entire group of flags can be read or set with a pair of instructions.

There are nine standard flags in all in the 8086. The EFLAGS register in later chips is a 32-bit location that stores 13-17 flags, depending on the processor. The Pentium supports 17 flags, for example, and the 386SX has 13 flag positions within the EFLAGS register. Six flags are used to indicate the results of arithmetic and similar operations: the zero flag, ZF, indicates a zero result (or equal comparison); the sign flag, SF, indicates a negative result; the carry flag, CF, indicates a carry to the next position; the auxiliary carry flag, AF, indicates a carry from the first four bits; the overflow flag, OF, indicates a too-large result; and, the parity flag, PF, indicates the odd or even parity of the result.

The three next flags are used for control purposes. The direction flag, DF, controls whether repeated operations (such as a byte-by-byte data move) go right to left or left to right. The interrupt flag, IF, controls whether or not interrupts are enabled or temporarily suspended. The trap flag, TF, causes the computer to generate a special "trap" interrupt after executing a single instruction. This makes it possible to step through a program, tracing the results of each individual instruction.

To these nine flags, the 286 processor adds two more special flags. One, called NT, is used for nested tasks, and the other, a 2-bit flag called IOPL, controls the I/O privilege level. The 386SX and 386 add two more flags: RF, resume flag, is used for debugging, and VM, virtual mode, switches the processor into virtual 86 mode. The 486 adds one flag: AC, alignment check, which is used to indicate whether or not references to memory locations are aligned properly with certain boundaries. Finally, the Pentium, with 17 flags in all, has a three additional flags: the virtual interrupt flag (VIF), the virtual interrupt pending flag (VIP), and the ID flag (ID).

The VIF flag replaces a required flag in multitasking environments that programmers previously had to emulate in software for 386 and 486 environments. Programs written for the 8086 sometimes set and clear the IF flag to control interrupts. In a multitasking environment, this can be a problem. Now, instead of having to maintain a virtual interrupt in software, the Pentium processor handles it. The virtual interrupt pending flag also helps in this process. Finally, the ID bit in the EFLAG register is used to help programs determine with which processor class a given application is running. Programs designed for earlier CPU environments traditionally determined the CPU class by setting a bit pattern within the flag register. Obviously, because early processors had only a 16-bit register for flags, if bits beyond that could be set, the processor must be in the 386 and above class. In addition, by testing for the capability to change the AC flag—unique to the 486 until the arrival of the Pentium—a programmer could determine when a 486 was present. Now, if a program can change the AC flag and set the ID bit, the processor must be a Pentium because the ID flag doesn't exist on 486 CPUs.

You can see and tinker with the flags, and all the other registers, by using the R command of DOS's DEBUG program. For example, if you activate DEBUG and then press R and Enter, DEBUG displays the current register contents and the settings of all the flags. The register dump of a 66MHz 486DX machine is listed below:

```
-r
AX=0000  BX=0000  CX=0000  DX=0000  SP=FFEE  BP=0000  SI=0000  DI=0000
DS=258D  ES=258D  SS=258D  CS=258D  IP=0100  NV UP EI PL NZ NA PO NC
258D:0100 8AFF          MOV     BH,BH
```

There is one remaining tool at the command of the processor that enables it to perform the complicated juggling act needed for the computer to do all the things that users want. As the computer is working, it gets buried in an increasingly complicated stack of work and needs a way to keep track of where it is and what it's doing. To switch from one part of its work to another, the computer also needs a way to put work on hold without losing sight of it. Thus, the stack serves as a computerized holding area that records all the current information about what the computer is doing. When the computer passes into a subroutine, or temporarily interrupts one task to look after another, the stack is used to take note of where the computer was and what it was doing so that the it can return to its interrupted subroutine or task without difficulty. As the computer switches to something new, information about the new operation is placed on top of the stack, indicating what is current. When the computer finishes the new work, information for that task is removed from the stack, and the prior work becomes the current and top item on the stack. In that way, the computer returns to its prior operation.

Now you have seen what processors can do—the general power and features of their instruction sets—and some of the tools they have to help them do it—the memory, stacks, and so on. However, I barely have mentioned interrupts, a driving force in the process. That's what I look at next.

Interrupts: The Driving Force

One of the key things that makes a computer different from any other kind of man-made machine is that computers have the capability to respond to the unpredictable variety of work that comes to them. The key to this capability is a feature known as interrupts. The interrupt feature enables the computer to suspend whatever it is doing and switch to something else in response to an interruption, such as the press of a key on the keyboard.

Interrupts solve what otherwise would be a very difficult problem in getting the computer to work effectively. On the one hand, you want the computer to be busy doing whatever work you've given it; on the other hand, you want it to respond instantly to any request for its attention, such as pressing keys on the keyboard. If the computer could only slog along doing just what it's been told to do in advance, it couldn't respond promptly to keystrokes unless it were constantly checking the keyboard for activity. Interrupts, however, make it possible for the processor to respond to keystrokes—or anything else that needs attention—even though it's busy working on something else. And, the interrupt processes enables this type of immediate response without having to waste CPU time and program code checking all of the possible side tasks that might need doing at any given time.

The computer's processor has the built-in capability to be interrupted combined with a convenient way of putting the work that's been interrupted on hold while the interrupt is being processed. The processor's stack (described above) is used for this. When an interruption occurs, a record of what the processor was doing at the time is stored on the stack, Thus, when the interruption has been handled, work can resume exactly where it left off. This is one of several uses to which the stack is put and is a very key one. Without the stack as a place to put work on hold, the interrupts wouldn't work.

Every part of the computer that might need to request the processor's attention is given its own special interrupt number. The keyboard has its own interrupt, so that every time you press a key on the keyboard (or, interestingly enough, release a key you've pressed), the processor finds out about it. The PC's internal clock also has its own interrupt to enable the computer's time-keeping program to know each time the clock has ticked—which is about 18 times each second. (That sounds like a lot of interruptions, and I'd be inclined to think that being interrupted 18 times a second would be a bother. However, the processor can perform many thousands of instructions between each clock tick, so the clock interrupts don't take up much of the processor's time.) The computer's disk drives and printers have dedicated interrupt numbers, too. The disks use theirs to signal that they have finished work that the program asked to be done; the printers use theirs to signal when they are out of paper.

Interestingly, interrupts were not part of the original concept of a computer. In fact, computers had been used for decades before the interrupt feature came into widespread use. Today it's hard to imagine a computer doing much of anything useful without the interrupts that enable it to respond to demands for its attention.

Although interrupts are used to make the processor respond to outside events, such as the printer running out of paper, that isn't the only thing that they are used for. The concept of an interrupt has turned out to be so useful that it has been adapted to serve a variety of purposes within the computer. There are essentially three kinds of interrupts used in PC computers. The first is the kind I already have discussed—an interrupt that comes from another part of the computer's circuitry reporting something that needs attention. This is called a hardware interrupt. The other two kinds of interrupts relate to software.

Sometimes, while the computer is running a program, something goes wrong with either the program or the program's data. It's as if you were reading along on this sentence and then suddenly found yourself reading rbnss zmc jduhm zmc gzqkdx— some gibberish that didn't make any sense. Although it's not supposed to, that also can happen to the computer. The processor might run into some instructions that don't make any sense or some data that drives it wild (such as trying to divide a number by zero). When this happens, the processor generates an exception interrupt.

The last category of interrupt, unlike the others, doesn't occur unexpectedly. The whole idea of interrupts is so powerful, that they have been put to use as a way of enabling programs to signal that they want some service to be performed by another part of the computer's programs. This type is called a software interrupt. I've mentioned before that PCs come equipped with built-in service programs called the ROM-BIOS. The computer's application programs need a way to request the services that the BIOS provides, and software interrupts are the way they do it. Software interrupts function in exactly the same way as the other kinds of interrupts. The only thing that's different about them is what causes the interrupt. In this case, instead of happening unexpectedly, software interrupts are generated intentionally by a program. There is a special assembly language instruction, called INT, that is used by a program to request an interrupt.

Another Look at Interrupts

There is a wider variety of types and uses for interrupts than you may imagine. In the text above, I outlined three broad categories of interrupt: hardware, exception, and software. But, there is another way of looking at interrupts that is closer to the way they are used in the PC family. You can break the basic interrupts into six different kinds.

First, there are the Intel hardware interrupts, which are the interrupts that are designed into the processor by its designer, Intel. These include the divide-by-zero interrupt mentioned before, a power-failure interrupt, and others. These interrupts are universal to any computer using an Intel 86 processor regardless of how unlike the PC family the computer might be.

Next are the IBM-defined PC hardware interrupts. These are interrupts that report hardware events—printer out of paper or disk action completed, for example—to the processor. The PC hardware interrupts are universal to the PC family.

Then there are the PC software interrupts. These also are defined by IBM and universal to the whole PC family. They are used to activate parts of the PC's built-in ROM-BIOS software—to display a message on the computer's screen, for example.

Then there are DOS software interrupts. Unlike the previous three types, these interrupts aren't built into the computer; they are added on by software—in this case by DOS. Because you normally use the same operating system all the time, these interrupts are, in reality, there all the time, even though they aren't fundamental to the computer's operation. These interrupts are defined and handled by routines internal to DOS (or any other operating system you may be using).

Next are the application software interrupts, which are established temporarily by the program you are running (including BASIC, which uses quite a few of its own special interrupts). These interrupts are defined and handled by the specific application programs.

The sixth category, the table interrupts, is an odd one because it doesn't truly involve interrupts at all. As you see in Chapter 17, part of the interrupt mechanism involves a vector table that holds the memory addresses of the interrupt handlers. This table is a convenient place to store some important addresses that actually have nothing to do with interrupts. For each of these, there's a corresponding interrupt number—one that can never be used because there's no interrupt-handling routine for it. All this table does is store the addresses where interrupt routines are stored. You can learn from this table where interrupt-handling routines are located.

Just how does an interrupt work? Each distinct interrupt is identified by an interrupt number. For example, one interrupt number is used for the disk drives (all drives share the same interrupt). The clock, the keyboard, and the printer all have their own interrupt numbers. For the BIOS services, interrupts are grouped by category; for example, there are over a dozen different BIOS services for different operations on the display screen, but they all share one interrupt number.

For each interrupt number there is a special program, called an interrupt handler, that performs whatever work the interrupt requires. A special table, kept at the very beginning of the computer's memory, records the location of each interrupt handler. When an interrupt occurs, the interrupt number is used to look up the proper interrupt-handling program. Before the interrupt handler begins work, however, the processor's interrupt-processing mechanism saves a record (on the stack) of the work that was in progress. After that is done, control of the processor switches over to the interrupt-handling routine.

The interrupt handler begins its operation temporarily protected from further interruptions, in case it has to perform critical or delicate operations that must not be disrupted. Usually, this involves changing the segment registers that control memory access and saving on the stack any further status information that's needed. After that is done, the interrupt handler safely can reactivate further interrupts of other types and do whatever work the interrupt calls for. When the work is done, the interrupt-handling routine restores the status of the machine to what it was before the interrupt occurred. Finally, the computer carries on with the work it was doing.

Looking at an Interrupt Handler

To give you an idea of what some of the program code in an interrupt handler looks like, I show you how to view some. The fragment I show you is unassembled from the ROM-BIOS of an AT computer. The particular code shown is taken from the beginning of the routine that handles requests for video (display screen) services.

Begin by activating the DEBUG program, as follows:

```
DEBUG
```

Tell DEBUG to unassemble some program code, which translates the computer's machine language into the slightly more readable assembly language format. I happen to know where to find the routine I want to show you, so I tell DEBUG to unassemble it at its hex address:

```
U F000:3605
```

In response, DEBUG gives an unassembled listing that looks like this:

```
F000:3605 FB        STI
F000:3606 FC        CLD
F000:3607 06        PUSH   ES
F000:3608 1E        PUSH   DS
F000:3609 52        PUSH   DX
F000:360A 51        PUSH   CX
F000:360B 53        PUSH   BX
F000:360C 56        PUSH   SI
F000:360D 57        PUSH   DI
F000:360E 55        PUSH   BP
F000:360F 50        PUSH   AX
F000:3610 8AC4      MOV    AL,AH
F000:3612 32E4      XOR    AH,AH
F000:3614 D1E0      SHL    AX,1
F000:3616 8BF0      MOV    SI,AX
F000:3618 3D2800    CMP    AX,0028
```

The very first column (F000:3605, etc.) is a set of reference addresses that you can ignore. The next column of information (FB, FC, 06, and so on.) is the actual machine language code, in hex. After this is what you're interested in—the assembly language equivalent of the program code you've unassembled.

The listing begins with the instruction STI, which reactivates interrupts. When an interrupt occurs, further interrupts are suspended in case the handler needs to do anything critical. In this case, there's nothing important to do, so the handling of other interrupts is turned on first.

The next instruction, CLD, sets the direction flag to its normal, forward state. This ensures that any data movement the program performs goes forward, not backward. This isn't a particularly important operation, but it's interesting to see that the programmer took the time to make sure the direction flag was set forward before anything else was done.

After that is something much more interesting: a series of nine PUSH instructions. The PUSH instruction saves data on the computer's stack. You see that each of these nine PUSH instructions names a register (ES, DS, and so on) that is being saved. These register values are being saved on the stack, so that this interrupt handler can be sure they are safeguarded. When the interrupt handler is done, it restores these values from the stack to the registers, so that regardless of how the registers have been used in the interim, they are returned to their former state.

After the register-saving PUSH operations, you find four data-manipulating instructions (MOV, XOR, SHL, and MOV) that grab a number and prepare it for comparison. Although it's not easy to tell just by looking at these instructions, what is going on here is fairly simple. This interrupt handler can provide a variety of display screen services, each of which is identified by a request code number. Before proceeding, the program gets its hands on that code number and puts it into the form in which this program wants it.

Having done that, the interrupt handler needs to make sure that the service code requested is a proper one, and that's what the last instruction does. Using the CMP (Compare) instruction, the computer compares the number with the value 28, which is the highest number corresponding to a proper service request. After that, the program branches on the basis of that test, either performing the service requested or rejecting the invalid service number.

This isn't an in-depth look at assembly language code, but it should give you a sampling of what assembly language looks like and how to go about decoding it. You can use the techniques shown here to inspect other parts of your computer's ROM-BIOS or other programs. When you do, remember that the ROM-BIOS varies from one model PC to another. The example shown here was from an old PC AT model. Unless you have the same computer, you will not find the same instructions at the same addresses.

Interrupt handlers, for the most part, appear in the computer's built-in ROM-BIOS programs or as a part of the operating system. However, they aren't restricted to just those systems programs. Applications programs—word processors, spreadsheets, and the like—also can have their own interrupt-handling routines. Any program can create an interrupt handler and use it either to replace a standard interrupt handler (so that its interrupts are handled in some special way) or to create a new kind of interrupt.

In the beginning of this section, I described interrupts as the driving force of the PC. Modern computers, which are designed to use interrupts, are said to be interrupt driven. That's because interrupts are the mechanism that connects the computer to the world around it (including users). Interrupts drive the computer because, one way or another, all the work that comes to the computer comes to it in the form of interrupts. More importantly, the internal organization of the computer is designed around interrupts—the forces that determine just where the processor turns its attention. Because the flow of interrupts directs the computer's attention where it's needed, it's quite accurate to think of interrupts as the driving force behind the whole machine.

Now that you've examined interrupts, you've seen all the basics that concern the PC's processor. You've covered the key things that are common to every member of the Intel 86 family. However, the more advanced processors—the 286, 386SX, 386SL, 386, 486SX, 486, and Pentium—add special features that are not part of the standard 8086/8088 architecture. These features, including virtual 86 mode and protected mode, are covered in Chapter 3.

Keeping Up with the Clock

To run at a particular speed, a processor needs something that can provide an electrical pulse at regular intervals, like a metronome. Such a component is called a clock.

Before the 486, PC processors were designed to use a clock that ran at twice the processor speed. For example, a 25MHz 386 computer uses a clock that runs at 50MHz; it just ignores every second beat. This is true for all the members of the Intel 86 family, from the 8086 to the 386. However, beginning with the 486, the newer CPUs use a clock with a matching speed. So, for example, a 25MHz 486 computer uses a 25MHz clock.

Some Things To Try

1. I've discussed how PC processors can do both 8- and 16-bit arithmetic. Is it really necessary to have both? What might be the benefits and costs of only having one or the other? What is the benefit of the 32-bit arithmetic that the newer processors offer?

2. You've seen, in the PC's arithmetic and in its logic looping instructions, some duplication—a variety of instructions that could be simplified into fewer instructions. What might be the advantages and disadvantages—for the computer's designers and programmers—of making a computer with lots of instructions that would provide many different ways of doing roughly the same thing or one with very few instructions that would provide just one way of doing things?

3. Few PCs have the 87 numeric coprocessor installed, and few programs can take advantage of the 87. Why do you think that came about? What might have made the 87 more popular?

4. Using BASIC's INP and OUT commands, write a program to explore the PC's ports. Do you find anything interesting?

5. In the "Looking at an Interrupt Handler" section, I show you how to use the DEBUG U (Unassemble) command. Try using it on your PC at various memory locations to learn what's there. For the most part, each computer system is different, and what you find within memory depends on the type of peripherals you have installed, what programs you are running, and the type of ROM-BIOS you are using. Remember that the U instruction in DEBUG doesn't hurt anything, so feel free to try it.

Disks: The Basic Story

T his chapter begins a six-chapter odyssey in which I discuss the computer's disks. Only one other aspect of our computers (the display screen) is as richly varied and has as many fascinating aspects as the disks. Because everything you use on your computer—all your programs and data—makes its home on disks, understanding disk storage has a great deal of practical importance in addition to being downright interesting.

In this chapter, you get the basics down so that you have a clear idea of just what a disk is. Because people use their disks under the supervision of DOS (Disk Operating System), Chapter 6 looks at disks from the DOS perspective, and Chapter 7 wraps up the discussion by inspecting some of the more technical aspects of disks. Chapter 8 describes disk utilities. Finally, Chapters 9 and 10 describe removable and optical disks, respectively.

Basic Disk Concepts

The disk storage that computers use is based on two things: a recording technology and a quick-access design scheme.

The technology is magnetic recording—the same technology used in the various forms of magnetic tape from audio cassettes to video cassette recorders (VCRs). The basis of magnetic recording lies in the fact that iron and some other materials can be magnetized. You probably remember from childhood science lessons how an iron bar becomes magnetized if you direct a magnetic field over it. The magnetic field is, in a crude sense, recorded in the iron. All of our sophisticated magnetic recording is nothing more than a refinement of that simple science lesson.

Magnetic recording was first and most widely used to record sound, which is an analog form of information. Only later was magnetic recording adapted for the digital recording that computers require.

Digital magnetic recording is done on a surface of magnetically sensitive material, usually a form of iron oxide that gives magnetic media its characteristic rust-brown color. The magnetic coating is quite thin; in fact, the thinner it is, the better it works. It's coated onto a supporting material, usually flexible mylar plastic for recording tape and floppy disks or rigid aluminum platters for hard disks.

Whether you're talking about tapes or disks, the way the information is recorded on the magnetic surface is the same. The surface is treated as an array of dot positions, each of which is treated as a bit that can be set to the magnetic equivalent of 0 or 1. Because the location of these dot positions isn't precisely determined, the recording scheme involves some ready-set-go markings that help the recorder to find and match up with the recording positions. The need for these synchronizing marks is part of the reason that disks have to be formatted before you can use them.

The second basis for disk storage is the quick-access design scheme of a disk. A magnetic tape essentially is linear because information must be recorded on it front to back; there's no quick way to skip to the middle of a tape. A rotating disk, however, is another matter.

Two things about a disk make it possible to get to any part of the surface quickly. The first is rotation. The disk spins around quickly, so any part of its circumference passes by any given point without much delay. A floppy disk spins at 300 RPM, which means it takes, at most, 1/5 of a second for any given part to swing into place; for a hard disk it's about 3,600 RPM, or 1/60 of a second per rotation.

The other thing that makes it possible to move around on the surface of a disk is the movement of the magnetic recording head—similar to the tone arm of a phonograph player—across the disk from outside to inside. For a floppy disk it takes an average 1/6 of a second to move to any desired location; for a hard disk, it takes from 1/25 to 1/70 of a second, depending on the type of disk.

When you combine the two factors—moving the read/write head across the disk surface and rotating the disk into position under the head—you see that you can get to any part of the disk very quickly. That's why computer disks are called random-access storage; you can get to (access) any part of the recorded data directly without having to pass through all the recorded information sequentially. You can see this concept illustrated in figure 5.1.

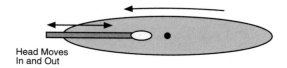

Head Moves
In and Out

Figure 5.1. *Direct disk access.*

Each of the concentric circles of a disk is called a track. The disk surface is divided into tracks, starting at the outer edge of the disk. The number of tracks varies with the type of disk. Today's most common disk, the 3.5-inch, 1.44MB version, has 80 tracks, as do the newer 3.5-inch, 2.88MB and the older 5.25-inch, 1.22MB disks. The low-capacity disks—the 3.5-inch, 720KB and 5.25-inch, 360KB versions—have 40 tracks. Hard disks typically have 300–1,000 tracks. The tracks, however many there are, are identified by number, starting with track zero as the outermost track.

You might expect the tracks to spread across most of the recording surface, but they don't; they cover a surprisingly small area. For example, a 3.5-inch, 1.44MB disk records data at 135 tracks per inch. Because there are 80 tracks, this means that the space between the first and last track is only 80/135 or about 0.6 inches (1.5 cm). (In the technical literature, tracks per inch often is abbreviated TPI; if you run into that term, you now know what it is.)

Just as the disk surface is divided into tracks, the circumference of a track also is divided into sections called sectors. The type of the disk and its format determine how many sectors there are in a circular track. For example, a 3.5-inch, 1.44MB disk has 18 sectors per track. The newer 3.5-inch, 2.88MB disks have 36 sectors per track. The hard disks that normally are used with PCs have 17 sectors per track.

On any given disk, all sectors are a fixed size. PCs can handle a variety of sector sizes from 128 to 1,024 bytes; however, 512-byte sectors have become a standard size, and PC manufacturers rarely deviate from this size. Figure 5.2 shows the relationship between tracks and sectors.

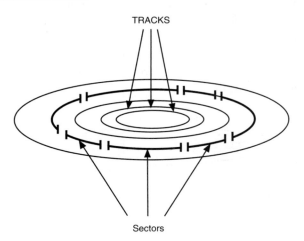

TRACKS

Sectors

Figure 5.2. *The tracks and sectors of a disk.*

All of the reading and writing of data that computers perform with disks is done in terms of complete sectors. As you see later, data can be any size and is made to fit snugly into the fixed storage size of sectors. However, the actual disk I/O that the computer performs is done only in complete sectors.

The sectors in a track, like the tracks on the surface of a disk, are identified by numbers, starting with one rather than zero. (Sector number zero on each track is reserved for identification purposes, rather than for storing data.)

There is one final dimension to a disk that I haven't mentioned—the number of sides. While a floppy disk, like anything that's flat, has only two sides, hard disk drives often contain more than one disk platter, so they can have more than two sides. The sides of a disk, as you might expect, are identified by number; as with tracks, the sides are numbered starting with zero for the first side. You can see the arrangement of a two-platter drive in figure 5.3.

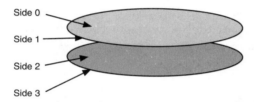

Side 0
Side 1
Side 2
Side 3

Figure 5.3. *The sides of a hard disk.*

Sometimes it is convenient to refer to the set of all tracks, one on each side, that lie at the same distance from the center of the disk. This is called a cylinder. If a drive has two platters, such as the one illustrated in figure 5.3, then each cylinder consists of four tracks.

Here's another example. Say that a hard disk has six sides, sides 0, 1, ..., through 5. Now consider the 26th track on each side—the 26th track on side 0, the 26th track on side 1, and so on. Collectively, these six tracks, the ones that line up at the same distance from the center of the disk, are referred to as the 26th cylinder. (You call it cylinder number 25 because tracks, like sides, are numbered starting from zero.)

On a hard disk, a cylinder includes one track on each of the recording surfaces. On a floppy disk, which has only two sides, a cylinder always consists of two tracks—one on each side.

When you combine all these dimensions, you arrive at the size, or storage capacity, of a disk. Multiplying the number of sides by the number of tracks per side by the number of sectors per track gives you the total number of sectors per disk. Multiply that by the number of bytes per sector—which is normally 512 bytes, or 0.5KB—to get the raw capacity of the disk. Naturally, some of that capacity is occupied with overhead of one kind or another, as you see in Chapter 6. But, the number you calculate in this way is essentially the storage capacity of the disk; it should be the same as, or close to, the capacity that's reported by the DOS utility program CHKDSK (Check Disk).

If you are interested in learning more about your disks, you can use the System Information program that comes with the Norton Utilities. If you have an old version of the utilities—before version 5.0—use the DI (Disk Information) program. These programs show you the four dimensions of your disk's storage together with some DOS-related information that you learn in Chapter 6.

There's one more thing to cover in this section on basic disk concepts. That's how disks are packaged and protected. This varies with different types of disks, so I defer it just briefly until after I describe the main varieties of disks.

Varieties of Disks

It may seem like there are more varieties of disks than can be used. It certainly isn't practical to undertake an exhaustive discussion of all the types of disks that exist; but, you can see the principal types, examine the more exotic varieties, and look more carefully at the most important kinds. That's what this section does. In this discussion, you need to keep clearly in mind that there are varying degrees of difference between the types; some differences are quite fundamental, and others, while important, are not major. Finally, some are purely minor variations. You see the distinctions as you go along.

(Keep in mind that disk storage technology moves forward rapidly. Between the time I write this and the time you read it, it's likely that the PC family will have gained some new disk formats. It's certain that more will appear in the future.)

5.25-Inch Floppy

The place to begin is where the PC family began, with the old-style, 5.25-inch floppy disk. Figure 5.4 shows a drawing of one.

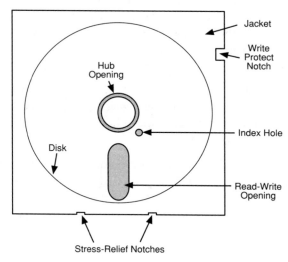

Figure 5.4. *A 5.25-inch floppy disk (top view).*

There are many variations on this disk, but before I get into them, I look at the common characteristics. The disk itself is made of soft flexible mylar plastic with a magnetically sensitive iron oxide coating. The coating is the same on both sides, even for single-sided disks that are intended to be recorded on only one side. The second side of a single-sided disk may not have its second side finished, polished, and tested, but it still has the same coating. Incidentally, not many people know it, but the active side of a single-sided disk is on the bottom, opposite the disk label, not on the top.

The disk has two holes in it. One is the hub where the disk drive grabs it. This hub may have a reinforcing hub ring on it to help ensure that the disk is properly centered. The other hole, the index hole, is just outside the hub. It provides a reference point that defines the beginning of a track.

Surrounding and holding the circular disk is the disk jacket, which usually is black. On the inside surface of the jacket, almost completely out of sight, is a white felt liner. The liner is designed specially to help the disk slide smoothly around and to wipe it clean at the same time. A large oval slot provides the opening through which the disk drive's read/write head touches the disk. The two small cuts on either side of the read/write slot are called stress relief notches; they help ensure that the jacket doesn't warp. Near the hub opening is an opening in the jacket for the index hole, which enables the disk drive to see the index hole in the disk. Finally, on one side, there is a write-protect notch. If this notch is covered, you cannot write to the disk.

You might encounter some variations in the holes and notches that appear on a disk jacket. Some disks don't have a write-protect notch; this means that they cannot be written to. These disks, such as the disks that DOS comes on, are used for the original copies of programs.

There are two types of 5.25-inch disks that you may run into—the 1.2MB version that made its debut with the PC AT and the older 360KB version that was used with the original PC and PC XT. Both these disk types look the same. You have to read the label to tell them apart. If a disk already is formatted, you can check it out by using the DOS CHKDSK command.

These days, 5.25-inch disks mostly are used by old-style, pre-PS/2 computers, although some people buy optional 5.25-inch disk drives for their PS/2s to read and write to the old disks. While many of the old-style computers use the high-capacity 1.2MB disks, almost all DOS software is distributed on the low-capacity 360KB disks.

Here is why. A 1.2MB disk drive can use both disk types; a 360KB drive can read only the low-capacity type. By distributing software on the 360KB disk, the lowest common denominator, software publishers are assured that users can read the disks regardless of what type of 5.25-inch drive they have. Of course, this means programs occupy four times as many disks (compared with high-capacity disks). However, it is easier than having to support three types of 5.25-inch disks. (You see the same thing with 3.5-inch disks.) And, of course, as the whole industry moves away from 5.25-inch disks entirely, there is a trend to distribute software by default on 3.5-inch disks. In the past, you could ask for 3.5-inch software distribution disks; increasingly, you have to ask for 5.25-inch disks.

The high-capacity 1.2MB disk drive can read and write both sizes. Be aware, however, that if you use a high-capacity drive to write on a 360KB disk, a 360KB drive may have trouble reading it. With newer drives this problem is not as common as it once was. However, if you want to be extra careful, format the 360KB disk with a 360KB drive before you use it in a 1.2MB drive.

3.5-Inch Floppy

The next kind of disk to consider is the 3.5-inch floppy disk. A drawing of a 3.5-inch disk is shown in figure 5.5.

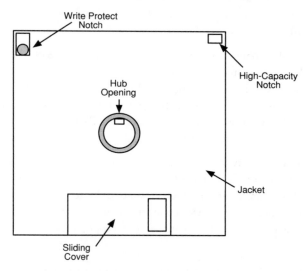

Figure 5.5. *A 3.5-inch disk (bottom view).*

The 3.5-inch disks are obviously smaller than 5.25-inch disks and are enclosed in a rigid protective case. Thanks to the smaller size and hard case, they are much easier and safer to mail and carry around (they fit nicely into a shirt pocket). Moreover, they hold more data than their older 5.25-inch cousins.

Inside, a 3.5-inch disk is the same familiar soft flexible plastic with a metal hub piece. Outside, the jacket is rigid, the hub opening is nearly covered by a hub piece, and the read/write opening is sealed by a spring-loaded sliding metal protector.

Write-protection is signaled by a sliding plastic tab. To write-protect a disk, simply slide the tab so that the little window is open. This works much better than the older 5.25-inch disks with the notches that had to be covered with sticky paper.

Almost all of today's computers use high-capacity, 3.5-inch disks that hold 1.44MB of data. The newest 3.5-inch disks hold 2.88MB. However, older PCs, such as the PC Convertible and the PS/2 models 25 and 30, use low-capacity, 720KB disks. Like the 5.25-inch drives, the 1.44MB drives can use either 720KB or 1.44MB disks.

What this means, unfortunately, is that, as with 5.25-inch disks, software distributors must cater to the lowest common denominator. The result is that most software distributed on 3.5-inch disks is on the low-capacity, 720KB disks. That, too, is changing. A lot of the software I have installed recently has come on high-density (1.44MB), 3.5-inch disks. As before, if the default disk format doesn't work for your machine, you usually can ask the software manufacturer for a version of the product in a different format.

If you look at a high-capacity, 1.44MB disk, you see a small hole in the corner opposite the write-protect switch (see fig. 5.5). This hole signifies that the disk is a high-density disk. In addition, most floppy manufacturers also print the letters HD somewhere on the disk case, either on the top beside the sliding metal cover or on the metal cover itself. The low-capacity, 720KB disks do not have either the extra hole or the printed HD letters.

Here is why. Many of the computers that originally sported the 3.5-inch disks did not have a controller that could set the data rate and write current properly. To get around this limitation, the high-capacity diskettes were identified by this special notch. A mechanical sensor enabled the disk drive to determine if the hole was present and to set the drive parameters appropriately.

These days, drive controllers are more sophisticated and do not make use of this notch. This means that, if you want, you can use a low-capacity disk as if it were a high-capacity disk. That is, you can format a 720KB disk to hold 1.44MB, as many people have done successfully. However—and let me make this perfectly clear—any time you use computer equipment other than according to the manufacturer's specifications, you do so at your own risk. If you want to save money (720KB disks are cheaper), go ahead and try. But, if you lose data, don't say that I didn't warn you. Besides, if you shop around, you should find that the actual difference in price between the low- and high-density diskettes is small enough that it isn't worth the risk of data loss.

If you have one of the new 2.88MB disk drives, you can read and write all three sizes of 3.5-inch disks—720KB, 1.44MB, and 2.88MB. However, the same warning applies. Do not try to format a low-capacity disk as a high-capacity disk. It may work because the read/write medium is essentially the same for all diskettes. However, diskettes designed for high-density service have been tested and certified for this density. If you use a low-density diskette in a high-density application, you may uncover some flaws in the medium that low-density disk testing didn't find. That could translate to data loss.

Hard Disks

Hard disks get their name from the fact that the magnetically coated disks themselves are rigid platters made of an aluminum alloy. Because of many factors, including the much faster speed of rotation and the higher recording density, hard disks need to be in an environment free from dust and other contamination. For this reason, hard disks are sealed inside the disk drive and usually are not removable like other media. Because of this, IBM uses the term fixed disk for what everyone else calls a hard disk. IBM also uses two other terms that you may run into when you read IBM literature: hard file and DASD. DASD (direct access storage device) is an older term that is used with IBM mainframe and midrange computers.

There are many varieties of hard disks. They differ in speed, the number of platters and active recording sides, the number of cylinders, the number of sectors per track, and other characteristics. Generally, they are all lumped together in the collective category of hard disk.

The IBM *Personal System/2 and Personal Computer BIOS Interface Technical Reference Manual* lists more than 30 different hard disk types that are supported by the BIOS. Where the smallest hard disks (now obsolete) held a meager 10MB, large new systems can hold well over 1GB. A typical PS/2 hard disk holds between 80 and 320MB. (Remember, though, that things change quickly. Don't be surprised if, by the time you read this, even these numbers are obsolete.)

Fortunately, all hard disks look pretty much the same from the users viewpoint, and people rarely need to know what type of hard disk they have. (There was a time, however, when DOS could not recognize hard disks larger than 32MB. That restriction was removed with DOS version 4.0. Before that, people with large hard disks had to use the DOS FDISK program to break them into partitions no larger than 32MB.)

Disk Controller Types

Now that I've talked about the physical design of hard and floppy disks, I spend a little time discussing how information is moved in and out of the drive. I've already discussed computer ports as a way for the processor to share information with peripherals. This is how data gets from the hard or floppy disk surface into memory and back out again. I say into and out of memory because, ultimately, this is where the data has to be for the processor to interact with it and for your programs to use it.

Disk drives interface with the computer through controller ports or controller cards. These are plug-in hardware boards that use either the main computer bus or, more recently, the VESA VL or PCI local bus. In addition, a number of computer motherboards are designed with the floppy and hard disk interface built in. Increasingly, when the disk interface is built into the motherboard it uses a local bus technology—VL or PCI—to communicate with the CPU and memory.

Beyond these general concepts, there are several popular disk controller standards, and any one of them may be in use on your computer. In general, as with much of the physical design of disk drives, it doesn't matter much which interface standard your machine uses. Your computer comes with the drive, the interface, and all the necessary cables preinstalled and preconfigured. You install whatever applications you want to use and go from there.

However, when it comes time to add another disk drive or replace a defective drive, what type of interface you have becomes somewhat important. I say "somewhat" because relatively few people actually pop the top on the computer case and put in a new disk drive and because, if you want to install a disk drive that uses a different interface from the one your original drive used, all you have to do is purchase an interface with the new drive, pull out the old card, and stick in the new one. Even when the controller circuitry is integrated with the motherboard, you still can change controller types when you replace the drive. All you have to do is disable the motherboard-based controller by throwing a few switches and then plug in the new card as if there were no controller built into your machine.

Still, you should be familiar with the popular disk drive technology and standards of the day, so I describe each one of them briefly in the next section. There are four basic hard drive interfaces used by personal computers today. Some are more popular than others. These are the AT (ST-506), ESDI, IDE, and SCSI interfaces.

AT

What now is called the AT interface was the original ST-506 standard used by the PC/AT and other machines. It still is (mostly) the interface used by floppy disk drives.

This was a pretty good interface at the time. Today, however, with the need for fast drive response and high transfer rates, the ST-506 really is too slow and limited by the size of disk it supports. For example, ST-506 is good only for 5 megabits per second data transfer, or about 625MB per second. That may sound like a lot of data, but it isn't when you're waiting on your computer to do some real work.

In addition, the ST-506 design isn't good for any drive bigger than 130MB or so. In today's marketplace, where 160–340MB drives are common, this is a severe limitation.

With ST-506 and similar controllers, there actually are several specifications for data transfer and for the way information is written to the drive. With the ST-506 design, the controller inside the computer handles nearly all of the work. The electronics inside the hard disk are designed to interface with the particular controller type, and then the controller takes over. Obviously, if your hard drive is not of the proper type, it doesn't work with your controller.

IDE

As this book is written, IDE (Integrated Drive Electronics, sometimes called "Intelligent" Drive Electronics) is by far the most popular hard disk interface. IDE was developed primarily because there were too many ways to interface a drive to the computer, causing manufacturers, vendors, and users too much trouble and expense.

Here's why I say that. There are three parts of the drive-to-computer interface problem. The computer has to talk to the controller (and vice versa), the controller has to manipulate the data, and the controller has to talk to the disk drive (and vice versa).

Until recently, the problem was approached from all three perspectives, and it was up to interface designers and drive manufacturers to make it all work. Most of the intelligence for moving data back and forth from the computer to the disk drive was on the controller card in the computer.

That meant that, to add a new hard disk or to replace an existing drive, you had to make sure your controller was completely compatible with the new hard drive. Moreover, this approach limited drive manufacturers in the amount of improvements and innovations they could provide because of the inherent limitations in the interface. The IDE controllers changed much of this. With IDE, the controller on board the disk drive takes on a larger role in data transfer, so the actual interface between the drive and the computer can be relatively simple.

As long as the drive you install can interface properly with the electronics of the IDE interface in your computer, it doesn't make much difference what goes on inside the drive, right? Now the "standard" for drive interface is merely to maintain this IDE link between the IDE controller on your computer and the IDE interface inside the disk drive. This simplifies the electronics inside the computer and leaves drive manufacturers more flexibility in how they design the electronics for their drives.

IDE is not the fastest interface available, but other developments have somewhat reduced the need for fast drive interfaces. The main advancement that has improved IDE performance is the local bus interface (see Chapter 2 for more information about local buses). By designing an IDE controller for the local bus, data transfer can take place on the wide and fast local bus instead of the crowded and relatively slow main bus.

You usually can spot an IDE interface in your computer. The interface board is much smaller and less complex than any other controller designs.

ESDI

The ESDI (generally pronounced "esdee") has been around since 1983 or so and is potentially faster than ST-506 and IDE, but it hasn't achieved particularly broad acceptance. ESDI (for Enhanced Small Device Interface), like IDE, was designed to support larger drives than ST-506, is capable of faster transfer rates, and offers manufacturers greater flexibility in their drive designs.

One advantage of ESDI is its recording technique. ESDI places information on a disk roughly twice as dense as ST-506. This is one reason ESDI data transfer rates are twice as fast as ST-506. In fact, some ESDI designs offer data transfer rates of 24 megabits per second, or about 3MB per second.

There probably are several reasons why ESDI is a less popular drive interface than IDE or SCSI (see the discussion of SCSI in the next section). For one thing, the industry specifications and standards for ESDI are relatively loose, leaving a lot of room for manufacturers to make their own decisions about the way information is manipulated and stored. For another thing, it took a long time after Maxtor proposed the design for the standard to be adopted; during that time, the IDE interface was embraced by most of the industry, reducing the pressure for acceptance of ESDI.

Finally, because the interface is used relatively less frequently than others, it costs more to purchase than an IDE-based interface. Because users always want to spend less, if possible, IDE is selected more frequently. And this becomes a chicken-and-egg issue.

SCSI

The SCSI (Small Computer Systems Interface; pronounced "skuzzy") also has been around a long time, but only recently has begun to rise in popularity among PC users. SCSI, like other interface standards, was first used by a drive manufacturer, Shugart Associates, and then moved into an industry standard as other vendors used it and refined it.

SCSI was first popular in the large computer world and moved onto the desktop when Apple routinely included a SCSI port with its machines. Workstation companies started using it next, and SCSI slowly began to move into the PC world.

SCSI is a good choice for PC disk interfaces because it is more of a bus than a simple interface. A SCSI port can daisy chain peripherals from the same interface card, supporting up to seven devices in addition to the interface board. This is important as the number of devices required in a PC continues to grow. Many users have more than one hard drive as well as a tape backup unit, an external or removable hard drive, a CD-ROM reader, and so on. If you must install a separate interface board for each device, you can run out of bus space, especially in today's smaller desktop systems, and out of electronic room, experiencing conflicts with interrupts and other common bus signals.

SCSI, on the other hand, can solve these problems, while providing a high-speed, 5–10MB transfer rate—a plus for today's high-end computer systems.

Some Things To Try

1. The original PC used single-sided disks. The reasons had to do with availability and time constraints. At the time the PC was developed, single-sided disks were readily available and well tested. Double-sided disks were newer and more expensive. The PC design team had a limited amount of time, so it chose to go with a proven, economical technology. Eventually, it switched to double-sided disks. What were the advantages of the original choice? What were the disadvantages?

   Suppose that you were a software vendor at the time that IBM made the switch to double-sided disks. What type of disks would you have used to distribute your software? If you used double-sided, it would have been a problem for all of your customers that had single-sided drives. However, if you used single-sided disks, you would have had to use twice as many disks.

   The same types of problems are with us today. Most DOS software vendors furnish both the old 5.25-inch disks and the new 3.5-inch disks. Moreover, distribution disks usually are the low-capacity versions.

   Many disks are wasted in this way. Is there a solution to this problem? What would you do to avoid similar problems in the future? Do these issues arise with other PC components, such as displays, printers, modems, and so on? What advice would you give to someone on how to buy technology that will last as long as possible?

   Thinking about these problems may help you understand a great deal about the realities that underlie personal computing.

2. An old IBM *Technical Reference Manual* states that a particular disk drive, which had 40 tracks, takes 5 milliseconds per track to move the read/write head. The manual says that the average move takes 81 milliseconds. Why is that and what does that tell you?

3. There are hard disks that have the same capacity but are shaped differently. For example, among the disk types that the PC AT can accommodate automatically, there is one with four sides and 614 cylinders and another with eight sides and 307 cylinders. The capacity of the two is identical. Is there any practical difference between them?

Disks: The DOS Perspective

6

I n this second chapter about disks, I take a look at computer disks from the DOS perspective; that is, how DOS lays them out and uses them. Disks, by themselves, are a kind of raw, unsurveyed land. It's only when an operating system, such as DOS, creates a map of how they are to be used that disks take on a useful form. Each operating system—the PC family has several—has its own plan for how the unbroken land of a disk should be turned into productive fields. Because DOS is the only operating system that most PC users encounter, DOS's way of organizing a disk is the only one I cover.

First, I look at the basics of how DOS uses a disk, followed by the technical specifics that underlie a DOS disk. Then, I explore key elements of what DOS data files look like, so you have a better understanding of the working contents of your disks. In particular, I focus on the most universal data format, ASCII text files.

This chapter gives you most of what you need to know about floppy and hard disks. What's missing here, you can find in Chapter 7.

DOS Disk Overview

In Chapter 5, when you looked at the basics of the computer's disks, you saw how a disk is defined by three or four elements. These elements—track or cylinder, side, and sector within a track—locate the position of each sector on the disk. The size of each sector—the amount of data that can be stored inside a sector—is the fourth element. Multiplying the first three elements gives you the total number of sectors on a disk, the number of working pieces DOS has at its disposal when it uses the disk. Multiplying the number of sectors by the sector size gives you the data capacity of the disk, the number of bytes DOS has at its disposal in which to store data.

Sectors are the fundamental units of disk activity. All reading and writing on a disk is done with full sectors, not with any smaller amount. An important part of understanding how DOS looks at a disk is seeing how it handles sectors. A key part of this is that DOS "flattens" a disk, ignoring some of the elements that define a disk. Of course, DOS can't completely ignore these elements. To read and write disk sectors, DOS has to work with sectors in terms of their location and identity. That, however, is just to accommodate the physical nature of the disk. For its own purposes, DOS thinks of a disk as a linear object.

This means that DOS treats the sectors of a disk as a sequential list of sectors, from the first sector on a disk to the last. The diagram in figure 6.1 shows how this is done. For its own purposes, DOS numbers the sectors sequentially, from 0 (for the first sector on the first side of a disk) to 1 (for the second sector on the first side) and so on to the last sector in the sequence (which is the last sector of the last side). Everything that DOS does in working with and planning the use of disk sectors is done in terms of these sequential sector numbers. Only at the last moment, when information actually is read or written on the disk, does DOS translate between its internal notation (the sequential numbers) and the disk's own three-element notation.

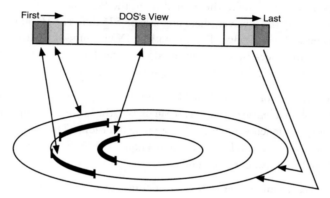

Figure 6.1. *A three-element disk meets a linear DOS.*

This linear approach greatly simplifies DOS's job of organizing a disk. However, it does have a price. One part of the price is that DOS can't take advantage of the fact that it takes quite a bit longer to move from one sector to another when they are located on different cylinders than it does to move between sectors in the same cylinder. Basically, DOS doesn't know which sectors are on the same cylinder because it ignores the cylinders. There used to be another price too. At one time, the traditional way that DOS handled disks set a limit on the size disk you could use. This limitation was removed with DOS 4.0.

The Old 32MB Limit

At one time, the linear, sequential approach that DOS uses to organize disks led to a limitation that wasn't expected to be a problem when DOS was young. The size of a disk DOS could use was limited to 32MB.

This limitation came about as the natural result of two simple things. First, the standard size of a disk sector for DOS is 512 bytes. Second, DOS numbers all the sectors sequentially.

At the time, DOS stored these numbers in the PC's most natural format—16-bit positive integers. However, there are only 65,536 different 16-bit positive integers (Remember 2^{16} = 65,536). This meant that DOS could work with, at most, 65,536 sectors. And, because each sector is 512 bytes long, this set a limit of 32MB (65,536×512 = 33,554,432) as the largest disk DOS could handle.

In the early days of DOS and the PC family, few people imagined that anyone would want a disk that big on a computer so small. But, the history of computing has proven that however much you have, it's not enough for long. The solution to the 32MB limit, which came with DOS 4.0, was to change the DOS file system so that it could use more bits to store sector numbers.

DOS takes a similar approach when it comes to storing data on the disk. As I've mentioned, all reading and writing of data on a disk is done in complete sectors. But, when you work with data—or when programs, acting on your behalf, work with data—it may be any amount of data. You can work byte by individual byte or can work with huge amounts at a time. This points to one of the main jobs that DOS performs in managing disks. It acts as a translator between the way the disk works with data (one 512-byte sector at a time) and the way you want to work with it (any of a hundred ways).

DOS's disk-management routines handle the conversion between the amounts of data you want and the amounts of data the disk stores. In effect, DOS does it by running a warehouse operation. It packages and unpackages data, so that the data is bundled in appropriately sized quantities. DOS can save any amount of data you want and writes that data to the disk in 512-byte sectors. This also works in reverse. DOS reads information stored in appropriately sized sectors and makes it available for you to use. You can see how this works in figure 6.2.

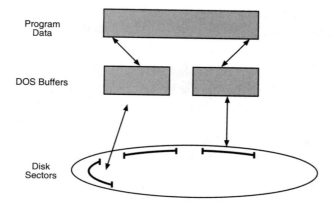

Figure 6.2. *DOS repackages data between disks and programs.*

Physical and Logical Formatting

The formatting of a disk has two parts: physical and logical formatting. You need to be aware of the distinction.

Physical formatting—sometimes called low-level formatting—involves the creation of sectors on a disk. The sectors are complete with their address markings (used like name tags to identify them after the formatting is done) and with the data portion of the sector (the part you and your programs know about) established and filled in with some dummy data. A new, unused floppy disk normally comes without physical formatting, while a new hard disk usually is physically formatted already.

Logical formatting is essentially the conversion of a disk to the standards of the operating system. When a disk is formatted for DOS, the DOS-style structure of the disk is created. The logical formatting is the road map that DOS, or any other operating system, uses to navigate through and make sense out of a disk.

In terms of physical and logical formatting, the FORMAT command of DOS acts differently on floppy disks than it does on hard disks, which is why it is important to understand the distinction between logical and physical formatting. Because logical formatting is essential to DOS's use of a disk, the FORMAT command always does that. What differs between floppy disks and hard disks is whether or not DOS is free to perform the physical formatting.

The FORMAT command performs the physical as well as the logical formatting for a floppy disk because a floppy disk "belongs" to the operating system that formats it. A hard disk, on the other hand, may be partitioned into sections that can belong to different operating systems (you see more about that in Chapter 7). On a hard disk, the FORMAT command does not dare perform the physical formatting, even within a partition that DOS "owns" because that may interfere with the rest of the disk.

DOS doesn't provide a program to physically format a hard disk, but you can find one in the IBM Advanced Diagnostics. With a PS/2, you enter the Advanced Diagnostics by starting the computer from the Reference Disk and pressing Ctrl-A when you see the main menu. With a pre-PS/2 computer, you need to obtain a special Advanced Diagnostics disk.

The DOS FORMAT program uses a special BIOS command (see Chapter 20) to format a disk track by track. The mechanism of physical formatting requires that the formatting for all the sectors in each track be laid down in one coordinated operation. This track-by-track disk formatting feature can be used as the basis of a copy-protection scheme, as you see in Chapter 7.

When FORMAT formats a floppy disk, it sets the sector data to a default value— hex F6—in each byte. Because the FORMAT command overwrites each byte of the disk, all old data on the disk is completely obliterated. Without a utility program or the latest version of DOS, formatting a disk eliminates any hope of recovering any data on the disk after it has been reformatted. However, FORMAT does not overwrite the old data on a hard disk, so it is possible to recover data from a reformatted hard disk.

Special features of DOS 6 and later make formatted data recovery a lot more reliable and a lot easier. Unless you tell DOS otherwise, an image of the original data is saved on disk before it is formatted, enabling you to recover as much information as is not physically overwritten between the time you format the disk and the time you try to unformat it.

If you have the Norton Utilities, you can use the Safe Format program to format disks in such a way that the data is not erased when using versions of DOS prior to 6.0. Not only is this faster, but it protects you from accidentally erasing the wrong data. If a disk is safe-formatted, you can unformat it as long as you have not already used the space for new data.

The Structure of a DOS Disk

To organize disks, DOS divides them into two parts: a small system area that DOS uses to keep track of key information about the disk and the data area, the bulk of the disk, where data is stored. The system area uses only a small portion of a disk—two percent for a floppy disk and several tenths of a percent for a hard disk.

The system area that DOS uses is divided into three parts: the boot record, the FAT, and the root directory. Figure 6.3 shows these disk components.

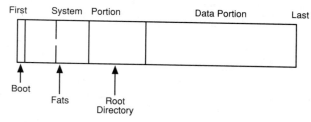

Figure 6.3. *The parts of a DOS disk.*

The Boot Record

The boot record is the very first part of a DOS disk. It holds a very short program—one that's only a few hundred bytes long—that performs the job of beginning the loading of DOS into the computer's memory. The start-up procedure is called booting because the computer is pulling itself up by the bootstraps. In this phase, DOS loads the programs that are necessary to carry on its work. When you have a DOS system disk (one that's been formatted with the /S system option), the disk contains the basic parts of DOS. The job of this boot record program is to begin the process of starting DOS from a disk by reading from disk to memory the first part of the DOS program. Interestingly enough, the boot record doesn't appear only on system formatted disks. It's on every disk and is clever enough to report the error if you try to boot from a disk that isn't formatted as a system disk (that is, a disk that doesn't include a copy of DOS on it).

The boot portion of a disk is very small—only a single 512-byte sector—so it occupies almost no space. Incidentally, some very interesting information is recorded on some disks' boot records. I look into that in Chapter 7 as well as some of the more technical information.

The next part of the system portion of a disk is called the file allocation table, or FAT. DOS needs a way to keep track of the big data portion of a disk, to tell what's in use and what's available for new data storage. The FAT is used to record the status of each part of the disk. To manage the data space on a disk, DOS divides it up into logical units called clusters. When a file is being recorded on the data portion of a disk, disk space is assigned to the file in these clusters. The size of a cluster varies from one disk format to another, but it can be as small as an individual sector or much bigger. Table 6.1 lists the cluster sizes that DOS uses for floppy disks. (Remember, 0.5KB, 512 bytes, is the size of one sector.)

Table 6.1. *Cluster Sizes for Floppy Disks*

Diskette Type	Cluster Size
3.5-inch 2.88MB	1.0KB = 1,024 bytes
3.5-inch 1.44MB	0.5KB = 512 bytes
3.5-inch 720KB	1.0KB = 1,024 bytes
5.25-inch 1.2MB	0.5KB = 512 bytes
5.25-inch 360KB	1.0KB = 1,024 bytes

FAT entries are 12 or 16 bits long, depending on the size of the disk. With a longer FAT entry, DOS can keep track of more clusters and therefore supports a larger disk. For floppy disks, DOS uses a 12-bit FAT entry. For hard disks, DOS uses a 12-bit entry if the disk is smaller than 17MB. For hard disks larger than 17MB, DOS uses a 16-bit entry.

In addition, the cluster size varies, depending on the total size of the hard disk and the way the disk is designed. Disks that hold 16MB or less, for example, usually are designed for a cluster size of eight sectors, or 4,096 bytes (4KB). Disks larger than 16MB usually are limited to four-sector clusters, or 2,048 bytes (2KB). However, depending on the manufacturer of your drive and whether you use additional driver software with it, you may discover that your hard disk has anywhere from 2 to 32KB or larger clusters.

Whatever the cluster size, DOS carves up the data portion of the disk into these relatively small clusters and then uses them as the unit of space that it allocates to the disk files. This allocation is managed by the FAT, which simply is a table of numbers with a place in the table for each cluster on the disk. The number that's recorded in each cluster's FAT entry indicates whether the cluster is in use by a file or available for new data. A zero in the cluster's FAT entry means the cluster is free. Any other number indicates it's in use. Because a data file may be larger than the size of a cluster, the numbers in the FAT are used to link clusters that contain one file's data.

The FAT gives DOS a place to keep track of the allocation of the disk's data space. This isolates the space and record-keeping function, which helps protect it from possible damage. If you think about it, you can see why the FAT is the most critical part of a disk, the part that most needs to be protected. In fact, the FAT is so critical that DOS records two separate copies of the FAT on each disk. Only the first copy is used; the second copy is there to help make it possible to perform emergency repairs on damaged disks.

The Root Directory

The last part of the disk's system area is the root directory. This is the file directory that every disk has; it's the basic, built-in directory for the disk. Disks also can have subdirectories added to them. However, subdirectories are an optional part of a disk that you create as necessary. The root directory is not an optional part of the disk.

The directory, of course, records the files that are stored on the disk. For each file, there is a directory entry that records the file's eight-character filename, the three-character extension to the filename, the size of the file, and a date and time stamp that records when the file was last changed. All those parts of a file's directory entry are familiar because they're shown in the DIR listing. Two other pieces of information about a file are recorded in its directory entry. One is called the starting cluster number, which indicates which cluster in the disk's data space holds the first portion of the file. The other is called the file attribute, which is used to record a number of things about the file. For example, subdirectories have a particular directory attribute marking; DOS's system files have a special pair of attributes called system and hidden. There are also two attributes that serve users more directly. The read-only attribute protects files from being changed or deleted, and the archive attribute is used to help keep track of which files on a disk already have or need backup copies.

The root directory of each disk, like the other items in the system portion of a disk, is a fixed size for each disk format. This size determines how many entries there are for files in the root directory. Each directory entry occupies 32 bytes, so 16 of them fit into a single sector. A 3.5-inch, 1.44MB disk has 14 sectors set aside for the root directory, so it has room for 224 (16×14) files in the directory. A 2.88MB disk has 15 sectors for the root directory, making room for up to 240 entries (16×15). Hard disks typically have something like 32 sectors, making room for 512 (16×32) directory entries.

I mentioned before that the FAT is used to chain together a record of where a file's data is stored. Here is how it works. Each file's directory entry includes a field that gives the number of the cluster in which the first part of the file's data is stored. The FAT table has a number entry for each cluster. If you look up the FAT entry for the first cluster in a file, it contains the number of the next cluster in the file, and the FAT entry for that cluster points to the next one. This way, the FAT entries are chained together to provide DOS with a way of keeping the contents of a file together. When the end of the file is reached, the FAT entry for the last cluster holds a special code number that marks the end of the file. Such a chain is called a linked list. You can see a typical file's space allocation in figure 6.4.

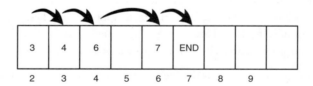

Figure 6.4. *A file's space allocation in the FAT.*

That finishes this survey of the system portion of a disk. What remains is the majority of the disk, the data portion. But you already know the basics about this part of a disk.

The Data Portion

The data portion is used to record the data contents of the disk files. The data space, as you've seen, is divided into units called clusters. (Clusters are made up of one or more sectors. Clusters on a disk are all the same size, but their size varies between disk formats and types.) Each file's data is recorded on one or more clusters, and the record of which clusters, and in which order, is kept in the disk's FAT. It's worth noting that a file's data can be scattered all over a disk in disjointed clusters. DOS generally tries to keep a file's data together in contiguous sequential clusters. However, after many disk reads and writes, files can end up being stored on different parts of the disk.

When too many files get scattered in bits and pieces all over the disk, the disk is said to be fragmented. When a disk is badly fragmented, it slows things down because DOS must constantly move the read/write head from place to place. If you have the Norton Utilities, you can use the Speed Disk program to eliminate hard disk fragmentation. In addition, DOS 6 and later have an integral disk defragmentation utility. Whichever one you have, vow now that you will use it relatively frequently. This keeps your drive running at optimum performance.

I've mentioned subdirectories, and at this point I should explain that each subdirectory acts like a mixture of a data file and the disk's root directory. As far as how a subdirectory is recorded on the disk, it's no different than any other disk file. The subdirectory is stored in the disk's data space, and a record of where the subdirectory is located is kept in the FAT, exactly like any other file. However, when it comes to using the contents of a subdirectory, a subdirectory acts like the disk's root directory. It holds a record of files and other subdirectories that are stored within it, and DOS works with subdirectories just as it works with the main, root directory. There are two major differences between subdirectories and root directories. One is that there is only one root directory on each disk, but there can be numerous subdirectories. The other is that each root directory has a fixed size and capacity, while subdirectories, like files, can grow to any size that the disk can accommodate.

What you've seen so far gives you all the fundamental information you need to understand the basics of the structure of DOS disks. There is more to know about them, of course; there are plenty of fascinating technical details left to explore. If you want to learn how to organize a large hard disk using subdirectories, read *Peter Norton's DOS 6 Guide*, which also is published by Brady Books.

Learning about File Formats

Each file stored on your disk potentially has its own unique data format, the structure of the data that's recorded in the file. The physical recording of data on the disk still must adhere to the format DOS and the drive's controller use, but the logical format of data varies with the application and the file type. It seems that there is little I can say about the format of disk files, and in many ways that is true. However, there are several important observations that I can make about files to help you understand what's going on inside your disks.

First, note that the three-character extension of a filename is intended to be used as an indication of the format and use of a file. Some filename extensions are standard and must be used to correctly identify the file type; most, however, don't have a strict use, just a conventional one.

The strictly enforced extensions primarily have to do with programs. DOS requires that all programs be recorded in one of two special program formats and that they be identified by the standard extension names of COM and EXE. Batch command files must use the BAT extension.

Most other filename extensions are optional, but application programs usually are designed to work more easily with files that have standard extensions. For example, the BASIC interpreter expects BASIC program files to have the BAS extension; Pascal expects program source files to have the PAS extension; and C expects source files to have a C extension. Similarly, programs such as spreadsheets and word processors have their own conventional extensions. For example, Microsoft Word files typically have the DOC extension, and Lotus 1-2-3 files have extensions like WK1. You may be able to use names that don't adhere to a particular program's extension convention, but working with files from within an application usually is easier if you use the filename convention the program expects.

The contents of data files can be very interesting, but you have to make a special effort to look inside your files by using snooping tools like DEBUG or the Norton Utilities, both described in Chapter 26. Often it's hard to decode or otherwise make much sense of what you see inside a data file. However, by looking, you sometimes can find some very interesting things.

There is one very good reason for taking a look at and learning about the data formats created by the programs you use: you may need to do repair work on your disks, such as unerasing deleted files or other such file-recovery operations. If you learn what your data looks like in advance, you have a better chance of recovering it in an emergency.

As a general rule, the data files created by programs have an internal structure that seems completely jumbled to the human eye. Certain parts—including such character text data as the names and addresses in a mailing list database—are easy to recognize. However, the parts of the data that hold numbers and the formatting information usually are recorded in a form that is cryptic and can be deciphered only by the programs that work with the data.

One special kind of file, though, has a pattern to it that you should be able to recognize fairly well. These are data files made up of what are called fixed-length records—a repeated pattern in which content of the data varies, but each element has the same length. This is the kind of data that BASIC uses for its random files. Because the data records in this kind of file are all the same length, BASIC can calculate its way to the location of any randomly specified record number without having to search through the file from the beginning. Whenever you look at a data file that is built from fixed-sized elements, you may be able to recognize the pattern and decode some of the file's data.

By exploring and digging through some file data, you can learn a great deal about how computers and programs work with disk data.

ASCII Text Files

The ASCII text file format is one file format about which every PC user needs to know. ASCII text files, which also are called ASCII files, or text files for short, are the closest thing the PC family has to a universal format for data files. While most programs have their own special way of recording data, the ASCII text file is a common format that can be used by any program and, in fact, is used by many of them.

ASCII text files are designed to hold ordinary text data, like the words you are reading. These files are used by many simple text editing programs, such as the DOS EDIT program, and some word processing programs also work directly with ASCII text files. However, most programs, including word processors, the BASIC interpreter, spreadsheet programs, and many others, use the ASCII text file format as an alternative to their own native data formats. These programs are prepared to work with ASCII text files simply because the ASCII text file format is something of a last resort way of transferring data from one program to another. Often, however, rather than a last resort, it's the only way to get data from here to there.

ASCII text file data is rather naked. It isn't clothed in the rich formatting that most programs use for their data. But, when you need to pass data from one place to another, it's often the only reasonable way to get it done.

When I say that most programs have their own special data formats, I am referring to applications programs such as databases and spreadsheets. There are many programs that expect to work only with ASCII text files. Programming language compilers and assemblers expect to read program source code from plain ASCII text files. Among programs that are, one way or another, writing tools, there is an informal division between the simple ones that use ASCII text files, such as many text editing programs, and the complex ones that use their own custom data formats, such as most word processing programs. Finally, batch command files, which enable DOS to carry out a series of commands with one instruction to the computer, use ASCII text files.

The data in a text file is composed of two character types: ordinary ASCII text characters and the ASCII control characters. The regular text characters are the principal data in an ASCII text file, while the control characters format the text, for example, marking line and paragraph divisions.

There is no strict definition of the way programs and computers are supposed to use ASCII text files. Instead, all programs that work with ASCII text files use the most basic elements of this file format, but some programs go further and use the less common formatting control characters as well. I start by describing the most common elements.

A pair of ASCII control characters is used to mark the end of each line. The characters Carriage Return and Line Feed—known in ASCII terminology as CR and LF—are character codes 13 and 10, or hex 0D and 0A. These two, taken as a pair, are the standard way to mark the end of a line of text.

One ASCII control character is used to mark the end of a text file. It's the Control-Z character, code 26 or hex 1A. In most tables of ASCII control characters, this code is called SUB, but because it usually indicates the end of a file, it also is called EOF. Normally, ASCII text files have an EOF character at the end of the text data.

The Horizontal Tab (HT) character is used as a substitute for repeated spaces. Its character code is 9. Tabs appear in many ASCII files, even though there is no universal agreement about just where the tab stops are. Most programs (but, unfortunately, far from all) handle tabs on the assumption that there is a tab stop every eight positions (at the 9th column, 17th column, and so on).

The Form Feed character is used to mark the end of one page and the beginning of the next. Its character code is 12, hex 0C, and the ASCII name is FF. This control character also is called Page Eject.

An ASCII text file can contain any control characters (these are summarized in table 14.1), but the most common ones are the five I just described. And, in many cases, even the last two—Horizontal Tab and Form Feed—are avoided to keep the coding as simple as possible.

There are several commonly used ways to indicate the division of text data into paragraphs. The most common form marks the end of each line of text with a Carriage Return/Line Feed pair. This is the form in which compilers expect to find their program source code. When this form is used to mark words, sentences, and paragraphs, it's common to indicate the end of a paragraph with a blank line (that is, two pairs of Carriage Return/Line Feeds in a row). Sometimes, though, you see ASCII text files in which each paragraph is treated as a single, very long line with a Carriage Return/Line Feed pair at the end of the paragraph, but nowhere inside the paragraph. Some word processing programs create ASCII text files like this.

Because there are different ways of laying out an ASCII text file, there often are conflicts between the way one program expects to find a text file and the way another program expects to find it. Different programs often are at odds with one another when you try to use ASCII text files as a way of transferring data between them. For example, if you try to use ASCII text files to pass something you've written from one word processing program to another, you may find that what one program considers lines in a paragraph the other program considers separate paragraphs. This sort of nonsense can be very annoying. Nevertheless, ASCII text files are the closest thing PCs have to a universal language. That's why you may find yourself working with ASCII text files more often than you expect.

People usually think of ASCII text files as containing either words, like the sentences and paragraphs you are reading here, or program source code, like the programming examples you have seen throughout this book. However, any form of data can be translated into ASCII text format. Thus, you may find some text files that consist only of numbers written in ASCII characters. Some programs use ASCII text files to exchange data that isn't made up of words. For example, the Data Interchange File, or DIF, standard uses ASCII text files to transfer data among spreadsheets and other programs that know how to interpret DIF data. DIF files are simply ASCII text files that describe, among other things, the contents of a spreadsheet.

To get a more concrete idea of what an ASCII text file looks like, here's an example. Suppose you have a text file with these two lines in it:

```
Columbus sailed the ocean blue
In fourteen hundred and ninety two.
```

To see what that looks like inside an ASCII text file, I write it out in a way that represents the text file data. Note the control characters <CR>, <LF>, and <EOF>.

```
Columbus sailed the ocean blue<CR><LF>
In fourteen hundred and ninety two.<CR><LF><EOF>
```

The more advanced the tinkering you do with your computer, the more likely it is that you will find yourself working with or looking at ASCII text files. When you do, you should know about one anomaly you may run into. It has to do with the way ASCII text files are ended and the size of the file.

I mentioned earlier that the Control-Z (EOF) character, code 26, normally is used to mark the end of a text file's data. There are several variations on how that is done. The cleanest and strictest form has the EOF character stored right after the last line of text (the way I show it in the example above).

The length of the file, as recorded in the file's disk directory, includes the EOF character in the size of the file. Sometimes, however, a file appears to be bigger, judging from the size recorded in the disk directory. This is because some programs work with text files, not byte by byte, but in chunks of, say, 128 bytes at a time. When this kind of program creates a text file, the Control-Z (or EOF) character shows up where the true end of the file is, but the file's disk directory entry shows a length that's been rounded up to the next highest multiple of 128. In such cases, the real length of the file is slightly smaller than you would expect based on the size in the directory.

There is another way that an ASCII text file may appear odd. It may be recorded without a Control-Z character. In that case, the file size recorded in the directory indicates the true size of the file, and there's no end-of-file marker on the theory that none is needed because the size tells you where the end is. Any time you take a close look at an ASCII text file or any time you write a program to read one, you should be prepared for variations like this in the way the end of the file is indicated.

Some Things To Try

1. If you have the Norton Utilities, use the System Information program to explore the dimensions of your disk. (If you have an older version of the utilities, before version 5.0, use the Disk Info program.) If you don't have the Norton Utilities, use CHKDSK from DOS. This intrinsic utility shows you the original size of your disk, how much of it is in use, what kinds of files are stored there, and more.

2. Why is the FAT the most critical part of a disk? What makes it more important than the directory portion? There is a DOS file recovery utility called RECOVER that can recreate a disk directory if the directory is damaged but the FAT is not. How do you think this is possible? Could there be a similar program to recreate a damaged FAT if the directory were intact?

3. To see how BASIC can record its program files in two forms—BASIC's own coded format and the ASCII text file format—enter a short BASIC program (just a line or two of any BASIC program) and then save it to disk in both formats, using these commands:

```
SAVE "BASFORM"
SAVE "TEXTFORM",A.
```

Examine the two files. Compare their sizes using the DIR command. See how their contents differ by using the TYPE command to print them on your computer's display screen. If you know how to snoop in files using DEBUG or NU, inspect the contents of the two files.

Disks: More Details

7

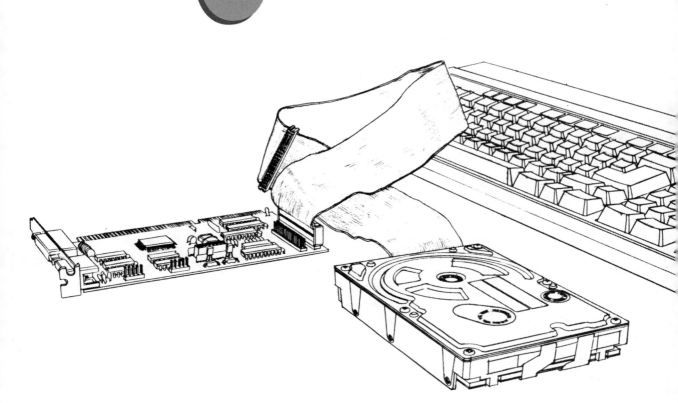

This is the last leg of our journey through basic disk storage technology. The next three chapters provide information on disk utilities and special disk types: removable and optical drives. In this chapter, I move into some of the more technical details of how computers use disks. I cover hard disks and the way computers work with them. Then I look at how DOS works with disks, expanding on what I covered in Chapter 6.

This chapter contains technical information, and readers who want to focus on understanding the PC can pass over the more technical parts. However, there is one part that I don't want you to miss—the discussion of hard disks and hard disk partitions. If you want to understand the most important practical things about the PC family, you need to know about hard disks.

Hard Disk Features and Partitions

Hard disks present some special challenges to the designers of computers. The most obvious thing is that a hard disk has a much greater storage capacity than a floppy disk. In nearly everything in life, there comes a point when a quantitative difference becomes a qualitative difference—when more isn't just more, it's also different. That's the case with hard disks. Their storage capacity is so much greater than the floppy disk's that they must be treated differently. Greater capacity and faster speed are part of what is special about a hard disk. Oddly enough, however, those two items do not constitute the most critical difference. What is most different about a hard disk is that it is not removable.

Or, I should say, it generally is not removable. For years hard disks have been called "fixed" disks because you couldn't access them from outside the computer or take them from machine to machine. However, this is no longer the case.

Now there are drive manufacturers, such as SyQuest, that make hard disk drives with removable platters. In nearly all other respects, these drives are like the nonremovable drives I've talked about already and describe further in this chapter. The difference is that the rigid platter (and sometimes the read/write heads as well) can be removed from the drive mechanism.

Also, a number of manufacturers offer very small, removable drives in which the entire drive mechanism is removed from a carrier so it can be put away for safe storage, carried to another computer to share data, or swapped for another disk with different information. As you might imagine, these removable drives are extremely popular with the new class of mobile computers because they enable you to remove a drive from the laptop or notebook machine, insert it into your desktop computer, and transfer files easily. They also are ideal solutions for areas where two or more people use the same computer. Removable hard drives enable each user to have one or more drives for personal programs or data.

In this chapter, I use the term "hard disk" because that's what nearly everyone calls them. IBM's term is "fixed disk." In the following discussion, I talk primarily about nonremovable disks rather than the removable cartridges or hard drives. But, especially with the removable hard drives, the technology is the same. It may be the same for some cartridge systems as well.

The fact that a hard disk is fixed presents a special problem. You're stuck with the disk that came with the computer; you can't easily switch it for another one in a different format or set it up to accommodate another operating system. While most people work exclusively within the framework that DOS creates, DOS isn't the only operating system around; other systems include OS/2 and UNIX.

With floppy disks, the fact that they are owned by an operating system such as DOS—owned in the sense that they have a format and logical structure that applies only to the program (DOS) with which they work—should not be a problem, just as there is no fundamental problem with a game program using its own peculiar disk format (which many do for copy-protection). Although odd floppy disk formats can be a nuisance, they do not present a fundamental problem because computers themselves aren't committed in any sense to always using the same format; you can switch disks any time you want.

With a (fixed) hard disk, the situation is completely different. If your hard disk is owned by one operating system, you can't use it with another operating system. Because almost everything you do with your PC is based on DOS, you may be tempted to ask, "So what?" That, however, is a very short-sighted sentiment. The world of computing is always changing, and it's quite likely that the operating system you use today will be different from the one you'll use in a few years. Even today, some PC users find good reasons to use systems other than, or in addition to, DOS. How do users accommodate different operating systems with incompatible ways of structuring disks on one hard disk?

The answer is partitioning, or dividing a hard disk into areas that can be owned by different operating systems. Within the confines of each partition, the disk can be formatted and logically structured to meet the needs of the operating system that owns the partition. Together all the partitions on a disk can occupy the entire disk or leave parts of it open.

This arrangement enables a great deal of flexibility, but relies on some across-the-board standards that every program using the disk must follow. There must be a master format within which all of the operating systems on the disk must operate. Part of this common ground is the physical formatting of the disk, which sets, among other things, the sector size that applies to every partition on the disk. This points up the distinction between physical and logical formatting (which was discussed in Chapter 6). However, a common sector size isn't all there is to the common ground and rules of coexistence that apply to a partitioned hard disk. There also must be a standard way of marking off the boundaries of a disk partition, and each operating system using a partitioned disk must agree to stay within its own bounds and not encroach on another partition's territory.

Here is how it's done. The very first sector of a hard disk is set aside for a special master record, which contains a partition table describing the layout of the disk. This table shows the dimensions of the disk, the number of partitions, and the size and location of each partition. A disk doesn't have to be divided into more than one partition; in fact, most PCs have only one partition, a DOS partition, which occupies the entire disk. Figure 7.1 illustrates a partitioned hard disk.

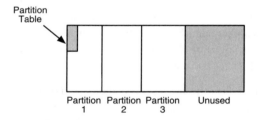

Figure 7.1. *A partitioned hard disk.*

Most PC owners ignore the extra possibilities and complexity that disk partitioning entails. Instead, most simply create a single DOS partition that fills the entire hard disk. This, in fact, is the most sensible thing to do. Until you need another partition, which may never happen, there is no reason to set aside hard disk space; you can take care of that problem when the time comes.

To deal with partitions on hard disks, DOS has a program called FDISK, which can display and change partition data. FDISK can list up to four partitions. Each partition in the list has a starting and ending location and size in disk cylinders. A typical listing of partition data is shown below:

```
Display Partition Information
Current fixed disk drive: 1
Partition Status  Type    Volume Label   Mbytes   System Usage
C: 1        A     PRI DOS   NORTON          115    FAT16  100%
Total disk space is 115 Mbytes (1 Mbyte = 1048576)
Press ESC to return to FDISK Options
```

The FDISK program enables you to manipulate the disk partitions while working with DOS. If you're working with another operating system, it should have an equivalent program. FDISK enables you to create or delete a DOS-owned partition. And, starting with version 5.0, DOS can delete non-DOS partitions; earlier versions of DOS could not do so. While this restriction of early DOS versions may seem like a good safety feature, it has disadvantages. If you ended up with an unwanted partition from another system, you couldn't delete it from DOS, so you could be stuck with a bum partition (this has happened to acquaintances of mine). If you're using a version of DOS prior to 5.0, one solution is to use the IBM Advanced Diagnostics (see Chapter 6) to perform a physical format, sometimes called a low-level format. Be careful, though—this wipes out all the data in all partitions.

Suppose you've devoted your entire hard disk to DOS and now want to surrender some of the space to make room for another partition. Can you simply give up the space? Unfortunately, because of the way DOS structures its partitions, you cannot simply shrink a partition to make room for another. If you need to resize a DOS partition, you must back up the contents of the partition (with the DOS utility BACKUP or another program that easily can remove and restore large blocks of data), delete the partition (with FDISK), create a new partition, format it (with FORMAT), and reload the data (with RESTORE). That can be a laborious process. As I said before, unless you know that you will need another partition, you're better off letting DOS use the entire hard disk and facing the chore of repartitioning if the need arises. Also, the majority of computer systems are delivered with the hard disk already partitioned and DOS and application software preinstalled.

In the FDISK listing above, notice that the sole partition is marked with status A. That means the partition is the active partition. On any partitioned disk, only one partition at a time can be active. This has to do with the start-up, or booting,

179

process. Remember that every ordinary disk has a boot program on its first sector, which begins the process of starting up the operating system. The same thing applies to a partitioned hard disk, but there is an extra step involved. The first sector of a partitioned hard disk contains a master boot program along with the table that describes the partitions. This master boot program looks at the partition table to see which partition is active. Then it fires up the boot program that starts that partition. Each partition has its own boot program (just as each floppy disk has a boot record), which is tailored to the needs of the particular operating system that owns that partition. The master boot record does the job of finding the right partition boot record and getting it going.

You can see that partitions are a special key to making the large storage space of hard disks work with extra flexibility not available with floppy disks. With this large capacity and extra flexibility, though, comes an additional degree of complexity. And, if you want to take full advantage your hard disk, you must master this complexity.

Next, I look at the structure DOS places on disks and see some of the fascinating technical details of how DOS manages disks.

Detailed Disk Structure

In this section, I take a closer look at the way DOS structures a disk to help you better understand what's going on with disks. That will help you appreciate and use your disk when everything is going right and may help you work your way out of trouble if something goes wrong.

As I described in Chapter 6, DOS divides each disk into two parts: the system part, used for DOS's record keeping, and the data part, where files are stored. The system portion has three parts: the boot record, the FAT (file allocation table), and the root directory. In the next sections, I give you a closer look at what's stored in each one.

The Boot Record

The boot record is always the very first item on the disk. As I said before, it's used to hold a short program that begins the process of starting DOS. The boot record is present on every disk, even those from which you can't boot (because they don't contain a copy of the DOS system files).

The boot program is small enough to fit easily into a single disk sector, so it doesn't require more than one sector. However, DOS allows for the possibility that the boot area may have to be larger in the future.

There are more interesting things in the boot record of a disk than you may imagine. You can use the DOS DEBUG program to inspect the contents of a boot record. It only takes the two simple DEBUG commands listed below. The first reads the boot record from the hard disk C into memory; the second displays the boot record's data in hex and ASCII.

```
L 0 2 0 1
D 0 L 200
```

The following information shows what a DOS version 5.0 boot record looks like:

```
1C7A:0000   EB 3C 90 49 42 4D 20 20-35 2E 30 00 02 04 01 00   .<.IBM  5.0.....
1C7A:0010   02 00 02 00 00 F8 9C 00-20 00 40 00 20 00 00 00   ........ .@. ...
1C7A:0020   E0 6F 02 00 80 00 29 85-4D 92 16 00 00 00 00 00   .o....).M.......
1C7A:0030   00 20 20 20 20 20 46 41-54 31 36 20 20 20 FA 33   .     FAT16   .3
1C7A:0040   C0 8E D0 BC 00 7C 16 07-BB 78 00 36 C5 37 1E 56   .....|...x.6.7.V
1C7A:0050   16 53 BF 3E 7C B9 0B 00-FC F3 A4 06 1F C6 45 FE   .S.>|.........E.
1C7A:0060   0F 8B 0E 18 7C 88 4D F9-89 47 02 C7 07 3E 7C FB   ....|.M..G...>|.
1C7A:0070   CD 13 72 79 33 C0 39 06-13 7C 74 08 8B 0E 13 7C   ..ry3.9..|t....|
1C7A:0080   89 0E 20 7C A0 10 7C F7-26 16 7C 03 06 1C 7C 13   .. |..|.&.|...|.
1C7A:0090   16 1E 7C 03 06 0E 7C 83-D2 00 A3 50 7C 89 16 52   ..|...|....P|..R
1C7A:00A0   7C A3 49 7C 89 16 4B 7C-B8 20 00 F7 26 11 7C 8B   |.I|..K|. ..&.|.
1C7A:00B0   1E 0B 7C 03 C3 48 F7 F3-01 06 49 7C 83 16 4B 7C   ..|..H....I|..K|
1C7A:00C0   00 BB 00 05 8B 16 52 7C-A1 50 7C E8 92 00 72 1D   ......R|.P|...r.
1C7A:00D0   B0 01 E8 AC 00 72 16 8B-FB B9 0B 00 BE E6 7D F3   .....r........}.
1C7A:00E0   A6 75 0A 8D 7F 20 B9 0B-00 F3 A6 74 18 BE 9E 7D   .u... .....t...}
1C7A:00F0   E8 5F 00 33 C0 CD 16 5E-1F 8F 04 8F 44 02 CD 19   ._.3...^....D...
1C7A:0100   58 58 58 EB E8 8B 47 1A-48 48 8A 1E 0D 7C 32 FF   XXX...G.HH...|2.
1C7A:0110   F7 E3 03 06 49 7C 13 16-4B 7C BB 00 07 B9 03 00   ....I|..K|......
1C7A:0120   50 52 51 E8 3A 00 72 D8-B0 01 E8 54 00 59 5A 58   PRQ.:.r....T.YZX
1C7A:0130   72 BB 05 01 00 83 D2 00-03 1E 0B 7C E2 E2 8A 2E   r..........|....
1C7A:0140   15 7C 8A 16 24 7C 8B 1E-49 7C A1 4B 7C EA 00 00   .|..$|..I|.K|...
1C7A:0150   70 00 AC 0A C0 74 29 B4-0E BB 07 00 CD 10 EB F2   p....t).........
1C7A:0160   3B 16 18 7C 73 19 F7 36-18 7C FE C2 88 16 4F 7C   ;..|s..6.|....O|
1C7A:0170   33 D2 F7 36 1A 7C 88 16-25 7C A3 4D 7C F8 C3 F9   3..6.|..%|.M|...
```

```
1C7A:0180   C3 B4 02 8B 16 4D 7C B1-06 D2 E6 0A 36 4F 7C 8B   .....M¦.....60¦.
1C7A:0190   CA 86 E9 8A 16 24 7C 8A-36 25 7C CD 13 C3 0D 0A   .....$¦.6%¦.....
1C7A:01A0   4E 6F 6E 2D 53 79 73 74-65 6D 20 64 69 73 6B 20   Non-System disk
1C7A:01B0   6F 72 20 64 69 73 6B 20-65 72 72 6F 72 0D 0A 52   or disk error..R
1C7A:01C0   65 70 6C 61 63 65 20 61-6E 64 20 70 72 65 73 73   eplace and press
1C7A:01D0   20 61 6E 79 20 6B 65 79-20 77 68 65 6E 20 72 65    any key when re
1C7A:01E0   61 64 79 0D 0A 00 49 42-4D 42 49 4F 20 20 43 4F   ady...IBMBIO  CO
1C7A:01F0   4D 49 42 4D 44 4F 53 20-20 43 4F 4D 00 00 55 AA   MIBMDOS  COM..U.
```

There are several obvious things that looking at this boot record tells you. The error messages and the names of the two DOS system files (IBMBIO.COM and IBMDOS.COM) give you an idea of some of the things that can go wrong during the boot process and also indirectly tell you that the boot program checks for these two names in the disk directory to see that it is a system disk. Also notice a version marker near the beginning of the listing that indicates the DOS version (IBM 5.0). Not so obvious, but quite interesting, is that this version marker is just the first element in a table that describes the characteristics of the disk to DOS. The table includes key information, such as the number of bytes per sector, sectors per track, and so on (the physical dimensions of the disk) as well as the size of the FAT and directory (the logical dimensions of the DOS structure on the disk). This table and an identifying signature at the end of the record (hex 55 AA) are included in all disks except those formatted for versions of DOS earlier than 2.0.

DOS must identify all the characteristics of each disk with which it works. In the earliest versions of DOS, when there were only a few disk formats, knowledge of those characteristics was built into DOS, and all DOS needed from a disk was a single-byte ID code (which was stored in the FAT) to know everything it needed to about a disk. Now that approach isn't really flexible enough, so DOS learns what it needs to know about a disk from the information table in the boot record.

If you want to decode the boot program to study it, you can use DEBUG's U (Unassemble) command. To see all of it, you have to unassemble it in pieces and look to the addresses used in any jump commands to see where other parts of the program code begin. For the boot record shown above, the following two commands get you started:

```
U 0 L 2
U 3E
```

The File Allocation Table (FAT)

Immediately following the boot record on each disk is the FAT, which controls the use of file space on the disk. As discussed in Chapter 6, the data portion of a disk is divided into clusters of segments, and the clusters are the units of space that are allocated to files. Each cluster is identified by a sequential number, beginning with 2 for the first cluster on a disk (clusters 0 and 1 are reserved for DOS). Regardless of the cluster size (which can be as little as 1 sector for a low-capacity disk to as much as 64 sectors for a 2GB hard disk), each cluster has an entry in the FAT that records its status.

Because what's stored in each cluster's FAT entry is the ID number of another cluster, the total number of clusters identifies how large a FAT entry needs to be. Originally, the FAT entries were stored as 12-bit numbers, which could accommodate numbers as large as 4KB and set a limit of about 4,000 on the possible number of clusters. However, newer hard disks may have many thousands of clusters, depending on how they are designed. This requires a larger FAT design. So, there are two FAT formats. One has 12-bit entries for smaller disks, and one has 16-bit entries for larger disks. The difference among these lies in how the FAT is stored; the way the FAT is used is the same for both sizes.

If a FAT entry is 0, that indicates that the corresponding cluster is not in use and is free for allocation to any file that needs it; 1 is reserved for a technical reason. For clusters that hold data, the FAT entry contains either the ID number of the next cluster or a special number that marks the end of a file's space allocation chain. The clusters in which a file is stored are chained together by the numeric links stored in the FAT. The file's directory entry indicates the first cluster number, and each cluster points to the next cluster or indicates the end of the chain (the end marker is hex FFF for a 12-bit FAT and FFFF for a 16-bit FAT). This enables DOS to trace the location of a file's data from front to back. Portions of a disk that are defective and shouldn't be used—bad track areas —are identified by a FAT entry of FF7 for a 12-bit FAT or FFF7 for a 16-bit FAT. Other special FAT codes, FF0 through FFF (12-bit FAT) and FFF0 through FFFF (16-bit FAT), are reserved for needs that may arise in the future. (Except, of course, FF7 and FFF7 which already are in use.)

Note that the special FAT codes are kept to the 16 highest values (for either FAT format). This is so that there are as many usable cluster numbers as possible—up to 4,078 for 12-bit FATs and 65,518 for 16-bit FATs.

Although both 12- and 16-bit FATs are used in the same way, each is recorded in its own way to take account of the difference in the size of the entry. There's nothing special about how a 16-bit FAT is stored; 16-bit numbers are part of the PC's natural scheme, so the numbers in a 16-bit FAT simply are stored as a list of 2-byte words. For 12-bit FATs, things are more complicated. The PC's processors don't have any natural and convenient way to record numbers that are 1.5 bytes long. To deal with this problem, the FAT entries are paired, so that two FAT entries take up 3 bytes. The method of coding two 12-bit numbers in 3 bytes is set up to be as convenient as possible to handle with assembly language instructions, but it's rather difficult to understand if you look at the hex coding for this kind of FAT.

Each FAT begins with the entry for cluster 0, even though the first actual cluster is number 2. The first two FAT entries are dummies and are used to provide a place to store an ID byte that helps DOS identify the disk format. The very first byte of the FAT contains this code. For example, the hex code F8 identifies a fixed disk.

To help safeguard the FAT, DOS records more than one copy. The two copies are stored one right after the other. From time to time, DOS checks one FAT against the other, making sure that they are identical. If they are not, DOS knows an error has occurred.

The Root Directory

The next and final element of the system portion of each disk is the root directory, which is stored immediately following the FATs. The directory works as a simple table of 32-byte entries that describe the files (and other directory entries such as a volume label) on the disk.

The directory entries record, as noted in Chapter 6, the 8-byte filename, the 3-byte filename extension, the size of the file, the date and time stamp, the starting cluster number of the file, and the file attribute codes. There are also unused bytes in each directory entry that can be used for future needs. There are many interesting things to discover in these directory entries. For example, there are two special codes in the filename field that are used in the first byte of the filename. If this byte is 0, it indicates that the directory entry (and any following entries in this directory) has never been used; this gives DOS a way of knowing when it has seen all the active entries in a directory without having to search to the end.

Another code, hex E5, is used to mark entries that have been erased. That's why, when you work with erased files (using my UnErase program or a similar utility), you don't see the first character of the erased file's name. When a file is erased, the first character of the filename is overwritten with this hex E5 erasure code. Incidentally, when a file is erased (or a subdirectory removed), nothing else in the directory entry is changed; all the information is retained. The only thing that happens when a file is erased is that the filename is marked as erased, and the file's space allocation in the FAT is released.

There's one more special and interesting thing to know about the filename and extension fields. For files and subdirectories, these two are treated as separate fields. But, when a directory entry is used as a disk's volume label, the two together are treated as a single 11-character field. When a disk's volume label is displayed (as it is by the DIR, CHKDSK, and VOL commands), the label isn't punctuated with a period the way filenames are.

The size of each file is stored in the file's directory entry as a 4-byte integer, which accommodates file sizes much larger than any disk you could use. This guarantees that files won't be limited by the size that can be recorded in the file directory. Incidentally, the file size is recorded only for true files. Other types of directory entries have their file size entered as zero. That makes sense for the directory entry, which serves as a volume label, but is a little surprising for subdirectories. Even though subdirectories are stored in the data portion of a disk the same way files are and even though a subdirectory has a size, it's not recorded in the subdirectory's directory entry.

The date and time stamp in each directory entry is formatted in a way that can record any date from January 1, 1980 to the end of 2099; the time stamp records times to an accuracy of two seconds, although DOS only displays the time to the minute. The date and the time are recorded separately in two adjacent 16-bit words, and each is coded according to its own formula. However, the way they are stored enables the two to be treated as a single 4-byte field that can be compared in a single assembly language instruction to learn if one stamp is earlier or later than another. The date is coded by the following formula:

$$date = day + 32 \times month + 512 \times (year - 1980)$$

The time is coded by this formula:

$$time = seconds/2 + 32 \times minutes + 1,024 \times hours$$

The final item of interest in a directory entry is the file attribute byte. This byte is treated as a collection of eight flags, each controlled by a single bit. Six of the eight are currently in use, while the other two are available for future use. Two of the six attribute bits are special and are used by themselves without any other bits set. One marks a disk's volume label directory entry; the other marks a subdirectory entry, so DOS knows to treat it as a subdirectory and not as a file. The other four attributes are used to mark files and can be set in any combination. One marks a file as read-only, not to be modified or erased; another marks a file as having been changed. This is used by the BACKUP and XCOPY commands to indicate which files need to be backed up.

The final two attributes, called hidden and system, are used to make a file invisible to most DOS commands. There is essentially no difference between hidden and system status. The two DOS system files that are on every bootable system disk are both marked as hidden and system. As an interesting oddity, hidden and system files are invisible to the DOS commands DIR, COPY, and DEL, but are seen by the TYPE command; you can verify that by entering the following command on a system disk (if you are using IBM DOS):

```
TYPE IBMDOS.COM
```

However, starting with DOS 5.0, you can use DIR with the /A (Attribute) option to display hidden and system files. Hidden files also are seen by the CHKDSK command when you use the /V option, which tells CHKDSK to display the name of every file along with the directory in which it resides.

Like the other elements of the system portion of a disk, the root directory has a fixed size for each disk, so DOS knows exactly where to find the beginning of the directory and the beginning of the data area that follows it. This means that the root directory can hold only so many entries, which is a rigid limit. Subdirectories, on the other hand, don't have that problem. While subdirectories work in essentially the same way that the root directory does, they are stored in the data portion of the disk just as though they were ordinary files and can grow to any size that the disk can accommodate. Using subdirectories, which were introduced with DOS version 2.0, avoids any arbitrary limit on the number of files a disk can hold.

As I mentioned, each particular disk format uses a fixed size for each element of the system area. The boot record is always 1 sector. The size of the FAT (file allocation table) varies. For example, on a 3.5-inch, 1.44MB diskette, each of the two FATs occupies 9 sectors; on a large hard disk, each FAT can use up to 256 sectors. The size of the root directory also varies.

If you have the Norton Utilities, you can use the System Information program to check out the size of each part of the disk. If you have an older, pre-5.0 version of the utilities, use the NU or DI (Disk Information) program. An example of this information (from the NU program) for a standard 1.44MB disk is listed below:

Menu 3.2

```
                     Technical Information

   Drive A:

   Type of disk:
       Double-sided, quad-density, 18-sector, high-capacity

   Basic storage capacity:
       1.4 million characters (megabytes)
       100% of disk space is free

   Logical dimensions:
       Sectors are made up of 512 bytes
       Tracks are made up of 18 sectors per disk side
       There are 2 disk sides
       The disk is made up of 80 tracks
       Space for files is allocated in clusters of 1 sector
       There are 2,847 clusters
       The disk's root directory can hold 224 files
                             Press any key to continue...
```

Data Storage Area

The final and largest part of each disk is the data space. As you can imagine, there aren't quite as many fascinating details to discover about this part compared with the system part of the disk. You know your file data can have any length, but the file data always is stored in complete 512-byte disk sectors, and the sectors are allocated to files in complete clusters. Because of this, there usually is some unused space in the last sector of a data file and there may even be completely unused sectors at the end of the last cluster.

When DOS writes data to a disk, it doesn't clean up any data that may have been previously recorded. Thus, slack space in the new data file can contain pieces of whatever was stored earlier in a sector or cluster. If you inspect the slack area at the end of a file, you can find odds and ends of previous files stored there.

Some Things To Try

1. Can you explain why the size of a DOS partition on a hard disk can't be changed without reformatting it? Is it possible to write a conversion program that can resize a partition? Describe the steps that would be involved.

2. Using the techniques described, inspect a boot record from one of your disks and compare it with the one shown. Then, using the U (Unassemble) command of DEBUG, get an assembly language listing of the boot program and discover how it works.

3. For every disk format that your computer handles—high-capacity, low-capacity, etc.—format a disk with the DOS files and then inspect the disk to see what the differences are in the boot record and other elements.

4. If you have the Norton Utilities, use the Disk Editor program to inspect the slack area at the end of your disk files. If you have a pre-5.0 version of the utilities, use the NU program. Select a file, display it, and then press the End key to jump to the end of the file. What do you see?

Disk Utilities

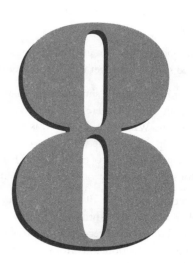

I wouldn't have spent so much time describing disk drives and how they work if I didn't believe this is an important topic. After all, you can spend a lot of time, energy, and money understanding how the processor works, how the computer uses memory, and procuring the best and fastest machine available, but if you can't store information safely, use it when you need it, and recover data if something goes wrong, then everything else is a waste.

In this chapter, I discuss some important software utilities and procedures you can use to keep your hard disk in good shape and to get the most out of it.

This isn't a comprehensive chapter because there simply are too many software programs out there for me to know about them all; there isn't even room in this book to tell you about all the ones I do know. What I do, however, is make you aware of some of the software available to help you manage your disks, describe briefly how they work, and discuss some of the pros and cons of using them. That way, you'll be ready to head off on your own for some investigation and research, if necessary.

The three main areas I discuss in this chapter are disk compression or disk doubler utilities, disk optimizers, and disk trouble shooting utilities. I already have mentioned my Norton Utilities package several times, and I recommend it to you again here. It is a comprehensive collection of disk inspection and error recovery that most users find indispensable. Obviously, there are other software utilities that you also may need. I talk about them in this chapter—by type, not by name—so you at least know what to look for.

Disk Compression (Doublers)

If you ever have purchased a new, larger disk drive in the hopes of finding enough storage for all those programs and data files you had a place to put, only to run out of room on the new drive, then you are a candidate for disk compression or disk doubler software.

Many companies offer these utilities, not the least of which is Microsoft with its DOS 6 and IBM with its DOS 6. Interestingly, these two system software giants have taken a decidedly different approach to disk compression. I talk about their differing views in a moment. First, I explain about the two sides of disk compression: the good and bad, the Dr. Jekyll and Mr. Hyde, sides.

As I mentioned, disk compression software can help you solve the never ending problem of running out of room on your hard drive. You can't just keep adding more space forever, of course, but with a good disk doubler you at least can double the amount of available space without buying another hard drive.

The technology of disk doubling is quite complex. A detailed explanation is well beyond the scope of this book. However, in general, here's how it works.

Nearly all the information you store in a data file or program file contains a lot of redundant information. Data files, particularly, may be full of spaces or information repeated over and over. You can see this concept by looking at a color computer screen. What is the background color? A dark blue, perhaps? Suppose that you were going to store the screen you're looking at as a data file, recording every piece of information faithfully to disk.

Can you see that the number of instructions for dark blue background dots is quite large, one for every location on the screen? If you have a 1,024×768 display, and every position is filled with a blue dot, that's a lot of dots. Blue, blue, blue, blue, and so on, and so on.

Now, suppose that you were to use a data compression utility to store the same information. The utility software looks at the data and notices that there are many blue dots. Sensibly, the software says, "Why not just store the blue dot once and then store some information about how many more blue dots are needed." In fact, that's what compression utilities do with the data they compress, whether the data is display information or text. Any time a file contains repetitive, redundant information, the software stores the repeated data once and notes how many times the information should be repeated.

To install such a utility, you need enough space on your hard drive for "scratch pad" work so that the software can inspect existing data, have room to work on it, and have room to move information around as it works with your drive. As you can imagine, if you have a couple of hundred megabytes of data already on a hard drive, it can take some time for the compression utility to scan all this data, decide how to compress it, and store it away on the disk in a new format. How much time isn't too relevant, however, because you can't use your machine for anything else while it is doing this. Thus, you can set the software in motion and go to lunch or home for the evening and find your disk storage magically doubled in size when you return.

I've used several of these utilities at one time or another. It truly is amazing to run a piece of software and then discover when you issue the DIR or CHKDSK command that you have about twice the free space you had before running the software. That's the good news, or part of it.

The bad news is that after the information on your disk is compressed in this way, neither DOS nor any other application that uses DOS or reads and writes directly to the drive can make heads nor tails out of it. So, after compressing a disk in this way, you always must run a driver when you boot your system. This TSR (terminate-and-stay-resident) software grabs any software calls to the disk drive, interprets the request to read or write information, and puts its own "spin" on the request.

If DOS or another program asks for something from the compressed disk, the utility finds it on the disk and then decompresses it before passing it to the requesting program. If a program writes something to the disk, the TSR grabs the write request and scans the data to remove as much redundant information as it can before storing the information to disk. In this way, anything you write to the disk, from word processor and spreadsheet data files to new programs you install, first goes through the compression routine so that you can continue to store about twice as much information as you could without a compression utility.

The further bad news is that, because this utility must always run for you to access compressed data, it takes up memory, either conventional or high memory. It also is bad news that you have to preread and prewrite data in this way. And, depending on how sophisticated the program you're using is, it may put an additional burden on you as you maintain your disk drive. You may not be able to use some of the tried-and-true utility software you have become accustomed to—in fact, it is almost certain that you cannot. You may have to use utilities (provided by the compression software company) especially designed to work with compressed data.

In addition to the fact that you effectively can double your disk space, there is another good side. Because the data is compressed into half the normal space, yet the rotational speed of your disk drive hasn't changed, you can read and write data noticeably faster with most compression software than you can without it. The improvement isn't twice as fast because there is some overhead in compressing and decompressing the information on the fly as you use it. A RAM-resident utility, however, usually can perform these conversion functions much faster than your drive can read or write uncompressed data. Thus, the overall result is an improvement in read/write speed with data compression software.

Is there anything else wrong with data compression? That depends on several factors, including which compression utility you are using, what other software you are using, what hardware you have, what operating environment you are using, and so on.

At the theory level, there should be no problem with data compression. The software takes out unnecessary information before the data is stored to disk, carefully remembering how it did so, and then reverses the process when you want to read the compressed data. That's the ideal situation.

The real world of computers is different from the ideal, as you probably already know. Why? People and machines do things the software designer didn't expect, unforeseen events occur, and errors occur. This was demonstrated graphically when Microsoft released DOS 6 with an integral disk compression utility.

In theory, bundling compression software with DOS made a lot of sense. Properly done, this approach could remove the objections and potential traps of on-the-fly data compression because the compression utility would be tightly coupled with the operating system. Unfortunately for Microsoft, this wasn't the case with the initial release of the DOS/compression package. Many people who upgraded from previous versions of DOS to DOS 6 and added data compression experienced problems ranging from software incompatibility to lost data.

It is unfortunate, but this early experience probably gave data compression in general a bad name, and it may take a while for the concept to bounce back. Eventually, I think everyone will compress their information on disk, but the utility may not be integrated with the operating system. More likely the utility will be incorporated as part of the hard disk controller hardware design so that it is outside of DOS and the perversities of RAM-resident software.

In fact, taking note of Microsoft's problems with its approach to disk compression, IBM released its own version of DOS 6, PC-DOS 6, without data compression software included. IBM did include a coupon so that users could upgrade to a compression utility (not the same brand as Microsoft used) if they wanted to.

I have, as I said, used a couple of these compression utilities on perhaps five or eight machines and, aside from an occasional inconvenience (which I describe in more detail in a moment), I never had any problems with the software. I eventually stopped using compression utilities because I install and uninstall so many different software packages for my use and for evaluation that it became too much trouble. However, I never experienced any data loss or serious problems.

Data Compression Details

With that background, I give you a little bit more insight into how data compression software functions. Each particular package is a little different, but the general operation I describe in this section shows you the basic theory and explains why it is sometimes very inconvenient to have compression software installed on your system, even if you never experience any data loss because of it.

Usually, when a data compression program finishes its work during installation you have two types of data storage on your hard disk—some that is compressed and some that is normal, uncompressed DOS data. If you think about this you see why it is important. Remember, I said that the compressed data doesn't mean anything to DOS or to any of your application programs and that you have to run a TSR to handle the translation.

Think about what happens when you boot your computer, however. You can't load this translator until after you have DOS running, and you can't get DOS running without the translator. The way out of this dilemma is to keep a portion of the disk uncompressed to store the boot information and DOS. Then you can place a command in your CONFIG.SYS or AUTOEXEC.BAT files to load the TSR and "turn on" compression after DOS is loaded.

In fact, some of these compression routines don't actually change the partition table of your drive at all. They merely place the required files for booting in your root directory on the C drive (or whatever drive you boot from) and then create a huge hidden data file that stores your compressed information.

Suppose that you have a 100MB hard drive. The compression routine may take 10MB for its own use at the head of drive C and then create a 90MB hidden file. If you boot the computer without loading the compression TSR, you have a single drive C with a few DOS and boot files that may take up a few megabytes, but if you do a DIR, you may have only a few megabytes of free space.

Use CHKDSK or DOSSHELL to view the contents of your disk. You find the 90MB hidden file. When you load the compression TSR, the utility logically switches the drive C or boot drive with the files stored in the hidden file. The files in the hidden file are now stored on drive C, and your DOS and other uncompressed data is on drive D. Now, with the TSR software running, instead of a 10MB drive, you have one 10MB drive (the "real" disk) and one 180MB logical drive, which is really the 90MB hidden file with everything compressed to half its normal size.

Normally, all this is handled automatically through routines that load during the boot process, so you never really have to be aware of it. In practice, it looks as if the install program created a drive D to hold your system files and compressed the data on your drive C. In reality, the opposite is true.

With the logical and physical drive letters swapped and your software installed and the TSR grabbing read/write requests, things can operate as usual, at least for a while. You can run into trouble when you install new software and when you use some types of software if that software doesn't handle all of its disk I/O strictly according to DOS. And, your compression TSR has to be pretty sharp to avoid problems, too.

Here's one example. Suppose that you want to install a new software package on drive C, which is really the hidden compressed file on your disk. The software has to make changes to your CONFIG.SYS file to function properly. Because you've installed the software on your drive C, the changes are made to CONFIG.SYS on drive C. But where is the *real* CONFIG.SYS? It is on drive D, the physical drive actually used during start-up. Some compression software can catch this potential problem and copy the changed CONFIG.SYS file on drive C to the drive D physical drive. Sometimes, however, because of the way the install process works, the new software can bypass this trap and write the changes to the wrong place.

I had a particular problem with a memory management utility I was testing that had to reboot the computer several times during installation. The software never could get straight where the correct CONFIG.SYS file was located, and I finally had to remove the compression utility from that drive to get the software to install properly.

This is the type of problem compression programs can cause. Although no data may be lost, it can be inconvenient. One suggestion is to install all the software you plan to use with a given computer before installing the compression routine. That way, only the data files you create with your programs will be written to the compressed disk. Another approach is to compress about half of your disk so that you have enough space to install new software on the boot drive. Then you can copy the new software over to the compressed drive (maybe) or simply use it from the uncompressed partition.

There's another problem that sometimes surfaces with compression software. It shouldn't cause you to lose data, but it can cause you to lose your patience. On average, these compression routines are capable of taking out about half of the information in your files. Some files, such as program files, don't compress nearly that much, if at all. However, graphics data and word processor information and database files usually compress considerably more than half. Thus, you can expect about a doubling of storage space.

As you use compression utilities, there is no way for some of them to know exactly how much they are compressing data. So they report 50 percent because that's a pretty good average across a sufficiently large sampling of data. However, on your system, the real compression ration may be only 35–40 percent. The utility, though, reports to DOS and your DOS utilities (such as CHKDSK, DIR, and the like) that compression is 50 percent. Thus, you may try to install a new software package, copy over a data file, or download information from an online service, believing that you have 10 or 20MB of free space, and run out of room. When you run out of room in this instance, it is not an orderly process as it is when DOS correctly reports to your applications how much memory you have.

When DOS says to an application, "Watch out, you only have 1,000 bytes left," the routine can judge its progress and then gracefully bail out of what it is doing when things get too tight. If DOS says, on the other hand, "Full speed ahead, you've got at least 10MB," when really there are only 2MB of free space, your applications can't bail out gracefully and they run full speed into a brick wall. Depending on what was going on and how well your application can handle the crash, you may or may not lose data. However, you're guaranteed to lose patience with this sort of surprise about the second or third time it happens.

Should you install data compression software? Maybe. It is much cheaper than buying another disk drive and, if used carefully with an understanding of some of the built-in limitations, it can work well. On the other hand, if your computing environment is one in which installed software changes frequently or in which the machines are used by inexperienced users who may have problems conceptualizing how data is stored, the best advice probably is not to use it.

Disk Optimizers

A disk optimizer is another sort of disk utility that you should have. This is a relatively broad class of software that can include a variety of features and functions. In general, disk optimizers are designed to handle some or all (and perhaps more) of the following functions:

- Defragment your disk

- Physically rearrange the files on your disk

- Locate and mark bad storage locations

- Determine and set the optimum disk interleave factor

- Provide disk read/write cache

Each of these features is discussed in the following sections.

Defragment Your Disk

Disk fragmentation occurs after DOS has written different versions of your files several times. When you first create a file, all the information in it is stored end to end in contiguous disk locations. If you create another file, either as data for an application or by installing a new program, this file starts right after the previous file on the disk and stores all its information contiguously as well. If you go back to the first file—say, a word processor document—and add several pages to it, when you store it, the entire file no longer fits in one place because you have stored another file behind it. In this case, DOS leaves the old piece of the file where it was and stores the rest of the file in the next available open space, which is at the end of the second file you saved. If you have two files, A and B, they may be stored something like this, where each letter represents a sector:

    AAAAAAAAAABBBBBBBBBBBAAA

If you add some data to file B and save it back to disk, the two files are stored like this:

    AAAAAAAAAABBBBBBBBBBBAAABBB

This is what happens, not with two files, but with hundreds on your disks. As you can see, over time your disk will look more like a pot of spaghetti someone dropped on the floor than an orderly arrangement of data files. Because you can't see the data on the disk, you don't care about the appearance, but it is a problem nevertheless. Each time DOS loads one of these fragmented files, it has to move the read head several times, perhaps jumping to wildly separated locations on the disk. This means that data retrieval can become extremely slow.

That's why you need to run a defragmenter utility on a regular basis. These programs scan the directory and FAT entries to determine which files are fragmented and then rewrite the files in new locations keeping them together. You should notice a definite improvement in disk performance when you clean up a heavily fragmented disk.

Another benefit to using most of the defragmenter utilities is that, while they are scanning the disk and moving all this information around, they scan the disk surface looking for bad locations. When a bad spot is found, the utility marks the spot in the FAT as questionable so that no new information will be written there.

Physically Rearrange the Files on Your Disk

Individual file fragmenting is only one way your disk gets slowed down. Another way is when you load more than one file at a time and these files are widely separated on the disk. This separation happens naturally as you create and delete files or run defragmenter utilities. It is better to have related files physically stored together on the disk.

Sometimes you also may want the files to be stored on the disk in the order that they appear in the directory. This can be a convenience and also can be the way the computer uses the files, depending on your applications.

For whatever reason, you can store files in a sorted order or an order you specify with a utility designed to physically move files. Sometimes this is done as part of the defragmenting process, and sometimes it is done with a separate utility. Either way, it can take a long time if you have a large disk and haven't sorted files in this way in a long time. If you run the routine once a week or twice a month, however, it won't take too long, and you may notice some benefits in improved computer performance.

Locate and Mark Bad Storage Locations

I mentioned this service in the discussion of defragmenting utilities. Some defragmenters test the surface of the disk before writing any new data to it, even if something else is stored there. Whether your defragmenter does or not, you may want to run a separate utility to do a surface scan and test each storage location. You need to do this because, if you write information to a portion of the disk that is not stable, you could lose some data. True, DOS handles this chore when you format the disk, but if it has been a while since you formatted the disk, there may be questionable storage locations lurking out there just waiting to jump up and bite you.

Determine and Set the Optimum Disk Interleave Factor

If your hard disk was properly installed and configured in the first place, then you don't need to reset the interleave factor. If a mistake was made during installation, however, you could speed up the operation of your hard disk considerably by correcting an interleave problem.

Disk interleave or the interleave factor is expressed as a ratio. It represents how many sectors your controller skips between each write operation. Information always is written to disk in multiples of whole sectors. This is because only so much memory is onboard the controller and inside your disk drive and, I suppose, because only so much data can be ready to write at any given time. Thus, the controller and disk work together to bundle up the information to be written to disk in a single operation. The bundle is sent to the disk read/write heads and recorded to disk.

Next, the electronics in the controller and disk have to fetch another cluster of information, send it down the wires to the read/write heads, and record it to disk. The hard disk platter, however, is spinning at 3,600 RPM. Unless the electronic process is pretty quick, a lot of blank disk has moved under the disk head before any data is ready to be recorded. The way around this problem is to specify how many sectors need to be skipped between writes to give the controller time to find the next block of data, format it, and get it to the drive's heads.

If the controller is fast (as most of them are today), then no sectors are skipped, and the disk interleave is 1:1. A 1:1 disk interleave means data can be written and read at disk speed without waiting for the controller to catch up. If one sector has to be skipped after each write, the interleave factor is 1:2 because every second sector is written. For a really slow controller, the interleave may be 1:9.

Again, if the drive were configured properly in the first place, you shouldn't have to adjust the interleave, but it doesn't hurt to check. A utility program that can check the interleave and adjust it if it isn't correct can improve disk performance.

Provide Disk Read/Write Cache

Even with the disk properly defragmented and the interleave properly set, the electronics inside your computer—the RAM, processor, and even disk controller card—are much faster than the physical drive. You simply can't read from and write to the disk as fast as the memory and the processor would like. Yet, if you could speed up read/write speed, the processor would be free quicker to go on about other duties.

That's where read/write cache come in. A cache program does a couple of things to help speed up data transfer. First, a segment of memory, either part of system RAM or dedicated memory on the controller, is set aside to store temporarily the data going to and from the disk. With cache memory established, when you write data to the disk it goes first to the cache memory. This is all electronic, and no mechanical mechanisms are involved that slow down the process. Then, when the processor has time between other tasks, it can write the data to the physical disk.

The opposite happens during a read operation. Information coming off the disk is read first into temporary RAM, the read cache. In fact, more data than the calling program asked for is read into memory. Now, when a program asks for information, the cache memory is searched first. If the required information is there, it is sent along without the need to go to the physical disk. And, depending on the sophistication of the caching program, this routine may be able to teach itself about the applications running at any given time, predicting with increasing accuracy what the next requested information will be. That means that, as the predictions get more and more accurate, the program has to read from the physical disk drive fewer and fewer times.

If you have Windows 3.1 or later, you have a cache routine. In fact, you already may be using it. The SMARTDRV utility usually is installed automatically when you install Windows. Likewise, if you have DOS 5.0 or later, you have SMARTDRV, which you can elect to install, depending on your needs.

In general, disk caching programs are a good thing, and I recommend that you use one. You should, however, be aware of several things. If you are using any type of high-density removable media, such as a SyQuest cartridge, make sure that your caching program can tell whether the disk has been swapped out. If your cache program doesn't recognize when you swap disks and then dumps the RAM buffer from the previous disk to a new disk, you will lose data.

Also, be aware of how your caching program handles file writes. If the writes are delayed (which they are in many cache programs to improve overall system performance), then you can't turn your computer off the moment you get a software indication that the write operation is complete. If you're working in DOS, for example, and save a file and exit the program, you might think it is safe to turn off the computer as soon as you see the DOS prompt. However, the cache buffer may still be full of the last data written, data that may not have gone to the disk. In this situation, you need to be aware of how long it takes to flush the write buffer and get in the habit of watching the disk drive light to make sure it has finished writing before turning your machine off or rebooting.

Troubleshooting and Repair Tools

Troubleshooting and repair software is like fire insurance. It is the most useless thing in the world—that is, until you need it. Then there is no substitute for having the software you need. Obviously, you can't wait until you need it to buy it, either. You can't buy fire insurance after the fire starts, you can't buy health insurance after you get sick, and you can't wait to buy troubleshooting software until after you have an emergency.

Among the features you can expect to find with this type of utility are the following:

- Unerase and unformat routines

- Finding lost or misnamed files

- Memory testing and reporting

- Backup

- Virus protection and other security features

- System speed testing

- Reporting on system information, including interrupts, disk, and ports

If you are using one of the new DOS products, you have access to some of these utilities already, but you will find that many third-party utilities go a step further than those built into DOS.

As you have seen in this chapter, disk utilities can be valuable additions to your computer setup. In the next two chapters, I discuss two more types of disks: removable and optical disks.

Disks: Removable Storage

9

W hen hard disks—or fixed disks—first became popular, they became popular for several very good reasons. One of the main reasons was the density of storage they offered. The only way, however, these drives could provide highly reliable, dense storage was to fix the read/write mechanism inside the drive and not enable the recording media to be removed from the drive.

It was this removing the media (usually along with the heads and other parts of the mechanical mechanism) that caused unreliable operation in previous removable rigid drives. When the fixed drive came along, users felt a new surge of confidence in the storage medium, so the limitation of not being able to remove the platters didn't seem particularly severe.

As drive technology advanced and users became accustomed to large amounts of storage, the desire to move back toward some form of removable medium was natural. After all, if 40MB of fixed storage was good, how much better it would be to have 40MB over and over again in the form of a removable disk?

To make a long story short, that's what happened over a period of years. Yes, there were times when the media weren't particularly reliable but, today, several technologies exist for providing high-density, removable, and reliable storage. I discuss these technologies briefly in this chapter.

Removable Disk Types

There have been a number of successful and not-so-successful removable disk designs over the years. For the most part, the PC world has settled on several drive types:

- Hard drives with removable rigid platters

- Floppy cartridge drives on which the read/write medium is soft instead of hard

- Removable hard drives on which the entire drive mechanism, including read/write heads, drive motors, and electronics slip in and out of a plug-in slot

Several designs exist in each of these broad categories, and a number of companies are competing for the top slot in each category. There are, however, some high-profile players already on the field.

Removable Hard Platters

Removable hard platter disks used to be the industry standard. These were huge, 14-inch or larger platters with two to four or more platters inside a (sometimes) clear cylinder with a large twist-off lid that looked more like a giant Tupperware container than a computer component. These drives carried 5–20MB of information. These were the disks of the day on minicomputers in the 1970s, but they were notoriously temperamental and prone to crashes. Nobody liked them, but they were the only way to achieve enough storage for office-based minicomputers that were doing work such as payroll, accounting, inventory, and billing. A different disk or set of disks was used for each task.

When fixed disks came out, people naturally forgot about removable high-density media because the fixed disks of the day had lots of storage in a small space, so no one worried about being able to take it out of the computer.

As data storage needs increased, various companies started working on removable hard disk media. There were and are several brand names of drives with removable hard disk cartridges; however, they all are made by one or two major companies. Perhaps the most common end-user label is SyQuest.

Removable Soft Platters

Several versions of the removable soft platter drive exist, but the most visible in the industry is the Bernoulli cartridge system from Iomega. This system uses cartridges with a floppy-type recording medium. Normally, you couldn't record multiple mega-bytes of data on a 3.5-inch floppy medium. Because of the way the cartridge is designed, however, the floppy becomes very rigid as it spins, enabling dense record-ing. These drives can hold up to 150MB on each cartridge (see the discussion of Bernoulli technology later in this chapter).

Floptical drives that use magnetic media and an optical-assisted positioning mechanism also are being offered. Although floptical drives haven't caught on like Bernoulli, they also are a viable technology. These drives can't hold as much data in a given floppy, and the hardware costs a little more than Bernoulli.

Removable Hard Drives

Removable hard drives are probably the newest of the technologies and (maybe) the one destined to see the broadest service. Removable hard drives are appearing in many laptop, notebook, portable, and other mobile devices. These drives are extremely small and light, don't make much noise, have low power requirements, and can be pulled out of one machine and put into another.

Removable hard drives fit into at least two categories: those that slide into a proprietary disk cage or slot and those that use one of the newer PCMCIA external expansion slots (for more information on PCMCIA, see the discussion in Chapter 2).

If you are using a drive with a proprietary hardware interface, you have to buy all your drives from the same manufacturer. And, if you want to install in your desktop machine a removable disk slot to match your laptop, you have to purchase the same kind of cage or slot from the same company that made the one in your mobile computer.

If you're using PCMCIA disks, on the other hand, the theory is that one drive should be able to slide into any compatible slot. As this new technology was getting under way, there were some problems with compatibility, and a few drives simply wouldn't work properly outside their manufacturer's environment. I expect this little unpleasantness was just early growing pains and should be a thing of the past as you read this. In any case, a standards-based drive should be a better choice for expandability and compatibility with other users.

Whatever the standard your removable disk uses, the concept is the same. A very small drive—frequently not much bigger than a credit card—slips into a hole in the case of your computer where it meets with a set of pins at the other end. Like plugging in an expansion card, you simply slide the drive into the case until it seats firmly, making power and data connections automatically. From that point, the disk operates as if it were a regular, hard-wired drive.

Removing the drive simply is the reverse. When you're ready to take the disk to another machine to exchange data, you simply pop the cover on the access door to the drive, pull a handle or press a lever that releases the drive, and pull it out of the slot.

The first time you see one of these drives, you may think someone is playing a not-so-funny joke. These units can be extremely tiny, making you wonder what possible good they could be in a real computing environment. These very small drives can hold up to 340MB of information, yet fit easily in the palm of your hand.

These tiny wonders are moving out of the mobile-only environment and showing up on desktop machines. Why not? They offer capacity similar to larger, hard-wired units, are smaller and lighter, require less power, and pop in and out as needed for information interchange or security purposes.

Removable Storage Advantages

The advantages to removable storage should be obvious. The most obvious advantage is the capability to use one piece of hardware for multiple blocks of storage. You pay for the drive electronics, read/write heads, motors, and so on, once and then can build the system to an unlimited amount of storage simply by adding new cartridges or disks.

Security is another obvious advantage. If you record sensitive data on a removable disk, you can take it out of the machine and lock it up in a secure place. Then, the chances of someone making off with your information are very slim. In fact, this is a popular application in military and industrial research circles. The Bernoulli and SyQuest drives are particularly popular because of the high-density storage they offer compared with the cost of the storage media.

You can use removable media to exchange data or whole software systems among different machines. I like to use some type of removable device to store installed software systems that I don't use very much, but which I need to be able to access. I can install the software, create any data files I need, and then put the disk away on a shelf until I need that particular package again. That way, I don't take up conventional hard disk space for an application that I rarely use, yet I have it when I need it.

207

Removable hard disks can be useful for backup as well. If you have very large systems, you can compress the data or use backup utilities and still place the information on a removable disk to cut down the number of disks required as compared with backing up to floppies. With smaller systems, you can treat backup as I just described for infrequently used applications. Simply dedicate an entire disk—40, 80, or 150MB—to a single application and copy the whole thing to the removable media. Now you have a backup that is more than a backup, it is also a working system. In the event that you need the backup, you don't have to copy it over to your regular hard disk because it is usable directly from the backup medium.

One problem is the question of reliability. In the early days of large removable drives, there were many stories of crashed drives and lost data. Today, even the worst drives have a mean time between failure (MTBF) of at least 30,000 hours, and some units report an MTBF of 150,000 hours or more. That's a rating of 3.5 years on the low end to 17 years on the high end. In fact, some manufacturers, including Iomega, makers of the Bernoulli drives, offer a 5-year warranty on the media itself—a long time in computer terms. This assumes normal usage. If you're looking for long-term archival storage, and assuming that you store the drives properly, the data should be quite safe indeed.

Removable Storage Disadvantages

There are a few disadvantages to using removable media, but only a few. Still, you should be aware of them so that you aren't surprised as you try to use the technology.

For one thing, with today's technology the basic removable drive costs more than a comparable fixed disk. That's because the removable part of the design adds complications and hardware to the basic disk. As you add more storage to the basic disk mechanism, however, the price falls fairly quickly. A basic SyQuest 40MB cartridge may cost only $50 or $60 through discount channels, for example. That's fairly cheap storage.

With most removable cartridge systems (not systems on which the entire drive is removable), you must run driver software so that DOS recognizes the drive. This requires another level of concern during system configuration and use, and these drivers take up system RAM.

Moreover, not all disk-caching software recognizes when a removable hard drive cartridge has been taken out of the drive. If you cache a removable drive with software that doesn't know when you've swapped disks, you could lose a whole platter's worth of data by swapping disks before the cache software has flushed the RAM buffer. The answer to this problem is to make sure that your caching software can recognize disk swaps or simply to turn off caching for that drive.

Depending on how you look at it, the required interface for removable drives may be a problem. By far the majority of removable storage units I know about use some form of SCSI interface—sometimes an industry standard interface and sometimes a proprietary interface based on the industry standard. If you already have a SCSI interface installed, then this is not a disadvantage (if the required interface is standard and the one you have is standard). If, on the other hand, you have to purchase a separate SCSI interface to use the removable drive, that raises the cost, requires another slot in your machine, and if the required interface is not standard, can lead to incompatibilities with future SCSI devices.

In general, however, SCSI is an excellent technology that I expect to become more popular in PCs as more drives use it. CD-ROM drives, for example, almost always use SCSI interfaces, and with the rise in popularity of removable drives requiring SCSI, you should see this high-speed, mostly standard interface showing up on more PCs in the future.

Removable Disk Technology

Removable technology matches the drive types I discussed earlier in this chapter: removable hard platters, removable soft platters, and removable drives. There's one more removable technology that is gaining popularity and, I expect, soon will take over. That is magneto-optical (MO) technology, which records on magnetic media but uses optical technology for very precise head positioning. I talk about MO technology in the next chapter when I discuss optical technology. For now, I look a little more closely at each of the conventional removable technologies.

Removable Hard Platters

At first look, a removable hard platter probably seems like the most reasonable solution to the removable media problem. After all, it was the first technology used by minicomputers, is well understood, and is accepted by the user community. In fact, it does work well and is a reasonable solution for many users.

Although they are marketed under different labels, today the majority of removable hard platter devices are manufactured by either SyQuest or Ricoh. For a long time, the standby standard for removable hard drives was the Sequester/Ricoh 44MB cartridge, which was about the size of a 5.25-inch floppy disk, except that it was 0.5 inches thick. Today, that same SyQuest drive may store 5 or 10 times as much data and can fit in a 3.5-inch form factor.

Whether the drive is sealed or uses removable media, a hard disk is composed of certain basic components:

- Rigid disks with magnetic media for data storage

- Read/write heads, usually one per surface

- Head movement mechanics

- Electronic interface between the heads and the computer interface

- A computer interface/controller

- One or more cables between the drive and computer

With current removable technology, the design is limited to only a single platter. With fixed devices, there may be two, four, or more platters; the more platters or disks, the more information a given drive can store.

The SyQuest design places very lightweight read/write heads above and below the spinning medium, floating on a cushion of air. Current drives can store up to 105MB, but the newer drives also are designed to read and write older 44 and 88MB cartridges.

Some users I've talked to about this technology have expressed concern over the integrity of data stored on a removable cartridge. However, from what I can determine, these drives are very reliable. It is true that some of the very early cartridge units had some reliability problems, but that was years ago.

Today's devices use essentially the same technology as conventional hard disks. The biggest weakness, I believe, is the potential for damaging the plastic case that encloses each cartridge. If the case is damaged, the platter might not rotate properly. The media, however, is no more susceptible to damage than a floppy disk and, because it is enclosed in plastic, maybe even less so.

Even early SyQuest cartridges were certified for a 36-inch drop to a hard surface. According to the company, the case shouldn't break and there should be no internal damage in a drop from this height. Although the cartridge actually may withstand much more abuse, the company doesn't guarantee it beyond that. This is, however, a pretty liberal rating. If you keep the cartridges in their soft plastic storage boxes when they aren't in use, then dropping them, shipping them, and any other normal wear and tear should be no problem.

One of the technical factors that makes these drives reliable is that the majority of the drive mechanism stays with the drive. Earlier designs removed the read/write heads and the positioning mechanics with the platters. Thus, when one of these cartridges was dropped, there was much greater potential for damage caused by misalignment.

Removable Soft Platters

High-density floppy cartridges use either a magneto-optical technology or a Bernoulli technology. I talk about MO drives in the next chapter.

The Bernoulli principle or law was first defined in the mid-1700s by Swiss mathematician Daniel Bernoulli, a specialist in hydrodynamic principles, calculus, and probability. The basic Bernoulli principle states that the higher the speed of a flowing fluid or gas, the lower the pressure. Conversely, as speed decreases, pressure increases.

This principle explains the lift of an airplane wing, among other things. An airplane flies because the wing is shaped to force air to travel faster across the top of the surface than it does underneath. This pressure differential exerts an upward force.

The Bernoulli cartridge from Iomega Corporation functions in this way. The Iomega box basically uses floppy disks that can store large amounts of information because they become semi-rigid in operation.

211

When the floppy disk spins rapidly inside a properly designed enclosure, the medium "flies," forming a reliable surface for high-density storage. In the Iomega design, the Bernoulli effect is caused by a rigid plate on top of the flexible medium. Air flowing between the plate and the medium causes the floppy disk to rise toward the plate. A read/write head protrudes through the plate, causing an even stronger and local Bernoulli effect, pulling the medium at the point very close to the head.

The disk is stabilized in 10 millionths of an inch of the head, which is even closer than standard hard disk tolerances. The read/write head does not actually touch the storage medium.

One of the advantages of this design is that the read/write head is on top of the medium. When the disk spins down, the floppy medium falls away from the head. There is no need for a special landing zone on the disk, nor is there a chance of a head crash in the event of mechanical or power failure.

Current Bernoulli boxes store from 35 to 150MB on each cartridge; 3.5- and 5.25-inch cartridges are available. One advantage to the Bernoulli design is the ruggedness of the cartridge. Because the storage medium is soft when at rest, the cartridge can withstand a lot of abuse without compromising data integrity.

Removable Drives

There's not much to be said for removable drives except that they have gotten smaller and smaller over the past few years. Inside, these drives are much like any conventional hard disk. The newest designs have some advantages over older drives manufactured just two or three years ago. They contain extremely lightweight components, such as read/write heads, making them quick and reliable. In addition, many of them use the new 3.3-volt power supplies that are becoming common in mobile and "green" computers. Together, these features mean that they run quietly, use a relatively small amount of energy, and are extremely tolerant of shock and other abuse, making them reliable. And, prices are less than you may think for this technology.

Some Things To Try

1. Removable technology of one kind or another can be a good primary or secondary storage choice for most users. One application is when your present storage needs are modest, 100MB or so, but you know that through data acquisition over the next months or years, you will need 1GB or more of storage.

   Suppose that this is your situation. How many removable cartridges that store 88MB would be required? What if you are using 150MB cartridges? You might need to know what the relative costs are of purchasing 1GB drive or of spreading the costs over several months by purchasing cartridges or removable drives. Many users compare prices by computing cost per megabyte. If the basic drive mechanism costs $1,200 and each 150MB cartridge is $235, what is the total per-megabyte cost of a 1GB drive? How does this compare with a 1GB hard drive that costs $2,695?

2. Consider your computing situation. How could removable technology fit into what you are doing? Would it save time or change the way you handle any of your computing chores? What about cost? Could changing at least some of your storage to removable media reduce costs in any area?

3. Think about the technologies I've described in this chapter. What are the relative benefits of each one? Can you think of one technological advantage to Bernoulli technology? Why would you choose a removable drive over a removable cartridge system?

Disks: Optical Storage

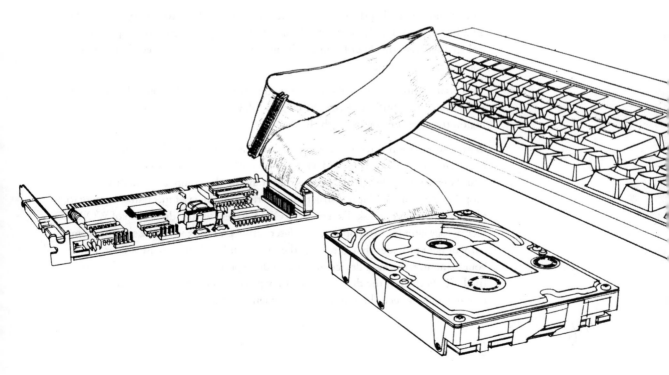

I've spent the last few chapters talking about the technology of magnetic storage. This is because magnetic disks form the foundation of computer storage today. Magnetic disks were the storage of the past, are the storage of the present, and will be the storage of the foreseeable future.

Another technology, optical-based storage, is gaining ground. Optical storage brings data integrity and data density that is unheard of in the world of magnetic storage.

Today there are three optical-based technologies in the PC world, each with a different application: CD-ROM, WORM, and magneto-optical (MO). CD-ROM is read-only technology; WORM enables you to write data once and read it many times; MO technology is read and write technology. None of these has even threatened to take over from conventional storage (at least not yet), but each has a strong place beside or inside your PC for some applications.

In this chapter, I describe the general optical technology and then talk a little about each of the major optical-based types of storage you're likely to find on a PC.

General Technology

The operation of all optical storage devices depends on laser technology. A laser is a highly focused, highly controlled beam of light. Depending on the type of technology involved, this laser beam can be used to record data on special media or to read prerecorded data.

This laser technology is similar to that used in the popular CD audio disks. In fact, many computer optical disks can be used to "play" computer data or music depending on the software you use with them.

When information is recorded on optical media, a laser beam burns out any location that stores a logical one and leaves blank any location that stores a logical zero. This laser is controlled by electronics that translate the computer data into the appropriate burn and no burn instructions and that tell the laser mechanism where to place the data on the disk. Except for WORM drives (see the discussion of WORM technology later in this chapter), such laser activity is reserved for the software company or data provider that generates the master disk. When you use a laser disk in your computer, the laser device inside your drive produces only enough light to read the holes burned in the disk or to precisely position a read/write head for conventional magnetic recording in the case of magneto-optical drives.

In most cases, the result is a rigid platter similar to a CD audio disk that contains 600MB or more of read-only data. You can place this disk into an optical reader that uses a laser beam to scan the disk, pick up the pitted locations, and—through electronics—translate that information into usable computer data.

Optical Advantages

The most obvious advantages to optical technology are storage density and data integrity. The latter feature is particularly important when WORM drives are used for data backup or archiving.

Just how reliable is optical technology? Consider your CD audio player. Sure, you should be careful in handling the platters, but even if you aren't, the sounds play back reliably, and except when scratches or other physical changes occur, you'd never know how dirty or often handled the disks were.

When WORM technology was relatively new, officials at Digital Equipment Corporation wanted to demonstrate just how reliable these devices were for its mini-computer customers. Computer industry writers were assembled at one of Digital's Boston-area facilities for sweet rolls and coffee and a slide show on optical technology. After everyone had eaten what they wanted from the tray of sticky doughnuts and rolls, Digital personnel dumped the remaining food off the tray, which turned out to be an optical platter. The "tray" was washed, wiped clean, and then placed into an optical reader where it performed flawlessly.

You still should store and handle your disks carefully, but optical media are extremely durable and reliable under normal use. Because the surface of the disk is never touched by anything but light and because the medium itself is virtually affected by moisture or temperature extremes, information written to an optical disk should last a very long time.

One reason optical technology is so reliable is that the read head is several millimeters away from the disk surface. Magnetic read/write heads, on the other hand, ride about 2,000 times closer to the disk surface than the heads in a CD-ROM reader. That means even a microscopic flaw in the disk surface, including particles of dust or smoke, can cause a head crash and loss of data.

Even if the read head were to somehow contact the optical disk surface, the chance of losing data is minimal. This is because the surface of the platter is physically strong, for one thing, and also because the electronics that read the data are smart enough to fill in the blanks where there is a minimal amount of data loss.

In addition, the actual data on a CD-ROM platter is isolated from the outside world by a strong protective layer of plastic. When the laser shines on the disk to pick up data, it isn't reading the very top surface of the disk where small scratches and dirt reside. It looks through such data detractors in much the same way as you can take a picture through a chain link fence and not see any of the fence if the lens is focused on a distant object.

Optical technology offers some advantages from the data distributor side as well. A master laser platter is made with an electronically controlled laser that physically burns or pits the surface of the disk as data is written. After this master disk is produced, however, distribution disks that contain graphics, maps, reference text, or computer software can be "pressed" in much the same way as old fashioned phonograph records.

You already see a good deal of software distributed on CD-ROM. This makes for relatively inexpensive software distribution and is changing the way people look at software. Have you received a software package on CD-ROM lately? I have several of them. Know what I miss? A real printed manual. All the information for using the software on a CD-ROM set is shipped on the disk instead of in a book. (With Microsoft Word and Bookshelf, you get a coupon to order a printed manual for an additional $49.) When help routines and CD access software catches up, you won't need manuals any more. That's the way the industry is going.

Optical Disadvantages

Although the disadvantages to optical storage are minimal, there are a few considerations of which you should be aware. One disadvantage is cost. You can purchase a good quality, dependable audio CD player for under $100. However, by the time you make the design more rugged, build it to exacting tolerances, add computer interface electronics and cables, and send it through the distribution chain, you pay $250–500 for a computer CD-ROM drive. If you specify faster performance or add any other extras, the price can climb to $800 or beyond.

Another disadvantage is that optical technology is primarily a read-only technology. You can't write to a CD-ROM drive. The data you read from these drives is written on large, expensive machines at a software house or data packager.

WORM drives enable you to write as well as read data, but you can write to each disk location only once. WORM drives store a great deal of data—1.2GB or so—but, if you write a lot of backup data, you eventually run out of room.

Magneto-optical drives are designed as read/write devices that use magnetic storage with optical head control. They can store 250MB or more on each side of a double-sided, 5.25-inch platter, but these platters are expensive, costing around $300.

With today's technology, you also have to be aware of access and transfer speed. Although a SCSI interface—the most common interface for optical devices today—is capable of 5–10MB per second data transfer, optical drives achieve less than 300KB per second (typically 250KB or so). In addition, except for magneto-optical technology, optical products offer extremely slow data access time when compared with most hard disks.

A typical internal hard drive can find the data your application asks for in 10–18 milliseconds, for example; a CD-ROM drive takes up to 300 milliseconds for the same task (that's nearly a third of a second!). Newer drives offer faster access times, but, if you need high-speed, online storage, a high-capacity hard disk is a better choice than a CD-ROM.

CD-ROM

CD-ROM technology is the most common optical technology in use with PCs. Particularly for software distribution and for multimedia applications, such as graphics, photographs, sound, and motion video, there simply is no substitute for this method of distributing information and for using it on your PC.

A CD-ROM disk is a rigid plastic platter 1.2 millimeters thick and 120 millimeters (4.7 inches) across with a center spindle hole that is 15 millimeters in diameter. Data is written to the disk by burning pits in the recording surface with a carefully focused laser. Each pit is 0.12 micrometers deep and about 0.6 micrometers in diameter. CD-ROM tracks are 1.6 micrometers apart for a track density of 16,000 tracks per inch (tpi). Compare this with the floppy disk track density of 96 tpi or a typical hard disk with a track density of only a few hundred tpi. CD-ROM data begins at the inside of the disk—the shortest tracks—and is written toward the outside.

Original data is enhanced with error correction information before it is written to the optical platter. Coupled with intelligent electronics in the ROM reader, this error correction code can help rebuild correct data even if the disk surface is damaged.

219

Data is written one sector at a time. Each sector consists of 2,048 bytes of data surrounded by error correction information: 16 bytes in front of each sector and another 288 bytes of error code. In addition, many systems write this entire sector again using a Reed-Solomon (cyclic redundancy check, or CRC) scheme. CRC breaks the encoded block of data into 24 bytes of information and adds another 8 bytes of error correction data before writing it to disk.

With all this error correction and the inherent physical reliability of the CD-ROM design, CD-ROM data is pretty reliable. For example, the mastering process is considered accurate to one bit in each quadrillion bits (10^{15} bits). That's actual wrong data read and detected. At the same time, because of error correction code, the electronics in your CD-ROM reader might fail to find a wrong bit once in two quadrillion disks—disks, not bits. Pretty good, huh?

Okay, so now it is time to consider purchasing a CD-ROM reader for your system. You could opt for the lowest cost unit you find. This unit will read data in standard PC formats, but you may find it is too slow for anything but text searches or software distribution.

As you look for a CD-ROM drive, keep the following specifications in mind and, believe me, it is worth spending the extra money to get a drive that meets at least these specifications:

- Average access time: 300 milliseconds or better

- Data transfer rate: 300KB per second or better

- Standard: CD-ROM XA (for extended architecture)

- Audio: direct audio out

Specifications are getting better across the board, and you can expect to pay a little extra for a drive that meets all these specifications. In the long run, you'll be glad you spent the money. If you purchase a conventional drive for a couple of hundred dollars less, you'll get access times of 500–900 milliseconds and transfer rates of 150KB per second. Try playing an interactive game with one of these drives or using it for any but the most basic multimedia application, and you'll soon pull out your hair.

The XA standard stores sound and picture data in an interleaved format (data, sound, data, sound, and so on) so that, during an animated or motion video read, the head stays in the same place reading display and sound data sequentially. As always, it is up to the application using the data to sort out the information and route it properly within the PC, but keeping sound and picture data together on the disk offers a considerable speed advantage.

Incidentally, the idea for this technique actually came from the existing audio disk process. Left and right stereo information is stored like this. The read head simply moves across the disk picking up first a little data for the left channel and then a little data for the right channel, and the electronics route it sequentially to the proper amplifier and speaker. The speed of the CD data access makes it seem like stereo sound.

Start looking around now for a CD-ROM drive. If you don't think you need one now, you probably will before long if you keep using computers.

Magneto-Optical Drives

MO drives use magnetic media to store information under laser control. MO drives use 5.25- or 3.5-inch cartridges filled with magnetic read/write media. The magnetic disk surfaces in an MO cartridge are slightly different from conventional magnetic material. MO offers more permanent data storage than conventional hard disks and floppies.

MO disks use the polarity changes that occur in magnetic material when it is heated. As the laser beam heats the magnetic material on the disk, it becomes very easy to change the polarity of the material. After the material cools, the polarity becomes fixed in the new orientation. Depending on which direction the magnetic material is polarized, it is interpreted as either a logical one or a logical zero.

Data is written in blocks of 512 bytes. The problem is that, to change a portion of this information, the disk must change all of it because there is no way to know which bits are ones and which are zeros. Thus, the entire block is initialized during the first pass, and the new data is written when the proper disk sector rotates around under the read/write heads the second time. Therefore, it takes twice as long to write MO data as to read it.

Until recently, MO drives were pretty much reserved for minicomputers. PCs didn't need this much storage, for one thing, and MO drives simply were too expensive for most PC users. Prices still are high—from $3,500 to $6,000 depending on interface and speed. But, if you need high-capacity, removable, secure data storage for a high-end PC workstation or network server, MO drives can be a good choice.

An MO drive uses a removable cartridge that is written on one side at a time. The most common format is 5.25-inch platters that can store about 300MB of data on each side. To access information on the other side of the disk, you have to remove the cartridge, flip it over, and put it back in the drive. Later, as technology evolves, it probably will become feasible, technically and economically, to read and write from both sides of the platter at the same time as is done with conventional hard disks. For now, though, you only can use one side of the disk at a time.

Magneto-Optical Advantages

Large data capacity and the removable platter design are two very strong MO advantages. In addition, manufacturers are promising a data shelf life of 10–15 years, which is another advantage for research and other archive data.

In addition, many full-sized (5.25-inch) MO drives also can read WORM disks, an advantage if you already are using WORM hardware elsewhere in your system. Just because the hardware reads WORM, however, doesn't necessarily mean that a particular computer system can use the data. You have to check this out before you depend on it. Compatibility is not a strong suit for any type of optical medium, except perhaps CD-ROM.

Magneto-Optical Disadvantages

The primary disadvantages to MO technology today are cost and compatibility. The price of the drive mechanism is far higher than most PC installations can justify, and the $300 or so for a 5.25-inch replacement cartridge is a relatively large chunk of change to lay out at one time, even if it does store 600MB of information.

The newer 3.5-inch MO packages are cheaper, typically $2,000–2,500, but also store less information. The 3.5-inch platter generally holds only 128MB. When compared with competing technology, such as the Bernoulli 150MB removable cartridge system, the cost is high. The Bernoulli system costs under $1,500 and stores only a little less data.

The standards issue also is a problem. You can't take an MO cartridge written on a Ricoh drive, for example, and play it back on a Sony drive. The formats are different enough to prevent even this level of compatibility. And, MO drives may be slower in access and data transfer than standard drives. This may not be an issue for archival and backup applications, but if you want to use the MO technology for primary, online storage, you have to pay a slight speed penalty.

WORM Disks

WORM technology is used mainly for archiving and backing up large systems rather than to distribute information in the way CD-ROM is used. WORM stands for write once/read many and works just the way the name implies. A laser source is used to burn information into the platter, like with a ROM computer chip or CD-ROM data. After the data is written in this way, you can't change it. You can read it as often as necessary and can rewrite the information to another portion of the disk, but you can't modify data that already has been written. WORM drives use either 12- or 14-inch platters in full-sized systems and 5.25-inch disks in compact systems.

You can put about 1.2GB on each side of a large removable cartridge and about 600MB on the 5.25-inch disks. The full-sized platters are designed to be used on both sides; the 5.25-inch platters usually are written only on one side.

An important consideration when using WORM drives is the type of emulation they use. Earlier WORM products in particular were designed to emulate tape products, which meant the read/write process was different than it was for a hard disk. Data was harder and slower to retrieve.

For best results, you want a WORM that emulates a standard hard drive. This works best when keeping archived data available online or nearly online as in the case of a platter that has to be turned over or manipulated by a jukebox mechanism. When disk emulation is used, the standard DOS commands for manipulating data on a hard disk can be used, and the drive becomes more or less transparent to the end user.

Currently, WORM drives use an approach similar to CD-ROM drives for storing data. The disk surface actually is burned by a laser or magneto-optical technology is used in a write-once format. The MO technology is the newer of the technologies and, in all likelihood, is the stepping stone to phasing out WORM altogether. After all, if write-once drives now use the same technology as the read/write magneto-optical drives, why maintain the two processes? If you need archived data of the type provided by WORM, it should be fairly simple to include a write-protect tab of some kind on the platters or, perhaps, for software to burn out a location to indicate that a disk is write-protected.

WORM jukeboxes (robotic units that automatically can maintain several terabytes of data for nearly online access) reduce costs of time and personnel required for backing up and accessing your important information. Jukebox hardware for 8-millimeter cartridges is available for about the same hardware costs as optical jukeboxes.

WORM Advantages

The main advantage of WORM technology is its data reliability and the fact that after data is written it can't be erased. This technology is very useful for data archiving or storing large volumes of data that don't change very much. This might include census data, scientific test results, long-term accounting, patient or customer records, engineering or architectural data, design drawings, and the like. Best estimates predict that WORM data is good on the shelf for at least 10 years.

WORM Disadvantages

As with other optical technologies, cost may be the primary deterrent to placing WORM technologies in most PCs. And, the fact that information can be written only once raises the cost of media for holding data over time.

One of the strengths of WORM—large data capacity—is also a disadvantage. After you have filled a few platters with data, how do you know where to find the information you need? This problem is somewhat alleviated by jukebox technology, but most serious WORM users also use a software utility to track information by platter name or number and even location. When you first start using such a technology, the amount of storage seems unlimited. As time goes on, however, and many disks fill up, careful management of stored information is an important part of its use.

WORM is an older technology that seems, at least, to be on its way out in favor of newer magneto-optical drives. For about the same money, you can have a drive that enables you to read and write data repeatedly like you do with your hard disk. That way, when you no longer need the data you have stored on a given location on the disk, you can erase it and replace it with something you do need. This reduces media costs for long-term, high-capacity storage. For the time being, the two technologies are destined to coexist, but look for MO to push WORM completely out of the marketplace over the next few years.

Video:
An On-Screen
Overview

11

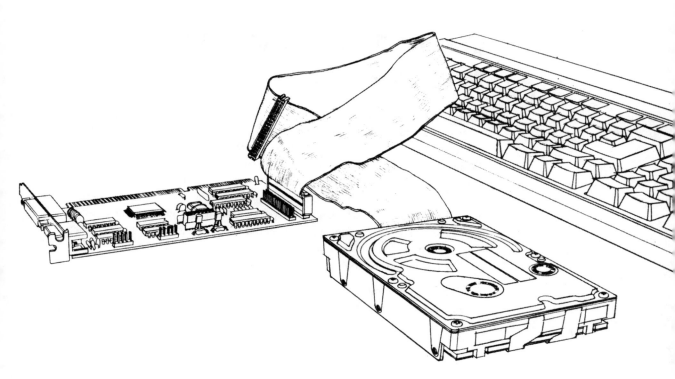

In one odd sense, I suppose you could say that the only part of the computer that really matters is the display screen. At least that's the way it can seem because most of the time you are interested in the results that appear on the screen, rather than the messy details of what it took to get those results. Besides, the screen and what's displayed on it form most users' only real interface with the machine.

I remember working with new computer users before the IBM PC was released when the computer and the display were separate units. Back then, the only way to communicate with the computer was with a serial terminal, which was a separate box bigger than today's computers that consisted of a keyboard and display with communications electronics. Almost always the terminal and computer were different brands, but the user almost never knew the company that made the computer. Users referred to the computer by the brand name or model number of the terminal.

The display hardware and how it appears is no less important today, and it's a lot more capable. In this chapter and the next two, you learn how the PC controls the display screen. You also learn what the display can do and what its limits are. The goal of this chapter simply is to understand how the computer screen works, so that you know what it can do. Then, in the next two chapters, I cover the two main screen modes: text mode and graphics mode.

How the Screen Works

The first thing to note about the computer's display screen is that it shows information, and that information has to be recorded somewhere. For maximum flexibility and speed, the PC keeps that information inside the computer rather than inside the display screen. That's in contrast with the way many computer terminals work. Consider, for example, the terminals used by travel agents. There, the display screens are located miles away from the computers that feed them. Those screens must hold their own record of the data that's displayed and talk to the remote computer only when new data is needed. That approach tends to make response on the display sluggish. By contrast, the display screen in the PC is so integrated with the computer that the screen and the computer can work together very closely.

That's done by placing the memory that holds the data that appears on the display screen inside the computer. The memory is inside the computer in two senses. It's there physically because the memory chips are inside the system unit, but it's also there in a logical sense because the display screen data is recorded in an integral part of the computer's memory space.

How much memory address space a PC has depends on its processor, but because of the history of the PC, the space that can be used to run programs and directly manage the system is 1MB. The very memory that the display screen needs to record its data is part of the PC's address space, so it's not in any way remote to the computer and the programs you run. The display memory is intimately connected with the computer, so there is no delay or inconvenience in getting to it. This helps make PCs very responsive.

The display memory is different from the rest of the computer's memory, however, because it must serve two masters. On the one hand, it must be accessible to the PC's microprocessor and programs, just like any other part of memory. On the other hand, the display memory also must be accessible to the display screen electronics and its internal programs, so the screen can "see" the information to display.

As a consequence, the display memory used by the PC has special circuitry. In effect, the display memory is a room with two doors. The rest of the computer's memory has only a single door, one way of being accessed, because only the processor uses that memory. However, two parts of the computer work with the display memory. The processor places data into the display memory to make it visible, and the display screen looks at that data to find out what to show on the screen. Both parts access the display memory, and each part has its own doorway into the memory so that the two do not get in each other's way. Memory that is set up in this way is called dual-port memory.

The programs running in the computer's microprocessor tap into the display memory only when they have to change what's being shown. The display screen, however, is constantly reading the display memory and creating a screen image that reflects the contents of the display memory. Roughly 70 times a second, the display screen's electronic circuitry reads the display memory and paints a new picture on the screen to reflect what's recorded in the memory. With the screen being repainted that often, new data placed in the display memory shows up right away on the screen.

The electronic servant behind all this is found in a part of the computer called the video controller. The early PCs had their controllers on adapter boards that you had to plug into the system unit. Nowadays, most PCs come with the video controller built into the main system board. However, even a computer with a built-in controller sometimes uses a plug-in adapter to get extra high performance.

For example, all PS/2s have a built-in display controller. Nevertheless, some people use a special adapter, called an 8514/A, to get extra high performance. Many non-IBM machines also still use plug-in video adapters. Actually, this can be a positive thing because it enables the manufacturer and user to respond to industry advancements. With a plug-in adapter, you can add the latest technology whenever it is available. You can do the same thing with a computer that has the video display circuitry built into the motherboard, but with the integral design, you leave the old hardware in place. With a plug-in adapter, you can move the old hardware to another machine or sell it to someone who is upgrading from a still-older technology.

In keeping with the idea of making the PC family's display screens changeable, the PC's design includes numerous video modes, or ways of presenting data on the display screen. Each display controller has its own repertoire of video modes. The video modes define what kind (and quality) of information you can show on the screen, and you select the display adapter hardware that best serves your purpose, although, when you select that hardware, you may not think of it in exactly those terms.

The computer's display screen works very much like a television set. The scheme is known as raster scan, and it works like this: the display screen is constantly being painted by a moving electron beam that traces a path through the entire screen roughly the way people read. The beam starts at the upper-left corner, scans the first thin line of the image from the left to right, lighting up the active parts of the screen, and then traces the next fine line from left to right. It proceeds from top to bottom, painting the entire image. As the electron bream moves over the screen, the display adapter's circuitry continuously reads data from the display memory and translates the data bits into the signals that control the electron beam. To minimize flicker, the image is sometimes painted in two interleaved halves; that is, every other line is painted from top to bottom, and the remaining lines are painted in a second scan. After two quick scans, the image is complete. Television sets use the same interleaved scan.

The Screen and Its Border

There is a border area on the display screen that surrounds the working part of the screen on which data is displayed. This border is an inactive part of the screen, and programs can't show any information there, but that doesn't mean that the border is necessarily blank.

The electron beam that traces out the working part of the screen also passes beyond the working area into what's called an overscan—the border area of the screen. While you can't put data into the border, you can set the border color. The results vary depending on which video mode you are using, although some video modes do not enable the use of the border. The main reason for setting a border color is to have it match the background color to make reading the screen easier on the eyes.

The PC's ROM-BIOS software provides a service that sets the border color. You can access this service thought the BASIC's COLOR statement. The following program demonstrates the border colors.

```
10   SCREEN 0,1 : WIDTH 80 : CLS
20   FOR BORDER.COLOR = 0 TO 15
30     COLOR , ,BORDER.COLOR
40     PRINT "Border color is ";BORDER.COLOR
50     PRINT "Press a key..."
60     WHILE INKEY$ = "" : WEND
70   NEXT
80   END
```

Note that, if you are using QBasic, this program does not work because the QBasic interpreter does not support border colors unless your system has an old CGA video adapter.

Those are the basic principles that govern the way the computer's display screen works. The fundamental ideas are very simple. The topic gets more interesting, however, when you look at what the PC display screen can do. I begin uncovering those details in an overview of the various video modes.

Video Mode Overview

Just about the most important thing to know about the computer's display screen is the variety of modes in which it can work. You need to be familiar with the different stunts that the screen can perform.

I start on the analytic side, looking at the basic differences among the display modes and showing how the video modes provide a multidimensional range of choices. Then I list all the modes and show which ones apply to which display controllers.

The first of two main divisions among the video modes is between text and graphics modes. In a text mode (and there are several distinct text modes), the display screen only can show the PC family's basic character set, the 256 basic PC characters. Strictly speaking, there is a way to redefine the character set via software, but it is seldom used. It's worth pausing to note again that the PC's character set is a rich one and provides plenty of opportunities for showing more on the screen than just written text. The box-drawing and other special characters that are part of the PC character set make it possible to create impressive character-based drawings on the PC screen.

In the text mode, the PC's screen is divided into specific character positions—usually 80 columns of characters across the width of the screen and 25 lines of characters from top to bottom. Chapter 12 covers the details of how computers work in text mode.

The alternative to text mode is graphics mode. In graphics mode, the screen is treated as an array of tiny dots, called pixels (short for picture elements), and anything that appears on the screen is created using these dots. The various graphics modes differ in the number of dots that can be displayed on the screen. This rating of possible dot display is called resolution. A typical high-resolution mode has 640 dots across the screen and 480 dots down the screen. You can draw anything you want using these dots, including the text characters, such as the letter A. The PC's built-in ROM-BIOS programs do the work of drawing characters dot by dot, so that programs operating in graphics mode don't have to take on that chore if they don't want to. (Sometimes they do, though, to draw characters in italics and other special ways.) Chapter 13 covers the details of how computers work in graphics mode.

Text versus graphics is one dimension of the video modes; color is the other main dimension. The black-and-white, or two-color, modes have no color range. In the other direction are color modes that can provide as few as four to up to millions of colors to choose from. In fact, one of the newest video modes, XGA-2, supports an extended graphics mode that can provide up to 65,536 colors, and some video display adapters that use their own video processors and graphics accelerators can display millions of colors. Finally, there are the monochrome modes, which don't have color in the ordinary sense but do have display attributes that are equivalent to a variety of colors. The monochrome display attributes include normal, high-intensity, reverse (dark characters on a light background), and underlined characters. There are color and black-and-white video modes for both text and graphics modes.

Within the four main possibilities that these two dimensions describe—text or graphics and colored or not—are a number of other variations in the range of video possibilities. These variations include the resolution (how many dots or characters the display screen holds) and the range of colors.

Overview of Video Standards

The next way to view the PC family's video modes is with respect to video standards. In Chapter 2, I introduced you to the various video standards that are used by the PC family. In this section, I look at the standards in more detail, relating each one to the modes it offers.

Take a look at table 11.1, which lists the names of the different standards.

Table 11.1. *PC Family Video Standards*

Name	Stands For	Introduced In
MDA	Monochrome Display Adapter	1981
CGA	Color Graphics Adapter	1981
HGC	Hercules Graphics Card	1982
EGA	Enhanced Graphics Adapter	1984
PGA	Professional Graphics Adapter	1984
VGA	Video Graphics Array	1987
MCGA	Memory Controller Gate Array (or Multi-Color Graphics Array)	1987
8514/A	(Named for IBM 8514 display)	1987
Super VGA	(VESA specification)	1989
XGA	Extended Graphics Array	1990

With the pre-PS/2 computers, the idea was that, because there were several choices (EGA, CGA, and MDA), the video controllers came on separate adapter boards so you could pick the one you wanted.

The PS/2 comes with built-in video controllers, and the controller chips usually are right on the main system board. In some models, they are on a separate adapter card. You can find the following video standards in the PS/2 line: MCGA (model 25), XGA (models P75, 90, and 85), and VGA (all the other models). Expect to see the new XGA standard on more computers in the future. If you have a 386- or 486-based VGA computer, you can buy an adapter from IBM and others to upgrade to XGA. In addition, high-end VGA-type upgrades are available from non-IBM vendors.

In a moment, I examine the various modes and what they offer, but first I quickly review the history of IBM video standards. For the original PC, there were two available standards: MDA and CGA. MDA was used with monochrome (one color) displays; CGA was used with color displays. MDA could work only with text and only in one color (green on the IBM display). However, the resolution (dots per inch) was high, and the characters looked especially good. CGA could work with text, graphics, and colors. However, the resolution was not as good as that of MDA, and many people found CGA unsuitable for work that made heavy use of characters (such as word processing).

This created a problem. People needed the quality text of MDA for some types of work and the color and graphics of CGA for other types. There were several solutions. First, a user could buy two displays and two adapters—one for monochrome and one for color. Both displays could be connected to the PC, and the user could switch from one to the other as necessary. There were even a few programs that supported the simultaneous use of color/graphics and monochrome/text on separate displays.

This was actually a fairly popular solution, and you could see many PCs with two monitors. You also were likely to hear users in earnest discussions about these two displays. Needless to say, opinions ran high on both sides of the graphics versus text issue.

Second, Hercules designed an adapter that could work with a monochrome display and still support graphics (in one color, of course). This adapter created a standard called HGC (for Hercules Graphics Card) and was quite popular. People who used the Hercules adapter had to buy only one display. But, of course, they were giving up color.

The third solution came from Compaq, which offered a color/graphics adapter that provided full CGA support and displayed text with a high resolution similar to MDA. However, this adapter worked only on Compaq computers.

The final solution came with IBM's introduction of EGA. EGA provided everything that MDA and CGA offered, but with some enhancements.

EGA remained the prevailing standard until the introduction of the PS/2s. The PS/2s introduced MCGA, VGA, and 8514. VGA offers almost everything that EGA, CGA, and MDA offer and adds a few more enhancements. MCGA, which is used only on the low-end PS/2s, has everything VGA has except a few of the EGA video modes.

Since then, IBM has introduced the XGA standard. Unlike previous video standards, XGA was designed to be a whole new video platform with many advanced capabilities especially designed to support graphical user interfaces (GUIs) such as Microsoft Windows and the OS/2 Presentation Manager. XGA encompasses all of the VGA video modes along with a few new ones for extra high performance. Moreover, the XGA controller was designed to provide sophisticated hardware graphics capabilities.

XGA offers a top resolution of 1,024×768 as well as a high-performance VGA mode, which is pretty good performance. The other side of the issue is that the screen output is interlaced, and IBM's XGA specification is intended for use solely in the proprietary MCA bus.

In addition to XGA, various vendors have their own enhanced VGA displays that are compatible with existing standards but which also offer a number of enhancements over standard VGA. These really high-end display adapters usually have their own dedicated processor coupled with a graphics accelerator and above average memory capacity.

Now that you know the history of IBM video standards, I give you a closer look at the various modes.

Most of the time, programmers access video modes by using the BIOS (for more information on the BIOS, see Chapter 19). For now, note that, when you write a program, you can call on the BIOS to perform for you by using a software interrupt (see Chapter 4). Each interrupt has a hexadecimal, base 16, ID number. (Hexadecimal is explained in Chapter 16.) The BIOS interrupt that performs the video chores is number 10 (hex).

You can use interrupt 10 for many purposes, one of which is to set the video mode. Each mode is identified by its own number. Like the interrupts (and many other computer numbers), the video mode numbers usually are expressed in hexadecimal. There are 21 video mode numbers: 0, 1, 2, 3, 4, 5, 6, 7, 8, 9, A, B, C, D, E, F, 10, 11, 12, 13, and 14.

Of these 21 video mode numbers, two, B and C, are reserved by IBM and are not used now, and the other three, 8, 9, and A, were used only by the PCjr.

This leaves 16 video modes that you can access via BIOS interrupt 10. In addition, XGA has two extra enhanced modes that are accessed differently. Of course, not all video standards support every mode. Take a look at tables 11.2 and 11.3. The first table lists each video standard and the number of modes it supports; the second table summarizes which standards support which modes.

Table 11.2.   *PC Video Standards and Number of Modes*

Video Standard	Number of Modes
XGA	18
VGA	15
MCGA	9
EGA	12
CGA	7
MDA	1

Table 11.3.   *Summary of Video Modes and Standards*

Mode (Hex)	Type	Video Standards				
0, 1	Text	XGA	VGA	MCGA	EGA	CGA
2, 3	Text	XGA	VGA	MCGA	EGA	CGA
4, 5	Graphics	XGA	VGA	MCGA	EGA	CGA

Mode (Hex)	Type	Video Standards				
6	Graphics	XGA	VGA	MCGA	EGA	CGA
7	Text	XGA	VGA		EGA	MDA
D	Graphics	XGA	VGA		EGA	
E	Graphics	XGA	VGA		EGA	
F	Graphics	XGA	VGA		EGA	
10	Graphics	XGA	VGA		EGA	
11	Graphics	XGA	VGA	MCGA		
12	Graphics	XGA	VGA			
13	Graphics	XGA	VGA	MCGA		
14	Text	XGA				
—	Graphics	XGA				
—	Graphics	XGA				

VGA

I start the discussion of video standards with VGA and the 15 modes it supports. To describe a mode, you must specify several pieces of information:

- Whether it supports text or graphics
- The resolution, that is, how many dots can be displayed on the screen
- The number of colors that can be displayed at one time
- The number of characters that can be displayed
- The number of dots that make up each character

Table 11.4 provides this information for each of the 15 VGA modes.

Table 11.4. *VGA Video Modes*

Mode (Hex)	Type	Resolution	Colors	Characters	Size
0, 1	Text	360×400	16	40×25	9×16
2, 3	Text	720×400	16	80×25	8×16
4, 5	Graphics	320×200	4	40×25	8×8
6	Graphics	640×200	2	80×25	8×8
7	Text	720×400	Mono	80×25	9×16
D	Graphics	320×200	16	40×25	8×8
E	Graphics	640×200	16	80×25	8×8
F	Graphics	640×350	Mono	80×25	8×14
10	Graphics	640×350	16	80×25	8×14
11	Graphics	640×480	2	80×30	8×16
12	Graphics	640×480	16	80×30	8×16
13	Graphics	320×200	256	40×25	8×8

To make sure that you understand this table, there are a few things I should explain. First, remember that all the mode numbers are in hexadecimal, base 16. Next, as you can see, each mode is either text or graphics. IBM has different terms for these that you may see in IBM manuals. Text is called alphanumeric and is abbreviated A/N. Graphics is called all points addressable because you have access to every dot on the screen and is abbreviated APA.

You can see from the table that VGA was an improvement over previous standards, yet VGA is not and was not the best video system, nor was it particularly revolutionary. Third-party displays available even before the VGA was introduced were sharper and offered more colors.

Next, take a look at the resolution column. The first number is the number of dots across the screen (row); the second number is the number of dots down the screen (column). Thus, you can think of the screen as a matrix of dots. For mode 11, for example, the matrix is 640×480 dots, or pixels. When you program in a graphics mode, you can control each individual dot if you want. In some cases, the actual resolution depends on the display being used. In the tables in this chapter, I have listed the default resolutions that apply to the most common types of displays.

The next column shows the maximum number of colors that can be displayed at one time. For the monochrome modes, there is only one color, which is usually green but can be orange or amber. For most of the other modes, the colors can be chosen (by a program) from a set of many possible colors. This set is called a palette.

This brings up the question of why you would want so many colors. For example, consider video mode 13, which can display 256 colors at the same time. (In fact, you can choose these 256 out of more than 256,000 possibilities—a very large palette indeed.) If you were to use this mode with a monochrome display, the 256 possible colors would be automatically converted into 64 shades of green.

The human eye cannot distinguish among 256 different colors or 64 shades of green. (These are called gray shades even though, in a case like this, they are green). Still, however, the large numbers are important because of the way in which the human mind perceives images.

Next time you watch television, notice how realistic the images look. Yet, if you sit as close to the screen as you do to your computer display, you see that the resolution is poor indeed; the pixels are relatively far apart and very noticeable. That being the case, why do television images look so good?

The answer is that television sets can display many, many gradations of color, and when the shading from one part of a picture to another is gradual, the human mind perceives it as a high-quality image. The computer display offers far fewer colors. The result is that people notice the change in shading in computer pictures (because it is less gradual), and the image quality seems poorer.

The fifth column shows the number of characters that can be shown on the screen at one time. Notice that both text and graphics modes can display characters. The difference is that text mode can display only characters. Graphics modes, because they are all points addressable, also can display pictures. The number of characters is expressed as the number of columns by the number of rows. For example, mode 3 can display 80 characters per row in up to 25 rows.

The last column shows how many pixels can be used to create a character. You can think of each character as fitting into a box. The number in the last column gives the size of the box. For example, for mode 3, the characters are generated within a box that is 9 pixels across by 16 pixels down.

Before I move on to the rest of the video standards, let me make a few comments about VGA and what you see in table 11.4.

First, some of the modes are identical: 0 is the same as 1, 2 is the same as 3, and 4 is the same as 5. This is because, on older equipment using older standards, these modes used to be slightly different. On newer equipment, they are the same.

Second, there are far more modes than you really need; most of them are there to be compatible with older standards. For example, modes 0 through 6 are CGA modes, most of which are included with VGA, so that VGA can support any program that was written for CGA. Mode 7 is the MDA mode; EGA includes these modes plus D, E, F, and 10. So, actually, of the 15 VGA modes, only 3—11, 12, and 13—are new.

Third, some of the modes display 40 characters on each line. These modes were originally designed for people who wanted to use the PC with a television set, on which 80 characters per line would be difficult to read. The 40-character-per-line modes now are rarely used.

Fourth, although VGA supports all 12 of the old modes, it does so in an enhanced manner. For modes 0, 1, 2, 3, and 7, VGA provides better resolution just as a matter of course. For example, in mode 0, CGA provides a screen resolution of 320×200, with 8×8 characters. In the same mode, VGA provides 360×400 with 9×16 characters. You can see this for yourself if you compare the tables that appear later in this chapter with table 11.3. The later tables show the details for the older video standards. You can see that, even for the same modes, the resolution is lower than VGA.

Finally, VGA adds enhanced support in one other way. All the modes that have a vertical resolution of 200 pixels—4, 5, 6, D, E, and 13—are displayed in a special way to make them look better. The VGA video controller writes each line of dots twice. This helps to fill in the gaps, so the speak.

I mentioned already that third-party products released prior to IBM's VGA actually were better than VGA. One offshoot of VGA improved basic VGA performance, but actually has served as little more than a stepping stone to even better products. This VESA (Video Electronics Standards Association) standard is Super VGA.

Super VGA

One problem with VGA was that it offered minimal improvement over EGA: 480 lines of resolution as opposed to EGA's 350 lines. In an effort to improve video standards, VESA specified a VGA display with 800×600 resolution, significantly better than the earlier EGA standard. Although a number of developers now include Super VGA support in their products, later technology raises the specifications to 1,024×768 and even to 1,280×1,024, making Super VGA's 800×600 resolution less attractive.

However, I should note here that the term "Super VGA" has become difficult to pin down. In the beginning, Super VGA meant the VESA specification for 800×600 displays. Today, however, the VESA committee (following the lead of manufacturers, users, and writers, I suspect) has broadened the term in at least some of its publications to include any video graphics products that implement a superset of the standard IBM VGA display adapter. That includes almost every adapter sold today.

As non-IBM vendors competed to improve PC video offerings, a problem arose that happened with frustrating regularity: there were no agreed upon standards to which designers could build display products. Consequently, software developers who wanted to support Super VGA products started having difficulties. Only by knowing how individual OEM products functioned could an application find out the precise display environment in which it was running. That meant constant updating of software or adding drivers to support specific video products.

In an effort to correct this problem, VESA proposed a standard Super VGA BIOS Extension (VBE) first in 1989 with an update in 1991. In this context, Super VGA meant any graphics display that went beyond IBM's VGA specification. People still talk about Super VGA when they really mean extended VGA, that is, features that go beyond standard and Super VGA standards. Boards that support resolutions of 1,024×768 and above are extended VGA products, for example. The VBE standard specified several BIOS functions that would answer application questions about the OEM manufacturer of the board, the current video mode, and the video modes the board could support.

Additional functions enabled a program to easily set the video mode directly without having to program it. Also, another function enabled an application to save and restore the current video mode without having to know anything about that mode. This enabled an application to take over the display, set it up for a specific operation, and then return it to the original state.

241

Among the advancements offered by the VESA Super VGA standard was an extended mode specification. As I showed earlier, standard VGA mode numbers range from 00 to 13 hex. These are 7-bit numbers, and by convention vendors established extended video modes in the range of 14 to 7F hex. The mode numbers in the VESA specification, on the other hand, were 15-bit numbers, beginning at 100 hex. One 7-bit mode number, 6Ah, was defined to set the real Super VGA mode of 800×600, 16-color , 4-plane graphics. A corresponding 15-bit number also was defined, as shown in table 11.5.

Table 11.5. *Super VGA Video Modes*

Mode (Hex)	Type	Resolution	Colors	Characters	Size
100	Graphics	640×400	256		
101	Graphics	640×480	256		
102	Graphics	800×600	16		
103	Graphics	800×600	256		
104	Graphics	1,024×768	16		
105	Graphics	1,024×768	256		
106	Graphics	1,280×1,024	16		
107	Graphics	1,280×1,924	256		
108	Text	—	—	80×60	
109	Text	—	—	132×25	
10A	Text	—	—	132×43	
10B	Text	—	—	132×50	
10C	Text	—	—	132×60	
10D	Graphics	320×200	—	—	32KB
10E	Graphics	320×200	—	—	64KB
10F	Graphics	320×200	—	—	16.8MB

Mode (Hex)	Type	Resolution	Colors	Characters	Size
110	Graphics	640×480	—	—	32KB
111	Graphics	640×480	—	—	64KB
112	Graphics	640×480	—	—	16.8MB
113	Graphics	800×600	—	—	32KB
114	Graphics	800×600	—	—	64KB
115	Graphics	800×600	—	—	16.8MB
116	Graphics	1,024×768	—	—	32KB
117	Graphics	1,024×768	—	—	64KB
118	Graphics	1,024×768	—	—	16.8MB
119	Graphics	1,280×1,024	—	—	32KB
11A	Graphics	1,280×1,024	—	—	64KB
11B	Graphics	1,280×1,024	—	—	16.8MB

The VESA Super VGA standard proposal raised another issue that was changing display adapter design: memory. Standard VGA adapters were designed around a 256KB video memory. This wasn't enough to support extended VGA modes, but the standard couldn't arbitrarily increase memory because the previous address space had to be preserved for backward compatibility. CPU video memory windows were established to enable applications to access extended VGA memory within the standard CPU address space.

Standard VGA CPU address space for 16-color graphics is generally at segment A000 hex for 64KB. By allocating 64KB for each of four planes, applications had access to 256KB. To access extended video memory, portions of the video memory were mapped into the standard VGA CPU address space.

Protected Mode Standard

With the growth of Microsoft Windows and other protected mode environments (UNIX and OS/2, specifically), there was a need for additional standards for video adapters. Just as with DOS-based video, too many different display drivers were evolving to support the various manufacturer's products in protected mode.

Again, VESA stepped in with its SVPMI (Super VGA Protected Mode Interface) specification in 1991. This standard established how applications developers could use configuration text files to specify hardware-dependent variables and procedures at run-time.

These run-time files consist of lines of ASCII text with a Carriage Return/Line Feed combination at the end. Interestingly, the file format specification does not provide for an end-of-file marker (like Ctrl-Z in DOS). By providing a more generic specification, the idea was that users in both DOS and UNIX environments could view the SVPMI files. The VESA specification describes precisely how data and command sections within this file should be organized.

In the next section, I turn my attention from VGA to two video standards that were designed to enhance VGA: XGA and 8514. I discuss XGA first.

XGA and XGA-2

XGA is the newest video standard for the PC family, having made its debut in October 1990. XGA-2 is an enhanced XGA specification that is shipping with current IBM computer models. As I mentioned earlier, XGA was developed by IBM as a strategic video platform suitable for graphical user interfaces. As you can see in table 11.6, XGA contains all the VGA modes plus three new ones.

Table 11.6.   *XGA Video Modes*

Mode (Hex)	Type	Resolution	Colors	Characters	Size
0, 1	Text	360×400	16	40×25	9×16
2, 3	Text	720×400	16	80×25	8×16
4, 5	Graphics	320×200	4	40×25	8×8
6	Graphics	640×200	2	80×25	8×8

Mode (Hex)	Type	Resolution	Colors	Characters	Size
7	Text	720×400	Mono	80×25	9×16
D	Graphics	320×200	16	40×25	8×8
E	Graphics	640×200	16	80×25	8×8
F	Graphics	640×350	Mono	80×25	8×14
10	Graphics	640×350	16	80×25	8×14
11	Graphics	640×480	2	80×30	8×16
12	Graphics	640×480	16	80×30	8×16
13	Graphics	320×200	256	40×25	8×8
14	Text	1,056×400	16	132×25	8×16
—	Graphics	640×480	256 or 65,535	—	—
—	Graphics	1,024×768	16 or 256	—	—

The first new mode is number 14. This mode was designed to display 132 characters on each line—the same as a standard computer printout. This mode is useful when you are working with, say, a large spreadsheet and want to be able to see as much data as possible at one time.

The other two modes are not accessed via the BIOS so they do not have video service numbers. These two modes, as well as the first mode, can be accessed in three ways: by programming the XGA hardware registers directly, employing an adapter interface, or using a device driver.

An adapter interface is used for running XGA with programs written for another video design. There is, for example, an 8514 adapter interface that enables you to adapt programs written for the 8514.

A device driver enables you to use specific software and take advantage of the extra capabilities of XGA, such as speed, higher resolution, and more colors. Many applications are supplied with XGA drivers that you select during installation of the program. In fact, some programs can detect which interface you are using automatically. If not, you specify XGA when you install the software, and, if the driver is available, it is installed for you.

As you can see from the table, the two XGA graphics modes have two sets of maximum colors. The first set, with fewer colors, is for XGA controllers that have 0.5MB of memory; the second set, with more colors, is for controllers with 1MB. Note that this is not regular system memory; it is the dual-port video memory that is part of the controller. As I explained earlier, this is the memory that stores the actual images to be displayed.

For most programs to use XGA, they must program the XGA controller's hardware registers directly. Such programs have a great deal of flexibility. For example, there is no built-in character set; a program can create any type of characters it wants, as long as the character fits on the screen. For this reason, it does not make sense to list a standard number of characters or a character size.

As with other video standards that have become common with PCs, what IBM started, the industry has taken over for its own. In May 1992, the Video Electronics Standards Association proposed VXE (VESA XGA Extensions) standard 1.0 to specify how third-party vendors could use the features of XGA outside the IBM MCA environment.

Among the specifications the VESA committee had to deal with was how to implement IBM's manufacturer ID scheme in non-MCA hardware. With true XGA designed for MCA, IBM assigns official manufacturer ID codes to be stored within a 7-byte hardware location. VXE specifies that developers who produce MCA and ISA/EISA XGA products must use the same ID in both products. VXE specifies additional ID locations that can be assigned by VESA.

In addition, VXE adds some extensions to the IBM-defined XGA register set, including the following:

- Bus identification

- Subsystem vendor ID

- Manufacturer expansion

- VESA-reserved registers

As with super VGA specifications, the VXE addresses BIOS issues, including how to return information about the video environment to applications and ways to assist applications in initializing and programming the hardware. At the same time, the specifications attempt to minimize the effects of these extensions on standard VGA BIOS, including the VESA VGA BIOS extensions.

8514

The second enhanced video standard is 8514. This standard was introduced as an adjunct to VGA. The idea was that you could buy a special adapter that, when combined with the VGA controller in your system, would offer three enhanced video modes suitable for applications such as computer-aided design. The basic VGA circuitry, remember, was on the system board while the 8514 enhancements were added as an option through a plug-in adapter.

For the most part, 8514 has been superseded by XGA, so I limit this discussion to a summary of the extra modes (see table 11.7). Like the XGA enhanced graphics modes, the 8514 modes are not accessed through the BIOS and do not have video service numbers.

Table 11.7. *8514 Video Modes*

Type	Resolution	Colors	Characters	Size
Graphics	1,640×480	256	80×34	8×14
Graphics	1,024×768	256	85×38	12×20
Graphics	1,024×768	256	146×51	7×15

The 8514 standard is still another example of an IBM-designed architecture that the rest of the industry adopted. And, as 8514 adapters started reaching the market from non-IBM vendors, a VESA committee proposed a standard for interconnecting the onboard VGA circuitry with the plug-in 8514 additions. This was the 1989 VGA pass-through connector specification, which was designed to provide an industry-agreed method for attaching extended feature adapters to existing VGA boards.

A number of display enhancements use the pass-through technique. For example, motion video and still capture boards may attach through the pass-through connector to display standard VGA data and external video data on the same screen.

MCGA

Now I look at MCGA, the video standard used with low-end PS/2s. This standard was used with the PS/2 model 25 and with the early version of the model 30. Table 11.8 shows the MCGA video modes.

Table 11.8. *MCGA Video Modes*

Mode (Hex)	Type	Maximum Resolution	Colors	Characters	Size
0, 1	Text	320×400	16	40×25	8×16
2, 3	Text	640×400	16	80×25	8×16
4, 5	Graphics	320×200	4	40×25	8×8
6	Graphics	640×200	2	80×25	8×8
11	Graphics	640×480	2	80×30	8×16
13	Graphics	320×200	256	40×25	8×8

If you check the tables carefully, you see that the differences between MCGA and VGA are, first, that MCGA resolution is not quite as good for modes 0, 1, 2, and 3 and, second, that MCGA does not support mode 7 (the MDA mode), mode D, E, or F (EGA modes), or mode 12 (VGA-only). MCGA was designed for more economical computers and for people who would be happy with fairly good text and graphics. For these purposes, MCGA works fine. And, in fact, MCGA runs almost all VGA software.

CGA, EGA, and MDA

To finish this section, examine tables 11.8, 11.9, and 11.10, which show the video modes for EGA, CGA, and MDA, respectively.

Recently, I was speaking to a programmer friend and asked him what he knew about video modes. "More than I want to know," was his answer. By now, you may be starting to feel the same way, so just take a quick look at the EGA, CGA, and MDA tables and move on. Later, if you feel so inclined, come back and take a closer look. You can see how the small details differ from the corresponding VGA modes.

Table 11.9 shows the EGA modes. EGA encompasses all of CGA and MDA plus four enhanced modes. Another way to put it is that EGA contains all of VGA—in lower resolution—except modes 12 and 13.

Table 11.9. *EGA Video Modes*

Mode (Hex)	Type	Maximum Resolution	Character Colors	Characters	Size
0, 1	Text	320×350	16	40×25	8×14
2, 3	Text	640×350	16	80×25	8×14
4, 5	Graphics	320×200	4	40×25	8×8
6	Graphics	640×200	2	80×25	8×8
7	Text	720×350	Mono	80×25	9×14
D	Graphics	320×200	16	40×25	8×8
E	Graphics	640×200	16	80×25	8×8
F	Graphics	640×350	Mono	80×25	8×14
10	Graphics	640×350	16	80×25	8×14

In addition to enhanced resolution over CGA, EGA made enough extra space available in the character matrix so descending and ascending characters on adjacent rows could not touch. With EGA, color text became as readable as on monochrome displays. You could say that EGA brought color to Hercules-quality graphics and text.

Interestingly, IBM followed EGA before too long with the Professional Graphics Controller (PGC), a technology that raised resolution to 640×480 and also supported square pixels. This was a significant improvement for professional users who needed to be able to reproduce on printers and plotters what they had displayed on the screen. You didn't and don't hear much about PGC, however, for two reasons: it didn't last that long before the VGA adapter was introduced, and the PGC controller card cost around $3,000. That's enough to slow down sales to any but the highest-end users. Then, when VGA and all of its improvements hit the street, PGC essentially went away.

Table 11.10 shows the CGA video modes. This was one of the video standards that was offered with the original PC. If you look at the text mode resolution—a screen of 640×200 and a character box of 8×8—you can see why CGA text was so poor.

Table 11.10. *CGA Video Modes*

Mode (Hex)	Type	Maximum Resolution	Character Colors	Characters	Size
0, 1	Text	300×200	16	40×25	8×8
2, 3	Text	640×200	16	80×25	8×8
4, 5	Graphics	320×200	4	40×25	8×8
6	Graphics	640×200	2	80×25	8×8

Table 11.11 shows the MDA video modes. MDA offered only one mode, for text, but it was high quality with a screen resolution of 720×350 and a character size of 9×14. This was almost as good as VGA and, on the small IBM monochrome screen, looked pleasing indeed.

Table 11.11. *MDA Video Modes*

Mode (Hex)	Type	Maximum Resolution	Character Colors	Characters	Size
7	Text	720×350	Mono	80×25	9×14

Hercules

I mentioned the Hercules adapter earlier in this chapter. Although it was an extremely popular and useful display type in the earlier days of the PC, it isn't that popular any more because advancement in VGA technology coupled with a drop in prices for display equipment has rendered it nearly obsolete.

However, in the days when users with text-based displays (using the IBM MDA adapter) were torn between MDA and CGA, the Hercules Graphics Adapter (HGA), or Hercules Graphics Card (HGC) as it was sometimes called, was a welcome alternative. The HGA added bit-mapped graphics to the character-mapped MDA.

Functionally, MDA and HGA worked identically in text mode, using the same frequencies, cabling, and displays. Characters were formed in the same 9×14 grid with a full-screen resolution of 720×350 pixels, a horizontal sync frequency of 18.1KHz, and a 50Hz frame rate. All attributes of the IBM MDA—underline, blink, high-intensity, and inverse video—are supported by the HGA. The HGA even included a parallel printer port with a base address of 03BC hex, the same as the MDA.

However, HGA is not compatible with any IBM graphic standard. Applications must be specially written to support HGA. Programs written for the CGA and other IBM graphic standards do not properly execute on the HGA unless they also have HGA support.

Local Bus Video

An important new avenue to improve the speed of transfer of video information from the microprocessor to the screen is to improve the highway that runs between them. That's the theory behind local bus video technologies that go around the I/O interface of the PC's expansion bus.

I provided more detail on the two most common local bus standards in Chapter 2, but I want to at least mention the local bus (sometimes called direct bus) here as well. It is an important part of the change taking place in PC design.

The new local connection can be hard-wired to video circuitry on the motherboard or plugged into an improved expansion bus and can operate at memory speed and with a full 32-bit bus width. This means the video information is off the 8MHz I/O bus and on a 25- or 33MHz (or faster in coming designs) local bus. In theory, this scheme enables an adapter to operate three to four times as fast as the fastest I/O bus adapter. An important advantage of such a scheme is that it should enable applications to operate at full speed without modifications or special drivers.

Graphics Accelerators and Coprocessors

Improved resolution and an increased numbers of colors aren't enough to support today's high-end applications, such as CAD programs, or user-friendly, graphics-based interfaces, such as Microsoft Windows. Graphics accelerators and graphics coprocessors now are being included with PC display adapters to provide the kind of performance these applications require. Coupled with a local bus interface, such display adapters can operate 10 times faster than conventional hardware.

Graphics accelerators and coprocessors are based on dedicated processors that offload some of the display processing from the main CPU. Graphics accelerators are decidedly faster than conventional display adapters, but full coprocessor designs are the fastest of all—and the most expensive.

Instead of building displays from character matrixes received from memory, these devices use coded and compressed instructions that describe how to generate patterns of pixels. For example, instead of sending a map of pixels to draw a box, the instructions might describe a box and indicate starting and ending points.

An accelerator has specific graphic functions, such as BitBlts, line drawing, and area fills. (A BitBlt is a bit block transfer; it's the function of a graphics card that copies a bit-mapped image from a source device to a destination device. For example, this could be the movement of information from memory to screen or from one location in memory to another. Microsoft Windows and other graphics front-ends depend heavily on BitBlts and benefit from accelerators that know about such matters.)

As I said, a coprocessor and an accelerator are similar. The difference is that the coprocessor board can be programmed. You can think of an accelerator as a fixed-function coprocessor hard-wired to perform certain functions. If the accelerator board offers a good match for the type of graphics-intensive applications you use, such as CAD programs, then the less-expensive accelerator board may be a good fit.

Windows Accelerators

Some accelerators are optimized for Microsoft Windows by including several of the most common Windows-type instructions right on the chip. That means instructions to a Windows-compliant system can execute many times faster. One such system that I tested recently, for example, could perform screen scrolling and other processor-intensive operations 10–20 times faster than a conventional VGA display on a 486-based computer.

This ends the discussion of the video modes. I end this chapter with a few words about how you can go exploring.

 # Exploring Video Modes

It's relatively easy to explore and tinker with most of the video modes. To begin, find out which video mode your computer currently is using. The PC's ROM-BIOS programs use a low memory area starting at hex address 400 to store information that the ROM-BIOS needs to keep track of. Part of that is current status information about the display screen, including the current video mode. The mode is recorded in a single byte located at hex address 449. Any tool that enables you to inspect data in memory can show you the video mode. You easily can do that with BASIC or DEBUG.

Two simple commands in BASIC do it. The first sets up BASIC to inspect low memory locations:

```
DEF SEG=0
```

The second command extracts the byte in which the video mode is located and displays it on the screen:

```
PRINT PEEK (&H449)
```

To try it yourself, fire up BASIC and enter those two commands.

To do the same thing with DEBUG, activate DEBUG and enter the following command:

```
D 0:449 L1
```

That tells DEBUG to display (D) one byte (L1) at the address you're interested in. DEBUG shows the mode, displayed in hex form, similar to the following:

```
0000:0440                    03
```

This example shows a video mode of 3, the standard VGA text mode.

If you do either of those two experiments, you see what mode your computer currently is in. It also is possible to change the mode and then inspect it. You can see only some of the possible modes because the tools you're using—DOS, BASIC, and DEBUG—operate only in certain video modes. And, of course, you can see only the modes that your computer is equipped to use. If your computer has only the standard monochrome adapter, the only mode you can see is mode 7. Even though you can't see every mode, the experiments I described enable you to tinker a bit and get a feeling for what it's like to be in control of the display screen's different modes.

There are two ways to change the mode, just as there are two ways to detect what mode you're in. One uses the DOS MODE command to set the mode; you can use this together with DEBUG to display the mode. The other method uses BASIC both to set and show the mode.

I explain MODE and DEBUG first. These two commands work in the standard DOS way, which accepts only text modes, so you can't try any of the graphics modes. To do this experiment, enter a MODE command to set the mode and then use DEBUG in the way you already have seen to show what mode you're in. The idea is to switch to a new mode with the MODE command and then use DEBUG to see if you actually got there. Set the mode like this:

```
MODE X
```

For X, you put MONO, CO80, BW80, CO40, BW40, 40, or 80. After you've done that, try DEBUG to see what mode you're in.

Starting with DOS 4.0, you also can use a new form of the MODE command:

```
MODE CON COLS=x LINES=y
```

In this form, x can be either 40 or 80, and y can be 25, 43, or 50. For example, to display 80 characters by 50 rows use the following:

```
MODE CON COLS=80 LINES=50
```

To use this form of the MODE command, you need to install the ANSI.SYS device driver. To display 43 lines, your PC must have EGA, VGA, or XGA; to display 50 lines, you need VGA or XGA.

If you use BASIC, you can perform the same sort of experiment in a way that also enables you to try the graphics modes. Here is an example that switches your computer into a medium-resolution graphics mode (if it is equipped to do so):

```
10  SCREEN 1
20  DEF SEG = 0
30  PRINT PEEK (&H449)
```

With QBasic, use the following:

```
SCREEN 1
DEF SEG = 0
PRINT PEEK (&H449)
```

You can tinker with the program by changing the first line to any of the screen modes available for your computer's BASIC. (By the way, don't be confused by mode numbers that BASIC uses in the SCREEN command; they aren't the same as the fundamental video mode numbers I've been describing in this chapter.) If BASIC reports an error when it tries to perform the SCREEN command, it means that the particular mode does not apply to your computer.

You can see a more elaborate version of this program under the name VIDMODE in Appendix C. Try running or studying that program to learn more about the video modes and how QBasic interacts with the PC family's video modes.

Now that I've covered the fundamentals of the computer's display screen, it's time to move on to see the specific details. The next chapter describes the text modes.

Some Things To Try

1. Try all the MODE commands suggested in this chapter. Also, check your DOS manual to see if there are any other MODE commands that apply to your display screen. New ones may have been added to the list.

2. Check your computer's BASIC manual to see if any new display modes have been added beyond the ones covered here. (If you are using QBasic, check the online help system.) You can find out by comparing the description of the SCREEN command options with the SCREEN commands that appear in the VIDMODE listing in Appendix C.

Video: Text Fundamentals

12

In this chapter, I explore the inner workings of the PC's display screen text modes. Although there is a growing shift toward graphical user interfaces (GUIs) with products such as OS/2 and Microsoft Windows, there's still a lot of work done on PCs in straight text mode, with only the PC family's text character set on the display screen. Even if you are using Windows, for example, when you enter a DOS window, you are in text mode, so this remains an important part of computer display technology.

Regardless of how you look at it, and even if you are a graphics enthusiast, the PC's text modes are very important. In this chapter, you see how text mode works and examine its capabilities and limitations. I begin with an outline of how the text modes are organized and how they work. Then I look at more of the technical details underlying the text modes; I finish up by exploring some tricks that can be used to add sizzle to a program's use of the text mode.

Text Mode Outline

Underlying the PC family's text screen modes is the division of the display screen into individual character positions, arranged in a grid of columns and rows. Each character position has two separate components: its data, which determines what character appears on the screen, and its attribute, which determines how that character appears (in color, blinking, and so on).

In the text modes, programs have full control over both the data and the attributes so that they can specify exactly what characters appear, where they appear among the predefined character positions, and how they appear in terms of the predefined color attributes, which I discuss shortly. However, programs have no control over other details, such as how the characters are drawn or the precise position of the character locations. That's strictly defined by the capabilities of the display adapter and the display screen. (By contrast, as you see in Chapter 13, when characters are used in the graphics modes, some or all of these things can be controlled.)

In short, in the text modes, programs work within a rigid framework of what can be shown on the screen. That predefined framework, though, frees programs from a great deal of overhead they otherwise would have to take care of, directly or indirectly.

The character positions on the screen are organized into 25 rows and, usually, 80 columns. But, as you saw in Chapter 11, two of the text video modes have only 40 columns. These 40-column modes were created to make it more practical to use a TV set as the display screen; the resolution and picture quality of a TV screen is not good enough to show 80 characters clearly. The 40-column modes, together with a few other features (like the cassette tape link), were designed into the PC when it was thought that many people might want low-budget minimally equipped PCs. As it has turned out, the 40-column modes are seldom used, and many programs do not accommodate them. Figure 12.1 shows how the display screen is organized into columns and rows.

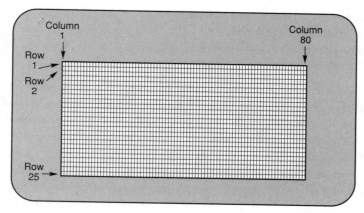

Figure 12.1. *Display columns and rows.*

You can conceptualize the screen as a series of horizontal lines or as a single continuous string of 2,000 characters (1,000 characters for 40-column mode). The PC family's text mode is designed to work either way. If a program asks for output to be placed in a particular row and column position, it appears there. On the other hand, if the program just pours data onto the screen, the data wraps from the end of one line to the beginning of the next.

Computer display screens can display all of the characters in the standard PC character set (for detailed information on the character set, see Chapter 14). However, getting some of the characters to appear on the screen can require special techniques such as POKE statements used in the programs ALLCHAR and REFCHAR in Appendix C. This is because the ASCII control characters, codes 0 through 31, have special meanings that can affect the way output appears, such as skipping to a new line. If any of these control characters are written to the screen—with the PRINT statement in BASIC, for example—they usually take action as control characters, but may appear as ordinary PC characters. The results vary depending on which character codes are being written and which programming language is being used.

Except for these ASCII control characters, though, all of the PC family's text character set easily can be shown on the display screen in any of the screen's character positions. The character that appears in each position is the data component of the character position.

There is also an attribute component, which controls how the character appears. A character's attribute is a control code that determines how it is shown, and each position has its own independent attribute. There are basically two sets of attribute codes—one designed for monochrome and one designed for color—but the two schemes are organized in a way that makes them as compatible as possible. I look at the color attributes first.

For color, each character position's attribute has three parts. One specifies the foreground color (the color of the character); the second controls the background color (the color around or behind the character); and the third specifies whether or not the character blinks. There are 16 foreground colors, numbered 0 through 15, as listed in table 12.1. The colors are made up of three components: red, green, and blue. The various combinations of those three elements give the eight main colors. And, adding a normal or bright variation of each gives a total of 16. There are eight background colors—the eight main colors without their bright variations. The final part of the color attributes is a switch that enables the foreground character to either blink or appear solid and steady.

Table 12.1. *Color Attributes*

Code	Appearance
0	Black (nothing)
1	Blue
2	Green
3	Cyan (blue and green)
4	Red
5	Magenta (blue and red)

Code	Appearance
6	Light yellow or brown (green and red)
7	White (blue, green, and red)
8	Gray (bright only)
9	Bright blue (blue and bright)
10	Bright green (green and bright)
11	Bright cyan (blue, green, and bright)
12	Bright red (red and bright)
13	Bright magenta (blue, red, and bright)
14	Bright yellow (green, red, and bright)
15	Bright white (blue, green, red, and bright)

Note that this 16-color scheme is the basic and original VGA 16-color mode. When you go to 256- or 65,000-color mode, more definition bits are required to specify the attribute.

For monochrome, attributes are used to control how characters appear, but in a different way. With monochrome, you don't have a color option, but you can make the characters appear in bright or normal intensity, blinking, underlined, or reverse video (black characters on a lit background). The various possibilities are listed in table 12.2. Not all combinations of these features are possible; for example, there's no reverse underlined.

Table 12.2. *Monochrome Attributes*

Code	Appearance
0	Invisible
1	Underline
7	Normal
9 (8+1)	Bright underline

continues

Table 12.2. *continued*

Code	Appearance
15 (8+7)	Bright normal
112	Reverse
129 (128+1)	Blinking underline
135 (128+7)	Blinking normal
137 (128+8+1)	Blinking bright underline
143 (128+8+7)	Blinking bright normal
240 (128+112)	Blinking reverse

That's the essence of the features of the PC's text display modes. What's left to learn about them are the technical details, including how the display data is laid out in memory, how the attributes are coded, and so on. I cover that in the next section.

Details of the Text Mode

The video controller shares video memory with the processor. This memory does not come out of the regular RAM. Instead, it is contained within the video array chip or, if a video adapter is being used, on the adapter itself. However, as I discussed earlier, the video memory is accessed via addresses that are part of the 8086/DOS 1MB address space. In particular, video memory is accessed as the A and B blocks. (The A block consists of the hex memory addresses from A0000 to AFFFF; the B block is from B0000 to BFFFF.)

Take a look at table 12.3. It shows each video mode and the memory addresses it uses. Notice that the B block is used for all the modes that originated with the old CGA and MDA video standards. The memory for the original CGA modes starts at B0000 and lies within the first half of the block. The memory for the original MDA mode starts at B8000 and lies within the second half of the block. The A block is used for the newer modes. If you look in Appendix C, you can see these addresses in the listings of some of the sample programs.

Table 12.3. *Video Modes and Their Memory Addresses*

Mode (Hex)	Starting Address (Hex)	Bytes per Page	Video Standards				
0, 1	B8000	2000	XGA	VGA	MCGA	EGA	CGA
2, 3	B8000	4000	XGA	VGA	MCGA	EGA	CGA
4, 5	B8000	16000	XGA	VGA	MCGA	EGA	CGA
6	B8000	16000	XGA	VGA	MCGA	EGA	CGA
7	B0000	4000	XGA	VGA		EGA	MDA
D	A0000	32000	XGA	VGA		EGA	
E	A0000	64000	XGA	VGA		EGA	
F	A0000	56000	XGA	VGA		EGA	
10	A0000	112000	XGA	VGA		EGA	
11	A0000	38000	XGA	VGA	MCGA		
12	A0000	153000	XGA	VGA			
13	A0000	64000	XGA	VGA	MCGA		
14	B8000	4000	XGA				

As you can see, different modes use memory at different locations. But, for the text modes, the way the data is laid out within the memory is always the same. Memory is used in pairs of bytes, with two bytes for each text position on the screen. The very first byte of the display memory holds the character data for the upper-left screen position, and the next byte holds the display attribute for that position. The next pair of bytes are for the second column on the first line, and so on, to the lower-right screen position (see fig. 12.2).

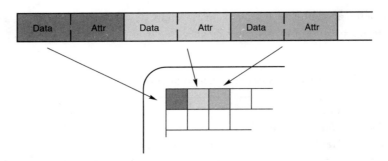

Figure 12.2. *Display memory and the screen in text mode.*

In the display memory, the screen is treated as a continuous string of 2,000 pairs of bytes, with nothing indicating the division of the display in lines. So, if information simply is stored in the memory, byte after byte, it appears on the screen automatically wrapping around from one line to the next. In the display memory, there are no lines, only continuous bytes of information. When the line and column positions matter to a program, it calculates the relative position of the appropriate bytes and sets its data there.

You can calculate the relative memory location of any position on the screen by using simple formulas. If you number the rows and columns on the screen starting with zero, you can determine the location of a data byte:

$$location = (row \times 80 + column) \times 2$$

This location points to the data byte and is relative to the beginning of the display memory. The formula is for 80-column mode; for a 40-column mode, multiply the row by 40 instead. To get the location of the attribute byte, all you need to do is add 1 to the location of the data byte.

The only way information ever appears on the display screen is for it to be copied to the display memory by a program. It can be done directly by the programs that you run or can be done by the computer's built-in ROM-BIOS services.

There are two schools of thought about which way it should be done. If a program places its data directly into the display memory, it can be done with great efficiency and impressive speed. Most or all of the flashy programs work like this. Programs that work this way have to know how the display memory is laid out and incorporate a fair amount of knowledge about how the display adapters work. Programs that work this way can't work with any display adapter that places its display memory at a new location.

On the other hand, if a program relies on the services of the ROM-BIOS to place data into the display memory, it can adjust easily to any changes in the display screen, such as a new location for the display memory or a windowing environment like Microsoft Windows that can move information around on the screen. Using the ROM-BIOS services uncouples programs from the peculiarities of the display screen and display memory, which makes programs more adaptable to changes in computers.

Seen from that point of view, it appears that all programs should use the ROM-BIOS services for screen data to get the maximum flexibility. However, there is an enormous penalty in using the ROM-BIOS services: these services take a surprising amount of time to work. Because of this heavy penalty, many programs perform their own screen output, moving data directly into the screen buffer.

It's clear that IBM originally wanted all programs to route display data through the ROM-BIOS, but things didn't work out that way. Because many programs do their own screen output, using the two key display adapter memory addresses of B000 and B800, it has become impossible for IBM radically change the way display memory works—at least for the text modes.

The Cursor

As you view data displayed on the screen, it is natural to feel that there is a close link between the cursor and the information displayed. But that is not true. Whatever information is placed in the display memory appears on the screen completely independent of the cursor. The cursor is simply a convenient way of indicating the active part of the screen, which can be very helpful for the person looking at the screen.

To reinforce that idea, the ROM-BIOS services that place information on the screen carefully match the writing of information with the placement of the cursor. For the ROM-BIOS, the cursor isn't only a visual clue, it also is a means of coordinating the screen, the ROM-BIOS, and the program generating the information. The cursor gives both the program and the ROM-BIOS only one way to indicate where information is to appear.

The blinking cursor that you're accustomed to seeing on the screen is a hardware feature of PC video controllers and only applies to the text, not graphics, modes.

Normally, the cursor blinks at the bottom of a character on the last two scan lines. The lines on which the cursor appears can be changed with a hardware command performed through the ROM-BIOS. You can experiment with changing the size of the cursor using BASIC's LOCATE statement. You can make the cursor start and end on any pair of the scan lines that make up a character position.

Many programs find that this hardware cursor doesn't suit their purposes, so they create their own logical cursor, typically by using reverse video to highlight the cursor area. One of the main reasons programs create their own cursor is to extend the cursor to more than one character position on the screen (the way a spreadsheet's cursor highlights the entire width of a cell, for example). Technically, a cursor like that is completely different from the hardware cursor, but the function of all kinds of cursors is the same—to indicate the active part of the screen.

When programs create their own logical cursors, they normally make the hardware cursor disappear, either by deactivating it or moving it to a position just off the edge of the screen.

Attribute Coding

Next I take a look at how the coding for the attribute bytes works. Although the attributes for color and monochrome are quite different, there is a common design that underlies each scheme. I start by looking at the common part and then get into the specifics for both color and monochrome.

The eight bits of each attribute are divided into four fields, as shown in figure 12.3.

```
7  6  5  4  3  2  1  0
B  .  .  .  .  .  .  .     Blinking (of foreground)
.  R  G  B  .  .  .  .     Background color
.  .  .  .  I  .  .  .     Intensity (of foreground)
.  .  .  .  .  R  G  B     Foreground color
```

Figure 12.3. *How each bit of an attribute is divided.*

The first four bits (0 through 3) control the foreground color; the first three bits specify the red, green, and blue components of the foreground color, and the fourth bit changes the foreground intensity, making the color bright or normal. The next three bits (4 through 6) control the red, green, and blue components of the background color; there is no background intensity bit. Finally, the last bit (7) controls foreground blinking.

All possible combinations of bits are faithfully produced based on this scheme. You can demonstrate them with the program COLORTXT listed in Appendix C. Every combination works regardless of how hard on the eyes or how bizarre. Some color combinations are very pleasing, such as bright yellow on blue (one of my favorites). Others are amazing, such as bright blinking blue on red (attribute hex C9, bits 11001001). If you have a color screen, you can try that combination in BASIC with the following command:

```
COLOR 25,4
```

The color mode uses these attribute bits exactly as you would expect. The monochrome mode matches this scheme as closely as it reasonably can. The normal display mode, lit characters on a black background, is coded hex 07 (in bits 00000111), which corresponds to the color attributes of white on black. Reverse video is coded just the opposite, hex 70, the equivalent of black on white. The code for underlined is hex 01, which makes the monochrome underlined attribute equivalent to the foreground color blue. The monochrome mode's invisible or nondisplay mode is coded hex 00, the equivalent of black on black. You might expect that the white-on-white code, hex 77, would give another invisible mode with the whole character area lit up, but it doesn't. The monochrome mode has only a handful of attribute modes. You don't get all the combinations of the monochrome mode's attributes that you might expect, which is why there is no reverse video underlined mode, for example. Monochrome mode displays only those combinations shown in table 12.2.

Although monochrome mode has only a limited number of display attributes, it works properly regardless of the setting of the attribute bits by using one of its standard ways of showing characters. In most cases, it shows the characters in the normal way, as if the attribute were set to hex 07. If your display has a monochrome mode, you can see how it responds to the possible combinations of attribute bits by running the COLORTXT program, the same program used to demonstrate color modes.

The attributes that I've been discussing control how characters appear on the screen in terms of color, blinking, and so forth. What they don't control is the appearance or shape of the characters, which is controlled by the display adapter. I discuss that aspect of the PC display in the next section.

The Character Box

In text modes, the characters you see on the computer's screen are drawn by the video controller, rather than by the PC software (which is the way they are drawn in graphics modes, as you see in Chapter 13). The quality of the characters displayed varies among the display adapters because of differences in what's called the character box.

The character box is the framework in which PC characters are drawn. The characters are drawn from a rectangular matrix of dots, although it's not easy to see that looking at the screen.

The size of the character box ranges from a high of 9×16 (XGA and VGA) to a low of 8×8 (CGA), although the 8514 mode provides a special extra high-resolution box of 12×20.

It's relatively easy to observe the vertical dimension of the character box by turning up the brightness on the display screen. Because the scan lines don't completely overlap, you can see where they fall. Horizontal resolution is more difficult to see; the pixels overlap and blur together so you can't see any separation between them. It's only by carefully observing and comparing the characters that you can judge how many dots across the characters are. If you want to see exactly how large a character box each video mode uses, check the tables in Chapter 11.

The character box defines only the framework within which the characters are drawn. Not all of the box is used for the characters; parts are set aside for the space between characters. To shown you how this works, I use MDA's character box as an example.

The complete MDA character box is 9×14. Of the nine columns across, the first and last are reserved for the space between characters, so the characters are actually seven dots across. Of the 14 rows, the top two and the bottom one similarly are used for the space between lines, so there are 11 rows with which to draw the characters. Of those, two rows are used for descenders, as on the lowercase letters p, g, and y. That leaves nine rows for the main part of the characters. Thus, the MDA's characters are said to be 7×9, referring to the main part of the character box, the part that a capital X fills. The working part of the character box, including the descender rows, is 7×11.

Setting aside areas for spacing—one column on each side, two rows at the top, and one row at the bottom—applies only to conventional characters. The special drawing characters, such as the solid character, code 219, and the box-drawing characters, which are mentioned and demonstrated in the BOXES program (see Appendix C), use all of the character box so that they can touch each other.

The finer a character box is, the more detailed a character can be. That's why high-resolution characters can have serifs—the tails on the ends of characters that dress them up and make them more legible.

That's most of what there is to know about the technical details that underlie the PC family's text modes. The next section contains even more details.

Text Mode Tricks

Special features and tricks inherent in the computer's text modes can be used to enhance the operation of programs and to produce some special effects. Of course, the full range of tricks is limited only by your imagination and cleverness; I can't begin to explain everything that can be done. However, there are some fundamental features and tricks that can help you understand the workings of the text mode. I begin by considering the uses of excess display memory.

Some video modes have just enough video memory to hold all the data, but others have extra memory. With these modes, you can divide the memory into parts, called display pages, each of which is large enough to hold one screen worth of data. At any time, only one display page is active, that is, being displayed. However, while one display page is active, a program can be preparing others. In this way, a program can quickly switch to a new page.

Whether or not a video mode supports multiple pages depends on how much room it takes to hold one screen of data and how much room is available. Table 12.4 shows the various video modes along with the number of available display pages. Notice that modes 2, 3, 4, 5, and 7 have varying numbers of display pages depending on what video standard is being used.

Table 12.4. *Video Modes and the Number of Display Pages*

Mode (Hex)	Number of Display Pages	Video Standards				
0, 1	8	XGA	VGA	MCGA	EGA	CGA
2, 3	4					CGA
2, 3	8	XGA	VGA	MCGA	EGA	
4, 5	1			MCGA		CGA
4, 5	2	XGA	VGA		EGA	
6	1	XGA	VGA	MCGA	EGA	CGA
7	1					MDA
7	8	XGA	VGA		EGA	
D	8	XGA	VGA		EGA	
E	4	XGA	VGA		EGA	
F	2	XGA	VGA		EGA	
10	2	XGA	VGA		EGA	
11	1	XGA	VGA	MCGA		
12	1	XGA	VGA			
13	1	XGA	VGA	MCGA		
14	8	XGA				

Figure 12.4 shows how this works for a video mode that has four display pages.

Any display page can be activated so that its information appears on the display screen. The video controller can switch quickly from one page to another. While only one page appears on the screen at a time, a program has access to all the data in all the display pages all the time.

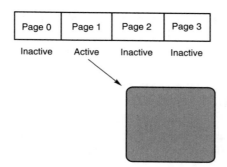

Figure 12.4. *Four display pages.*

That's the point of having and using multiple display pages. While it may take a noticeable amount of time for a program to generate information for the screen, the information can be made to appear instantaneously by switching from one page to another. While you're looking at one screen of information, the program can be building another screen off stage in another display page. When you're ready to have it appear, it can do so nearly instantaneously.

Multiple display pages can be put to any use. They might, for example, be used to hold completely new information or slightly changed data. If you build four or eight versions of a character-based drawing, you can page through them rapidly, creating an animation effect.

Programs switch between pages via a simple command to the display adapter that tells it to paint the screen image from another part of the display memory. The BA-SIC SCREEN statement enables you to work with multiple display pages. The third parameter of BASIC's SCREEN statement, apage, is the active page, and it controls which page the program is working with (that is, if the program is writing information to the screen, which screen page is being changed by the program). The fourth parameter of the SCREEN statement, vpage, is the visible page, and it controls which page image currently is on the screen.

While BASIC provides features that do the basic tasks of screen page control, programs written in other languages have to do this with the assistance of features provided by the ROM-BIOS. One of the things that the ROM-BIOS does for programs is keep a separate cursor location for each page. However, whether the program takes advantage of BASIC's features, uses the ROM-BIOS's features, or does all the screen page control itself, the multiple-page feature is there to be used.

Although some video modes do not have multiple display pages built into them, programs can, and often do, adopt the paging idea to make their screen images appear instantaneously. This is done by setting aside a portion of the program's conventional memory as an improvised display page, where a complete screen image is constructed. When the data is ready, it's moved into the real display memory in one quick assembly language operation. The mechanics are different from those of true display pages. With true pages, the display data is not moved. Instead, the display adapter switches from looking at one page of memory to another. A pseudo-page operation, on the other hand, actually moves data from another location to the display memory. Moving a full screen of data takes such a small fraction of a second that it appears to happen as quickly as true page switching does.

If any of the programs you work with present unusually snappy screen displays, it's likely that they use the private paging technique I described. My Norton Utilities program uses this technique as well.

There is more that can be done with the screen display than just moving data into or out of it. It also is possible, with assembly language tricks, to blank out the data that's on the screen or to change the display attributes—the colors—in a flash. The slow and laborious way to change the data on the screen is to do it one character at a time, changing each position on the screen individually. However, there are faster and more efficient ways.

For example, if you want to clear the whole screen, you can do so with just a few assembly language instructions. To blank the screen properly, you set each data byte to a blank space (ASCII code 32, hex 20) and each attribute byte to the "normal" color (which is usually 7, hex 07). You can set the first screen position to a blank space with a normal attribute by using the assembly language instruction that places a two-byte word anywhere you want in memory. The word you use is hex 2007, which combines the blank space character (20) with the normal color attribute (07). A variation on this instruction that moves a single word into memory can be used to repeat this operation, so the same data is propagated over the whole screen.

A variation on the same trick can be used to change only the color attributes, leaving the data unchanged, or vice versa. That's done with the assembly language instructions that AND and OR data, so that you can turn the bits on or off. Using these tricks, just a couple of instructions can paint a new color across the entire screen faster than the eye can see.

In addition to the tricks that programs can perform on their own, the PC's ROM-BIOS contains service routines that do most of the things that you might want done, including some fancy steps that you rarely see. One of these ROM-BIOS services enables you to define a rectangular window anywhere on the screen, and inside that window, you can display information and scroll it off the window without disturbing the data outside the window. That service is among the ones that I describe in Chapter 19.

But, before I move on to new topics, I explore more of the computer's video capabilities, the graphics modes, in Chapter 13. Graphics modes are a special dimension beyond the text modes you've just seen.

Some Things To Try

1. In BASIC, or any other programming language, write a program that prints the 32 ASCII control characters, codes 0 through 31, on the display screen. See what happens with each and note which ones appear as their PC characters and which ones work as control characters. Compare your results with the information on these control characters in Chapter 14.

2. Figure out what memory addresses are used for the eight display pages that a VGA display uses when it's working in video mode 3 (80-column text mode).

3. The MDA controller (on the old MDA adapter) had 4,096 bytes of video memory even though it only needed 4,000. Why is this? Why is it a bad idea for programs to attempt to use the leftover 96 bytes?

4. Experiment with text pages using the BASIC SCREEN command to switch pages and the PRINT command to place some information in each page.

Video: Graphics
Fundamentals

13

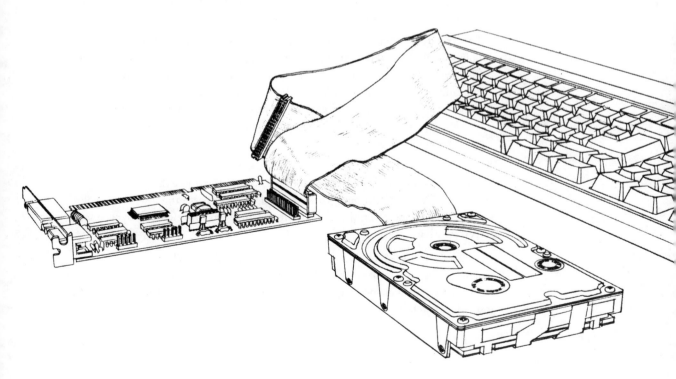

I n this chapter, I discuss the unique characteristics and capabilities of the graphics modes. You learn what the main features of the graphics modes are, and I repeatedly contrast the graphics modes with the text modes to highlight the differences. Then I look at the variety of modes available. Finally, I finish the discussion with a look at some of the technical details that underlie the workings of the graphics modes.

Graphics Modes Outline

In each of the graphics modes, the PC's display screen is divided into a series of dots, called pixels. The pixels are arranged in a rectangular grid of rows and columns, and each pixel can be set individually to show some color within the range of colors available. In those respects, the graphics modes are not fundamentally different from the text modes. And, even though there are many more pixels in the graphics modes than there are text characters in the text modes (640 pixels across and 480 down, for example, compared with 80 characters across and 25 down), that's mostly a difference of degree rather than a fundamental difference in kind.

What is really different about the graphics modes is that each pixel on the screen is simply a small splash of light that has no form to it. In the text modes, each position on the screen is a rich entity in itself: it holds a character that has its own unique shape, and the shape is made visible by the contrast between the colors that fill the foreground and background of the character position. But, with pixels in the graphics modes, there is only a dot of light with no unique shape and no distinction between foreground and background.

In the text modes, each screen position has three elements. First, there are the two main elements of data (which character is shown) and attribute (how the character is shown). Then, the attribute part is divided into two parts, the foreground color and the background color; therefore, there are three separate elements to each text screen position.

By contrast, in the graphics modes, each pixel has only one element, the color to which it is set. In graphics modes, there is no data (in the sense that each text mode position has a data element) nor is there background color, only the color of each individual pixel.

The background color in a graphics mode is the default color to which you set all the pixels so that they contrast with the color (or colors) with which you're drawing. That's a practical convention (and a sensible and necessary one) that has to do with the way pictures are made, but has nothing to do with the fundamental way the graphics modes operate. In text mode, the background color is a technical reality as well as a visual reality. In graphics mode, the background color is just a visual convention that has nothing to do with the technical way graphics modes work.

There is one other thing that the graphics modes lack: blinking. In the text modes, you're used to seeing blinking in two things: the cursor and characters. The graphics modes have neither. There is no blinking cursor in the graphics modes; in fact there is no cursor at all in the technical sense. (For more on that, see the next section, "The Graphics Cursor.") In addition, one aspect of the "colors" that are available in the text modes is blinking. Of course, blinking isn't a color in any real sense, but in the text modes, as you learned in Chapter 12, characters can be made to blink, and the blinking feature is controlled in the same way that true color is controlled. Thus, for the text modes the blinking feature is, in effect, a special kind of color. XGA, VGA, and EGA provide blinking; MCGA and CGA do not. Software can do almost anything, so programs can make things blink simply by changing the screen image at a regular interval. There is no inherent (or hardware-supported) blinking feature in any of the graphics modes.

The Graphics Cursor

If you activate BASIC, you see a flashing cursor of the type you're most used to. If you switch to a graphics mode (by using the SCREEN 1 command in BASIC, for example), you still seem to have a cursor on the screen, although it appears as a solid block rather than in the normal flashing form.

What's going on here? A trick! In the hardware sense, there is no such thing as a cursor in graphics mode. The standard flashing cursor, as you learned in Chapter 12, is a designed-in feature of the video controller that applies only to the text modes. This hardware cursor flashes and appears on just one character space at a time. Normally, it just underlines the current position on the screen and is created specifically by the display adapter hardware circuitry. Its appearance requires no special effort from your software other than the occasional command to position the cursor where you want.

What you see as a cursor in the graphics modes is a software-created effect that serves the purpose of a cursor, indicating the active location on the screen. Functionally, it's no different than the hardware cursor, but technically it's a totally different animal because it's created in a completely different way.

When a program, such as BASIC, operating in a graphics mode wants to create a cursor on the screen, it simply does whatever is necessary to produce the right kind of effect. Usually, that's nothing more than changing the background color where the cursor should be. This same thing can be done in a text mode to supplement or replace the blinking hardware cursor. You're used to seeing this sort of software-generated cursor in spreadsheet programs, which place a cursor on the current cell by making the cell appear in reverse video.

In text mode, programs have the option of using the hardware cursor or creating their own software cursor. In the graphics mode, there's no choice because there is no hardware cursor.

You may encounter the two main conventions for showing a cursor in graphics mode. One, which BASIC uses, is the old standard of indicating the cursor location by changing the background color. The other is a newer standard popularized by the Apple Macintosh computer and used more and more in software for the PC family. This standard shows the cursor as a thin vertical line that may blink (the blinking is a software-generated effect). This line cursor can be hard to see and use, but it has the advantage of being able to appear anywhere, even between characters, not just on top of a character.

Regardless of what it looks like, anything that acts like a cursor in one of the graphics modes is simply a visual effect created in software to serve the same purpose as a hardware cursor.

Instead, of text and cursors, graphics modes have available at their command a palette of colors to which each pixel position on the screen can be set. Each graphics mode has its own repertoire of colors, which, along with the number of dot positions, is what distinguishes the various modes from one another. What they all have in common is the grid of dots and the capability to set each dot to a solid color chosen from a palette of colors.

If that seems remarkably simple and primitive to you, then you understand the essential character of the graphics modes. They are at once cruder and more powerful than the text modes. They are cruder because they can display only colored dots, but more powerful because from those dots you can construct rich and complex drawings that are not possible in text modes. You can do a greater variety of things with the graphics modes, but getting those things done requires more work because everything must be drawn, dot by dot, by the software. This includes text and numbers.

Writing Text in Graphics Mode

The ROM-BIOS routines that supervise the graphics modes provide services to write text characters on the screen, just as they do for the text modes. The reason is simple enough: if the ROM-BIOS provides character writing services for any mode, it ought to provide it for all modes. In addition, any part of any program ought to be able to display an error message on the screen if it gets in trouble. Having a universal set of text output routines in the ROM-BIOS that work in every mode provides a common way for programs to send up an emergency flare.

Text mode programs, including the ROM-BIOS, write messages on the screen by outputting the ASCII character codes, and the video controller hardware takes on the job of producing a recognizable character. In the graphics modes, however, characters can appear on the screen only if they are drawn like any other picture.

To do this, the video memory for VGA, MCGA, and EGA contains a table that describes how each of the 256 ASCII characters is to be drawn, bit by bit. With the old CGA standard, the video controller used a table that was kept permanently in the ROM at location F000:FA6E. This table, however, contained patterns for only the first 128 ASCII characters. If a CGA program needed to display the other 128 characters, it had to initialize an auxiliary table and leave its address in a particular memory location. (By the way, this is what the DOS GRAFTABL command does.)

The bits in this drawing table are used to indicate the pixel settings, on and off, used to draw each character. For the standard table, eight bytes represent each character. The bits of the first byte give the eight pixel settings for the first scan line, and so on. Appendix C contains a program called GRAPHTXT, which decodes this table and displays each character drawing in enlarged form so that you can see how each character is drawn. You can use the GRAPHTXT program with any display adapter because it recreates the drawings with characters, so you don't have to have a graphics screen to use GRAPHTXT.

When programs use the ROM-BIOS services to display characters in a graphics mode, the ROM-BIOS looks up the character's drawing in the table and uses the information stored there to set the appropriate bits in the display memory so that a drawing of the character appears on the screen. The technique used is roughly the same as the one used by the GRAPHTXT demonstration program.

It's common for game programs and other light-duty programs that use graphics to rely on the ROM-BIOS's services to display any text information that needs to be shown. However, heavy-duty programs usually paint their own character data when they work in a graphics mode. This is because these programs have demanding needs for the way characters should appear, and by doing their own character drawing, they can control character size, type style, and attributes (such as bold or italic). The same is true of word processing programs that work in graphics mode.

Regardless of which approach a program uses—do it yourself or leave it to the BIOS— any text characters that appear when a computer is in a graphics mode are drawn on the screen, pixel by pixel, through the work of software, not by hardware as in the text modes.

Now you have a basic idea of what the graphics modes are generally about. It's time to consider the range of graphics modes and examine the characteristics and potential of each.

A Tour of the Graphics Modes

Table 13.1 shows all the graphics modes and the video standards that support them. As you can see, there are 11 different modes (4 and 5 are the same). This section examines these modes and gives you an idea of the variety available. Note that the last two XGA modes are not accessed via the BIOS, so they do not have mode ID numbers.

Table 13.1. *Summary of Graphics Video Modes and Standards*

Mode (Hex)	Type	Video	Standards			
4,5	Graphics	XGA	VGA	MCGA	EGA	CGA
6	Graphics	XGA	VGA	MCGA	EGA	CGA
D	Graphics	XGA	VGA		EGA	
E	Graphics	XGA	VGA		EGA	
F	Graphics	XGA	VGA		EGA	
10	Graphics	XGA	VGA		EGA	
11	Graphics	XGA	VGA	MCGA		
12	Graphics	XGA	VGA			
13	Graphics	XGA	VGA	MCGA		
—	Graphics	XGA				
—	Graphics	XGA				

Obviously, 11 video modes, each supported by three or more standards, makes for many details. I begin by taking a tour of the most important graphics standard, VGA. To start, take a look at table 13.2.

Table 13.2. *VGA Graphics Video Modes*

Mode (Hex)	Type	Maximum Resolution	Colors	Characters	Size
4,5	Graphics	320×200	4	40×25	8×8
6	Graphics	640×200	2	80×25	8×8
D	Graphics	320×200	16	40×25	8×8
E	Graphics	640×200	16	80×25	8×8
F	Graphics	640×350	Mono	80×25	8×14
10	Graphics	640×350	16	80×25	8×14
11	Graphics	640×480	2	80×30	8×16
12	Graphics	640×480	16	80×30	8×16
13	Graphics	320×200	256	40×25	8×8

281

It is clear that modes 4, 5, and 6 are low quality. For the most part, the resolution is low, and few colors can be displayed. You might wonder why these modes are supported at all.

The reason is to be compatible with CGA. The original PC's color graphics hardware could support only rudimentary modes. To this day, the newest video standards still support modes 4, 5, and 6. This means that you can run programs that demand a CGA standard, even though it is unlikely that you would use CGA to write new programs.

One nice thing about using VGA to run a CGA program is that it looks much better than on the original CGA display. This is because VGA displays each line of pixels twice. On an old CGA display, you can see gaps between the lines of pixels. This is especially vexing when you are working with characters. With VGA, these gaps are filled in, so a vertical resolution of 200 isn't quite as bad as it sounds.

The next four modes—D, E, F, and 10—are EGA modes. Like the CGA modes, these are supported for the sake of compatibility. When EGA was announced, it combined the features of CGA and MDA. For the first time, an official IBM video standard supported both graphics (like CGA) and sharp, crisp text (like MDA).

Like VGA, EGA supported the old 4, 5, and 6 modes. What was most important, however, were the new modes, especially mode 10, which provided much higher resolution than CGA (640×350 compared with 320×200) along with characters that looked almost as good as MDA. And, where CGA offered at most 4 simultaneous colors, the new EGA modes offered up to 16.

Mode F, which also is an EGA mode, is interesting. It was designed to display graphics on the old monochrome monitors, just as the Hercules Graphics Card (HGC) did. At one time, HGC was very popular because it offered both graphics and high-quality text on one display. Mode F was IBM's analog of HGC. (To compare, the EGA mode F provided a resolution of 640×350; HGC provided 720×348.)

These days, however, the most important standard VGA modes are 11, 12, and 13. Most of the time, mode 12 is the mode of choice because it provides excellent resolution with a reasonable number of colors.

When fine gradations of color are necessary, however, mode 13 is the one to use. It offers up to 256 simultaneous colors at the price of some resolution. Mode 12 has a resolution of 640×480; mode 13 drops to 320×200, which is no better than the old CGA. In fact, you could consider mode 13 to be a reincarnated CGA mode 5, the difference being, of course, that mode 13 has 64 times as many colors (which is very important). Because mode 13 has a vertical resolution of 200, however, the VGA controller automatically draws each line of pixels twice, just as it does with modes 4, 5, and 6. This makes a big difference.

And, as I showed you in Chapter 11, newer Super VGA adapters are really the norm today; few vendors offer adapters that support only conventional VGA. With Super VGA, resolution is better and more colors are supported.

So far, I have talked about colors. What happens when you display these colors on a monochrome display? I already have mentioned mode F, which supports graphics on the old MDA monochrome displays. The PS/2 family, however, uses newer, high-quality monochrome displays that are capable of interpreting the advanced VGA color modes.

As you may know, a video system creates color by displaying three separate signals—one each for red, green, and blue. When the PS/2 video logic automatically senses a monochrome display, it calls on the BIOS to convert the three colors into one by combining them. Interestingly enough, the BIOS does not treat each color equally as you might expect. Instead, the recipe it follows is 30 percent of the red component, 59 percent of the green component, and 11 percent of the blue component.

Thus, VGA provides a wide variety of graphics modes. Some are for compatibility, and some provide a new, enhanced standard. In fact, the overall VGA design philosophy can be summed up as follows: to support every mode on every display. As you see in a moment, however, the VGA set of modes has been expanded by the newest standard, XGA.

Now that you know a bit about the VGA graphics modes, look at VGA's baby brother, MCGA. MCGA was designed to be a cost-effective video system for the low-end PC/2s, the models 25 and 30. Thus, it is not necessary for MCGA to support every mode on every display. The MCGA design philosophy is to support all the modes that a customer with a PS/2 model 25 or 30 would reasonably need. Table 13.3 shows the MCGA graphics modes.

Table 13.3. MCGA *Graphics Video Modes*

Mode (Hex)	Type	Maximum Resolution	Character Colors	Characters	Size
4,5	Graphics	320×200	4	40×25	8×8
6	Graphics	640×200	2	80×25	8×8
11	Graphics	640×480	2	80×30	8×16
13	Graphics	320×200	256	40×25	8×8

If you compare this table with table 13.2, you see that MCGA is a subset of VGA. Missing are the newer EGA modes (D, E, F, and 10) and one of the new VGA modes (12). This means that people who use MCGA make two sacrifices. First, they cannot run software that demands EGA; second, when they use high-resolution VGA graphics, they must be content with two colors (mode 11) instead of 16 (mode 12).

The next stop on this tour of graphics modes is the enhanced video standard, XGA. As explained in Chapter 11, XGA was designed to be a strategic video platform. It supports all the VGA modes and three new modes. Of these, one is a text mode, which I discussed in Chapter 12; the other two are graphics modes. Table 13.4 summarizes the XGA graphics modes. Note that the two new modes are not accessed via the BIOS, so they do not have mode ID numbers.

Table 13.4. XGA *Graphics Video Modes*

Mode (Hex)	Type	Resolution	Colors	Characters	Size
4,5	Graphics	320×200	4	40×25	8×8
4,5	Graphics	320×200	4	40×25	8×8
6	Graphics	640×200	2	80×25	8×8
D	Graphics	320×200	16	40×25	8×8
E	Graphics	640×200	16	80×25	8×8
F	Graphics	640×350	Mono	80×25	8×14
10	Graphics	640×350	16	80×25	8×14
11	Graphics	640×480	2	80×30	8×16
12	Graphics	640×480	16	80×30	8×16

Mode (Hex)	Type	Resolution	Colors	Characters	Size
13	graphics	320×200	256	40×25	8×8
—	graphics	640×480	256 or 65,535	—	—
—	graphics	1,024×768	16 or 256	—	—

The first nine graphics modes work exactly as they do with VGA. The next two modes are new to XGA. They sometimes are called enhanced graphics modes to distinguish them from the VGA modes.

As explained in Chapter 11, these modes are accessed not via the BIOS but through the video hardware (an adapter interface or a device driver) directly. These modes do not have built-in characters, so it does not make sense to describe a standard number or size of characters. A programmer can use any number of characters that fit on the screen.

The XGA controller comes with either 0.5 or 1MB of VRAM (video memory), the memory that holds the images to be displayed. The number of colors each mode can support depends on the amount of VRAM. With 0.5MB of memory, the 640×480 enhanced mode can display up to 256 colors. With 1MB, the number increases to 65,535 colors. This is an extremely large choice of colors and enables display of images that approach photographic quality. Similarly, the 1,024×768 enhanced mode can display either 16 colors with 0.5MB of VRAM or 256 colors with 1MB.

These two modes also support a different way for programmers to access the video memory. As explained in Chapter 11, video memory is dual-port memory in that it can be accessed both by the video controller and by a regular program. A program reads from and writes to this memory by using preassigned addresses. These addresses lie either in the A or B block of memory, depending on the video standard.

The two enhanced XGA graphics modes use a large amount of video memory— either 0.5 or 1MB. There are three ways for a program to access this memory.

First, a program can access up to 64KB at a time by using a "window," whose address starts at the beginning of either the A block (A0000) or the B block (B0000). The program controls the value stored in a special index register, which indicates which

64KB of video memory should be mapped onto the window. (The setup is conceptually similar to the bank-switched system of expanded memory. See Chapter 17 for more details.)

Because the 64KB window lies within the standard 1MB DOS address space, this method of accessing the XGA video memory works with any PC.

The second way a program can access XGA video memory is by using a special set of memory addresses that maps onto the full 1MB of memory, as opposed to only 64KB. The starting address is set by the Micro Channel configuration program and must lie on an exact 1MB boundary.

The advantage of this method is that it enables a program to work directly with the entire 1MB of video memory rather than just 64KB at a time. Because this system requires access to memory addresses above 1MB, however, it works with only a 286-, 386-, or 486-based computer. Actually, this is not much of a restriction in that only 8088- and 8086-based computers lack the capability to address more than 1MB of memory, and it is unlikely that you would use XGA on one of those computers.

The third way a program can access XGA video memory is similar to the second, except that it enables a program to access 4MB at a time. Again, the base address is assigned by the Micro Channel configuration program. In this case, the address must lie on an exact 4MB boundary. This system is not used now; it is for future graphics systems that will have very large amounts of video memory—up to 4MB. Because of the addressing restrictions, you probably will see this XGA facility only on 386-, 486-, or Pentium-based computers.

To finish the discussion of the graphics modes, look at the 8514 standard. As you already know, the 8514 uses the built-in VGA controller for all the regular VGA modes. What the 8514 adds is three extra graphics modes. The details are shown in table 13.5.

Table 13.5. *8514 Graphics Video Modes*

Type	Maximum Resolution	Character Colors	Characters	Size
Graphics	640×480	256	80×34	8×14
Graphics	1,024×768	256	85×38	12×20
Graphics	1,024×768	256	146×51	7×15

As you can see, the 8514 modes provide especially high resolution and a large number of colors. However, the 8514 video controller (which comes on the 8514/A adapter) offers even more. It can move a large amount of video data from one place to another very quickly, automatically draw lines and areas, extract rectangular areas of the display image for special processing, and manipulate video data in sophisticated ways.

As you might imagine, the 8514/A adapter and the special 8514 display usually are used only by people who employ graphics-intensive software, such as computer-aided design (CAD) or desktop publishing programs. Nowadays, the 8514 standard has been surpassed by XGA.

Color Mapping

In the discussion of the various graphics modes, you may have noticed that each mode supports a number of colors. This is the maximum number of different colors that can be displayed on the screen at one time.

The monochrome modes can display only one color. The special 8514 modes and VGA/MCGA mode 13 can display up to 256 colors. Between, there are modes with 2, 4, and 16 colors.

Earlier in this chapter, I discussed how, in a graphics mode, the video memory contains the information necessary to specify the color of each pixel to be displayed. You also saw how the various graphics modes display pixels in particular resolutions and colors.

VGA, however, supplies an important service beyond what you have seen. It enables a program to specify which 256-, 16-, 4-, or 2-color combinations out of a total of 262,144 (256×1,024) possibilities to use. Of course, you can't distinguish so many shades, but, as discussed in Chapter 11, using many colors enables programs to display fine gradations of shading that are pleasing to the eye.

This set of color possibilities is called a palette. How a program chooses colors from the palette is called color mapping. Color mapping works this way. The PC video system has a component called the digital-to-analog converter, or DAC. The job of the DAC is to convert a request for a particular color into the red, green, and blue signals that are sent to the display. The DAC contains 256 registers (memory locations) in an area called the color lookup table, or CLUT. Each CLUT register contains 18 bits.

Now, 18 bits can express 2^{18}, or 262,144, possible values. At any time, each of the CLUT registers contains a bit pattern that specifies 1 of the 262,144 possible colors. This means that to choose a color, all a program has to do is specify the number of a CLUT register. The DAC looks in the register, reads the 18-bit pattern, and uses it to generate the proper color.

Of course, for this system to work, the appropriate 18-bit patterns must be loaded into the CLUT registers. When the video system is initialized, the CLUT registers are set to certain default values. However, a program that wants its own color combinations can change these values whenever it wants. The question is, how does a program specify a particular CLUT register?

Because there are only 256 CLUT registers, you need, at most, 8 bits to specify which one you want. (In 8 bits, you can store 2^8, or 256, possible values.) These 8 bits are stored in the video memory in the location that describes the particular pixel you want to display. When a pixel is to be displayed, the VGA chip extracts the 8 bits from the video memory and sends them to the DAC. The DAC uses them to choose one of the 256 CLUT registers, reads the 18-bit pattern, and then uses it to generate the proper combination of red, green, and blue signals.

Now, suppose that instead of 256 colors you are satisfied with 16. That is, you are interested in only 16 of the CLUT registers. In that case, you need only 4 bits to specify which CLUT register you want. You need to store only 4 bits of information in the video memory for each pixel. Thus, in the same amount of video memory, you could refer to twice as many pixels.

Because more pixels means better resolution, you can see why there is always a trade-off between many pixels and many colors. The various video modes distinguish themselves by using particular combinations of the number of pixels and the number of colors. You also can see why higher-resolution displays need additional memory.

Ultimately, the bits in the video memory that describe a pixel are converted to an 18-bit value that specifies a color. I finish this section by showing you how the DAC turns the 18 bits into colors.

It's actually quite simple. The DAC divides the 18 bits into three groups of 6 bits, each of which represents one of the basic colors, red, green, or blue. With 6 bits you can express 2^6, or 64, different values. The DAC interprets each group of 6 bits as specifying 1 of 64 possible signal strengths for a particular color. Thus, each color is a combination of 1 of 64 shades of red, 1 of 64 shades of green, and 1 of 64 shades of blue. That is why you can have up to 64×64×64, or 262,144, possible colors.

When the BIOS converts a color to monochrome, it combines the three 6-bit values into one 6-bit value. This is why VGA supports up to 64 gray shades.

With XGA, color selection is much the same except for the enhanced graphics mode, which offers up to 65,535 colors (with 1MB of video memory). To specify a choice from so many different colors requires 16 bits (because 2^{16} is 65,536). These bits are divided into three groups:

- 5 bits to specify red
- 6 bits to specify green
- 5 bits to specify blue

Because the DAC requires 18 bits (6 bits for each color), you still need 2 bits more, 1 bit each for red and blue. These are supplied by the palette controller, which looks at the 16 bits and, based on the colors in the CLUT, creates the extra 2 bits.

One of these extra bits is added to the red bits, and the other is added to the blue bits. The choice of extra bits are made to harmonize with the values already in the CLUT (which a program can change if necessary).

After these extra 2 bits are combined with the 16 bits from the video memory, the resulting 18 bits are sent to the DAC, which generates the proper color.

Some Things To Try

1. Experiment with the GRAPHTXT program shown in Appendix C. The program stops with character code 127. What would happen if it went further? This program assumes that the table it displays is at a certain memory location (F000:FA6E). Can you think of a reasonable way to recognize such a table if you had to search for it?

2. For something more ambitious, try using GRAPHTXT as a starting point and create a program that enables you to create your own character drawings in large scale.

3. Imagine that you are creating specifications for the PC's hardware engineers and want to add a cursor to the graphics modes. How would you have it operate? Can you work out the reasons why the graphics modes don't have a cursor? Can you think of ways to overcome these problems?

The PC
Character
Set

14

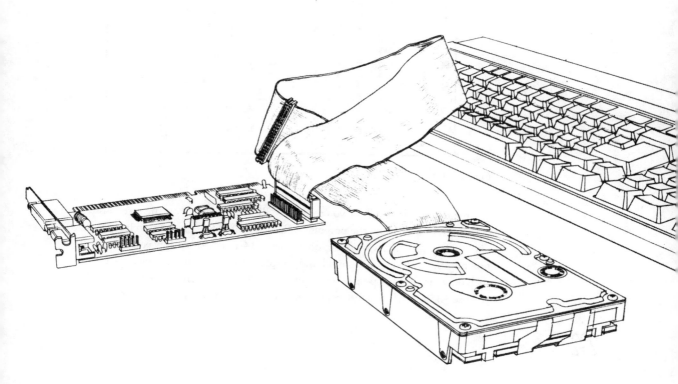

I n several previous chapters, I mentioned the PC's character set, but I haven't spent any time really describing what it is and how it works. That's because this is such an interesting subject that I've set aside this chapter to take a closer look. First, I give you an overview of the whole character set, then I show you how the PC's characters relate to a widespread standard known as ASCII, and, finally, I dig into and analyze the full set of special PC characters.

A Character Set Overview

Characters in the PC, as in most modern computers, occupy an 8-bit byte, so that there can be as many as 2^8, or 256, distinct characters. These characters are shown in figure 14.1.

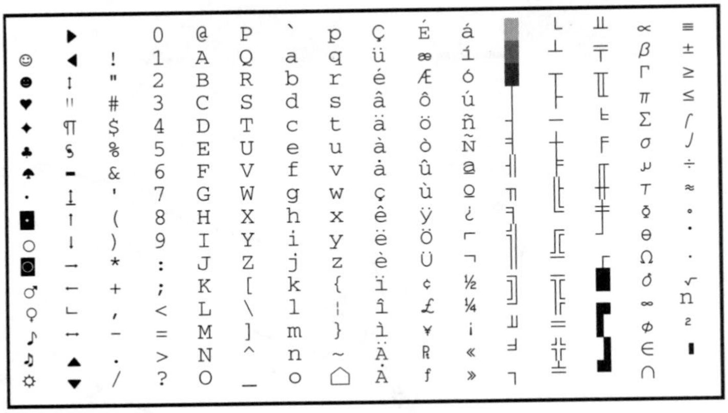

Figure 14.1. *The full PC character set.*

There are two easy ways for you to display all the characters on the screen of your computer. One is to use the program called ALLCHAR (you can find it in Appendix C). This program was used to create figure 14.1. The other way is to use a utility program that offers a quick and handy display of the PC's full character set. Some such programs even pop-up on top of other applications when you need them. When you use ALLCHAR or a utility program, you see the PC character set in exactly the way your computer's screen shows them, which can vary somewhat depending on the type of display you have (for more information on video displays, see Chapters 11–13). Figure 14.1 shows the characters in more or less their ideal form and gives you a quick and accurate way of seeing just what each character is like.

For reference, figure 14.2 shows each character's appearance together with the numeric character codes in decimal and hex. For each character, the decimal and hex code have the same numerical value but different representations. I refer to this figure frequently throughout this chapter. If you want to see the information from this figure on your computer screen, you can use either the REFCHAR program listed in Appendix C or a utility program.

Char	Dec	Hex	Char	Dec	Hex	Char	Dec	Hex	Char	Dec	Hex	Char	Dec	Hex	Char	Dec	Hex	Char	Dec	Hex	Char	Dec	Hex
	0	0		32	20	@	64	40	`	96	60	Ç	128	80	á	160	A0	└	192	C0	∝	224	E0
☺	1	1	!	33	21	A	65	41	a	97	61	ü	129	81	í	161	A1	┴	193	C1	β	225	E1
☻	2	2	"	34	22	B	66	42	b	98	62	é	130	82	ó	162	A2	┬	194	C2	Γ	226	E2
♥	3	3	#	35	23	C	67	43	c	99	63	â	131	83	ú	163	A3	├	195	C3	π	227	E3
♦	4	4	$	36	24	D	68	44	d	100	64	ä	132	84	ñ	164	A4	─	196	C4	Σ	228	E4
♣	5	5	%	37	25	E	69	45	e	101	65	à	133	85	Ñ	165	A5	┼	197	C5	σ	229	E5
♠	6	6	&	38	26	F	70	46	f	102	66	å	134	86	ª	166	A6	╞	198	C6	µ	230	E6
•	7	7	'	39	27	G	71	47	g	103	67	ç	135	87	º	167	A7	╟	199	C7	τ	231	E7
◘	8	8	(	40	28	H	72	48	h	104	68	ê	136	88	¿	168	A8	╚	200	C8	Φ	232	E8
○	9	9	)	41	29	I	73	49	i	105	69	ë	137	89	⌐	169	A9	╔	201	C9	Θ	233	E9
◙	10	A	*	42	2A	J	74	4A	j	106	6A	è	138	8A	¬	170	AA	╩	202	CA	Ω	234	EA
♂	11	B	+	43	2B	K	75	4B	k	107	6B	ï	139	8B	½	171	AB	╦	203	CB	δ	235	EB
♀	12	C	,	44	2C	L	76	4C	l	108	6C	î	140	8C	¼	172	AC	╠	204	CC	∞	236	EC
♪	13	D	-	45	2D	M	77	4D	m	109	6D	ì	141	8D	¡	173	AD	═	205	CD	φ	237	ED
♫	14	E	.	46	2E	N	78	4E	n	110	6E	Ä	142	8E	«	174	AE	╬	206	CE	∈	238	EE
☼	15	F	/	47	2F	O	79	4F	o	111	6F	Å	143	8F	»	175	AF	╧	207	CF	∩	239	EF
►	16	10	0	48	30	P	80	50	p	112	70	É	144	90	░	176	B0	╨	208	D0	≡	240	F0
◄	17	11	1	49	31	Q	81	51	q	113	71	æ	145	91	▒	177	B1	╤	209	D1	±	241	F1
↕	18	12	2	50	32	R	82	52	r	114	72	Æ	146	92	▓	178	B2	╥	210	D2	≥	242	F2
‼	19	13	3	51	33	S	83	53	s	115	73	ô	147	93	│	179	B3	╙	211	D3	≤	243	F3
¶	20	14	4	52	34	T	84	54	t	116	74	ö	148	94	┤	180	B4	╘	212	D4	⌠	244	F4
§	21	15	5	53	35	U	85	55	u	117	75	ò	149	95	╡	181	B5	╒	213	D5	⌡	245	F5
▬	22	16	6	54	36	V	86	56	v	118	76	û	150	96	╢	182	B6	╓	214	D6	÷	246	F6
↨	23	17	7	55	37	W	87	57	w	119	77	ù	151	97	╖	183	B7	╫	215	D7	≈	247	F7
↑	24	18	8	56	38	X	88	58	x	120	78	ÿ	152	98	╕	184	B8	╪	216	D8	°	248	F8
↓	25	19	9	57	39	Y	89	59	y	121	79	Ö	153	99	╣	185	B9	┘	217	D9	·	249	F9
→	26	1A	:	58	3A	Z	90	5A	z	122	7A	Ü	154	9A	║	186	BA	┌	218	DA	·	250	FA
←	27	1B	;	59	3B	[	91	5B	{	123	7B	¢	155	9B	╗	187	BB	█	219	DB	√	251	FB
∟	28	1C	<	60	3C	\	92	5C	|	124	7C	£	156	9C	╝	188	BC	▄	220	DC	ⁿ	252	FC
↔	29	1D	=	61	3D	]	93	5D	}	125	7D	¥	157	9D	╜	189	BD	▌	221	DD	²	253	FD
▲	30	1E	>	62	3E	^	94	5E	~	126	7E	₧	158	9E	╛	190	BE	▐	222	DE	■	254	FE
▼	31	1F	?	63	3F	_	95	5F	⌂	127	7F	ƒ	159	9F	┐	191	BF	▀	223	DF		255	FF

Figure 14.2. *The PC character set with decimal and hex codes.*

The characters in the PC character set are designed to do many things, and some of them take on a different quality, depending upon how they are used.

If you glance at figure 14.1, you see that it begins with two columns of very curious characters (the first 32 characters, with decimal codes 0 through 31) followed by six columns of the characters with which you are most familiar: the digits 0 through 9, the letters of the alphabet in upper- and lowercase, and a lot of punctuation characters. These eight columns are the first half of the PC's character set. They are called the ASCII (American Standard Code for Information Interchange) characters because they follow a widespread standard used in most computers.

ASCII proper consists of only 128 characters—the characters with decimal codes 0 through 127. The PC character set has twice as many entries, including the codes 128 through 255. These higher codes, which make up the other half of the PC character set, usually are called the extended ASCII characters. Strictly speaking, only the first half, the codes 0 through 127, are ASCII characters, but you often find people using ASCII to refer to any character or the coding scheme that defines how characters are represented in patterns of bits. There's no harm in that, but you ought to be aware that, depending on how it's used, ASCII can have a precise technical meaning or a broader meaning.

The ASCII half of our character set has an official meaning and definition that ranges far beyond our PC family. ASCII is a universal code used by many computers and other electronic devices. The extended ASCII characters, however, are another story. There is no universal convention for which characters codes 128 through 255 should represent, however, the characters shown in figures 14.1 and 14.2 were especially designed for the PC. Because of the importance and popularity of the PC, these particular extended ASCII characters have been used not only by the entire PC family but also by many computers that are only distant relatives of the PC.

This particular group of characters has become a de facto standard, usually referred to as the IBM character set. However, you may find that some non-IBM printers do not support the second half of the character set. In fact, printers, word processors, spreadsheets, and other applications can decide (well, their programmers and designers do) what characters to support and what characters to display or print when certain codes are entered. In today's computer world, you can use many more than 256 characters simply by using a software or firmware font that supports other characters. However, for the purposes of this book, I describe the basic—and mostly standard—PC character set.

It's time to dig into the details of the PC character set. I do that in three parts—two covering the ASCII characters (first the ordinary ASCII characters and then some special control characters) and one discussing the extended ASCII characters and some other unique characteristics of the PC character set.

The Ordinary ASCII Characters

The ASCII character set, character codes 0 through 127, breaks into two different parts that can be seen in figures 14.1 and 14.2. The first part, which I discuss separately, are the first 32 characters, codes 0 through 31. These are called the ASCII control characters and are quite different from what they appear to be in figures 14.1 and 14.2. I come back to them after I talk about the more conventional characters, codes 32 through 127.

If you look at the characters represented by codes 32 through 127, you see that these characters are the ones usually thought of as characters—the letters of the alphabet, digits, and punctuation. Although these characters look ordinary, there actually are quite a few subtle details of which you should be aware.

It is obvious that there are separate characters for upper- and lowercase—that **A** isn't the same as **a**—but there is something else here you shouldn't miss. Whenever you're using any program that arranges data in alphabetical order or searches for data, this matters, unless the program takes special pains to treat upper- and lowercase characters the same (some programs do, some don't, and some enable you to choose). A search for the letter **a** may not find the letter **A**, and unless you specify otherwise, in alphabetical order, lowercase **a** (decimal ASCII code 97) comes after capital **Z** (decimal ASCII code 90). You also should note that numbers come before uppercase letters.

The next characters you need to consider are the punctuation and other special symbols. One thing to note is that they are scattered all around the digits and letters—before, after, and in between. This means that the punctuation characters as a group don't sort into any one place relative to the alphabet and digits. For example, the commercial "at" sign (@) is decimal ASCII code 64, just before capital **A**, while left bracket ([) is decimal ASCII code 91, after capital **Z**. Falling before the numbers is forward slash (/), the plus sign (+), the dollar sign ($), and some other symbols. And, way down in the list numerically speaking are the braces ({ and }), vertical bar (|), tilde (~), and more. As you work with these characters—particularly if you need to sort or display them—keep figures 14.1 and 14.2 handy.

The blank space character has a decimal character code of 32—the lowest of all the punctuation characters, so it appears at the beginning of any alphabetic sort. (In the character charts in figures 14.1 and 14.2, you see three different characters that appear to be a blank space. See the "Spaces and Nulls" section for more about that.) Note that besides parentheses, ( ), there are two other pairs of characters that can be used to enclose things—the brackets, [ ], and the braces, { }. People also use the less-than and greater-than characters, < >, as a way of enclosing things, like <this>. It's good to know about all four of these embracing pairs because they all come in handy.

Consider quotation marks. In the type used in a book, you see left and right quote marks, but ordinary typewriters don't have them; neither does our PC character set. The PC character set has only one double-quote mark ("; decimal ASCII code 34) and one single-quote mark, or apostrophe ('; decimal ASCII code 39). Using the PC character set, the same double-quote mark is used to both open and close a quotation. There is also a curious character known as a reverse quote (`)—the one just before the lowercase **a** with a decimal character code of 96. This character should not be paired with the ordinary single-quote character. The reverse quote is used in combination with letters of the alphabet to form non-English characters. Other characters used this way include the circumflex (^; code 94), the tilde (~; code 126), the single-quote ('; code 39), and the comma (,; code 44). This idea of combining characters works only when you can overstrike one character on top of another, which you can do on a computer printer or a typewriter but (usually) not on a computer display screen. To make them easier to use, these non-English alphabetic characters have been incorporated into the extended ASCII characters. I talk more about them in a few pages.

There are other characters that call for a brief mention. In addition to the regular slash character (/; code 47), there is a backslash (\; code 92). As far as I know, use of the reverse slash is limited to computing. For example, in the BASIC programming language it indicates whole-number division, while a regular slash indicates regular division, including fractional results. When working with DOS, the backslash indicates directory paths. Also take care not to confuse the hyphen character

(-; code 45) with the underscore character(_; code 95). Finally, the circumflex (^; code 94) is sometimes used to indicate special control characters (or a number raised to a power in some text programs) rather than standing as an independent character. This can cause confusion, so when you see a circumflex, check carefully to see whether you are dealing with the circumflex character or a reference to a control character.

Spaces and Nulls

In figures 14.1 and 14.2, you see three characters that appear to be blank spaces. Only one of them actually is the proper blank character—the one with character code 32. The characters with codes 0 and 255 are called nulls, or null characters. They aren't supposed to be treated as true characters, but as inactive nothings. For example, if you send code 32 (the true space character) to a computer printer, it leaves a space and moves on to the next location. However, if you send one of the null characters, nothing happens. The printer ignores the character—it doesn't move to the next location or leave a blank space.

In the proper ASCII character set, there are two nulls—codes 0 (NUL) and 127 (DEL). In the PC character set, code 127 is a real, visible character with an appearance something like a little house. To substitute for the ASCII null code 127, the PC character set treats code 255 as a null.

Null characters don't have any everyday use. They are used primarily in communications to mark time; transmitting nulls is a way of keeping a line active while no real data is sent.

The ASCII Control Characters

The first 32 places in the ASCII character set, codes 0 through 31, have a very special use that has nothing to do with their appearance. For the moment, I ignore their appearances because this section looks at these characters from an entirely different perspective.

When a computer talks to a printer, it must tell the printer what to print and how to print it. It must indicate, for example, where the ends of the lines are and when to skip to the top of a new page. The ordinary ASCII characters, which I discussed earlier, are the what-to-print part of the ASCII character set. The how-to-print part is the subject of this section.

The first 32 codes in the ASCII character set are reserved for passing special information to a printer, to another computer through a telephone line, and so forth. These codes aren't used to pass information or data, but to provide action commands, formatting signals, and communication control codes. I cover the main items here to give you a broad perspective on these characters and their uses.

First, you should know that these 32 codes have special names when they are used as ASCII control characters rather than the picture characters shown in figures 14.1 and 14.2. Table 14.1 provides a summary of these codes and their names.

Table 14.1.   *ASCII Control Characters*

Decimal Code	Hex	Code Control	Key Name	Description
0	00	^@	NUL	Null Character
1	01	^A	SOH	Start of Header
2	02	^B	STX	Start of Text
3	03	^C	ETX	End of Text
4	04	^D	EOT	End of Transmission
5	05	^E	ENQ	Enquire
6	06	^F	ACK	Acknowledge
7	07	^G	BEL	Bell
8	08	^H	BS	Backspace
9	09	^I	HT	Horizontal Tab
10	0A	^J	LF	Line Feed
11	0B	^K	VT	Vertical Tab
12	0C	^L	FF	Form Feed
13	0D	^M	CR	Carriage Return
14	0E	^N	SO	Shift Out
15	0F	^O	SI	Shift In
16	10	^P	DEL	Delete
17	11	^Q	DC1	Device Control 1

Decimal Code	Hex	Code Control	Key Name	Description
18	12	^R	DC2	Device Control 2
19	13	^S	DC3	Device Control 3
20	14	^T	DC4	Device Control 4
21	15	^U	NAK	Negative Acknowledge
22	16	^V	SYN	Synchronize
23	17	^W	ETB	End of Text Block
24	18	^X	CAN	Cancel
25	19	^Y	EM	End of Medium
26	1A	^Z	SUB	Substitute
27	1B	^9	ESC	Escape
28	1C	^/	FS	File Separator
29	1D	^:	GS	Group Separator
30	1E	^^	RS	Record Separator
31	1F	^@	US	Unit Separator

Before I look at these control characters in greater detail, I should mention a few things about table 14.1. The first two columns of the table are, of course, the numeric character codes in decimal and in hex. The third column shows the key combinations that evoke the characters. Each of these characters can be keyed in directly from your keyboard by holding down the Control key and the Shift key and pressing the indicated character—A (for code 1), B (for code 2), and so on. The conventional way of indicating these Control-Shift codes is to place a circumflex (^) before the name of the key to be pressed, as shown in the third column of the table. When you see ^A, it doesn't means the circumflex character (^) followed by the character A. It means Control-A, which is invoked by holding down the Control key and the Shift key and pressing the a key. This combination is sometimes shown as Ctrl-A.

This "circumflex notation" is used quite often. You may run across ^Z or ^C— Control-Z or Control-C—both of which have special meaning for the PC, as you see shortly.

In the fourth column of table 14.1, you find a two- or three-letter code, which is a standard abbreviation for the full descriptive name of the control code character.

299

You sometimes find these short codes used in writing about computers and communications. And, in the last column, is a descriptive name for each of the 32 special codes.

Some of the ASCII control characters are interesting and useful; others have rather obscure and technical uses. Instead of discussing them from first to last, I cover them in order of their importance.

First, I talk about the ones that are on your keyboard.

Keyboard Control Codes

As I mentioned, any of these characters can be entered easily from the keyboard. But, the most important keyboard control codes also have regular keys assigned to them. There are four of these: Backspace (BS, code 8), Tab (HT, 9), Enter or Carriage Return (CR, 13), and Escape (ESC, 27). The Delete key on your keyboard is not, however, equivalent to the ASCII Delete (DEL, 16) code.

Notice the relationship between the control codes and the other characters on your keyboard. When you hold down the Control-Shift keys and press a character, the keyboard routine subtracts 64 from the value of the letter. (Applications can make use of Shift-Ctrl-character, but in DOS if you press Ctrl-character, the uppercase character is assumed by the keyboard conversion routine.)

To discover what keys to press to duplicate some of the control codes, simply add 64 to the value of the control code. To enter a Backspace (BS, 8) from the keyboard, for example, you either can press the Backspace key or hold Control and press H. The BS code is ASCII 8. If you add 64 to that, you get 72, the ASCII code for the letter H. The Line Feed code is Ctrl-J. LF is ASCII code 10. When you add 64 to that, you get 74, the code for the letter J.

Here's an example of when this information is useful. There's no Line Feed key on the keyboard. You can use this knowledge when you are talking with another user online and don't have your communications software set up to add a Line Feed when the Enter (Return) key is pressed. If the software you are using doesn't automatically add a Line Feed, then each subsequent line overtypes the previous line. To avoid this, press Enter and then press Ctrl-J to move the cursor on the remote machine to the next line.

One group of these control codes is used to indicate the basic formatting of written material. They function as both logical formatting codes, which help programs make sense out of data, and as printer control codes, which tell printers what to do. The most common ones include some I already have discussed, such as Backspace (BS), Tab (HT or Ctrl-I), and Carriage Return (CR). Others are Line Feed (LF, code 10, or Ctrl-J), which is used in conjunction with Carriage Return; Form Feed (FF, code 12, or Ctrl-L), which skips to a new page; and Vertical Tab (VT, code 11, or Ctrl-K).

Several other characters are of general interest and use. The Bell character (BEL, 7) sounds a warning bell or beep. If you send this character to a printer or console, you get an audible signal. Want to "ring the bell" on a remote system with which you are communicating via modem? Hold down the Control key and tap the letter G. (The BEL code is ASCII 7. When you add 64 to that, you get 71, the ASCII code for the letter G.)

The Control-C character (ETX, 3) also is known as the Break character. Pressing Ctrl-C usually has the same effect as pressing the Ctrl-Break combination. The Control-S (DC3, 19) and Control-Q (DC1, 17) characters sometimes can be used as Pause and Restart commands, particularly when you're working with a communications service such as CompuServe or MCI Mail. The Control-S Pause command is not, however, the same as the Pause key on your computer (for more information, see Chapter 15). (If your computer has an old-style keyboard, the Pause key is the Ctrl-NumLock, and Break is Ctrl-ScrollLock.) The Pause key actually stops your computer, while the Control-S Pause command pauses only the program with which you're working.

DOS follows the Ctrl-S and Ctrl-Q convention. If you type DIR at the DOS prompt, you can use Ctrl-S to stop the scrolling of a long directory listing and you can use Ctrl-Q to start continue the listing. In some early versions of DOS, however, the Ctrl-Q combination can cause the display to lock instead of releasing. If you have this problem, just repeat Ctrl-S to start the display again instead of using Ctrl-Q.

Another useful control code character is the Ctrl-Z key combination (SUB, 26). This code is used to mark the end of text files stored on a disk. I discussed this code and the Carriage Return and Line Feed codes in Chapter 6.

Those are the ASCII control characters that are of the widest interest. I finish this section with an overview of some of the more technically oriented control characters. You can skip over the following paragraphs if you're not interested.

Other Control Codes

The rest of the ASCII control characters are used for a variety of purposes that assist in communications, data formatting, and the control of printers and other devices. I don't cover this topic exhaustively, but I do give you an idea of what these characters do.

Codes 1 through 4 (SOH, STX, ETX, and EOT) are used in communications transmissions to indicate the boundaries of header (descriptive) information, text data, and the entire transmission. Those codes are oriented particularly toward text data. Other codes, such as 28 through 31 (FS, GS, RS, and US), are used as punctuation marks in other forms of data and to mark the boundaries of files—groups, records, and units—that take on different meanings depending upon the type of data being transmitted.

Other codes are used for the control of communications. For example, Acknowledge (ACK, 6) and Negative Acknowledge (NAK, 21) are used to indicate if data is passing successfully. ENQ, SYN, ETB, CAN, and other codes also are used in the control of communications (which is much too complex and specialized a subject to get into here).

A number of the ASCII control codes are used to control printers and other devices. Although the exact control codes vary widely from printer to printer, some of the more commonly used codes are worth mentioning. The Shift Out (SO, 14) and Shift In (SI, 15) codes commonly are used to instruct a printer to print wide or compressed characters. The four Device Control codes (DC1–4, 17–20) also are used by many printers for such commands as turning off wide printing.

However, because most printers have more formatting and control commands than there are ASCII control characters available, it is normal for the Escape character (ESC, 27, or Ctrl-[) to be used as a catch-all command prefix. When a printer receives an Escape character, it knows that a special command follows. Instead of printing the next few characters, the printer interprets them as a command—a command to set the location of the tab stops or turn on underscoring, for example. If you want to know more about printer control codes, see the reference manual that comes with the printer you are interested in.

A Cast of Odd Characters

It's time to look at the special characters that make up the extended ASCII characters, codes 128 through 255, and the PC-specific character pictures, codes 0 through 31. I discuss these characters in groups, pausing to make comments and point out interesting features.

Before proceeding, I need to discuss again a major source of confusion. There are two completely different ways of viewing the first 32 characters, codes 0 through 31. I discussed one way—interpreting them as ASCII control characters—earlier in this chapter. When these characters are interpreted as ASCII control characters, there is no displayed image associated with them. They serve as hidden codes to control communications or a printer, so there is nothing to see. In this section, I examine the other interpretation of these character codes—as characters that have an image or symbol associated with them, as shown in figures 14.1 and 14.2.

What determines whether the same character code is interpreted as an ASCII control command or as a visible character? Basically, it all depends on how the code is used. In most circumstances, these codes are treated as ASCII control characters. But, if you manage by one means or another to get them to appear on our PC's display screen, then they take on their other interpretation, which is as part of the PC's special character set. It is up to the application you are running to make this interpretation.

If you look at the pictures of the first 32 characters in figures 14.1 and 14.2, you see that they form a fascinating hodge-podge of graphic characters that can be used for a variety of purposes, none of them really essential. Because the use of these character codes is relatively restricted (they usually are interpreted as control characters), IBM decided to put the most important special characters into the extended ASCII area and use this section for some of the more amusing and dispensable characters.

Nevertheless, you can find some useful characters, including the card group (codes 3 through 6), the paragraph and section marks (codes 20 and 21), the arrow group (codes 16 through 31), and the "have a nice day" group (codes 1 and 2). There are real uses for these characters, but they frequently are used in entertainment contexts.

Moving on to the extended ASCII characters, codes 128 through 255, you find more special characters. They are organized into three main groups—the foreign characters, the drawing characters, and the scientific characters.

The foreign characters use codes 128 through 175 and include essentially everything that is needed to accommodate all of the major European languages other than English. (ASCII is oriented toward the needs of the English language.)

There are three main subparts to the foreign character group. One part, codes 128 through 154 and 160 through 167, provides the special alphabetic characters (with diacritical marks) used in various European languages. I mentioned earlier that the regular ASCII character set contains most (but not all) of the diacritical marks needed for European languages. They only can be used, as on a printer, when you can overstrike them onto letters of the alphabet, something you can't do on the PC's display screen. These special alphabetic characters solve that problem in an attractive way. The necessary diacritical marks are part of the defined extended character.

The second part of the European set provides currency symbols: the cent sign (code 155), the pound sign (156), the Japanese yen (157), the Spanish peseta (158), and the franc (159). The dollar sign (36) is part of the regular ASCII set.

The third part of the European set provides some special punctuation, including the Spanish inverted question mark and exclamation point (codes 168 and 173) and the French-style quotation marks (codes 174 and 175). These French quotes are worth noting because they can be used for many graphic purposes as well as their intended use.

Buried among the European characters are four symbols that have general use—the one-half and one-quarter symbols (codes 171 and 172) and two angle marks (169 and 170). Look them up in case you might have a use for them.

The next major section of the extended ASCII character set includes the drawing or graphics characters. These are characters enable programs to produce drawings using only the PC's character set. There are three subgroups of drawing characters.

The most interesting and most widely used set of drawing characters are the box-drawing characters. These characters enable you to draw precise rectangular outlines (boxes) on the computer's display screen. These box-drawing characters are sophisticated enough to draw vertical and horizontal dividing lines within an outline and to draw with either single or double lines. There are four sets of characters for box drawing—a set for double lines, another for single lines, and two mixed sets for double-horizontal, single-vertical lines, and vice versa. Figure 14.3 illustrates all four sets and shows the character codes used to call them. If you want to see the boxes in action on the screen, the program called BOXES, listed in Appendix C, reproduces figure 14.3.

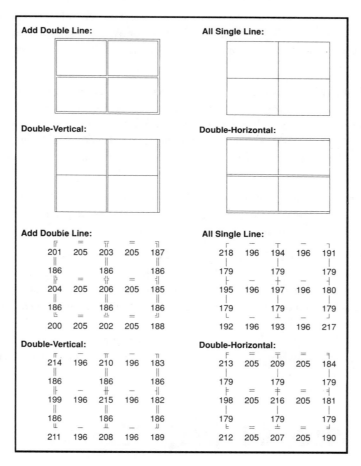

Figure 14.3. The box-drawing characters.

Because they look so good on the computer's display screen, practically every important program for the PC makes heavy use of these box-drawing characters. I've taken the trouble to produce figure 14.3 and the program that draws it to make it easy for you to look up the codes for these box-drawing characters and use them in your work.

The next group of drawing characters is used to provide shaded areas. Code 176 provides the lightest fill, approximately one-quarter dense; code 177 is one-half dense; code 178 is three-quarters dense; and code 219 is completely solid. Together with the blank character, they provide a range of four or five shades of gray that can be used either to fill an area on the screen or to produce bar charts of distinctly different appearance.

The final group of drawing characters consists of codes 220 through 223. Each of them is half of the all-solid character (219) that just mentioned. One is the top half, another the bottom, another the right, and another the left. They can be used to draw solid, filled-in shapes that are twice as fine-grained as could be drawn with the all-solid character alone. For example, they can be used to make more detailed bar graphs.

Many amazing drawings can be produced on the screen of the PC using just the PC's standard characters, including all the drawing characters mentioned here along with some of the regular characters. With some imagination you can do wonders this way.

The final part of the PC's extended ASCII special character set consists of the scientific character group, codes 224 through 254. These include the Greek letters commonly used in math and science, the infinity symbol (code 236), various special mathematical symbols, including two (244 and 245) that, when stacked together, form a large integral sign. There are even square and square-root symbols (253 and 251). While these symbols don't cover everything that might be needed for mathematics, science, and engineering, they do take care of some of the most common requirements.

Some Things To Try

1. Experiment to find out how your computer's screen and printer respond to the 32 ASCII control characters. Write a program in BASIC, for example, to send these characters one by one to the screen and printer. (Hint: if you precede and follow each control character with an X, you can get a clearer idea of what the response is to each control character.)

2. Do your computer's printer and display screen respond differently to the same control characters? Try to explain why.

3. Look at the ALLCHAR and REFCHAR programs in Appendix C that generate figures 14.1 and 14.2 on your computer's screen. Find how they write the characters onto the screen. Why don't they use the ordinary PRINT command?

4. If a program sorts data treating upper- and lowercase letters alike (which is often what you want), it either treats both as uppercase or both as lowercase. Does it matter which way? What effect does that have on punctuation?

5. The design of the PC's drawing characters was limited by the number of character codes available. Suppose there were another 50 or more codes available. What sort of additional drawing capabilities might have been added? Try to produce your own extensions to the PC's set of drawing characters.

Keyboard Magic

15

Now that you've looked at the PC family's display screens and character set, it's appropriate that the next topic be the keyboard—the other half of your interface with the computer. While the keyboard may seem simple in comparison with the display screen, the PC's keyboard contains complexities that make it much more interesting to explore than you might think. You see why in this chapter. You also see how some programs work with the keyboard in some very unusual ways.

Basic Keyboard Operation

To understand what's going on with the computer keyboard, you need to understand two key things. First, there is more to keyboard operations than you may think, and, second, keyboard information undergoes several transformations before it emerges as what you might expect. To make sense out of this, I begin by explaining why the keyboard works so indirectly and then show you how it works.

You may expect the keyboard to work in a relatively crude way: press the A key, and the keyboard says to the computer "A." It doesn't work that way for a simple reason: if the keyboard is assigned the task of making the A key mean the letter A, then the keyboard is in the business of giving meaning to what you do when you pound away on the keyboard. There are two things wrong with that. One is that it's not the business of computer hardware to assign meaning to what you're doing. Hardware is supposed to be like a blank slate. Software, on the other hand, is supposed to bring the hardware to life, giving it activity and meaning. So, the first thing that is wrong with the keyboard deciding that the A key means the letter A is that the hardware is intruding on a job that belongs to software.

The other thing wrong is the inflexibility of that scenario. You may think that it is stupid for the A key to mean anything else, but that's not the issue. As much as possible, a computer should be flexible and adaptable, and if the hardware doesn't impose any meaning on keystrokes, so much the better.

In fact, under certain circumstances it may be convenient to change completely the way the keyboard works. The keyboard layout commonly used is called the QWERTY design, named after the letters in the top-left of the keyboard. Another layout, the

Dvorak (named after a person, not a letter arrangement), was designed to be easier to use. Because PCs have a flexible software-based keyboard system, you can change the position of the keys by telling the computer which key represents which letter and have a Dvorak keyboard.

Those are the ideas behind what may seem like a curious relationship between the keyboard and the computer (and the built-in ROM-BIOS programs). Here is what actually happens when you press a key on your computer's keyboard: the keyboard recognizes that you've pressed one of the keys and makes a note of it. (The keys are assigned an identifying number, called a scan code, and that scan code is what the keyboard notes.)

After the keyboard notes that you've pressed a key, it tells the computer that something has happened. It doesn't even say what; it just says that something has happened on the keyboard. That's done in the form of a hardware interrupt. The keyboard circuitry sends your computer's microprocessor an interrupt using the interrupt number assigned to the keyboard, interrupt 9. Interrupts, as you learned in Chapter 4, cause the microprocessor to put aside what it is doing and jump to an interrupt-handling program. In this case, the interrupt handler is an integral part of the ROM-BIOS software.

At that point, the keyboard interrupt handler swings into action and finds out what took place on the keyboard. It does that by sending a command to the keyboard to ask what happened. The keyboard responds by telling the ROM-BIOS which key was pressed. These commands and responses are sent via ports (which also were discussed in Chapter 4). The ROM-BIOS issues its command by sending a command code out to a port address to which the keyboard responds. The keyboard replies by sending the scan code of the key to the port address that the ROM-BIOS reads. In a moment, you see what the ROM-BIOS does with that information, but first you need to know what takes place in the keyboard itself.

The keyboard, of course, must keep track of which key was pressed and wait until the ROM-BIOS asks for it. (It isn't a long wait—usually less than 1/10,000 of a second; still, for computer hardware, that's a wait.) To do this, the keyboard has a small memory, called the keyboard buffer, which is large enough to record a number of separate key actions in case the microprocessor does not respond to the keyboard interrupts before more keys are pressed. Although it's rare for the microprocessor not to respond immediately, the keyboard design makes allowances for that possibility. After the keyboard reports the details of a key action to the microprocessor, that action is flushed from the keyboard's memory, making room for new scan codes.

There are two more things you need to know about the keyboard, the first of which is critical. The keyboard doesn't just note when you press a key; it also notes when you release a key. Each separate key action is recorded by the keyboard, turned into an interrupt, and fed to the ROM-BIOS on command. To distinguish between the press and release of a key, there are separate scan codes for both actions.

That means that the ROM-BIOS is interrupted twice as often as you may have guessed. It also means that the ROM-BIOS knows whether a key is being held down or has been released, enabling it to know, for example, if you're typing in capital letters by holding the Shift key down.

The other thing you need to know about the keyboard is that the keyboard hardware governs the repeat-key action. The keyboard hardware keeps track of how long each key is held down and, if a key is held down for more than a certain period of time (about half a second), the keyboard hardware generates repeat-key scan codes at a regular interval. These repeat-key signals appear to the ROM-BIOS just like regular keystroke signals. If it needs to, however, the ROM-BIOS can distinguish keys held down by the absence of key release scan codes.

IBM calls this repeat-key action the Typematic feature. If you want, you can change the initial delay and the repeat rate by using the DOS MODE command like this:

```
MODE CON RATE=r DELAY=d
```

For this command, r is a number between 1 (slow) and 32 (fast), and d is a number between 1 (short delay) and 4 (longer delay). Note that this command is not available with versions of DOS prior to 4.0 and does not work with most pre-PS/2 PCs.

What I've described so far is exactly how the standard PC family keyboards work. The older members of the PC family, however, use different keyboards. However, the older keyboards work in more or less the same way but have different layouts. This is discussed in the "Keyboard Differences" section later in this chapter.

Advanced Keyboard Functions

It's natural to think that keyboard information flows in only one direction. After all, you press the keys, and the data ends up in the computer. Actually, the keyboard system is a complex mechanism. Because keyboard information is passed back and forth to the main processor, the keyboard requires its own controller, just like any other I/O device. (Note that the low-end PS/2s, the models 25 and 30, do not have a separate keyboard controller, and the following discussion does not apply to them.)

The keyboard controller used with modern PC keyboards is called the 8402 and resides on the system board. The 8402 first was used with the PC AT where it acted primarily as a keyboard interface. With the PS/2s, the 8402 has an expanded role: it enhances the keyboard function by adding password security and controls a pointing device (such as a mouse) as well as the keyboard.

The PS/2s offer several variations of password security, all of them dependent on the keyboard. First, you can set a power-on password. This means that, when you turn on the computer, it doesn't start until you type in the correct password.

Second, you can set a keyboard password. This enables you to lock the keyboard without turning off the computer. When the keyboard is locked, it does not respond until you type in the correct keyboard password. This is useful if you have to leave your desk for a short time and want to ensure that no one can play around with your PC while you are gone.

Third, you can set a network server password. This is important when a PC is acting as a file server for a local area network. In such a case, the PC provides data to the network and must be left on, unattended, all the time. In this situation, you don't want people to be able to enter commands at the keyboard. You can set the PC so that the keyboard is locked but so that other computers on the network can access the hard disk. To unlock the keyboard, you type in the network server password.

Starting with the PS/2s, the keyboard controller can control a pointing device as well as the keyboard. Usually, this is a mouse, although it can be a touchpad, trackball, or special keyboard. To provide this support, the keyboard controller maintains a special serial interface for the pointing device.

Notice that the password and mouse controller keyboard features I've just described are available on IBM PS/2s, but they may or may not be available on non-IBM brand computers, even in the same class. In fact, other vendors offer other keyboard features that may or may not be available on the PS/2s. Gateway 2000, for example, supplies a keyboard with its machines that can be programmed for special key functions, including keyboard-level macros.

As you can see, the keyboard has a great deal more functionality than most people think. To help you understand this, table 15.1 summarizes the keyboard-type services that the BIOS provides for programs with the help of the keyboard controller.

Table 15.1. *BIOS Keyboard Services*

Service	Description
Keyboard identification	Find out the keyboard ID number. (Different keyboard types have different ID numbers.)
Scan codes	Find out if any scan codes are available from the keyboard buffer or if it is empty. Read scan codes from the keyboard buffer. Write scan codes to the keyboard buffer, just as if those keys had been pressed by the user. (This is useful if a program wants to simulate the pressing of keys on your behalf.)
Status keys	Find out the current status of the Insert, CapsLock, NumLock, and ScrollLock keys. Find out if one of the Shift, Alt, Ctrl, or SysReq keys is being pressed. Reinitialize the keyboard and turn off NumLock, CapsLock, and ScrollLock. Find out the current state of NumLock, CapsLock, and ScrollLock. Set NumLock, CapsLock, and ScrollLock off or on.
Typematic support	Set the Typematic (repeat-key) delay and rate. Find out whether or not the keyboard supports changeable Typematic features (the older keyboards do not).
Security	Enable or disable the keyboard's capability to pass data to the system. Turn the keyboard password security system off or on. Set a specific keyboard password. Set which scan codes should be ignored when a password is being typed in. (For example, it shouldn't matter if you press a Shift key while you are typing a password.) Lock the keyboard until the correct password is typed in. Unlock the keyboard after the correct password has been typed in.

314

To see what some different keyboard types look like, refer to figures 15.1, 15.2, and 15.3. These are fairly standard, IBM offerings that are duplicated by a number of computer and keyboard manufacturers. There's no need to study these samples too closely. Just look at the general shape and layout. The fact is that no two keyboards are the same. If you sit down to a computer keyboard other than your own, you will find yourself groping for one or two keys. (This is true even if the keyboard is from the same manufacturer as yours but not produced with a month or so of yours because designs are refined constantly.) There are various models of keyboards even within the same computer line, and the keyboard supplier sometimes changes the design even for the same model number.

Figure 15.1. The enhanced keyboard. (Photo courtesy of IBM.)

Figure 15.2. The space-saving keyboard. (Photo courtesy of IBM.)

Figure 15.3. *The host-connected keyboard. (Photo courtesy of IBM.)*

Keyboard Differences

There are three principal keyboard designs used with PS/2 computers. The most common is the standard keyboard shown in figure 15.1. IBM calls this the enhanced keyboard. This name was given when the keyboard was first introduced (with the last model of the PC AT computer). The name refers to the new features this keyboard offered compared with the oldest PC keyboards.

The original keyboard that came with the PC and PC XT and a second version that came with the first PC AT preceded the enhanced keyboard. Although most PCs sold these days use the enhanced keyboard, you may run into an older machine with one of the PC or PC AT keyboards. For this reason, I have made sure that the sample keyboard programs in this chapter and in Appendix C work with all the variations.

And, of course, there are many non-IBM vendors that supply keyboards of their own design. Some of these, as I said, include programmable features. Other keyboards are hybrids of the old-style and the enhanced keyboard. They may, for example, have a set of function keys along the top of the keyboard plus a set of function keys at the left of the keyboard. Other designs may include additional keypads or cursor movement keys and some vendors frequently duplicate some frequently used keys such as the asterisk (*) or backslash (\ ). Individual placement of keys varies from keyboard to keyboard and from brand to brand

In addition to the enhanced keyboard and its variations, another current keyboard is the space-saving keyboard shown in figure 15.2. This keyboard is similar to an enhanced keyboard without the numeric keypad. The design was created for people who can do without the keypad and want a smaller keyboard. The space-saving keyboard comes with the smallest PS/2, the model 25, and can be used with other PS/2s.

The final keyboard design is the host-connected keyboard shown in figure 15.3. This is used with PS/2 systems that are connected to a host mainframe computer. The keyboard looks like the one that comes with the IBM 3270 terminal—the terminal usually used to connect to IBM mainframes.

How Scan Code Works

When the ROM-BIOS's keyboard interrupt handler springs into action, it receives one of the scan codes from the keyboard and must interpret that code. The ROM-BIOS quickly goes through several stages of analysis to discover how it should interpret and what it should do about the key action. First, it tests to see if the key action applies to one of the shift-type keys—the left and right Shift, Alt, and Ctrl keys. If so, the ROM-BIOS makes a note of the shift state because this affects the interpretation of any action that follows. Next, the ROM-BIOS tests to see if the key action is one of the toggle keys—the CapsLock, NumLock, ScrollLock, and Ins keys. The toggle keys, like the shift keys, affect the meaning of other keys, but the action is different. The shift keys apply only when they are held down, and the toggle keys apply depending upon whether they are toggled on or off.

For both the shift and toggle keys, the ROM-BIOS must keep track of the current state of these keys. This record is kept in two bytes of low memory. Each of the bits in these two bytes separately records one part of the keyboard status, recording if one of the keys is pressed or whether one of the toggle states is on or off. You can inspect and play with these keyboard status bits using the KEYBITS program listed in Appendix C. KEYBITS demonstrates how the keyboard status is recorded and shows you some surprising things about the information that the ROM-BIOS tracks.

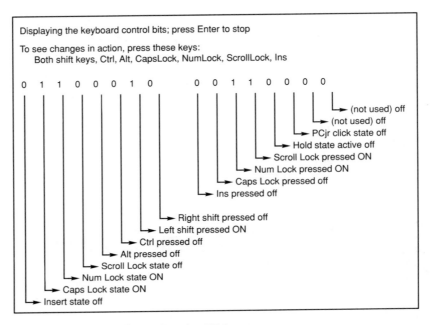

Figure 15.4. *Keyboard status bits of an IBM system.*

You see, for example, that the ROM-BIOS keeps separate track of the left and right Shift keys and whether the toggle keys are pressed. Experimenting with KEYBITS tells you a lot about how the ROM-BIOS works together with the keyboard. Using the KEYBITS program, you can find out the status of the various bits, as shown in figure 15.4.

There is another memory location that is used only with newer keyboards. This location stores the bits that tell whether or not the right Alt or Ctrl key has been pressed. These keys do not appear on the old-style keyboards. Because the KEYBITS sample program was designed to work on all keyboards, it does not test these bits. You may want to extend the program to do so.

After the ROM-BIOS has taken care of the shift and toggle keys, it needs to check for special keys and key combinations, such as Ctrl-Alt-Del, which reboots the computer, and the Pause key. I discuss these special keys and key combinations in the next section.

About Ctrl-Alt-Del, Pause, PrintScreen, and More

The keyboard ROM-BIOS routines do more than supervise the raw keyboard input and translate it into meaningful characters. They also oversee some built-in features of the PC family.

The three best-known features that the keyboard routines invoke are the system reboot (invoked by the Ctrl-Alt-Del key combination), print screen (Shift-PrintScreen), and system pause (Pause). (On the old keyboards, print screen was invoked by pressing Left Shift-Asterisk, and the system pause was invoked by pressing Ctrl-NumLock.)

Both reboot and print screen are services that always are available to any program that wants to invoke them. Print screen, for example, is invoked by issuing an interrupt 5. In the case of these two services, the keyboard routines simply provide the user with a way of getting at a service that normally only is available to a program.

Pause, however, is a special feature peculiar to the keyboard ROM-BIOS. When the keyboard routines recognize this key combination, the ROM-BIOS makes a note of it and goes into a never-ending, do-nothing loop, effectively suspending the operation of any program running. When this pause state is in effect, the machine is not locked up, and it continues to respond to any hardware interrupts that occur, such as disk and timer interrupts. However, when those interruptions are completed, control passes back to the keyboard routine, which refuses to return control to the program that has been suspended. Only when you press one of the PC's regular keys does the ROM-BIOS reset its pause bit and return the microprocessor to active duty. If you run the KEYBITS program, you can see the pause bit that the ROM-BIOS uses to keep track of this state. However, KEYBITS can't show the pause bit set because, when this bit is set, no program, including KEYBITS, can run.

Finally, if a key action passes through all that special handling, it means that the key is an ordinary one and can be assigned a meaning—that is, if the action is the key being pressed and not released. Releasing a key ordinarily means nothing unless the key is one of the special shift or toggle keys. When you press an ordinary key, the ROM-BIOS recognizes it and produces a keyboard character in the ordinary sense, such as the A key. To give an ordinary key meaning, though, the ROM-BIOS must translate the key into its character code. This is the point at which the A key becomes the letter A. In this translation process, the shift states are taken into account to distinguish letter a from A and so forth.

When a keystroke is translated, it can have one of two sets of meanings. The first is one of the ordinary ASCII characters, such as A or Control-A (ASCII code 1). The second is for the PC's special keys, such as the function keys. These keys, which include the function keys, the cursor keys, and the Home key, have special codes that distinguish them from the ordinary ASCII character keys.

The Alt-Numeric Trick

There is one more special trick that the keyboard ROM-BIOS routines perform that many PC users don't know about. I call it the Alt-numeric trick.

Most of what you want to type is right there on the keyboard in plain sight—the letters of the alphabet and so forth. And, much of the more exotic stuff can be keyed in by combining the Ctrl key with the alphabetic keys; for example, Ctrl-Z produces the ASCII code 26, which is used as an end-of-file marker for text files. But, you can't key in every item in the PCs character set that way. For example, if you wanted to key in the box-drawing characters that you saw in Chapter 14, you could not do that.

To make it possible for you to key in virtually anything, the ROM-BIOS provides a special way to enter any of the characters with ASCII codes 1 through 255. Oddly, though, you can't key in ASCII code 0 in any way.

To key in the ASCII codes 1 through 255, hold down the Alt key and then key in the ASCII code number. You enter the code in decimal and must use the numeric keys on the right side of the keyboard, not the number keys on the top row. When you key in a character this way, the ROM-BIOS makes a note of it and calculates the code number you keyed in. When you release the Alt key, it generates an ASCII character just as if you had pressed a single key that represented that ASCII character.

To try it yourself, you can use the ASCII code for capital A, which is 65. Hold down the Alt key, press and release 6 and then 5 on the keypad, and then release the Alt key. The letter A should appear on your screen, just as if you had typed in a capital A.

This special scheme works under most, but not all, circumstances. BASIC (and many applications programs such as graphics-oriented word processors or drawing programs that take over control of the keyboard) changes the keyboard operation, so it doesn't work. However, under most circumstances, you have access to this special ROM-BIOS facility.

To accommodate both the plain ASCII codes and the PC's special codes, the ROM-BIOS records each key character as a pair of bytes. If the character at hand is an ASCII character, the first of the two bytes is non-zero and holds the ASCII character. (In this case, the second character can be ignored. It generally holds the scan code of the key that was pressed.) The special PC characters are identified by a zero in the first byte. When the first byte is zero, the second byte contains the code identifying which of the special key characters is present.

BASIC gives you access to these two-byte keyboard codes with the INKEY$ function. With it, you can inspect the keyboard codes. The little program below shows you how. Just run this in BASIC and start pressing keys. The Enter key stops the program.

```
100  CLS
110  FALSE = 0
120  TRUE = 1
130  FOR I = 1 TO 10 : KEY I, "" : NEXT
140  DONE = 0
150  WHILE DONE = FALSE
160    K$ = INKEY$
170    L = LEN(K$)
180    IF L = 1 THEN PRINT "ASCII Character "; ASC (LEFT$(K$,1))
190    IF L = 2 THEN PRINT "Special Key Code "; ASC (RIGHT$(K$,1))
200  IF K$=CHR$(13) THEN DONE = TRUE
210  WEND
```

Here is the same program in QBasic:

```
DO
  K$ = INKEY$
  L = LEN(K$)
  IF L = 1 THEN
    PRINT "ASCII character  "; ASC(LEFT$(K$, 1))
  ELSEIF L = 2 THEN
    PRINT "Special key code "; ASC(RIGHT$(K$, 1))
  END IF
LOOP WHILE K$ <> CHR$(13)
```

After a real keystroke has been recognized and translated into its two-byte meaning, it's stored in the ROM-BIOS's keyboard buffer. This is the second time that the keyboard information is stored in a buffer—once in the keyboard's internal memory and then in the ROM-BIOS's storage area. The ROM-BIOS has a buffer large enough to store 32 characters. If it overflows, the ROM-BIOS issues the complaining beep on the speaker to which experienced PC users are accustomed and then throws away the latest key data.

After key actions have been received and translated into meaningful characters by the ROM-BIOS, they are available for programs to use. Programs can either take them directly from the ROM-BIOS, using the ROM-BIOS keyboard services, or get them from DOS, using the DOS keyboard services, which indirectly takes them from the ROM-BIOS. Either way, programs end up using the keyboard characters that have been constructed by the ROM-BIOS from key actions.

That, anyway, is the way things work when things proceed in a straightforward way. However, the whole elaborate scheme for processing keystrokes that I've described so far is intended to enable programs to sidestep the normal keyboard operation and start pulling rabbits out of hats. Next you see how some of that is done.

Keyboard Tricks

The PC's design enables programs to work with the keyboard in many, many ways. Even when a program isn't doing anything exotic, it has a choice between two ways of obtaining its keyboard data: either obtaining it directly from the ROM-BIOS or getting it through the DOS services. However, those certainly aren't the only ways a program can come by keyboard information.

I can't give you an exhaustive rundown of keyboard tricks for many reasons. One is that ingenious programmers are inventing new keyboard tricks all the time. The biggest reason is that the tricks are far too technical. They are advanced programmer's tricks that have nothing to do with the goal of this book, which is to help you understand the PC family. However, more and more, users find themselves using programs that are based on keyboard tricks, and it's very worthwhile to know the basics of how they work.

There are a number of unusual ways in which a program can respond. One of them is indirectly demonstrated in the KEYBITS program. Any program can monitor the keyboard status bytes and act accordingly. Here's an example:

```
10  DEF SEG = 0
20  PRINT "Please press both shift keys at once!"
30  WHILE PEEK (&H417) MOD 4 <>3 WEND
40  PRINT "Thank you."
```

Here is the same program in QBASIC:

```
DEF SEG = 0
PRINT "Please press both shift keys at once!"
WHILE PEEK(&H417) MOD 4 <> 3: WEND
PRINT "Thank you!"
```

This code enables a program to treat the shift-type keys in a special way. While ordinary programs have no good reason to do something like that, I'm not talking about ordinary treatment of the keyboard. Often the designers of game programs want to do something rather special, particularly with the shift keys. For example, a pinball program may want to use the right and left Shift, Alt, or Ctrl keys to control the right and left pinball flippers. To do that, the program must recognize when either of those keys is held down, which it can do simply by monitoring the keyboard status bits.

One of the most interesting types of programs used on PCs is the memory-resident programs that sit, inactive, in the computer's memory until they are activated with a special key combination. I will show you some of the ways that this can be done.

Recall from Chapter 3 that the PC has an internal clock that ticks about 18 times a second. The clock tick is made audible, so to speak, by a special clock-tick interrupt, interrupt 8. Normally, the ROM-BIOS receives that interrupt and uses it to update its time-of-day record. However, the ROM-BIOS also makes the ticking of the clock available to programs by generating another interrupt, interrupt 28 (hex 1C), which does nothing unless a program has set up an interrupt vector to receive it. If a program has set up such a vector, it is activated 18 times each second (or as many times per second as there are clock ticks).

Consider how a memory-resident program might use this technique to spring into action. Say that the program is waiting for you to press a particular combination of keys. One way the program could do that simply is to use the timer interrupt to give it a frequent chance to check the keyboard status bits to see if you have both keys pressed (similar to the way the sample BASIC program above checks for shift keys). If the bits are not set, the program simply returns control from the timer interrupt, and very little time has been wasted. However, if the bits are set, the program can keep running, performing its special magic.

In this example, the timer interrupt does not interfere in any way with the normal flow of keyboard data. Instead, it makes use of the timer interrupt and the keyboard system's willingness to enable a program to see the state of the shift keys.

That, however, is far from the only way a program can make special use of the keyboard. For even more exotic operations, a program can interpose itself in the middle of the keyboard data flow so that it can monitor, and possibly modify, the information.

If a program wants to take control of the keyboard or at least know exactly what's going on in the keyboard, it can interpose itself in the path of the keyboard hardware interrupt simply by placing an interrupt vector pointing to the program in place of the standard vector that directs keyboard interrupts to the ROM-BIOS. Then, when the keyboard causes a hardware interrupt, the new program, instead of the ROM-BIOS, sees the interrupt.

There are two main things that such a program might do. One simply is to take full control of the keyboard data so that the ROM-BIOS never sees it. This can be done by a program that wants to take ruthless and total control. Most programs that intervene in the keyboard data process, though, aren't interested in stopping the flow of information from the keyboard to the ROM-BIOS; they merely want to monitor it and, when appropriate, modify it. This sort of program inspects the keyboard data as it goes by, but generally permits the normal flow of information. That's how most keyboard-enhancing programs work. They step in to monitor and modify the keyboard data. To do that, they may have to replace the ROM-BIOS processing programs with their own program steps, but they don't stop the processing of the keyboard data in the way in which the ROM-BIOS normally does.

When you look at the wide selection of software available for the PC family, you find many programs that treat the keyboard in special ways, and if you look under their surfaces, you find different degrees of programming. What I've discussed concerning memory-resident programs represents the extreme case. There are, however, much less radical, but still special, ways to handle keyboard data.

Consider the example of Framework. Framework makes special use of the so-called gray plus and gray minus keys, the plus and minus keys that are on the far right side of the keyboard. In an ordinary program, there is no difference between these plus and minus keys and the plus and minus keys located in the top row of the keyboard. However, Framework (as well as WordPerfect for DOS and other programs) uses these gray keys to perform a special operation. Framework uses these keys to move up or down a logical level within its data scheme. To do that, however, Framework must be able to recognize the difference between the gray plus and the regular plus key. You might be tempted to think that Framework would have to tinker with the keyboard data, but it doesn't.

As you saw earlier, when the ROM-BIOS presents keyboard data to a program, it presents it as a two-byte code in which the first byte indicates the ASCII code of the character data. Whether you press the gray plus key or the other plus key, this byte of information from the ROM-BIOS is the same (ASCII code 43). However, the second byte that the ROM-BIOS makes available to the program reports the scan code of the key that was pressed, so it is very easy for a program like Framework to tell the difference between the gray plus and the regular plus key. It also easily can tell when you generate the plus code by using the Alt-numeric scheme that I described earlier in this chapter.

Framework can respond to the special gray plus and minus keys simply by making full use of the standard information that's available, without having to perform any special magic or interfere with the operation of the ROM-BIOS or the flow of keyboard information.

That's an important thing to know because people often assume that it's necessary to use special and potentially disruptive tricks to accomplish special objectives in programs. This example illustrates that it is possible to accomplish what you need to accomplish without breaking out of the standard conventions that keep PCs working smoothly.

Some Things To Try

1. For the toggle keys, like the CapsLock key, the ROM-BIOS keeps track not only of the current toggle state but also of whether the key is pressed. Even though programs have no normal use for this information, there is a simple logical reason why the ROM-BIOS records it. Can you discover why?

2. The scheme used to separate the PC's special character codes from the ASCII codes works quite well, but it has one technical flaw. Can you find it? How could you correct it?

3. There are some ways (though devious) in which a program can detect the keyboard pause state. Can you imagine how it might be done?

4. Earlier, I discussed the data areas that show which shift-type keys have been pressed. The KEYBITS program in Appendix C accesses the data area at locations 417 and 418 (hex). This program distinguishes between the left and right Shift keys but not between the left and right Alt and Ctrl keys.

   The BIOS keeps another data area at location 496 (hex) that shows whether or not the right Alt or Ctrl key has been pressed. If the right Alt key has been pressed, bit 3 is set on; if the right Ctrl key is pressed, bit 2 is set on. (The bits are numbered so that the rightmost bit is 0.)

   Modify the KEYBITS program so that it checks the data area at location 496 (hex) to distinguish between the two Alt and Ctrl keys.

16 Data!

I n this chapter, I introduce you to the basics of computer data and the main data formats that the PC uses. When I'm done, you should have a clear foundation for understanding what the PC really works with—data!

Bits, Bytes, and Characters

The starting point of computer data, the smallest, most fundamental unit, is called a bit. The word *bit* is a contraction for binary digit. Everyone is familiar with the 10 decimal digits, 0 through 9, used to express the numbers with which we work. Binary digits, bits, are similar, but there are only two different values, 0 and 1.

The bits 0 and 1 represent off and on, false and true, and no and yes. Inside the computer, these values actually are represented by the presence or absence of voltage. When voltage is present at a given location, that location is interpreted as holding the value 1; when no voltage (or a relatively lower voltage, sometimes) is present, that location is interpreted as holding the value 0. These 1s and 0s also have the obvious numerical meaning; the bit value 0 really does mean zero, and 1 does mean one. As I mentioned in Chapter 1, it is the concept of the bit that makes information-handling machines (computers) possible. Because it's practical to make electronic machines that work with on/off signals at great speed, it's possible to make machines that work with information that process data. It all depends, however, on the capability to match information that's meaningful with the model of information with which the computer can work. And that depends on the capability to construct real information out of the simple bits of 0 and 1.

Commonsense and some heavy mathematical theory both indicate that a bit is the smallest possible chunk of information. Bits serve as building blocks that enable the construction of larger and more meaningful amounts of information. By themselves, bits usually aren't of much interest, and only on occasion do I talk about individual bits in this book. It's when bits are strung together into larger patterns that something useful and interesting is made.

The most important and interesting collection of bits is the byte. A byte is eight bits taken together as a single unit. Bytes are important because they are the main practical unit of computer data. You undoubtedly know that the memory capacity of a computer and the storage capacity of a disk are measured in bytes. (Large numbers of bytes are measured in kilobytes, megabytes, and gigabytes, which I discuss shortly.)

That's because the byte is really the main unit of data; a bit may be the smallest grain of sand of computer data, but the byte is the brick, the real building block of data. Although computers can work with larger aggregates of bytes and get into the bits in a byte, they are designed to manipulate and work with bytes.

A byte contains eight bits, which means that there are eight individual 0 or 1, off or on, settings in each byte. Therefore, if eight bits each have two settings (0 and 1), then the number of possible distinct combinations of bit settings in a byte is 2^8, which is 256. Thus, there are 256 different values, or bit combinations, that a byte can have. This number is important; you see it again and again, so you need to remember it. (Remember in Chapter 14 that I said there were 256 basic elements in the PC character or symbol set. Now you see the reason for this seemingly arbitrary number.)

Most of the time, you won't be interested in anything smaller than a byte. However, there will be times when I need to refer to the individual bits in a byte—particularly when I get into some of the more technical matters. I give a brief introduction to this level of computer logic in the next section.

The Bits in Bytes and Words

Before you can examine the bits in a byte, you need a way of referring to them. This is done by numbering them from the far right, or least significant, bit starting with the 0, as shown in table 16.1. This method of specifying numbers is called binary (I already have talked about decimal and hexadecimal numbers in previous chapters). *Bi* means two, and there are only two values possible in this numbering system. The more familiar decimal system has 10 digits (0 through 9), and hexadecimal uses 16 numbers (0 through 9 and A through F).

Table 16.1. *Binary Bit Pattern and Values*

Bit Pattern	Bit Position	Numeric Value	Power of 2
00000001	0	1	2^0
00000010	1	2	2^1

continues

Table 16.1. *continued*

Bit Pattern	Bit Position	Numeric Value	Power of 2
00000100	2	4	2^2
00001000	3	8	2^3
00010000	4	16	2^4
00100000	5	32	2^5
01000000	6	64	2^6
10000000	7	128	2^7

It may seem odd to number the bits from the right and to start numbering them from 0, but there is a good reason for doing this. When interpreting the numeric value of a byte and the bits in it, the bit number is the power of 2 that corresponds to the numeric value of the bit. For example, bit 3 has a numeric value of 8, and 23 is 8.

A similar scheme applies when you're looking at two bytes that make up a word. (A word is 16 bits [two bytes] in some computers and 32 bits [four bytes] in others. In fact, as processors get more powerful, there is talk about 64-bit [eight-byte] words.) Instead of numbering the bits in the individual bytes or a word separately, they are numbered together: 0 through 15, 0 through 31, and so on.

A byte inside a computer is raw data that can be used for anything. Two of the most important things that you do with your computer is work with numbers and manipulate written text like the words you are reading here. Bytes are the building blocks of both numbers and text (character) data.

There is nothing fundamental about a byte, or any other collection of data, that makes it either numeric or text. Instead, it is simply a matter of what you want to do with your computer. If you're working with numbers, then the bytes in the computer are treated as numbers, and the bit patterns in the bytes are given a numerical interpretation. On the other hand, when you work with text information, the bytes are interpreted as characters that make up the written text information. Each byte represents one character of text.

Basically, bytes work as either numbers or characters, depending on what program you are using. The same pattern of bits could be, for example, the letter A or the number 65, depending on what you are doing.

Most of the rest of this chapter discusses how bytes can be used as numbers and characters and how several bytes taken together can be treated as more complicated numbers or strings of text characters.

By the way, when I refer to a computer as an 8-, 16-, or 32-bit computer, I am talking about the amount of data it can deal with in a single gulp. The PC family members are 16-, 32-, or 64-bit computers, depending on which processor they use (this is discussed in Chapter 3). Despite this, most of the time computers and the programs that make them go handle data in individual bytes. Besides, even machines based on the 32-bit 386 and 486 processors still handle data 16 bits at a time in real mode, which is what DOS runs under.

Finally, look at four more basic terms concerning computer data: the kilobyte (KB), the megabyte (MB), the gigabyte (GB), and the terabyte (TB).

It always is handy to be able to talk about things in round numbers, particularly when you're dealing with large quantities. Computers deal with large numbers of bytes, so people started expressing these values in round numbers, which are an approximation of the actual binary value. The most common of these terms is the kilobyte, which is 2^{10}, or 1,024. The *kilo* in kilobyte comes from the metric term for thousand. In a computer context, however, kilobyte represents 1,024, not 1,000, bytes. When you hear people talking about 64KB, they mean 64×1,024, or 65,536, bytes.

Similarly, a megabyte is roughly one million bytes. To be exact, a megabyte represents 2^{20}, or exactly 1,048,576, bytes. The sizes of computer hard drives often are expressed in megabytes. The last two terms have become important in recent years as disk sizes have grown. Gigabyte refers to 2^{30}, or 1,073,741,824, bytes. Terabyte refers to 2^{40}, or 1,099,511,627,776, bytes. These relationships are summarized in table 16.2.

Table 16.2. *Number Suffixes and Powers of Two*

Term	Power of 2	Approximate Value
1 kilobyte	2^{10}	one thousand
1 megabyte	2^{20}	one million
1 gigabyte	2^{30}	one billion
1 terabyte	2^{40}	one trillion

Now you're ready to move on to learn more about computer data. You can learn about the fearsome hexadecimal system and go on to explore numeric data in greater detail.

Learning about Hexadecimal

If you really want to understand the inner workings of the PC or any other computer, you need a good working grasp of the computer-oriented number system known as the hexadecimal (or hex) system. Understanding hex certainly isn't necessary for you to be a very capable (even expert) user of the PC. However, if you want to comprehend the machine and use some of the more sophisticated tools for the PC, including the DEBUG program that is a part of DOS, you must have a working knowledge of hex.

The smallest building blocks of computer data are bits that individually represent the values 0 and 1. If you write computer data in its binary, or bit, form, you get a rather long string of 0s and 1s. Just writing out a single byte in binary form is rather long—01010101, for example. Because each byte, or character, contains 8 bits, it takes 88 bits to write out the pattern that represents the word hexadecimal (a typical floppy disk can store approximately 15 million bits). When you want to write out the exact data in the computer, you need a way to represent all the bits, a way that isn't as long and tedious as binary. This is where hexadecimal comes in.

Hex, simply put, is a practical solution to a tedious problem: expressing the exact data that's coded inside the computer. Hex is a shorthand for binary notation, in which one hexadecimal digit represents four binary digits (bits). If you look at bits individually, they have two values, 0 and 1. If you grouped them in pairs, there would be four possible combinations of bit values: 00, 01, 10, and 11. Taking that idea two steps further, if you organize four-bit groups, there are 16 possible patterns, starting with 0000 and ending with 1111. (The math of it is that the number of distinct combinations of the two-bit values taken four at a time is 2^4, or 16.)

In the decimal numbering system, you use 10 symbols, 0 through 9, to represent 10 digit values. You then combine these decimal digits to make larger numbers, like 100. The same principle applies to binary notation; you can combine the two-bit symbols, 0 and 1, to make larger numbers. This same idea applies to hex, but instead of the two binary digits or the 10 decimal digits, hex uses 16 hexadecimal digits to represent 16 values. The 16 hex digits are 0 through 9 (which have the same numerical meaning as the decimal digits 0 through 9) plus six additional hex digits, which are written using the letters A, B, C, D, E, and F. These last six hex digits, A through F, represent the six values after the value nine: A is 10, B is 11, and so on, to F, which has a value of 15.

Each of the 16 hex digits represents a value between 0 and 15; it also represents a pattern of four bits. The hex digit A, for example, represents the bit pattern 1010, and F represents 1111. Table 16.3 shows a list of the 16 hex digits, their decimal equivalents, and their binary equivalents.

Table 16.3. *The 16 Hex Digits*

Hex Digit	Decimal Equivalent	Binary Equivalent
0	0	0000
1	1	0001
2	2	0010
3	3	0011
4	4	0100
5	5	0101
6	6	0110
7	7	0111
8	8	1000
9	9	1001
A	10	1010
B	11	1011
C	12	1100
D	13	1101
E	14	1110
F	15	1111

There are two ways to view these hex digits (and the four bits that each represents), and it's important to understand the distinction. It's a distinction that applies to all the computer data that you view. When you consider a hex digit, say B, you might be interested in the numerical value that it represents (which is 11) or the pattern of bits that it represents (1011). Bear in mind that whether you're talking about hex, bits, or any other computer data, the same data takes on different meanings, depending on how you look at it. And, at the same time, regardless of how you (or an application program) interprets the data, it is stored in the computer only one way, as a pattern of 1s and 0s.

One question that might come to mind is, "Why hex?" It's easy to understand that bit notation is too long and clumsy and that something more compact is needed to express several bits at a time. But why hex? Why four bits at a time, when that leads to using the unfamiliar digits A through F? The answer is that hex is a reasonable compromise between what's closest to the machine and what's practical for people to work with. Because the most common unit of computer data is the byte, hex can conveniently represent all the bits in a byte with two hex digits, each one representing four of the byte's eight bits. Hex fits neatly into the fundamental scheme of computer data.

So far I've talked about individual hex digits, but you also need to work with larger numbers expressed in hex. Later in the book, I talk about the memory addresses used in the PC family that use four- and even five-digit hex numbers. Therefore, you need to have a sense of the size of larger hex numbers and be able to do some arithmetic with them.

Hex arithmetic, of course, works just like decimal arithmetic, but the values of the numbers are different. The largest decimal number is 9, and the number after it, 10, is written using the individual digits 1 and 0. The same principle applies in hex (or any other number base). The largest hex digit is F (which has a value of 15), and the number after it is written 10, which has a value of 16; next comes 11 (which is 17), and so on.

Two hex digits are all you need to express all the possible bit combinations in a byte. With eight bits in a byte, there are 2^8, or 256, bit patterns (00000000 through 11111111) to a byte. In hex, the binary 00000000 and 11111111 are hex 00 and FF. The first four bits are represented by the first hex digit, and the last four are represented by the second hex digit.

You can use table 16.3 to translate between any pattern of bits and its hex equivalent. That's what you do when you're just looking at hex and bits as arbitrary data.

When you want to interpret hex digits as a number (which you do from time to time in this book), you need to know how to convert between hex and decimal as well as how to do simple arithmetic in hex.

First, I show you how to evaluate a hex number. It helps to pause and think of how you evaluate decimal numbers, say 123. The number 123 really means 3 + 20 + 100. Each position has a value that's 10 times higher than the place to the right. The same principle works in hex, but the multiplier is 16, not 10. So, if you interpret 123 as a hex number, it's $3 + 2 \times 16 + 1 \times 16^2$ (which is 256). Thus, 123 in hex is equivalent to 291 in decimal. Table 16.4 lists the decimal equivalents for the round hex numbers from 1 to F0000.

Table 16.4. *Hex Value Table*

Hex	Decimal	Hex	Decimal
1	1	10	16
2	2	20	32
3	3	30	48
4	4	40	64
5	5	50	80
6	6	60	96
7	7	70	112
8	8	80	128
9	9	90	144
A	10	A0	160
B	11	B0	176
C	12	C0	192
D	13	D0	208
E	14	E0	224
F	15	F0	240

continues

335

Table 16.4. *continued*

Hex	Decimal	Hex	Decimal
100	256	9000	36864
200	512	A000	40960
300	768	B000	45056
400	1024	C000	49152
500	1280	D000	53248
600	1536	E000	57344
700	1792	F000	61440
800	2048	10000	65536
900	2304	20000	131072
A00	2560	30000	196608
B00	2816	40000	262144
C00	3072	50000	327680
D00	3328	60000	393216
E00	3584	70000	458752
F00	3840	80000	524288
1000	4096	90000	589824
2000	8192	A0000	655360
3000	12288	B0000	720896
4000	16384	C0000	786432
5000	20480	D0000	851968
6000	24576	E0000	917504
7000	28672	F0000	983040
8000	32768		

If you want to convert between decimal and hex manually, you can use table 16.4 to look up the equivalents. To convert, for example, the hex number F3A into decimal, look up the value of hex A (it's decimal 10), hex 30 (48), and hex F00 (3,840). Adding them, you get 3,898 as the decimal equivalent of hex F3A.

To convert decimal into hex, you work the other way, subtracting as you go. For example, to convert the decimal number 1,000,000 to hex, you look up the largest entry in the hex table that's not over the decimal number. In this case, it's hex F0000 at the end of the table. Subtract its decimal value (983,040) from the starting number and continue the process until there's nothing left. Then the series of hex numbers you subtracted combine to make the hex equivalent of the decimal number. In this case it is hex F4240.

Fortunately, there are tools that do the work of hex-to-decimal conversion, so you don't have to resort to this manual process. First, there are pop-up programs designed for programmers. Such programs usually can convert values and do arithmetic in hex, decimal, and binary. Second, there is BASIC, which comes free with DOS. Here are two little programs that demonstrate BASIC's capability to convert numbers between hex and decimal:

```
10   ' Convert hex to decimal
20   '
30   INPUT "Enter a new Number", X$
40   PRINT "The decimal equivalent is " ; VAL("&H"+X$)
50   GOTO 30
```

```
10   'Convert decimal to hex
20   '
30   INPUT "Enter a decimal number ", X
40   PRINT "The hex equivalent is "; HEX$(X)
50   GOTO 30
```

If you ever need to do any arithmetic with hex numbers, you can use a programming utility or use BASIC's capability to both do arithmetic and convert between decimal and hex. If you're forced to do hex arithmetic the hard way or just want to try your hand at it, type in the program HEXTABLE in Appendix C. When you run this program, it generates a handy conversion table.

Standard Numbers

Because numbers are so important to computers, you need to look at the kinds of numbers with which PCs can work. I start this section with the simple number formats that are part of the PC's basic repertoire of numbers, the numbers that the PC has a native capability to work with. In the next section, I look at some more exotic types of numbers that the PC can use when you stretch its skills.

You might be surprised to realize that the PC basically can work with only whole numbers (integers), and rather small numbers at that. The PC can work with only two varieties of numbers: one- and two-byte (one-word) integers.

Although today's PCs are 16-, 32-, or 64-bit machines, they operate in DOS in real mode (16-bit mode). That means the PC's built-in arithmetic skills can be applied only to single 8-bit bytes and 16-bit (two-byte) words. With the assistance of clever programs, the PC can work with larger numbers by combining two 16-bit words into a larger 32-bit number, for example. However, this can be done only with special software. When you're talking about the PC's natural skills, you're talking about only 8- and 16-bit arithmetic.

Just how big can 8- and 16-bit numbers be? Not very big really. As you already know from looking at 8-bit bytes, an 8-bit byte can have only 256 (2^8) distinct values. A 16-bit, 2-byte word can have 2^{16} (65,536) distinct values in all. That sets a rather tight limit on the range of numbers that you can work with using bytes and words. (If you want to explore 2-byte words or other longer integer formats, you need to know about back-word storage. See the "How Words Are Stored" section in Chapter 17.)

Each of these two sizes of integer can be interpreted in two ways, doubling the number of possible numeric formats. The two interpretations depend on whether you want to allow for negative numbers. If you don't have to work with negative numbers, the entire range of values of each of these two sizes of integers can be devoted to positive numbers. For a one-byte integer, the range of numbers can run from 0 to 255, using all 256 bit patterns. For a two-byte word, the range of positive integers is from 0 to 65,535.

On the other hand, if you need negative numbers as well, half of the range of values is devoted to negatives, and you can have numbers only half as large. In the case of bytes, the range of values is from -128 to +127; for words, the range is from -32,768 to +32,767. You don't get to choose the range, so you can't get a wider range of positive numbers by giving up some of the negative ones. (For more on negative numbers, see the following "How Negatives Are Represented" section.) Notice that the range of negative numbers is one greater than the range of positives (there is a -128 but no +128). That's just an odd by-product of the way negative numbers are handled. Table 16.4 summarizes the range of numbers handled by the four integer formats.

Table 16.4. *Range of Integer Formats*

Integer	1 Byte	2 Bytes
Unsigned	0 to 255	0 to 65,535
Signed	-128 to +127	-32,768 to +32,767

As mentioned before, the processor in your PC can do all of its standard arithmetic (add, subtract, multiply, and divide) on these four integer formats, but that is the extent of the basic calculating the PC can do.

As you might imagine, few programs can get along with just those four simple integer formats. BASIC, for example, uses three kinds of numbers. Only one of them, called integer in BASIC's terminology, is of these four formats (it's the signed two-byte word format). The other two, which BASIC calls single-precision and double-precision, have to be created by going beyond the PC's ordinary skills.

How Negatives Are Represented

Negative integers are represented inside the PC in a form known as two's-complement. It's a commonly used scheme in computers and is closely related to the borrow-and-carry tricks you were taught when you first learned to add and subtract. It's easiest to explain with an example done with decimal numbers that you make three digits long; that's analogous to the fixed length one- or two-byte binary numbers with which the PC calculates.

In the example three-digit decimal numbers, zero is written 000 and one as 001. If you subtract 001 from 001, you get 000. How can you subtract 001 again to get minus one? You can do it by borrowing from an imaginary one in the fourth place. Think of 000 (and all other positive numbers) as having a one in front that can be borrowed like this:

$$
\begin{array}{ll}
(1)000 & \text{zero} \\
\underline{-001} & \text{subtract one} \\
999 & \text{gives minus one}
\end{array}
$$

Thus, -1 is represented as 999; -2 is 998, and so on.

The positive numbers start at 000, 001, 002, and go up to 499. The negatives are 999 (-1), 998 (-2), and go down to 500, which really means -500. The same trick works with the binary numbers inside your computer.

Notice that the value of a number can depend on whether you interpret it as signed or unsigned. As a signed number, 999 means -1; as an unsigned number it means 999.

Hot Numbers

Most of your computing needs go beyond the simple integers that are native to the PC. Whether you're doing financial planning with a spreadsheet program, performing engineering calculations, or just balancing your checkbook, you need numbers more powerful than the integers discussed so far. Just dealing with money, the integers discussed so far couldn't handle anything more than $655.35 if you figure down to the penny. So you need some more numbers.

There are two ways that the PC can give you a wider range of numbers and two ways to calculate with those numbers. I look at the kinds of numbers first and then show you how those numbers can be calculated.

The first way to extend the range of numbers with which your PC can deal is simply to make longer integers. You already have seen one- and two-byte integers. You also can use integers of three, four, and more bytes. Anything is possible, but the most practical extra length of integer is four bytes, which gives you a range of numbers of about -2,000,000,000 to +2,000,000,000.

To handle fractional amounts and extremely long numbers, computers use a concept known as floating point. Floating point works like something you may have learned about in school called scientific or engineering notation. In this scheme, numbers are represented in two parts. One part represents the digits that make up the number; the other part indicates where the decimal point is located. Because the decimal point can be moved around freely, floating-point numbers can become very, very large (astronomical) or very, very small. Regardless of how large or small the number becomes, it remains accurate because the digits that determine accuracy, or precision, are independent of the numbers that specify where the decimal point is.

In the BASIC programming language, the style of numbers known as single- and double-precision are both floating-point formats. The difference between them is that double-precision has more digits of accuracy. Other programming languages use floating point, too. Spreadsheet programs also use floating point to represent their numbers because it gives them greater flexibility and greater precision in the calculations they perform.

The PC's number scheme can be extended in two ways: longer integers and floating point. As I mentioned, however, the PC's microprocessor, its brain, has the natural capability to work with only the four simple integer formats covered earlier. How do you get any arithmetic done in these extended formats? The answer is through software and hardware.

Software is the most common solution. Every programming language, including BASIC, and nearly every calculating program, including spreadsheets, contain program routines that can perform calculations on floating-point numbers or long integer formats. These subroutines use the PC's basic arithmetic and logic skills as building blocks to perform the more complex calculations necessary to work with these other number formats. This goes on at a cost, however. Although the PC can perform its own integer calculations very quickly—typically, for a 386 or 486, in a less than a millionth of a second—a floating-point subroutine takes perhaps 100 times as long to do an equivalent calculation simply because the subroutine has to perform its work using 100 elementary steps.

For many purposes, the speed of these software-based calculations is fast enough, but not as fast as it could be. To get more speed, you must look to a hardware solution.

The processor inside the PC has an optional companion, the coprocessor, designed for just one task: fast mathematical (floating-point) calculations. These components are members of the Intel 87 family of math coprocessors. The 486 and Pentium processors come with a built-in coprocessor so they have no need for the 87 family. When a coprocessor is installed and a program knows how to use it, the speed and accuracy of floating-point calculations can be improved enormously.

It's worth bearing in mind that many programs just don't do any floating-point calculations. Word processing programs, for example, have no use for floating-point numbers. These programs aren't slowed down by floating-point subroutines or sped up by the presence of an 87 coprocessor. (However, some of today's word processors include math or spreadsheet functions or links to external programs that handle numbers. In these cases a coprocessor could be used.) And, some programs that do perform floating-point calculations don't take advantage of a coprocessor. Older versions of BASIC, for example, ignore any coprocessor that might be present; spreadsheet programs, on the other hand, use the coprocessor whenever it can help.

Unlike integer formats (discussed in this chapter) and unlike the PC character set (discussed in Chapter 14), there are no universal standards for the kinds of longer integers and floating-point numbers that can be used by a program. Next, I look at some of the most common extended number formats.

First, I look at longer integers. Programs can work with any number of bytes to make a long integer, but one size is by far the most common: four-byte signed integers. These numbers can range from slightly over -2,000,000,000 to just over +2,000,000,000. Math coprocessors are designed to work with both four- and eight-byte integers, which get as large as nine billion billion. These coprocessors also can work with a special decimal integer format that holds 18 decimal digits, which is also in the billion billion range. This special decimal format is a unique example of a decimal orientation; everything else that your computer does is essentially binary rather than decimal.

Next, I look at what floating-point can do for you. The two most common sizes of floating-point numbers occupy four or eight bytes of storage, like BASIC's single- and double-precision formats. Four-byte, floating-point formats give the equivalent of about 6 decimal digits of accuracy, and eight-byte formats give about 16 digits of accuracy. The range (how large numbers can get) is in the neighborhood of 10^{38} power. Because there are several ways to code a floating-point number, there is some variety in the amount of precision and the range in size of floating-point numbers, so the figures I give are rough estimates. The 87 processors also can work with a slightly larger format that occupies ten bytes; it provides about 18 digits of accuracy.

The kind of numbers with which you can work depends on the kinds of programs you use. The discussion in this chapter applies to most programming languages, but specialty programs may have their own unique number formats. It's common, for example, for spreadsheet programs to use their own variations on the idea of floating-point numbers. This chapter should give you a clear idea of the kinds of hot numbers that can be at your disposal when you work with your computer.

Stringing Along

Character or text data (letters of the alphabet and so forth) are very important in your use of the computer. In fact, computers are used more for working with text data than with numeric data, which is ironic because computers are, first and foremost, fancy calculators. However, people have learned how to make these fancy calculators do a lot of useful work manipulating written text. For example, the words you are reading have been handled by a computer from the moment they were written. It's important to understand some of the fundamentals of how computers handle text data.

Text data is made up of individual characters, such as the letter A. Each letter is represented by a particular pattern of bits and occupies a byte of storage. A coding scheme is used to define the standard way of determining which pattern of bits represents which letter.

Individual characters aren't terribly useful until you put them together to form words and sentences. Similarly, inside the computer, groups of character bytes are more significant than individual bytes. String is the technical term used to describe a group of characters handled as a single entity. A string is a group of consecutive bytes that is treated as a unit.

All computer programming languages and many of the most important kinds of software, such as spreadsheet programs, work with strings of character data. Word processing programs are designed to work primarily with character strings.

Even though strings are important, there isn't a great deal to say about them. There are, however, a few key things that you ought to know, particularly about how they are stored and the limitations that are sometimes placed on what sort of string data you can use.

Inside the computer's memory and on the computer's disks, strings are stored just as commonsense indicates: the character bytes are recorded one right after another. That's nothing special. What is special about strings is that something has to tie them together. Earlier in the chapter, you learned that every kind of numeric data has a specific format that rigidly defines the size of the number—how many bytes it occupies. Strings, however, are special because they don't have any fixed length. Some are long; some are short. Still, something has to define a string's length to tie together the characters that make it up.

This is not done in any universal way. Different programs use their own methods and rules to define what a string is and what holds it together. Although I can't give you any universal rules that say exactly how strings are defined, I can discuss some of the most common methods to give you some insight into how programs work with strings and why the limitations on strings come about.

Programs define the length of a string in two main ways. One simply is to keep track of the length of the string as a number that is recorded separately from the string (usually this length-of-string number is placed just before the beginning of the string). Here's an example:

```
4This2is1a6string2of5words
```

As you can see, each word in the example is a separate string, and the number of character bytes in each word is recorded just before it. This is a very common technique for dealing with strings and determining how long they are. If you think about it, you realize that this method places an inherent limit on the length of any individual string. The number that represents the length of the string is recorded in a numerical format like the ones I discussed. The maximum number that format allows sets a limit on the length of the string.

It's very common for the length of a string to be recorded as a single unsigned byte, which can't be larger than 255. Many programs limit the length of the strings they work with to 255. (Sometimes the limit is a few less than 255 because one or two bytes may be needed for overhead.) The ordinary BASIC in your computer works this way, so strings in BASIC can't be over 255 characters; but compiled BASIC records its string lengths as two-byte words, so the string length for compiled BASIC can be over 32,000. Some word processing programs hold each line as a separate string and use a one-byte string length counter; these programs limit the length of a line to 255 characters.

There is another way to determine the size of a string that doesn't place any arbitrary limit on string length. With this technique, the length of the string isn't recorded; instead, the end of the string is marked with some sort of delimiter. Here's another example, using asterisks as delimiters:

```
This*is*a*string*of*words*
```

The delimiter is used to mark the end of the string, but is not considered part of the string itself. There are two delimiters that are widely used. The first is a zero-byte, a byte with all the bits off. (A zero-byte isn't a bad choice of delimiter because it is not normally used as an ordinary text character.) The second commonly used delimiter is a byte with a numeric code of 13. Thirteen is the code for a Carriage Return character, which is normally used to mark the end of a line of text. Because it's common to treat each line of text as a separate string, it makes sense to use the same byte code to mean both end of line and end of string.

One obvious disadvantage to using a special end-of-string delimiter code is that the string can't include that code value in the string. This may not be a major problem in most circumstances, but it is a disadvantage and a limitation of which you should be aware.

Some Things To Try

1. BASIC easily can convert numbers between hex and decimal as long as the numbers aren't any bigger than the equivalent of four hex digits. Try writing a program that converts larger numbers between hex and decimal.

2. Try your hand at some hex arithmetic. Add 1234 to ABCD. Subtract 1A2B from A1B2. Multiply 2A by 2 and by 3.

3. Can you figure out a way to test either the accuracy or range of numbers that a program can handle? Try writing a BASIC program that tests how large a number can become or how precisely a number is represented.

4. Analyze the problems inherent in the two ways of defining a string. Think of practical situations in which the limitations might matter. Can you think of a scheme that places no limit on the length or contents of a string? Are there any disadvantages to your scheme? Write a program in BASIC (or any other programmable software, such as a spreadsheet) that finds out how long a string can be by increasing a string character by character.

345

The Memory Workbench

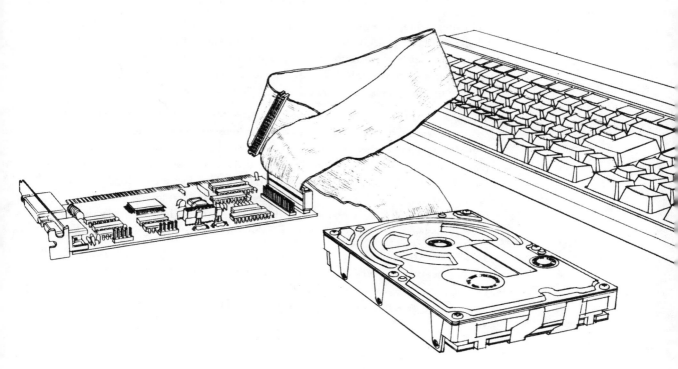

N ow it's time to get to know the computer's memory. In this chapter, I quickly look at what memory is and how data is stored in it. Then I look into the complex but fascinating details of how programs gain access to the memory. You see how the PC's designers subdivided the memory into different uses and then take a look at two kinds of additions to the PC's memory. This may sound like a lot, but it's all intriguing.

Memory Overview

You already know, from earlier parts of this book, most of the underlying ideas about the PC's memory, so I really don't need to introduce you to the fundamentals of computer memory. But, to help make sure that you're on the right track, I briefly pause to summarize the key things about computer memory. Then I dive into the really interesting details.

The computer's memory is a scratchpad where working information, which includes both program instructions and data, is kept while it is being worked on. For the most part, what's in the computer's memory is temporary working information (for the exception, see the discussion of read-only memory later in this chapter).

Computer memory is organized into units of bytes, each made up of eight bits. (See Chapter 16 for more details on how this works.) The same bit pattern can be seen as a number, a letter of the alphabet, or a particular machine language instruction, depending upon how you interpret it. The same memory bytes are used to record program instruction codes, numeric data, and alphabetic data.

While the computer's memory is divided into bytes, those bytes can be combined to create larger aggregates of information. One of the most important is the word, which is two bytes taken together to form a single 16-bit number. When four bytes are taken together to form a single 32-bit number, it's called a double-word. (Remember that the 386 and 486 series can work with 32-bit quantities. For an interesting sidelight on that, see the "How Words Are Stored" section.) When you interpret a series of bytes together as alphabetic text, it's called a character string. There are endless ways to combine bytes into meaningful data, but these are some of the most important.

To work with the computer's memory, each byte of the memory has an address, that is, a number that uniquely identifies it. The memory addresses are numbered, beginning with zero. The same numbers used as computer data also can be used to specify memory addresses, so the computer can use its capability to do arithmetic to find its way through its own memory. This integration of arithmetic, data, and memory addressing gives the computer astonishing power.

That's the essence of the computer's memory. Now, I take a closer look.

How Words Are Stored

If you plan to explore the computer's memory, want to work with assembly language, or, like me, just want to know everything you can about your computer, you need to know about what's whimsically called back-words storage.

When you write down either numbers or names, you put what's called the most significant part first. That's the part that matters the most when you arrange names or numbers in order. In the number 1776, the 1 is the most significant, or high-order, part; in the name California, the C is the most significant letter.

In PCs, it doesn't go exactly that way. For character string data, which is the format used to store names like California, the most significant letter is stored first, in the leftmost byte (the byte with the lowest address), just as you write it. Numbers, however, are stored the other way. For numbers that take up more than one byte (such as a 16-bit number), the least significant byte is stored first. In effect, the number you know as 1776 is stored in the computer as 6771. (Please don't take that example too literally for reasons you'll see in a moment.)

This way of storing data, with the least significant byte first, is called the little endian data format. (If the processor stored data with the most significant byte first, it would be called the big endian data format.) However, the term that is used more often is back-words. This term indicates that a word (a 16-bit, two-byte integer) has its bytes stored backward from what you might expect. This doesn't apply just to two-byte words; it also applies to longer integer formats, such as 32-bit, four-byte long integers. It also applies inside the complex bit coding used to represent floating-point numbers.

While PCs can work with any numeric format, the one that they use most is the two-byte word format. That's because 16-bit words are used in every aspect of the PC's memory addressing (as you'll see in more detail below) and because 16-bit words are the largest numbers that the PC's instruction set handles when the processor is in real mode.

To explain the idea of back-words storage, I gave the example of the (decimal) number 1776 written back-words as 6771. But that doesn't exactly tell you what's going on. Back-words storage concerns binary integers stored byte-by-byte in reverse order. When you see binary integers written down, you see them in hex notation, which uses two hex digits for each byte. For example, when you write it front-words, the decimal number 1776 in hex is 06F0. To write the same hex number back-words, don't reverse the order of the individual hex digits, reverse the bytes (which are represented by pairs of digits). Hex 06F0 back-words is F006 with the two hex pairs (06 and F0) reversed.

Knowing about this back-words storage is more than a matter of simple intellectual curiosity. Any time you work with computer data represented in hexadecimal, you must know whether you're seeing numbers represented front-words (the way you write them) or back-words (the way they actually are stored). Generally speaking, whenever data is formatted for the users consumption, it is in front-words order; whenever it's being shown as stored in the machine, it is in back-words order. You have to be careful not to get confused about which way you're seeing it.

Here's an example of how you may be shown a number in both forms. If you work with some assembly language, using either DEBUG or the assembler, and have an instruction to move the hex value 1234 into the AX register, you see something like the following:

```
B8 3412    MOV   AX,1234H
```

On the right side, you see the number in people-oriented, front-words form (1234); on the left side, you see the number as it actually is stored, back-words.

Getting into Memory

There's a messy little problem inside the PC's processor, a problem that makes it complicated for programs to find their way around the computer's memory. The problem centers around 16-bit arithmetic.

Remember that when you use DOS the processor is working in real mode (or perhaps virtual 86 mode). It is emulating an 8086, which means that it works best with 16-bit numbers, which can be no larger than 65,536. Because the computer uses numeric addresses to find its way through the memory, that suggests that the memory can't be larger than 64KB.

Experience has shown that 64KB is laughably too little memory for serious computer applications; as you know, many PCs are equipped with megabytes of memory. So how can you work your way into a larger memory and still use 16-bit numbers to access it?

The solution that Intel designed into the 8086 processor family involves segmented addresses. Segmented addresses are built by combining two 16-bit words in a way that enables them to address 1,048,576 bytes (1MB) of memory. To see how it's done, you have to look at two things: the arithmetic involved in combining the two words of a segmented address and the way these segmented addresses are handled in the processor.

The arithmetic involves what is called shifted addition, which enables you to create a 20-bit binary number (which goes up to 1,048,578) from two 16-bit numbers. Suppose that you have two 16-bit words, which, in hexadecimal, have the values ABCD and 1234. Remember that each hex digit represents four bits, so four hex digits (ABCD or 1234) represent 16 bits all together. Take one of these two numbers, say ABCD, and put a 0 at the end: ABCD0. In effect, this shifts the number over one hex place (or four binary places); you can say that it has multiplied the value of the number by 16. The number is now five hex digits (or 20 bits) long, which brings it into the million range. Unfortunately, it can't serve as a complete 20-bit memory address because it has a 0 at the end; it can represent only addresses that end in 0, which only are every 16th byte.

To complete the segmented addressing scheme, take the other 16-bit number (1234) and add it to the shifted number, like this:

$$
\begin{array}{r}
ABCD0 \\
+\ \underline{1234} \\
ACF04
\end{array}
$$

When you combine these two 16-bit numbers, you end up with a 20-bit number that can take on any value from 0 to 1,048,577. That's the arithmetic scheme that underlies the PC's capability to work with 1MB of memory using 16-bit numbers.

The two parts of this addressing scheme are the segment and offset parts. In this example, ABCD is the segment value, and 1234 is the offset value. The segment part specifies a memory address that is a multiple of 16—an address that has a hex 0 in its last place. These memory addresses that are multiples of 16 are called paragraph boundaries, or segment paragraphs.

The offset part of a segmented address specifies an exact byte location following the segment paragraph location. Because the 16-bit offset word can range from 0 to 65,535, the offset part of the segmented address enables you to work with 64KB of memory, all based on the same segment address.

There is a standard way of writing these segmented addresses, which you encounter often when you're dealing with technical material about the PC. It's done like this: ABCD:1234. The segment part appears first, then a colon, and then the offset part. If you do anything with assembly language or use the DEBUG program, you see plenty of segmented addresses written this way. If you look at the DEBUG listing that appears later in this chapter, you see segmented addresses in the right column.

Usually, addresses inside the computer's memory are referred to in their segmented form. Occasionally, however, you need to see them in their final form, with the two parts of the segmented address combined. Whenever you need to do that, they are called absolute addresses, so as not to be confused with segmented addresses. In the example of combining ABCD and 1234, ACF04 is the resulting absolute address.

That's the arithmetic behind the segmented addressing scheme. Now, how does it work inside the computer? The segment part of segmented addresses is handled entirely by a set of four special segment registers, which I mentioned in Chapter 6. Each of the four is dedicated to locating the segment paragraph for a particular purpose. The code segment (CS) register indicates where the program code is. The data segment (DS) register locates the program's main data. The extra segment (ES) register supplements the data segment, so that data can be shifted between two widely separated parts of memory. And, the stack segment (SS) register provides a base address for the computer's stack.

(As I mentioned in Chapter 3, the 386 and 486 series processors have two extra segment registers, FS and GS. These generally are not used by DOS programs which, for the most part, follow the rules of the 8086 architecture.)

Most of the time these segment registers are left unchanged, and programs waltz around within the base set by the segment paragraph. Detailed addressing is done by working with the offset part of the address. While the segment part of an address can be used only when it's loaded into one of the four segment registers, there is much greater flexibility in how offsets can be used. A program can get its address offsets from a variety of registers, including the general-purpose registers AX, BX, etc., and the indexing registers SI and DI. Offsets also can be embedded in the program's machine language instructions or calculated by combining the contents of registers and the machine language instructions. There is a great deal of flexibility in the way offsets can be handled.

The way that the PC's processor uses segmented addresses has many practical implications for the way programs work. For an important aside on that, see the "Banging into 64KB Limits" section.

Fortunately, the tedious details of working with segmented addresses are kept out of the user's way as much as possible. For the most part, only if you're doing assembly language programming do you have to bother yourself with the tricky problems of segmented addressing. However, if you want to explore segmented addressing, BASIC gives you a way to do it. The DEF SEG statement in BASIC enables you to specify the segment part of a segmented address, and the number that's used with the PEEK and POKE statements provides an offset part that's combined with the DEF SEG's segment part. So, if you want to try your hand at tinkering with segmented addresses, you can do it with these features of BASIC. For some examples of how to use segmented address, see the program listings in Appendix C, especially the ALLCHAR program.

Banging into 64KB Limits

Once in a while, you may encounter what are called 64KB limits. For example, when you use older dialects of BASIC, you're limited to a maximum of 64KB of combined program and data memory. Other programs mention that they can handle no more than 64KB of data at one time. Some programming languages can't build programs with more than 64KB of program code.

You know, of course, where the 64KB number comes from. It's the maximum amount of memory that can be addressed with one unchanging segment register value. Why are you restricted to one fixed segment pointer and why do you encounter such 64KB limitations in real mode? The answer lies in something called the memory model, which is based on the degree of sophistication that a program has in manipulating the segment registers.

As a program runs, it has to find its way to the various parts of the program and to its data. In simplified terms, each program uses the code segment (CS) register to locate parts of the program and the data segment (DS) register to locate the data. While the program is running, these registers can be independently treated as fixed or changeable. If either of them is fixed (that is, not being changed by the program), then that component (program code or data) can't be any larger than the 64KB that a single segment value can address. But, if either can be dynamically changed during the program's operation, there is no such limit on the size of that component. If both are fixed, you have the small memory model, which limits a program to 64KB of code and another 64KB of data. With both changeable, you have the large model, which is without the 64KB limits. There are two more models, which have one segment fixed and the other changeable.

Although the advantage—no 64KB limits—of changing the segment registers is obvious, the price isn't so obvious, but it's quite real. When a program manipulates the segment registers, it takes on both an extra work load, which slows down the operation, and an extra degree of memory management, which can complicate the program's logic. There is a clear tradeoff to be made between speed, size, and simplicity on the one hand and power on the other.

As it turns out, the design of the processor's instruction set makes it relatively easy and efficient to change the CS register that controls the program code and relatively clumsy to control the data's DS register. Thus, you find a fair number of programs that are larger than 64KB but work with only 64KB of data at a time. Fortunately, both the art of programming the PC and the PC's programming languages are becoming increasingly sophisticated, so you run into the 64KB limit less and less frequently.

And what about BASIC? Why does it have a single limit of 64KB for program and data combined? BASIC is a special case. When you use BASIC, the program that runs in the computer is the BASIC interpreter. To the BASIC interpreter, a BASIC program and its data are accessed with one 64KB data segment. That's why BASIC has a quite distinct kind of size limit.

With the new BASIC interpreter, QBasic, which comes with DOS 5.0 and later, the constraints are relaxed. QBasic can change the program CS register. Thus, every procedure (subprogram) can be up to 64KB long. Similarly, you can use up to 64KB worth of data. If you use arrays—lists of data elements—each one can be up to 64KB long. However, there is one overall limitation: because of the way QBasic programs are handled internally, the total size of your program (code plus data) must be less than 160KB.

The PC's Memory Organization

One of the most useful things you can learn about the inner workings of your PC is how the memory is organized and used. Knowing this helps you understand how the PC works, comprehend many of the practical limits on the kinds of work the PC can undertake, know how the display screens work, and learn the basis for the often-mentioned but little-understood 640KB memory limit. All of that, and more, should become clear when I take a look at the basic organization of the PC's memory space. As you read on, bear in mind that I am describing how things work in real mode or virtual 86 mode (which is what DOS uses).

You know, from seeing how the PC addresses memory through its segment registers, that there is a fundamental limit on the range of memory addresses with which the PC can work. This limit is roughly one million different addresses, each representing a byte of memory. That means that the PC has an address space of 1MB.

A computer's address space is its potential for using memory, which isn't the same thing as the memory that the computer actually has. However, the basic address space provides a framework for the organization of the computer's workings. When the designers of a computer figure out how it's going to be laid out, the scheme for the address space is a very important part of it. I explain how the PC's designers laid out the use of the PC's address space.

The easiest way to see it is to start by dividing the entire 1MB address space into 16 blocks of 64KB each. You can identify each of these blocks of memory by the high-order hex digit that all addresses in that block share. So, the first 64KB of memory is called the 0 block because all addresses in that block begin with 0 (i.e., 0xxxx in five-digit absolute address notation and 0xxx:xxxx in segmented address notation). Likewise, the second block is the 1 block. Thus, the 1MB address space is made up of sixteen 64KB blocks, the 0 block through the F block. Table 17.1 summarizes how this memory generally is used. I give you more detail on that in the following sections.

Table 17.1. *The PC's Memory Blocks*

Block	Address Space	Use
0	1st 64KB	Ordinary user memory to 64KB
1	2nd 64KB	Ordinary user memory to 128KB
2	3rd 64KB	Ordinary user memory to 192KB
3	4th 64KB	Ordinary user memory to 256KB
4	5th 64KB	Ordinary user memory to 320KB
5	6th 64KB	Ordinary user memory to 384KB
6	7th 64KB	Ordinary user memory to 448KB
7	8th 64KB	Ordinary user memory to 512KB
8	9th 64KB	Ordinary user memory to 576KB
9	10th 64KB	Ordinary user memory to 640KB
A	11th 64KB	Video memory
B	12th 64KB	Video memory
C	13th 64KB	ROM extension area
D	14th 64KB	ROM extension area
E	15th 64KB	System ROM-BIOS
F	16th 64KB	System ROM-BIOS and ROM-BASIC

It's very important to note, when talking about these blocks, that there is no barrier of any kind between the blocks. Memory addresses and data flow in smooth succession through all of memory and across the artificial boundaries that separate these blocks. They are referred as distinct blocks partly for convenience, but mostly because the overall scheme for the use of the PC's 1MB of memory is organized in terms of these blocks.

Low Memory Goodies

The very lowest part of the computer's memory is set aside for some important uses that are fundamental to the operation of the computer. There are three main divisions to this special use of low memory.

The first is the interrupt vector table, which defines where interrupt-handling routines are located. The first 1,024 bytes of memory are set aside for the interrupt vector table, with room for 256 interrupts—quite a few more than are routinely used. This occupies absolute memory addresses 0 to hex 400. (You learn more about this later in this chapter.)

The second area is used as a workplace for the ROM-BIOS routines. Because the ROM-BIOS supervises the fundamental operation of the computer and its parts, it needs some memory area for its own record keeping. This is the ROM-BIOS data area, one of the most fascinating parts of the computer's memory. Among the many things stored in the ROM-BIOS data area is a buffer that holds the keystrokes you type before your programs are ready to receive them, a note of how much memory the computer has, a record of the main equipment installed in the computer, and an indicator of the display screen mode.

An area of 256 bytes is set aside for the ROM-BIOS data area in absolute memory addresses hex 400 to 500. There are some amazing things in this area. If you want to learn more about them take a look at my book *The New Peter Norton Programmer's Guide to the IBM PC & PS/2*. You might also want to use one of my software tools, *The Norton Online Programmer's Guide for Assembly Language*. Both of these references will help you poke into low memory to your heart's content.

The third part of the special low memory area is the DOS and BASIC work area, which extends for 256 bytes from absolute address hex 500 to 600. This region is shared by both DOS and BASIC as a work area, similar to the ROM-BIOS work area that precedes it.

This low memory area is just loaded with goodies for the interested explorer. Anyone who wants to learn about the inner workings of the PC can get a graduate education in PC tinkering simply by digging deeply into this part of memory.

The key working area of memory is the part used for programs and their data. That's the area made up of the first 10 blocks, the 0 through 9 blocks. This area often is called the user memory area to distinguish it from the rest of the address space, which is, in one way or another, at the service of the computer system itself. When I talk about the amount of memory that PCs have, what I really am talking about is the amount of user memory installed in this area. In theory, user memory could be as little as 16KB or as much as 640KB with all 10 blocks of memory installed. Whatever amount of memory is installed forms one contiguous chunk from the 0 block to wherever the end of the memory is.

There are actually several different kinds of memory, and the kind installed here is regular read/write random-access memory (RAM). Two things characterize RAM memory. First, as read/write memory it can have the data in it inspected (read) and changed (written). Second, it is volatile, meaning that the data in it is preserved only as long as the computer is running.

This memory is dedicated to holding programs and data while the computer is working with them. The amount of RAM installed here in many ways determines the size and scope of the operations that the computer can undertake.

The basic design of DOS sets aside only 10 of the 16 blocks in the address space for this main working memory area. That's just over 60 percent of the total. Today, that 640KB area seems much too small for today's problems, but at the time the PC was designed it seemed like a very generous amount. At that time, typical personal computers were limited to perhaps 64 or 128KB of total memory, and the DOS's 640KB limit seemed enormous. (Underestimating the need for growth and expansion is a mistake that has occurred over and over again in the history of computing.)

It is possible to expand the 640KB user memory area slightly by encroaching on some of the system area that follows, but that isn't really wise because the memory blocks that come after the 640KB user area are reserved for some special uses that should not be sabotaged. However, there are new memory management routines—including those available with DOS 5.0 and 6.0—that do a pretty good job of using these memory areas safely. Third-party utilities also are available to make use of some of this memory between 640KB and 1MB. Note that few, if any, applications use this memory directly. They do so only through the manipulations of these DOS or third-party utilities. That's a safer and more predictable way to go.

Not every single bit of the user memory area is available for programs to use. The very first part of it, beginning at memory address 0, is set aside for some essential record keeping. You can find some deeper technical information about one part of it in the next section. But, except for that small (and interesting) part, this entire

640KB section of memory is set aside for use by programs. On the other hand, the rest of the memory blocks have some fascinating characteristics.

The Interrupt Vector Table

When I introduced interrupts in Chapter 4, I explained that the interrupt mechanism causes the current program to be put on hold while an interrupt-handling program is activated. The processor needs a simple and straightforward way to find that interrupt-handling program, and that's accomplished using the interrupt vector table, a very simple table of the addresses of the stored interrupt-handling routines beginning with the vector (the pointer to the beginning of the routine) for interrupt number 0 at memory location 0. Each vector address is four bytes long; the vector for any interrupt number x is found at memory location $x \times 4$.

The vectors are simply the complete memory address, in segmented form, of the routine to be activated when the interrupt occurs. A segmented address is made up of a pair of two-byte words, so you can see why vectors are four bytes each.

You can inspect the interrupt vector table in your computer very easily by using DEBUG. Use the D (Display) command to show the beginning of memory like this:

```
D 0:0
```

DEBUG shows you the first 128 bytes, or 32 vectors. An example is shown below. When you try it on your computer, you probably will get different numbers. What you see depends on several factors, including the version of DOS you are using, the type of computer you have, and whether or not you have installed any memory-resident programs.

```
0000:0000   E8 4E 9A 01 00 00 00 00-C3 E2 00 F0 00 00 00 00
0000:0010   F0 01 70 00 54 FF 00 F0-05 18 00 F0 05 18 00 F0
0000:0020   2C 08 51 17 D0 0A 51 17-AD 08 54 08 E8 05 01 2F
0000:0030   FA 05 01 2F 05 18 00 F0-57 EF 00 F0 F0 01 70 00
0000:0040   90 13 C7 13 4D F8 00 F0-41 F8 00 F0 3E 0A 51 17
0000:0050   5C 00 B7 25 59 F8 00 F0-E2 0A 51 17 9C 00 B7 25
0000:0060   00 00 00 F6 8E 00 DE 09-6E FE 00 F0 F2 00 7B 09
0000:0070   27 08 51 17 A4 F0 00 F0-22 05 00 00 00 00 00 F0
```

The vectors are stored back-words, the offset followed by the segment. For example, the first four bytes that DEBUG shows above (E8 4E 9A 01) can be translated into the segmented address 019A:4EE8.

Generally, you find three kinds of addresses in the vector table. There may be ones that point to the ROM-BIOS, which you can identify by a hex F leading the segment number. There may be ones that point into main memory, as in the above example. These may be pointing to routines in DOS or in a memory-resident program or to DEBUG itself because DEBUG needs to have temporary control of the interrupt. Finally, the vectors may be all 0 because that interrupt number is not currently being handled.

If you want, you can chase down any of the interrupt-handling routines by first decoding its interrupt vectors as shown above and then feeding that segmented address to DEBUG's U (Unassemble) command to inspect the program code inside the interrupt handler.

Immediately following the user memory area is a 128KB area consisting of the A and B blocks, which is set aside for use by the display screens. The data that appears on the screen of the computer has to be stored somewhere, and the best place to store it turns out to be in the computer's memory address space. That's a good idea because it enables programs to manipulate the display screen data quickly and easily. So, to make that possible, the 128KB area of the A and B blocks is set aside for the display screen's data. (I discussed in Chapters 11–14 how the display screens work and how they use this memory.)

In the original PC design, only part of the B block was used for the display screens; the A block was reserved but not used. This is why it has been possible for some PCs to have an additional 64KB of user memory installed. This has never been a wise thing to do, though, because it breaks important design conventions of the PC family. The first official use of the A block came with the appearance of the IBM Enhanced Graphics Adapter, which needed more working display memory than the previous display adapters.

The memory installed for use by the display screens operates just like the conventional RAM. Normally, it has one extra feature that helps speed the operation of the computer: it has two doorways, so that programs (using the processor) and the display screen can work with it simultaneously without interfering with each other. This is called dual-port memory. I show you an interesting example of how such interference can cause problems in the next section.

Video Snow

The display circuitry and the processor usually can access the dual-port video memory at the same time without getting in each other's way. With the old Color Graphics Adapter (CGA), however, the display and the processor clashed under certain conditions. The result was video interference that showed up as snow.

To circumvent the problem, old software installation programs asked the user whether such snow was noticeable. If the user answered yes, the software took steps to avoid the interference.

There were two choices. The software could refrain from accessing the video memory directly and use the facilities of the BIOS. However, on older computers, this slowed down the program. Or the software could access the video memory directly but only during the intervals in which the electron beam that actually displays the dots was not in use. These times are called the horizontal and vertical retrace intervals. They occur when the beam is moving from the end of one row to the beginning of the next or from the bottom to the top of the screen.

After the display memory area come two blocks, C and D, which are set aside for some special uses. They are rather nebulously called the ROM extension area. There is no hard-and-fast assignment for this memory area. Instead, it is used for a variety of purposes that have arisen in the evolving history of the PC family. One use, which gives this section its name, is as a growth area for the very last section of memory, the ROM-BIOS which occupies the E and F blocks. When new equipment is added to the PC family and it requires built-in software support, the additional ROM-BIOS programs are added here. Another use for the ROM extension area, one which was not designed by IBM, is to support extended memory, which I discuss shortly.

The final part of the PC family's memory address space includes the E and F blocks, which are used to hold the computer's built-in ROM-BIOS programs. The memory used here is a special kind known as read-only memory (ROM). ROM is permanently recorded, so it can't be written to or changed, and isn't volatile, so turning off the computer does not disturb it. As you can see, ROM is very different from RAM, although their names are easy to confuse. I give you some additional information about ROM-BIOS in the next two chapters.

Extended Memory

As discussed earlier, the amount of memory that the standard 8086/DOS architecture can use is 1MB. Out of this 1MB, only 640KB is available for programs and data. However, today's computers have multiple megabytes of memory. With DOS, any ordinary memory over 640KB is not directly accessible and is called extended memory.

OS/2 and other protected mode operating systems can take advantage of all this memory. And, special DOS control programs such as Microsoft Windows can as well. But what can you do with plain vanilla DOS to avoid wasting this extra memory?

The BIOS provides a service to transfer blocks of data in whatever size you need back and forth to extended memory. There are some special programs that take advantage of this feature to provide facilities that would normally not be available.

For example, DOS comes with a program—named either VDISK.SYS or RAMDRIVE.SYS depending on your version of DOS—that enables you to create a virtual disk. (A virtual disk is an area of memory that is used to emulate a real disk.) You activate VDISK.SYS by placing the appropriate command in the CONFIG.SYS file. If you want, you can instruct DOS to have VDISK.SYS create a virtual disk in extended memory. This saves as much room as possible of the low-end 640KB for your programs and data.

When VDISK.SYS uses the BIOS transfer service to move data in and out of extended memory without having to change into protected mode or to manipulate the extended memory area directly.

If you carefully read the instructions in your DOS manual for setting up the CONFIG.SYS (configuration) file, you will see that there are a few more system programs that can use extended memory if you so desire. This is usually a good idea as the space below 640KB is precious.

Virtual Memory

Remember that today's processors—the 286, 386, 486, and the Pentium—can use virtual memory in addition to real memory. Virtual memory is a service provided by a protected mode operating system (such as OS/2) working in conjunction with the built-in features of the processor to use external storage (such as a disk) to simulate large amounts of real memory.

Back when the mainframe was king and all types of storage were expensive, it was said of virtual memory that "you pay for it, but you only think it's there."

Table 17.2 shows the maximum real and virtual memory with which various PC processors can work. Take a look at this table and then read on for an explanation of how virtual memory is implemented.

Table 17.2. *Maximum Real and Virtual Memory Available to PC Processors*

Maximum Processor	Real Memory	Virtual Memory
8088	1MB	—
8086	1MB	—
286	16MB	1GB
386	4GB	64TB
386 SX	4GB	64TB
386 SL	4GB	64TB
486	4GB	64TB
486 SX	4GB	64TB
Pentium	4GB	64TB

To put this in perspective, tables 17.3 shows the same information expressed in bytes.

Table 17.3. *Maximum Real and Virtual Memory Available to PC Processors (in Bytes)*

Maximum Processor	Real Memory	Virtual Memory
8088	1,048,576 bytes	—
8086	1,048,576 bytes	—
286	16,777,216 bytes	1,073,741,824 bytes

continues

Table 17.3. *continued*

Maximum Processor	Real Memory	Virtual Memory
386	4,294,967,296 bytes	70,368,744,177,664 bytes
386 SX	4,294,967,296 bytes	70,368,744,177,664 bytes
386 SL	4,294,967,296 bytes	70,368,744,177,664 bytes
486	4,294,967,296 bytes	70,368,744,177,664 bytes
486 SX	4,294,967,296 bytes	70,368,744,177,664 bytes
Pentium	4,294,967,296 bytes	70,368,744,177,664 bytes

Virtual memory is a sleight-of-hand operation that involves some carefully orchestrated cooperation among the processor, a virtual memory support program, and the disk drive.

When a program is being set up to run in the computer, the operating system creates a virtual memory space, which is a model of the amount of memory and the memory addresses the program has at its disposal. Then, a portion of the computer's real memory is given over to the sleight-of-hand operation that is the core of the virtual memory concept. Using a feature that's an integral part of the processor, the operating system's virtual memory support program tells the processor to make the real memory assigned to it appear to be at some other address. This other address is the virtual address that the program will use. A memory mapping feature in the processor makes the real memory appear to have a working memory address other than its true address.

So far what I've described is just a shuffling act, a trick that makes some real memory addresses appear to be, and work as, some other virtual addresses. The most important part of virtual memory comes in the next step, when a program tries to use more virtual memory than there is real memory.

A program starts out with some of its (large) virtual memory space mapped into a part of the computer's (smaller) real memory (see fig. 17.1). As long as the program is working with only that part of its virtual memory, all goes well. The program actually is using different locations in memory than it thinks it is, but that doesn't matter. What happens when the program tries to use some of the large virtual memory that hasn't been assigned a part of the smaller real memory? When that occurs, the processor's mapping table discovers that the program is trying to use an address that doesn't currently exist; the processor generates what is called a page fault.

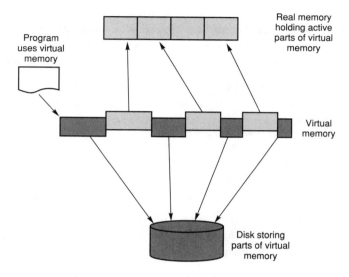

Figure 17.1. *How virtual memory works.*

When there is a page fault, indicating that a program is trying to use a virtual address that isn't actively mapped into real memory, a special virtual memory support program swings into action. It temporarily places the program on hold while it deals with the crisis. The support program chooses some part of the virtual memory currently in real memory and saves its contents temporarily on the disk; that's called swapping out. That freed-up part of real memory is recycled to act as the needed part of virtual memory. When the swapped-out part of memory is needed again, it's copied back in from disk. As you can see, the disk is used as a warehouse for storing the parts of virtual memory that aren't in current use.

Depending on how things go, the virtual memory operation can run very smoothly or can involve so much swapping in and out of memory that a lot of time is wasted waiting for the swaps to take place. The latter is called thrashing; when a virtual memory system starts thrashing, very little work gets done. The practical operation of a virtual memory system can involve a very sensitive balancing act known as system tuning.

Using More than 640KB of Memory

The future of the PC family's evolution belongs to the 486- and Pentium-based processors and to new operating systems, like OS/2, Microsoft Windows NT, and UNIX, that can take full advantage of the hardware. However, there are still millions of DOS-based machines that are dependent on the old 8086-based architecture.

As I explained earlier, the 8086/DOS architecture enables programs to directly access only 1MB worth of addresses. Moreover, the top 384KB of this area are reserved, leaving only 640KB of addresses that can be used by programs.

Remember that each byte of memory requires an address to be accessed by a program. Because DOS has only 640KB worth of nonreserved addresses, DOS programs can access only 640KB of general RAM.

When the PC was first developed, this was fine. Indeed, the very first PCs had only 64KB of RAM. Nowadays, however, 640KB is far from adequate. Indeed, DOS has been straining at the seams, so to speak, for some time. Although today's computers have plenty of memory, DOS has no easy way to use it.

Through the years, solutions have been developed. However, these solutions aren't perfect, and not one of them is universally employed. The basic problem—that the memory addresses from 640 to 1,024KB have been reserved and that thousands of DOS applications are written to expect this—is a fundamental flaw within DOS. Even control programs, like Microsoft Windows, have problems because they are based on DOS. The only complete solution is to change to an operating system like OS/2 or Windows NT that is designed to access large amounts of memory. Such programs don't "remember" the old requirements and can make more efficient use of available system resources.

The Expanded Memory Specification: EMS

Having said that, I take a look at some of the solutions that have been developed to help DOS solve this problem. I start with expanded memory, the first important solution.

You know that DOS can access any memory with addresses from 0 to 1,024KB. Expanded memory uses a 64KB block of addresses to access extra memory. Here is how it works. You buy a memory adapter board (or plug additional memory into the proper slot on the motherboard) that contains extra memory (RAM) chips. The board has a number of 64KB banks of chips. These banks are not assigned permanent addresses; instead, they are accessed one at a time using a 64KB page frame.

Here is an example. Your computer has an expanded memory board that has 16 banks of memory, each of which contains 64KB of RAM. When you install the board, you also install a program called an extended memory manager, or EMM. The EMM sets up a 64KB area of memory as a page frame.

Now, when your programs want to use expanded memory, they call on the EMM to fulfill the request. The EMM sends a signal to the memory board that turns on the appropriate bank. The EMM then helps your program access the bank via the 64KB page frame. The system that makes this all work is called the Expanded Memory Specification, or EMS. (Sometimes, this specification is known as LIM-EMS. LIM stands for the names of the three companies who developed the design—Lotus, Intel, and Microsoft.)

EMS usually uses a 64KB page frame that lies in the reserved area of DOS memory, which is somewhere between 640 and 1,024KB. Usually, this window is in the D or E block of memory and sometimes in the C block (see table 17.1).

To enable your program to access the data in the page frame, the EMM divides the frame into four windows, each 16KB long. Any program that knows how to use EMS can call on the EMM to swap data in and out of a window (see fig. 17.2).

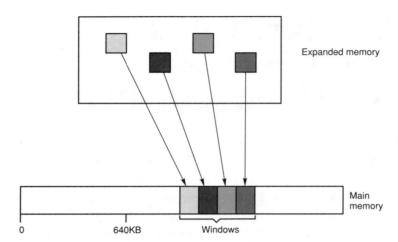

Figure 17.2. *How expanded memory works.*

For EMS to work, however, several conditions must be met. First, you must have a special memory board, one that has the necessary hardware to perform bank switching. Second, the program you run must be written to take advantage of expanded memory. Finally, you must install an expanded memory manager to run the show.

The newest processors—the 386 and 486 families and the Pentium—have built-in facilities that can simulate bank switching. Thus, if you have a newer PC, you can use regular extended memory—plain vanilla extra memory—to simulate expanded memory. This means that you can use EMS-savvy programs without having an expanded memory board. All you need is a memory manager designed to take advantage of the enhanced capabilities of these processors. Starting with DOS 4.0, such a program is included with the operating system. (Your DOS manual has the details.)

The Extended Memory Specification: XMS

The good thing about the EMS scheme is that it enables you to avoid DOS's 640KB memory limitation. There are two drawbacks, however. First, only programs that are written to use EMS can use expanded memory. The big memory hogs—the spreadsheets, databases, and so on—are, for the most part, written in this way. However, the vast majority of DOS programs do not support EMS, and no Microsoft Windows program can make use of expanded memory. In fact, if you are running Windows as your exclusive operating environment, you need not configure any memory as expanded. It is simply a waste of memory.

The second drawback is that, even if a program can use the extra memory, it cannot be accessed all at once. Although a program may think it is using a lot of memory, DOS only can access 64KB, that is, just the amount that fits into the page frame. And, within a program, data must be accessed via 16KB windows. Even with a fast computer, this can slow things down.

A newer solution enables DOS programs to access extended (extra) memory by using the Extended Memory Specification, or XMS. As with EMS, a program must be explicitly written to use XMS. However, after this is done, the memory can be accessed quickly; the program does not have to work via continued bank switching.

To use XMS, you need a 386-, 486-, or Pentium-based computer and an extended memory manager. (Such a program is included with DOS 5.0 and later as well as with Microsoft Windows.) As the use of extended memory becomes more and more common, you should find very few new programs that can't make use of it. In fact, as Microsoft Windows gains in popularity, the number of programs that require, or that even can use the older EMS standard, is waning.

The memory managers that come with DOS are called EMM386.EXE (expanded memory) and HIMEM.SYS (extended memory). You can find more information on how these programs work with DOS and how you can use them to enhance your system in my DOS book, *Peter Norton's DOS 6 Guide*, published by Brady Books. And, of course, your DOS manual is a good source of information on these program utilities. In fact, some newer applications check your system configuration to make sure that one or both of these programs is installed properly.

Some Things To Try

1. Explain why the segmented addresses 1234:0005, 1230:0045, 1200:0345, and 1000:2345 all refer to the same memory location. Which of these refers to a different location than the other two: A321:789A, A657:453A, and A296:824A? Is there an ideal way to divide the two halves of a segmented address?

2. Using the DEBUG program's U (Unassemble) instruction, unassemble some of your computer's ROM-BIOS. For example, enter the following:

```
U F000:A000 L 100
```

Try to pick out examples of back-words storage.

3. How could you write a program in BASIC that finds out how much memory is installed in the computer by experimental means? Can this operation disrupt the computer? Write such a program and see what happens. (Incidentally, you can find a very fast version of such a test in the System Information program as a part of the Norton Utilities program set.)

4. What do you think are the advantages and limitations of expanded (bank-switched) memory? What does a program have to do to take advantage of it? What might the problems be for a program working with 16KB windows of data?

5. If you try using the MSGHUNT program, which searches through the ROM-BIOS looking for messages, you may find that it gives some false alarms; for example, one "message" that it detects on my computer is "t'<.u"—nothing very fascinating or meaningful. That's because the program accepts as a possible message all characters from a blank space to a lowercase z. That enables you to capture punctuation inside of a message, but it also finds spurious messages, like the one above. What sort of test can you add to the program to filter out this nonsense? Try adding such a filter to MSGHUNT. Experiment with making your rules for an acceptable message tighter or looser and see what the result is.

Built-In BIOS: The Basic Ideas

18

I n this chapter, I begin to explore the software heart of the PC, its built-in ROM-BIOS. The task here is to understand the basic ideas behind the ROM-BIOS—the philosophy of how it is organized and what it tries to do. This lays the groundwork for Chapter 19, where I explore the details of the services that the ROM-BIOS performs.

Before proceeding, to avoid confusion, note there are two things in the computer called BIOS. One is the ROM-BIOS, a built-in software feature; that's the topic for this chapter and the next. The other is the DOS-BIOS, the part of DOS that performs a similar service (but on a quite different level) for DOS.

The Ideas behind the BIOS

The ROM-BIOS has a clumsy name that only hints at what it's all about. ROM-BIOS is short for Read-Only Memory Basic Input/Output System. Ignore the name and concentrate on what it does. The ROM-BIOS is a set of programs built into the computer that provides the most basic, low-level, and intimate control and supervision operations for the computer.

Software works best when it's designed to operate in layers, with each layer performing some task and relieving the other layers above of concern for the details of a task. Following this philosophy, the ROM-BIOS is the bottommost layer. It is the layer that underlies all other software and operations in the computer. The task of the ROM-BIOS is to take care of the immediate needs of the hardware and to isolate all other programs from the details of how the hardware works.

Fundamentally, the ROM-BIOS is an interface, a connector, and a translator between the computer hardware and the software programs that you run. Properly speaking, the ROM-BIOS is simply a program like any other. However, if you want to understand the ROM-BIOS, you should think of it as if it weren't just software but some kind of hybrid—something halfway between hardware and software. Functionally, that's exactly what the ROM-BIOS is. (As a matter of fact, software that is permanently stored in hardware chips is called firmware.)

What's in the ROM-BIOS?

The ROM-BIOS holds a key set of programs that provides essential support for the operation of the computer. There are three main parts to the ROM-BIOS programs. The first part is used only when the computer is first turned on; these are test and initialization programs that check to see that the computer is in good working order. The delay between when you turn on the computer and when it starts working for you is caused primarily by these test and initialization programs, which sometimes are called the power-on self-test (POST).

The second and most interesting part of the ROM-BIOS are its routines. These programs provide the detailed and intimate control of the various parts of the computer, particularly the I/O peripherals, such as the disk drives, which require careful supervision (including exhaustive checking for errors). The ROM-BIOS, to help support the operation of the computer, provides a very long list of services that are available for use both by the operating system (DOS or OS/2) and by application programs. I have much to say about this part of the ROM-BIOS throughout the rest of the book.

The third part of the ROM-BIOS, which applies only to the older members of the PC family made by IBM, is the built-in ROM-BASIC. This was designed into the machine in the days when every user had to do a lot of programming to make the machine do much useful work. In fact, the earliest IBM machines didn't even have disk drives. They used cassette tape to load programs and store data. And, because there were no disk drives, there was no Disk Operating System (DOS). The machine started in BASIC, and this was the operating environment you used to interact with the machine, build programs, and load other applications. This BASIC was the core of the BASIC programming language, which is used either by itself or as part of the old dialect of BASIC (BASICA) that comes with IBM DOS. The new dialect of BASIC (QBasic) that comes with DOS 5.0 and later versions, does not depend on the ROM-BASIC, of course. And, the new IBM PCs don't include BASIC as part of the ROM. It simply isn't needed with DOS.

All of the ROM-BIOS programs are contained very compactly within the 128KB area of the E and F blocks of memory (E000 and F000 hex). (See Chapter 17 for more information on memory allocation and usage.) The amount of this block used varies from model to model in the PC family. Generally speaking, the more complex computers need more software crammed into the ROM-BIOS. Thus, the E block is used for this purpose only in newer computers from IBM (the PS/2 family) and other vendors. In older PCs, the ROM-BIOS is confined to the F block.

Some of the PS/2s and newer third-party computers have an important addition to the BIOS, ABIOS, which is described later in this chapter.

What Does the ROM-BIOS Do?

What makes the ROM-BIOS so special? What does it do that makes it seem to be midway between hardware and software?

The answer lies in what the ROM-BIOS has to do and how it does it. The ROM-BIOS is designed to control the hardware directly and respond to any demands that the hardware makes. How it does this is largely through use of the ports that you learned about in Chapter 2. For the most part, all of the PC's components are controlled by commands or parameter settings sent through the ports, with each part of the circuitry having special port numbers to which it responds.

You already know that there are many important aspects of the hardware that don't work through ports, such as the memory addresses used to control what appears on the display screen. Most of the exceptions to the general rule that the hardware is controlled through the ports are exactly the part of the computer that it's okay for programs to work with directly. These are the parts that the ROM-BIOS doesn't have to supervise.

I don't want you to get the impression that the ROM-BIOS concerns itself only with ports; it doesn't. Ports best symbolize what is special about the ROM-BIOS; it's the software that works most intimately with the computer's hardware and that takes care of hardware details (like ports) that other programs shouldn't have to touch.

What's Special about the BIOS?

What's special about the ROM-BIOS is that it is written to work intimately with the computer's hardware. That means the ROM-BIOS incorporates lots of practical knowledge about how the hardware works. It isn't always obvious just what that knowledge is.

Up until the debut of the PS/2s, IBM published the listings of the programs that make up the ROM-BIOS. If you study these listings (which, of course, are out of date for PS/2s), you easily can see what's so special about BIOS programming—using the right ports to send the right commands to the PC's hardware components. What isn't anywhere near so obvious is that there is magic going on as well.

Not everything that it takes to make computer circuits work correctly is clear from their basic specifications. There are many subtleties as well, including things such as timing or just how errors actually occur.

For example, some circuits can accept a command at any time, but need a short amount of time to digest one command before they are ready to take another. In other cases, two separate steps may have to be performed with as little intervening time as possible. Hidden inside the ROM-BIOS are subtle factors like that. You might see a sequence of commands that appear straightforward and simple but that have a hidden element in them as well, such as carefully worked-out timing factors.

This is a part of what makes BIOS programming so special and why many programmers think of BIOS programming as something of a magical art—an art that involves not just the logical steps from which all programs are built but also close cooperation between the programs and the computer hardware.

How Does the ROM-BIOS Work?

Although the complete details of how the ROM-BIOS works are really of concern only to accomplished assembly language technicians, the basics of how the ROM-BIOS is organized and works are of importance in helping you understand your machine. That's what I sketch out in this section.

To start with, the ROM-BIOS is roughly divided into three functional parts, as diagrammed in figure 18.1.

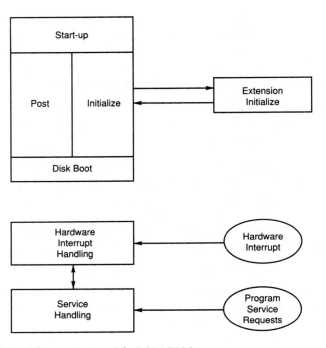

Figure 18.1. *The organization of the ROM-BIOS.*

The first part of the ROM-BIOS contains the start-up routines, which get the computer going when you turn on the power. There are two main parts to the start-up routines. The first, as I mentioned a little earlier in this chapter, is the power-on self-test (or POST) routines, which test to see that the computer is in good working order. They check the memory for defects and perform other tests to see that the computer isn't malfunctioning. The second part of the start-up procedure is the initialization.

The initialization involves such things as creating the interrupt vectors, so that when interrupts occur the computer switches to the proper interrupt-handling routine. Initialization also involves setting up the computer's equipment. Many of the parts of the computer need to have registers set, parameters loaded, and other things done to get them ready to go.

The ROM-BIOS knows the full complement of standard equipment that a PC can have and performs whatever initialization each part needs. Included in this initialization are steps that tell the ROM-BIOS what equipment is present. Some of that is learned by checking switch settings inside the computer (in the case of the original PC) or by reading a permanent memory that records the equipment the computer has (in the case of the newer PCs). In some cases, the ROM-BIOS can find out if equipment is installed simply by electronically interrogating it and checking for a response. Whatever it takes, the ROM-BIOS checks for and initializes all the equipment that it knows how to handle.

Of course, you can add new equipment to your PC; people do it all the time. Some of this equipment is standard stuff, such as additional memory or extra serial and parallel output ports, but not all of it is. There is some optional equipment that isn't taken care of in the standard ROM-BIOS routines that need special ROM-BIOS support. To take care of that situation, the ROM-BIOS is prepared to search for additions to the BIOS.

How Do You Add to the ROM-BIOS?

The ROM-BIOS in the PC is a fixed part of the computer's equipment, which leads to a fundamental problem: how do you add support for new options? The answer lies in an automatic feature, called ROM-BIOS extensions, that allows for additions to the ROM-BIOS.

The scheme is simple. Additions to the ROM-BIOS are marked so that the standard ROM-BIOS can recognize them and give them a chance to integrate themselves into the standard part.

Just as the main ROM-BIOS appears in memory at a specific location—the high, 128KB, E and F blocks of memory—additions have a standard memory area reserved for them as well—the C and D blocks.

Any new equipment requiring special ROM-BIOS support, such as an optical disk, places its read-only BIOS memory somewhere in that block and includes in it a special marking, hex 55 AA, in the first two bytes. The ROM-BIOS can't be located just anywhere. It has to be in a unique location that doesn't conflict with any other ROM-BIOS extensions and must begin on a 2KB memory boundary.

The standard (or you might say, master) ROM-BIOS, as part of its start-up routines, searches the ROM-BIOS extension area for the identifying 55 AA signature. When it finds one, it passes control over to the beginning of the ROM-BIOS extension. That enables the ROM-BIOS extension to do whatever it needs to do to initialize its equipment and integrate itself into the rest of the ROM-BIOS. For example, a ROM-BIOS extension for a new kind of display adapter might change the interrupt vector for video services to direct them to the ROM-BIOS extension rather than to the old ROM-BIOS video routines.

A ROM-BIOS extension performs whatever start-up and initialization work it has to do when the main ROM-BIOS passes control to it during the start-up procedure. When the ROM-BIOS extension is initialized, it passes control back to the main ROM-BIOS, and the computer proceeds in the usual way. Now, however, new equipment and new ROM-BIOS support for that equipment has been added.

All this is made possible by the mechanism that enables the main ROM-BIOS to search for and recognize ROM-BIOS extensions.

ABIOS: The Advanced BIOS

So far, the BIOS and the memory usage I have discussed have been based on the 8086 architecture that is still used by DOS. With PCs that are based on the newer processors—the 286, 386, 486, and Pentium series—DOS runs in either real mode or virtual 86 mode. This means that, unless special control programs are used, DOS cannot take advantage of the protected mode features of these processors, such as large memory facilities, multitasking, and so on.

Other operating systems—in particular, OS/2 and Microsoft Windows—can take advantage of protected mode. However, such operating systems require a lot of system support that the regular BIOS does not provide. This support is provided by the Advanced BIOS, usually referred to as ABIOS.

If you want, you can write a short BASIC program that hunts through the ROM-BIOS looking for messages. In Appendix C, you find the listing for a short program, called MSGHUNT, that hunts through the whole F block looking for a string of five letters or punctuation characters in a row. When it finds them, it displays them and goes on hunting. If you want to learn more about what's inside your computer's ROM-BIOS, try MSGHUNT. After you have experimented with MSGHUNT, you might try to modify it to search another area of memory, such as the 0 or E block.

There's one final and quite interesting thing to know about the ROM-BIOS. In the original PC, IBM placed an identifying date at the end of the BIOS. I was among early users who found out where that date was located and talked about it in the original version of this book and in articles. I showed people how to find the date and display it with a simple BASIC program, like the one below:

```
10 ' Display ROM-BIOS date
20 DEF SEG = &HFFFF
30 DATE.$ = "
40 FOR I = 5 TO 12
50 DATE.$ = DATE.$ + CHR$(PEEK(I))
60 NEXT
70 IF PEEK (7) <> ASC("/") THEN DATE$ = "missing"
80 PRINT "The ROM-BIOS date is ";DATE$
```

Here is the same program in QBasic:

```
' Display ROM-BIOS date
DEF SEG = &HFFFF
BiosDate$ = ""
FOR I = 5 TO 12
BiosDate$ = BiosDate$ + CHR$(PEEK(I))
NEXT I
IF PEEK(7) <> ASC("/") THEN BiosDate$ = "missing"
PRINT "The ROM-BIOS date is "; BiosDate$
```

After the days of the original PC, when other vendors started making PCs and writing BIOS code for them, an interesting thing happened. BIOS vendors, intent on duplicating the PC to the last detail, also included this date location. However, they weren't exactly sure how applications were using this date, so some companies were afraid to change the date. (One way the date was used was to tell an application whether the PC was capable of speed switching, which was implemented on late model PC ATs.) In Phoenix BIOS firmware, this date stayed the same for a long time. Then, sometime after 1990, the company decided it was probably okay to change the date for any major upgrades. Thus, you may find some later dates in your Phoenix BIOS if you poke around. And, Phoenix sold some BIOS packages to third-party companies who were licensed to take it and use it as they wanted. Some of these companies kept this original version of BIOS up to date with new processor and other computer technology, but they never did change the date inside the code.

Some computer vendors ignore this date when they install BIOS, others try to keep it current. One of my contacts at CompuAdd told me recently, for example, that they didn't used to change the date that the BIOS vendor used. However, so many customers complained about the date of their BIOS that they had to start maintaining that date. Even so, the date in your BIOS is probably not the precise date when the BIOS was updated.

Most manufacturers don't change this location with every minor change or version modification. They change it once a year or when there are major changes made to the BIOS. In short, don't be concerned if your BIOS date is relatively old. It really doesn't mean much.

That's why, even on newer machines, you may find very old dates when you run this program. The machine I used to write this book, for example, is a new 486DX66 with VESA local bus. It uses a Phoenix BIOS dated 1988. Obviously, if the BIOS were actually that old, the machine wouldn't run with all of its new equipment. It still can be fun to poke around in the BIOS and see what is there.

In addition to the date stamp, IBM has created a loosely defined model ID code, which can be used by programs that need to know when they are running on some of the more unusual models of the family. This simple BASIC program displays the ID byte:

```
10 ' Display machine id byte
20 DEF SEG = &HFFFF
30 ID = PEEK (14)
40 PRINT "The id byte is";ID;"hex ";HEX$(ID)
```

Here is the same program in QBasic:

```
' Display machine id byte
DEF SEG = &HFFFF
ID = PEEK(14)
PRINT "The id byte is"; ID; "hex "; HEX$(ID)
```

There are a number of codes that you may come across. They follow two separate patterns. At first, IBM decided to give each model of personal computer its own ID code. Later, they changed the scheme to focus on the architecture of the processor. Table 18.1 shows the model/architecture ID codes.

Table 18.1. *The IBM Model/Architecture ID Codes*

ID Code	Model/Architecture
FF	PC
FE	PC XT (early version)
FB	PC XT (later version)
FD	PCjr
F9	PC Convertible
FA	8086-based computers
FC	286-based computers
F8	386- and 486-based computers

For example, the PS/2 model 90, being a 486-based computer, has an ID code of F8. The PS/1, as an 8086-based computer, has an ID code of FA. Non-IBM manufacturers have followed this code convention up to a point. To ensure PC compatibility, BIOS manufacturers (nearly all of them, I think) store FC in this location, indicating to any application that needs to know that the machine is PC AT compatible. Note that if the computer uses an ISA or EISA bus it is PC AT compatible, even if it uses a newer processor.

If you want more details on how the various members of the PC family are identified within the BIOS, take a look at the "System Identification" section in the *IBM Personal System/2 and Personal Computer BIOS Technical Reference Manual*.

Because each model of computer has its own subtle but distinct characteristics, it can be beneficial for programs to make appropriate adjustments in the way they operate based on the machine ID. From this viewpoint, it's unfortunate that the most important of the non-IBM members of the family may not be easily identified by either a model ID byte or by the ROM-BIOS date. However, remember from the discussion in Chapter 3 that the newest processors include registers that, when properly accessed by applications, show what processor is being used.

ROM-BIOS Boot Routine

The very last part of the start-up routines in the ROM-BIOS is the boot routine, which tries to fire up DOS or any other operating system you may be using. The boot process involves the ROM-BIOS attempting to read a boot record from the beginning of a disk. The BIOS first tries drive A. If that doesn't succeed and the computer has a hard disk as drive C, it tries the hard disk. If neither disk can be read, the ROM-BIOS goes into its non-disk mode. In PS/2s, this means displaying a drawing that prompts you to insert a disk and press the F1 key. In other machines, an error message of one kind or another is displayed, indicating that no valid boot device is available.

Normally, the ROM-BIOS can read a boot record from the disk and hands control of the computer to the short program on the boot record. As discussed in Chapters 6 and 7, the boot program begins the process of loading DOS (or another operating system) into the computer.

After the start-up routines are finished, the computer is ready to go. The other two parts of the ROM-BIOS play key roles in running the computer. These two parts are hardware interrupt handling and service handling routines. They function as two distinct but closely cooperating kinds of routines.

The service handling routines are there solely to perform work for programs (and for DOS) by carrying out whatever services the programs need. You see in more detail what these services are in Chapter 19. They include such things as requests to clear the display screen, switch the screen from text mode to graphics mode, read information from the disk, or write information on the printer. For the most part, the ROM-BIOS services that the service handling routines perform relate to hardware devices, such as the screen, keyboard, disks, printers, and so on. These are the basic input/output services that give the BIOS its name. However, there also are other services that the ROM-BIOS performs that aren't I/O related. For example, the ROM-BIOS keeps track of the time of day and reports the time to programs.

To carry out the service requests that programs make, the ROM-BIOS has to work directly with the computer's I/O devices. That's where the intimate and tricky part of the BIOS comes in, that is, using ports to issue commands and send and receive data to and from various devices. The key job of the ROM-BIOS here is to relieve the program of the tedious details involved in performing these tasks.

The program doesn't need to know which port is used to send data to the printer; it just asks the ROM-BIOS to send data to the printer, and the BIOS takes care of the details. That shields the program from the details of how the printer works, but even more important it shields the program from the very annoying and messy problems of error recovery. Surprisingly, the equipment that makes up a computer often is balky and can act up temporarily. Part of the job of the ROM-BIOS is to check for errors, retry operations to see if the problem is only temporary (as it often is), and only in the case of stubborn failure, report the problem to the program.

While some of the hardware parts of the computer require attention only when you want them to do something (that is, when a program is requesting a service from the BIOS), other parts call for attention completely separate from what the programs are doing. You already have seen a few examples of this: you know that, when you press a key on the keyboard, it generates a keyboard interrupt that demands attention from the ROM-BIOS.

Likewise, the PC's internal clock creates clock interrupts every time it ticks, about 18 times a second. There are other hardware interrupts as well: for example, the disks use an interrupt to signal when they need attention from the ROM-BIOS. To handle these needs of the hardware, there is the final part of the ROM-BIOS, the hardware interrupt handling section.

The hardware interrupt handling part takes care of the independent needs of the PC's hardware. It operates separately but in cooperation with the service handling portion. In Chapter 15, where I discussed how the keyboard operates, you saw a good example of how that works. The keyboard handling routines are divided into two separate but related parts that work together.

The hardware interrupt part of the keyboard handling responds to your actions on the keyboard, recording what you do and holding the resulting characters ready for use when your programs need them. The service handling part of the keyboard routines accepts requests for keyboard data and passes on the keyboard characters that the interrupt handler has received. These two parts face in different directions— one to the hardware, and the other to the software—and service different demands. Together, they make the keyboard work for you and your programs.

That captures the essence of the ROM-BIOS and what it does for computers. With that groundwork in place, Chapter 19 shows what sort of services the ROM-BIOS can perform for programs.

Some Things To Try

1. If you have the Norton Utilities, you can use the SI (System Information) program to search for the BIOS signature that identifies additions to the BIOS. Try using it on your computer and see what you find.

2. Analyze how the interrupt handling and service handling parts of the keyboard ROM-BIOS routines work with each other. How do you think these two parts interact safely and successfully?

3. What do you think are the special needs and requirements to initialize an extension to the ROM-BIOS? How would an extension smoothly integrate itself into the rest of the BIOS without creating any disruption?

Built-In BIOS: Digging In

19

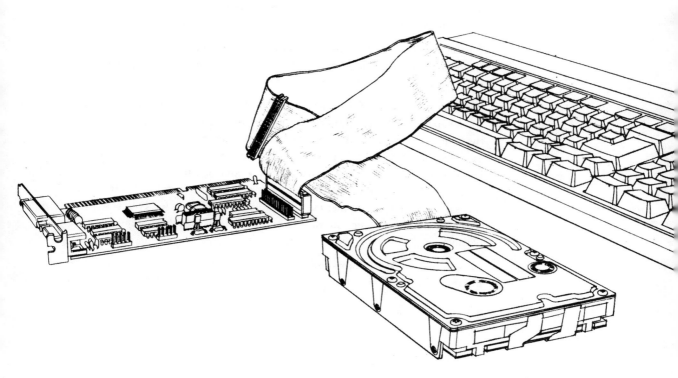

T his chapter takes a more detailed look at what the PC family's built-in ROM-BIOS does for you and your programs. It focuses on the standard services that the BIOS provides. This isn't, however, an exhaustive reference guide. Instead, it is a guided tour of the power that the BIOS puts at your command. The objective is to give you a feel for what the BIOS can do.

Before beginning the BIOS tour, though, you need to look at some of the principles and problems that underlie the services.

Working Principles and Machine Problems

If you want to understand the workings of the ROM-BIOS and the list of the BIOS services and comments that follow in the next section, it helps to understand some of the principles that underlie the way the BIOS works and the way it's organized as well as some of the design problems that are inherent in any software as sensitive as the PC family's ROM-BIOS.

The BIOS has to operate in a way that provides maximum flexibility, places the least caretaking load on the programs that use it, and works with the greatest possible safety (safety against disrupting the workings of the computer).

You already saw some of the ways the design of the BIOS works toward these ends when you learned about one of the BIOS's interrupt handlers in Chapter 4. One of the design considerations that the BIOS routines must meet is to suspend interrupts as seldom as possible. It's important not to shut down or even suspend interrupts because interrupts are the force that keeps the computer running. Recall from the discussion of the interrupt handler that interrupts are immediately activated. Sometimes this can't be done; sometimes it's necessary to perform a few critical steps free of the possibility of being interrupted, but the BIOS keeps those steps as short as possible.

Because the BIOS performs the bulk of its work with interrupts active, other interrupt-driven BIOS service calls can be invoked while the BIOS is carrying out an earlier service request. To avoid tripping over its own feet or confusing the work-in-progress of one service call with that of another, the BIOS routines must be programmed following a special discipline called reentrant coding. Reentrant programs, such as the ROM-BIOS, are designed to keep the working data and status information that pertains to each service call separate from the others. This is done by keeping all data either in the stack or in registers that (by programming convention) are preserved on the stack if another interrupt occurs.

Although reentrant coding is not difficult to do, it must be done carefully and places restrictions on the ways in which information can be passed between the BIOS and any program requesting BIOS services. Much of the design of the BIOS stems from the requirement that it be reentrant.

As a separate but related issue, the BIOS services must be organized in a modular fashion. As you learn in the next section on the details of the basic BIOS services, these services are organized into groups. All the services for the display screen, for example, are grouped together under one interrupt number, and no other BIOS services use that interrupt.

This modular organization by group and interrupt has two obvious benefits. First, for the programs that use the BIOS services, the grouping makes it easier to deal with the complexities of the services. Second, if it becomes necessary to modify the operation of any particular kind of BIOS service—for example, modifying the video services to accommodate the special features of a new display adapter—it can be done in a relatively clean and uncomplicated way simply by replacing one interrupt handler.

There is one fundamental complexity and difficulty that has not been dealt with very well in the ROM-BIOS. There are two families of IBM PCs, the original ones and the PS/2s. Then, of course, there is the entire "other" family of desktop and deskside computers designed and manufactured by non-IBM companies. Each family has multiple members, and each member has its own version of the BIOS. Although much of the BIOS is the same for all PCs, different services are offered for different models.

This book covers BIOS only generally because, not only do different manufacturer's products have different BIOS designs, each motherboard in a product line has a different BIOS. The general operation and theory are the same, of course, but specifics, such as services offered, memory locations used, the size of program, and other details, are motherboard chip set dependent. By "chip set," I mean not only the CPU (processor) used, but the support set that handles memory I/O, manages the ports, and conducts other CPU interface duties. These chip sets are provided by several vendors (one of the most common is Chips and Technologies). It is the technology of these chip sets (around which the rest of the motherboard is built) that determines the precise design and function of the BIOS on any given computer.

Fortunately, IBM's reference manual explains every BIOS feature (for IBM machines) thoroughly, showing exactly which services apply to which computers. In the old manuals, IBM used to print listings of the BIOS programs. Nowadays, this information, which is copyrighted, is considered proprietary and is not published. The interfaces to the BIOS are well documented, however, and for those with a smattering of assembly language, easy to understand.

Other companies publish their own version of this manual to show programmers and system designers how to use the BIOS services available in a given BIOS design.

Obtaining the BIOS Reference Manuals

IBM publishes a detailed reference manual, the IBM *Personal System/2 and Personal Computer BIOS Interface Reference Manual*, which contains a wealth of fascinating information about the BIOS and the Advanced BIOS (ABIOS). There is also specific information regarding the various computers and devices.

If you have an old version of this manual, you can get supplements to bring it up to date. Some of these supplements come with the manual; others must be ordered separately. You can order these manuals and supplements from your local IBM branch office. Alternatively, you can call (800) 426-7282. The current price of the manual is $55. It is somewhat outdated, so to get the latest information, you need two additional publications: *BIOS Technical Reference Update* ($55.75) and *BIOS and ABIOS Update* ($18.25). So, to get the whole package with all current information, you need to lay out about $129.

When ordering IBM manuals, it helps to know that all publications have eight-character form numbers that begin with letters. If the letter is G, the publication is generally available (that is, free). If the first letter is S, the manual is for sale, and you must pay for it.

For details on BIOS from other companies, contact those companies directly or contact their distributor. American Megatrends, Inc., for example, a producer of a popular BIOS product included in many third-party computers, publishes its *BIOS Technical Reference Manual*, available directly from AMI distributor Washburn and Company at (716) 248-3627 and, perhaps, other bookstores or computer companies. The current price for this book is $45.

A similar book, *System BIOS for IBM PC Compatibles and EISA Computers*, is available on Phoenix BIOS. This book is available through many bookstores, especially those that cater to the technical audience.

On a technical level, a great deal more can be said about the design and workings of the ROM-BIOS, but I've covered the most basic and important part. In the next section, I cover the full list of ROM-BIOS services that are universal to the entire PC family, the PC's basic complement of services. It's a more technical treatment that some readers may want to skip, but reading it offers two benefits. First, you learn what services the ROM-BIOS puts at the disposal of your programs. This helps you understand how programs get things done and may give you ideas for ways in which your programs can benefit from these services. Second, skimming through the list of BIOS services gives you a feeling for their level, an understanding of where they stand in the spectrum between simple and complex programs.

# The BIOS Services

The ROM-BIOS services are organized into groups, with each group having its own dedicated interrupt. Table 19.1 summarizes the groups as used by IBM computers. I cover them one by one, beginning with the richest, most complicated, and most interesting—the video services.

Notice that in table 19.1 the BIOS services are identified by a hexadecimal number. This is the usual case. This table does not show every BIOS interrupt, just the ones that offer groups of services to programs. Unless it is specified otherwise, you can assume that an interrupt number is in hex. Likewise, all the services in a group are identified by their own hex number. Remember, too, that computer (and therefore

BIOS) technology is changing rapidly. Although this table, and the information and tables that follow, generally are true, you may find individual differences in specific BIOS code used with specific computers. It isn't practical to try to give you a fully up-to-date list in this book because, even in a single vendor's line, things tend to change frequently.

Table 19.1. *The ROM-BIOS Service Interrupts*

Interrupt (Hex)	Service Group
05	Print screen
10	Video
11	Equipment determination
12	Memory determination
13	Floppy and hard disk
14	Asynchronous (serial) communication
15	System services (miscellany)
16	Keyboard
17	Printer (parallel ports)
18	ROM-BASIC (old)
18	Network interface card
19	Bootstrap loader
1A	System timer, real-time clock
4B	Advanced services (SCSI, DMA)

Video Services

There are 16 separate video screen services in the PC family's basic ROM-BIOS services. These 16 are the original complement used on the very first PC model, and they form a base for the video services of every member of the family. The services are numbered 00 through 0F. In addition to these basic services, there are nine other services used with the newer members of the PC family. The video services are summarized in table 19.2.

Table 19.2. *The Interrupt 10 Video Services*

Video Service (Hex)	Description
00	Set mode
01	Set cursor type
02	Set cursor position
03	Read cursor position
04	Read light pen position
05	Select active display page
06	Scroll active page up
07	Scroll active page down
08	Read attribute/character at cursor position
09	Write attribute/character at cursor position
0A	Write character at cursor position
0B	Set color palette
0C	Read dot
0D	Write dot
0E	Write teletype to active page
0F	Read current video state
10	Set palette registers
11	Character generator
12	Alternate select
13	Write string
14	Control character set for LCD display
15	Return information about active display
1A	Read/write display combination code
1B	Return functionality/state information
1C	Save/restore video state

Bear in mind that all video services, the basic ones as well as the new ones, are accessed via interrupt 10 (hex). You may wonder how the BIOS knows which service you want. The answer is that an application prepares for interrupt 10 by loading the AH register with the code number of the service requested. Then the application invokes the interrupt. As soon as the interrupt handler takes over, it checks the contents of the AH register to see which service is requested.

Loading certain registers with specific values before invoking an interrupt is the standard way to pass information to the BIOS. Conversely, the BIOS passes information back to an application by loading data into registers before returning to the program. One of the main purposes of a BIOS technical reference manual is to describe what each interrupt and service expects in the way of register usage.

The 16 Basic Services

The first service, number 00, is used to change the video mode. This service is used by the program to switch the display screen into whatever mode is needed. As you see later, there is a complementary service that tells the program what the current mode is.

Video service 01 controls the size and shape of the cursor. It sets the scan lines on which the cursor appears. This is the ROM-BIOS service that underlies the BASIC program statement LOCATE ,,,X,Y.

Video service 02 sets the cursor location on the screen, corresponding to the BASIC program statement LOCATE X,Y.

Video service 03 reports the shape of the cursor and where it is located. This service is the opposite of services 01 and 02 combined. It enables the program to record the current state of the cursor so that it can be restored after the program is done. You see an example of how useful that can be when I discuss the print screen interrupt.

Video service 04 is the sole service supporting the PC's little-used light pen feature. (Actually, support for pen computing is growing. Several manufacturers offer pen-based computers, but compared with regular PC products, pen computing is still a little-used technology.) When a program invokes this service, the BIOS reports whether the pen is triggered and where it is touching the screen. Interestingly, the service reports the pen position in two different ways: in terms of the grid of text character positions and in terms of the graphics pixel locations.

Video service 05 selects which display page is active (shown on the screen) for the video modes that have more than one display page in memory (see Chapter 11 for more information).

Services 06 and 07 are a fascinating pair that perform window scrolling. These two services enable an application to define a rectangular window on the screen and scroll the data inside the window up from the bottom (service 06) or down from the top (service 07). When a window is scrolled, blank lines are inserted at the bottom or top, ready for the program to write new information into them. The purpose of these services is to enable the program to write information on just a part of the screen and leave the rest of the screen intact. This capability wasn't used very much in the early days of program development. Nearly all programs today, however, support some form of windowing interface; the capability to control (and scroll) multiple windows is an important feature.

The next three video services work with text characters on the screen. Video service 08 reads the current character (and its attribute) from the screen (or rather out of the screen memory). This service is clever enough, in graphics mode, to decode the pixel drawing of a character into the character code. Video service 09 is the obvious complement to service 08; it writes a character on the screen with the display attribute that you specify. Service 0A also writes a character, but it uses whatever display attribute is currently in place for that screen location.

The next three services provide operations for the graphics modes. Video service 0B sets the color palette, service 0C writes a single dot on the screen, and service 0D reads a dot from the screen.

Video service 0E is a handy variation on the character writing service, 08. This service writes a character to the screen and advances the cursor to the next position so that it's in place for the next character. (The other services require the program to move the cursor as a separate operation.) This is a convenient service that makes it easy for a program to use the display screen like a printer, printing out information with a minimum of fuss (and flexibility). Therefore, this service is called write teletype.

The final basic video service, 0F, is the inverse of the first. It reports the current video state so that the program can adjust its operation to the video mode or record the current mode so that it can return to it after changing the mode. This service tells you what video mode is set but not what video standard is being used (XGA, VGA, and so on). To determine this type of information, you can use video service 1A.

That covers the 16 basic video services. Next, I discuss the 9 newer services.

The Nine Newer Services

For the most part, these nine services are used with only EGA and newer video standards (rather than with the older CGA and MDA standards).

Service 10 sets the registers in the hardware that control the colors displayed.

Service 11 is an interface to the character generator. You can change which character set is used for either text or graphics. You can specify one of the built-in character sets or even design your own. It sounds like fun to set up your own character set, but it requires a fair amount of work. You must first initialize a table of bit patterns to define each character.

The name of service 12, alternate select, comes from its original purpose, which is to specify an alternate way of handling the print screen function (more on this in the discussion of interrupt 05). With newer displays, alternate print handling is necessary to print screens that have more than 25 lines of text. The new functions added to this service are unrelated to printing; for the most part, they involve very technical display settings.

Video service 13 enables an application to write an entire string of characters to the display in one fell swoop. This is easier and faster than repeatedly calling on a video service, such as 09, 0A, or 0E, to display characters one at a time.

The next two services are used with the PC Convertible, which has a special liquid crystal display (LCD). Service 14 loads a particular character set, and service 15 returns information about the active display, which can be either the built-in LCD or a separate display. The PC Convertible is no longer a current model, but other machines do have LCD displays. Remember, as technology changes, BIOS designs change. This information should be considered as general. The market is so broad today that an exhaustive list of all services, such as these BIOS calls, is all but impossible.

Services 16–19 are not used with PS/2s. These numbers may or not be used with other vendor's hardware. Service 1A tells you what type of display standard is currently being used with what category of display (MDA with a monochrome display or VGA with a color display, for example). You also can find out whether there is an unknown display or even no display at all. By using this service, you can tailor a program to act appropriately with different types of systems.

Service 1B returns a table of detailed information about the current video mode and video hardware. This service provides a way for programs to determine the capabilities of the video system currently in use.

Finally, service 1C enables you to preserve the state of the video BIOS and hardware. You can change the current setup by changing video modes or reprogramming the color palette, for example, and later restore the setup to its previous condition.

These video reading and writing services constitute the officially approved way for programs to put information on the screen. Using these services has the advantage of ensuring that output heading for the screen is handled in a standard way and can be automatically adapted to new hardware. However, many programs avoid these services because the overhead involved is disappointingly high. Screen output can be performed much faster when programs do it themselves rather than using the ROM-BIOS services.

The Print Screen Service

The next thing I look at is a special service, the print screen interrupt, which is different from all the others. The majority of the ROM-BIOS services work with specific peripheral devices, such as the display screen or keyboard. The remaining services are basically informational, handling the time of day or indicating the amount of memory installed in the computer. The print screen service, though, is a different animal.

The print screen service is designed to read from the screen the information displayed and route it to the printer. You can invoke this service directly by pressing the PrintScreen key on the keyboard. What makes this service particularly interesting is the fact that it is built from other ROM-BIOS services; it does nothing unique in itself. It just combines services to perform a new and useful service.

Print screen begins work by using video service 03 to determine the current cursor position and service 0F to check the dimensions of the screen. It saves the cursor position so that it can later restore the cursor to its original position. Then, print screen moves the cursor through every location on the screen from top to bottom. At each location, it uses video service 08 to read a character from the screen and a printer output service to copy the character to the printer. When this is done, print screen restores the cursor and returns control to the program that invoked it.

You may think of the print screen service as strictly an adjunct of the keyboard, something you get by pressing the PrintScreen key. Not so. Print screen is a standard ROM-BIOS service that can be invoked by any program just as any other service is invoked—by issuing an INT (interrupt instruction; for interrupt 05, in this case). The PrintScreen key works because the keyboard ROM-BIOS routines monitor keyboard activity to see whether you have pressed this key. Whenever you press the PrintScreen key, the keyboard ROM-BIOS uses interrupt 05 to request the print screen service. Any other program could do the same. This nifty service can be placed at the disposal of any program to be used in any way.

Disk Services

This section covers the other device services first and then the information services.

All the disk services are invoked with interrupt 13. You can divide these services into three groups: those that apply to both floppy and hard disks, those for hard disks only, and those for floppy disks only. The disk services are summarized in tables 19.3 and 19.4.

Table 19.3.   *The Interrupt 13 Hard Disk Services*

Hard Disk Service (Hex)	Description
00	Reset disk system
01	Read status of last operation
02	Read sectors to memory
03	Write sectors from memory
04	Verify sectors
05	Format a cylinder/track
06	Format a cylinder and set bad sector flags
07	Format drive starting specified cylinder

Hard Disk Service (Hex)	Description
08	Read drive parameters
09	Initialize drive pair characteristics
0C	Seek
0D	Alternate disk reset
10	Test drive ready
11	Recalibrate
15	Read disk type
19	Park heads
1A	Format unit

Table 19.4. *The Interrupt 13 Floppy Disk Services*

Floppy Disk Service (Hex)	Description
00	Reset disk system
01	Read status of last operation
02	Read sectors to memory
03	Write sectors from memory
04	Verify sectors
05	Format a cylinder/track
08	Read drive parameters
15	Read disk type
16	Change line status
17	Set disk type for format
18	Set media type for format

Services Used with Floppy and Hard Disks

This discussion begins with the disk services used with both hard disks and floppy disks. These are services 00 through 05, 08, and 15.

397

The first, service 00, is used to reset the disk drive and its controller. This is an initialization and error recovery service that clears the decks for a fresh start in the next disk operation. Related to it is disk service 01, which reports the status of the disk drive so that error handling and controlling routines can find out what's what.

Disk service 02 is the first of the active disk services. It reads disk sectors into memory. The sectors don't have to be read individually; the service reads as many consecutive sectors as you want, as long as they are all on the same track. Disk service 03 works similarly, except that it writes sectors instead of reading them.

Disk service 04 verifies the data written on a disk, testing to ensure that it is properly recorded. This often misunderstood service underlies the DOS option VERIFY ON that you see in the VERIFY command and the VERIFY feature of DOS's configuration file (CONFIG.SYS). It does not check the data stored on disk to see that it matches data in memory (data that you may have just read or written). Instead, the verify service simply checks to see whether the disk data is properly recorded, which means testing for parity errors and other recording defects. As a general rule, that helps ensures the data is correct, although it's no guarantee. If you have the wrong data properly recorded, the verify service reports that it's fine.

Disk service 05 is used to format a track of a disk. This is the physical formatting that underlies DOS's logical formatting of a disk. This formatting service is a fascinating business because it specifies, for each track, the number of sectors, how the sectors are identified, the order in which the sectors appear, and the size of each sector. Normally, all the sectors on a track are the same size (512 bytes) and are numbered sequentially beginning with 1. On floppy disks, sectors physically appear in numeric order (they also may appear in sequential order on hard disks, but on slower hard disks, they don't).

The next service, 08, provides information about the hardware characteristics of a particular disk. Finally, service 15 tells you what type of disk you have (hard disk or floppy).

This ends the discussion of the disk services that apply to both hard disks and floppy disks. Next I discuss the nine services used with only hard disks.

Services Used with Hard Disks

Services 06, 07, and 1A augment the formatting capabilities of service 05. Service 06 is a variation of 05 that can format a defective cylinder; service 07 formats an entire disk, starting with a specified cylinder; and service 1A formats an entire ESDI (Enhanced Small Device Interface) drive.

The next service, 09, is used to initialize a hard disk that is not recognized automatically by the BIOS.

Service 0C positions the disk's read/write head at a particular cylinder.

Three services help set up the hard disk. Service 0D resets the drive. It is similar to service 00, except that service 0D does not reset the floppy disk drive automatically. Service 10 tests to see whether a disk is ready, and service 17 recalibrates a disk.

Services Used with Floppy Disks

The last set of disk services includes those that apply only to floppy disks. There are three such services: 16, 17, and 18.

With certain floppy disk drives, you can use service 16 to see whether the disk in the drive has been changed. This feature is called change line status. Actually, this service can tell an application only whether the disk drive door has been opened. If this is the case, you can have a program check an identifier, such as the volume serial number, to see whether the actual disk has been changed.

The last two services are used to prepare for formatting. Before you can use service 05 to format, you must use either service 17 or 18 to describe the disk. With service 17, you specify what type of disk; with service 18, you specify the number of sectors and tracks. This sort of knowledge is interesting, but generally you use features of

DOS (such as FORMAT with its various switches) to handle this level of disk management for you. And, as DOS has gotten more sophisticated, it becomes less necessary for users to know the specific BIOS locations and calls that make all this happen.

Serial Port Services

The serial port (RS-232, communications line) services are invoked by interrupt 14. Sometimes these services are called asynchronous communications, reflecting the back and forth nature of the way in which data flow is controlled between serial devices and the computer. Table 19.5 summarizes the six serial port services.

Table 19.5.   *The Interrupt 14 Serial Port Services*

Serial Service (Hex)	Description
00	Initialize a serial port
01	Write a character
02	Read a character
03	Write sectors from memory
04	Initialize a PS/2 serial port
05	Control modem control register

Using the serial port is fairly simple. Everything is compared with the screen and the disk drives, and only six services are needed. Service 00 initializes the communications port, setting the basic parameters (discussed in Chapter 25), the baud rate, and so forth. Service 01 is used to write a byte to the port; service 02 reads a byte. Service 03, the last, is used to get a status report, which indicates things such as whether data is ready.

Services 04 and 05 are advanced services used with only PS/2s and newer AT-class machines that have improved serial ports. Service 04 is used instead of service 00 to initialize a port. Service 04 adds such features as support for communications rates above 9,600 bps. Service 05 reads from and writes to a special modem control register.

Other BIOS Services: Miscellaneous, Keyboard, Printer

The next interrupt, 15, was at one time used only to control a cassette tape interface. However, IBM has expanded the interrupt to offer a grab bag of miscellaneous system services. Table 19.6 lists some of the more interesting services provided by this interrupt.

Table 19.6. *The Interrupt 15 Miscellaneous Services*

Service (Hex)	Description
21	Read the error log from the power on self-test
80	Open a device
81	Close a device
82	Terminate a program
83	Wait for an event to happen
84	Support a joystick
85	Test to see whether the SysReq key has been pressed
86	Wait for a particular length of time
87–89	Support extended memory and protected mode
90	Signal that a device is busy
C0	Find out the system configuration parameters
C2	Support a pointing device such as a mouse

The keyboard services are activated with interrupt 16. Service 00 reads the next character from the keyboard input buffer. The characters are reported in their full two-byte form, as discussed in Chapter 15. When a character is read by service 00, it is removed from the keyboard input buffer. Not so with service 01; service 01 reports whether there is any keyboard input ready. If there is, this service also previews the character by reporting the character bytes in the same way that service 00 does, but the character remains in the keyboard buffer until it's officially read with service 00.

The final keyboard service, 02, reports the keyboard status bits, which indicate the state of the Shift keys and so forth. (This is discussed in Chapter 15, and you can see it in action in the KEYBITS program in Appendix C.) Although you know where to find that information in the low memory location where the BIOS stores it, this service is the official and approved way for programs to learn about keyboard status.

Services 00, 01, and 02 were designed for the old-style keyboard. Starting with the last version of the PC AT computer, IBM introduced what is now the standard 101/102-key keyboard. (American keyboards have 101 keys; some non-American keyboards have 102 keys.) All PS/2s use some version of this keyboard.

Because this keyboard has extra keys, it requires new services to replace 00, 01, and 02. These services are 10 (read), 11 (status), and 12 (shift status).

Service 03 controls the typematic rate, that is, how long you have to hold down a key to get it to repeat and how fast it repeats.

Service 04 was used with only the PCjr and PC Convertible. The keyboards on these computers did not make a clicking noise on their own, so a sound had to be generated via the speaker. This service was used to turn the clicking sound off and on.

Table 19.7 summarizes the keyboard services.

Table 19.7. *The Interrupt 16 Keyboard Services*

Keyboard Service (Hex)	Description
00	Read (old keyboard)
01	Status (old keyboard)
02	Shift status (old keyboard)
03	Set typematic rate
10	Read (new keyboard)
11	Status (new keyboard)
12	Shift status (new keyboard)

The next of the device support services are for the parallel printer port, using interrupt 17. There are three simple services: 00 sends a single byte to the printer, 01 initializes the printer, and 02 reports the printer status, such as whether the printer is out of paper.

The final interrupt that provides device services is a new one, 4B. This interrupt actually does two jobs. First, it provides services to control SCSI devices. SCSI is an interface that enables you to daisy-chain devices to use only a single port. IBM offers high-capacity SCSI hard disks on the high-end PS/2s.

The second set of services offered by interrupt 4B involves DMA, Direct Memory Access, which is the capability to transfer data between a device and memory without the constant control of the main processor. This part of interrupt 4B actually is supplied by the operating system, not by the BIOS.

That finishes off the ROM-BIOS services that are directly used to support the PC's I/O peripheral equipment. It's worth noting that there are two other I/O devices in the PC's standard repertoire, the speaker and joysticks, that have no support in the BIOS whatsoever.

The Rest of the BIOS Interrupts

The remaining ROM-BIOS services are used to control information or to invoke major changes in the PC.

Interrupt 11 is used to get the PC's official (and now rather out of date) equipment list information. The equipment list was designed around the facilities of the original PC model and hasn't been expanded to include the new equipment that has been added to the family (mostly, I think, because it hasn't turned out to be necessary). The equipment list reports the number of floppy disk drives the machine has, but says nothing about hard disks or other disk types. It reports the number of parallel ports and serial ports. It also reports whether there is an internal modem installed, some rudimentary video information, whether a pointing device such as a mouse is installed, whether a math coprocessor is installed, and whether a boot disk is present.

A companion service to the equipment list reports the amount of memory the computer has up to 640KB. Officially, it's requested with interrupt 12. The amount of memory is reported in kilobytes. (The amount of extended memory is reported by interrupt 15, service 88.)

The third and last of the pure information interrupts is 1A. This interrupt provides services that have to do with time. Some of the more interesting services are setting the time and date, using a timer, and using an alarm. The BIOS keeps a time-of-day clock in the form of a long, four-byte integer, with each count representing one clock tick.

The PC's hardware clock ticks by generating a clock interrupt 18.2 times a second, and the interrupt handler for the clock adds one to the clock count each time. The clock count is supposed to represent the number of ticks since last midnight. It shows the right time (that is, the right count) only if it has been properly set, for example, by the DOS TIME command or the battery-powered, real-time clock.

When you turn the computer on, the clock starts counting from zero, as if the time were midnight, until something sets the correct clock time/count. DOS converts the clock tick count into the time of day in hours, minutes, seconds, and hundredths of seconds by simple arithmetic. The BIOS routines that update the clock check for the count that represents 24 hours. At that point, the clock is reset to zero, and a midnight-has-passed signal is recorded. The next time DOS reads the clock count from the BIOS, DOS sees this midnight-has-passed signal and updates the record it keeps of the date.

Newer PCs have BIOS code to handle BIOS shadowing, as well. I've pointed out before that a computer's ROM operates much slower than RAM. Depending on the type of memory you are using, system RAM may be 70 percent or more faster than ROM in handling memory I/O. This is due not only to the speed of memory itself (ROM may operate at 200 nanoseconds, for example; RAM moves along at 70 nanoseconds), but also to the way ROM and RAM move data. ROM may be handling only 8 bits at a time; system RAM may handle 32 bits at a time.

The solution is to copy ROM-BIOS out of ROM and into system RAM as soon as the boot process is complete. Then by disabling ROM, you can locate the RAM-based BIOS at the same memory address as the ROM-based BIOS. That's how "shadow" BIOS works. For each ROM address, there is an equivalent RAM address. So, even if you have shadow BIOS, it may be located at F000 or E000 just as it would be without shadow. It just runs a whole lot faster.

There are, finally, two more interesting BIOS service interrupts. They are used to pass control to either of two special routines built into the BIOS. One is the ROM-BASIC (on older machines; network interface on newer machines), and the other is the start-up routines. (By the way, keep in mind that only IBM's own older models of the PC family have the built-in BASIC; other family members, such as Compaq computers, do not.)

Many of today's computers use interrupt 18 (the old ROM-BASIC) for network interface card (NIC) control. One routine that is fairly common, for example, is for interrupt 18 to be called during start-up if both the floppy and the hard disk fail. That could mean that there are no local disk drives on the PC and that the DOS boot routine is handled by a ROM on board the NIC. You can boot a system over a network with the proper bootstrap ROM installed on the network interface card.

The normal way to activate the bootstrap program is by pressing Ctrl-Alt-Del. And, usually, you do not activate the ROM-BASIC at all. However, it's also possible for any program to activate either of these routines simply by invoking their interrupts. Unlike the ordinary service routines, which do something for the program and then return processing to the program that invoked them, these two routines are one-way streets. They take full charge of the machine and never return control to the program that invoked them.

If you do decide to play with these interrupts, remember two things. First, there is more to rebooting than invoking the bootstrap interrupt. You may hang up the machine so thoroughly that it must be turned off and on again. Second, if you do start up ROM-BASIC (something you only can do with an old PC anyway), there is no way to save any work that you do. ROM-BASIC was designed originally for a cassette device and cannot save files to disk. With those warnings in mind, the following is a simple way to test these interrupts by using DEBUG.

Start the DEBUG program (DEBUG is discussed in Chapter 26). The DEBUG prompt is a hyphen (-). When you see the prompt, enter the Assemble command (**a**). This enables you to enter an assembly language command. Enter **int 18** (for ROM-BASIC or to access your NIC) and **int 19** (for bootstrap). Press Enter to end the assembly. Finally, enter the Go command (**g**) to execute the interrupt statement.

BIOS Future

Like the rest of your PC, the BIOS isn't sitting still. It is changing as new technology evolves that requires some basic changes to this important, internal logic area of your machine. For now, many of the changes are handled through DOS-level drivers and BIOS extensions that are part of add-on boards. In the near future, however, I expect some rather fundamental changes to BIOS and BIOS standards. As you move further and further away from the original PC and PC AT, it becomes less necessary to preserve some of the old code and conventions that have been cherished and maintained for so long. Although not many users had a say during the evolution process of the PC, the industry now can cooperate with users to make some important and necessary changes to PC conventions.

The push toward "green" PCs (those that use less power and are more efficient), for example, probably will require some basic BIOS changes before long. The video services will be expanded to provide ways to turn off or power down video displays, for example, and hard drives will be turned off if they aren't used for an extended period. You already see these types of services on laptop machines; now laptop technology is starting to move to the desktop. IBM and others are marketing flat color displays that can be powered from the system unit and controlled by software, for example, and desktop machines are showing up with PCMCIA expansion slots. Already, some laptop machines have BIOS changes to permit booting from PCMCIA cards. This may not seem like something you need on a desktop machine yet, but just wait. When you can carry in your shirt pocket or purse your own, personalized PCMCIA card with enough ROM, RAM, and storage space for your tasks, the concept of sitting down at any PC in any office, inserting your personal card, and starting to work, has a lot of appeal.

Another area of interesting change is an emerging IEEE standard to enhance the computer's parallel port. When the dust settles around this one, I expect that you will have BIOS support for an enhanced parallel port standard that could improve printer performance 10 times or more and also could permit multiple, addressable devices to be attached to the parallel port as with SCSI interfaces now.

The move toward PCI local bus will mean some BIOS changes, eventually, especially as manufacturers of other types of computers, such as RISC machines, incorporate it. This gives these manufacturers a doorway into the PC world and a chance for PC manufacturers to offer another level of industry-wide standardization. Making these changes at the BIOS level can relieve third-party vendors of the task of providing this support.

Other areas of PC technology cry for basic BIOS control changes, but they may come slower. Support for sound and motion video, for example, could mean basic system changes. You do it today with DOS drivers and add-on hardware. If, at some point, sound and video support become as common and as necessary as a hard disk and video display, surely the computer's BIOS would change to reflect that.

In addition, as CD-ROM becomes more common, and if speed improves, you may see a move toward booting some systems from CD. That would necessitate a BIOS change to enable the system to look for the CD-ROM drive. Also, CD-ROM support currently is handled through special drivers loaded from CONFIG.SYS or AUTOEXEC.BAT. With the increasing popularity of CDs, it makes sense to me that BIOS designers will work a way to support the CD directly just as they support hard disks and floppies now.

That completes the coverage of the ROM-BIOS, the PC's lowest level of software support. Now you're ready to move on to the next basic level of software, DOS itself. The next three chapters take a close look at DOS.

Some Things To Try

1. What would be the effect of combining all the ROM-BIOS services under one interrupt? Or giving each service its own separate interrupt?

2. Can you think of reasons why the bootstrap loader and the PC's built-in ROM-BASIC would be invoked by interrupts? Do you think it was to make them available for use by any program or just to make them easier to use by IBM's system programs?

3. At the end of the first section of this chapter, I mentioned that one of the reasons to study the BIOS services is to understand their level. Consider how the level of the services might be higher or lower. Take one example from the services and see how you could change its definition to be more primitive or more advanced. Analyze the video services and rank them in terms of relatively high or low levels.

The Role
of DOS

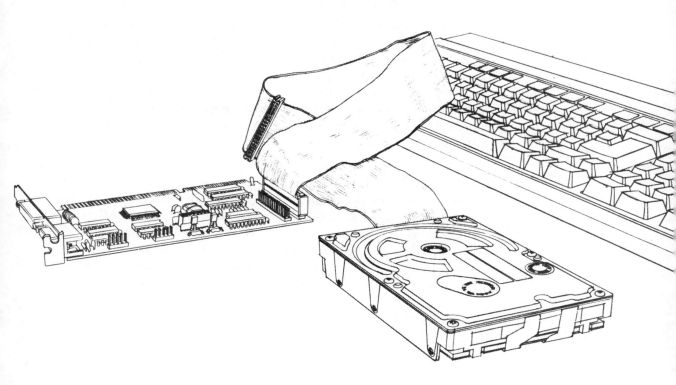

T his chapter begins a three-chapter tour of DOS, the last major part of the PC epic. The next two chapters investigate how DOS works for you directly and how it works for your programs. However, before I get into that, I need to set the stage with some background information on DOS, and that's what this chapter is for. I start by looking at operating systems in general. Then I discuss the forces that shaped the character of DOS and the ideas that formed the basis for its design. Then you learn how DOS can be expanded in ways that are internal (such as device drivers) and ways that are external (such as visual shells).

What Any DOS Is About

The DOS that you use on your PC is just one example of a class of computer programs that are known as supervisors, control programs, or operating systems. Operating systems, such as DOS, are probably the most complex computer programs that have ever been built. The task of an operating system basically is to supervise and direct the work, the operation, of the computer.

It's a tribute to the power and flexibility of computers that they are able not only to do computing work but to take on the complex job of looking after their own operation. And, it's a marvelous irony that the most sophisticated programs are created not to deal with the user's work but to take care of the computer's own work. Computers are the most powerful tool man has ever created. They are so powerful, in fact, that users must have the intermediary of an operating system to make the tool manageable. Users give computers the task of supervising themselves so that they don't have to concern themselves with the extraordinary problems involved in making a computer work.

In Chapter 6, when you learned about interrupts, you saw just how demanding the task of supervising a computer can be. Every physical part of the computer's equipment requires some looking after, and some of those parts demand a lot. The PC's clock, for example, which is used to keep track of the time of day, demands attention with an interrupt 18.2 times each second. The keyboard, as you learned in Chapter 14, demands attention every time a key is pressed or released. When you type the word *keyboard*, you cause the computer to be interrupted 16 separate times just to note the keystrokes, and an enormous, additional load of work is done after the keystrokes are recorded.

The task of orchestrating, coordinating, and supervising the breathtaking array of events that take place inside computers falls to the operating system. For PC users, this is DOS.

So what does the operating system do? Essentially, it manages devices, controls programs, and processes commands.

DOS's work in managing devices (printers, disks, screens, keyboards, and other peripherals) involves everything needed to keep the computer running properly. On the lowest level, that means issuing commands to the devices and looking after any errors they report. That's exactly the job that the PC's ROM-BIOS performs. In the broadest sense, any operating system that works on a PC includes the ROM-BIOS as one of its key components. On a much higher level, the operating system performs a major organizing role for the computer's devices. This is particularly evident with the disks. An important, even dominant, part of the operating system's responsibility is to work out the scheme for recording data on disks. This includes management of disk space, efficient storage of data, and quick, reliable retrieval.

The second broad job that DOS undertakes is the control of programs. That involves loading programs from disk, setting up the framework for a program's execution, and providing services for programs (more on this in Chapter 21). On more complex and sophisticated computer systems than the PC family, the control that operating systems perform also involves things that aren't possible on PCs, such as setting the limits on what parts of memory and what parts of the disk storage the program can access. Because of the relative simplicity of the PC, every program has full access to any part of memory and all the disk storage. On larger computers, however, that isn't true, and one part of the task of controlling programs on those computers is controlling the limitations and restrictions within which programs work.

The third major task that DOS performs is command processing, which is the direct interaction that DOS has with the user. Every time you type something at the DOS command prompt, you are working with the command processing aspect of DOS. In the case of DOS, your commands are essentially requests to execute a program. In more complex operating systems, commands can take on a wider scope, including things like directing the workings of the operating system. Whatever the scope of commands that an operating system provides, an important task for the operating system is to accept and carry out the user's commands.

That, in summary, is the heart of what any operating system does. Now, it's time to take a look at the history of DOS so that you can see some of the concepts that underlie the way DOS works.

History and Concepts of DOS

The real history of DOS begins with the early planning for the IBM Personal Computer and the operating system used with the generation of personal computers that preceded the PC.

The PC was planned and designed at a time when most personal computers used an 8-bit microprocessor, and the dominant operating system for those machines was CP/M (Control Program/Microcomputer). Even though the PC was to be a much more powerful 16-bit computer, IBM wanted to build on the experience and popularity of CP/M machines. Although the PC was going to be quite different, and even though 8-bit CP/M programs couldn't be used directly on the PC, making the PC's operating system similar to CP/M would make it easier to adapt programs (and users' experience and skills) to the new machine.

Apparently, IBM intended to have an updated, 16-bit version of CP/M, which became known as CP/M-86, as the PC's primary operating system, but that didn't work out. For whatever reason, IBM decided to use a new operating system created for the PC by Microsoft. That operating system was DOS.

Today, after several years of developing and changing, there are two basic versions of DOS: IBM's and everybody else's. IBM's DOS is called PC DOS; everybody else's is called MS-DOS. Beyond that, there are multiple versions of everybody else's DOS, which are not that much different, but different, nevertheless. That's because Microsoft doesn't sell DOS to end users, it sells DOS to computer companies. And, as with other areas of computing and technology, each designer believes its way of doing things is the best. This results in slight differences in the external routines included with DOS and within DOS itself. For the most part, you don't notice these differences, unless there is an external program with your machine that isn't on someone else's. I don't know what the numbers are today, two DOS versions later, but when the current version of DOS was 4.01, Microsoft told me there were 26 different versions of MS-DOS, based on differences among the implementations of different manufacturers.

Although DOS was favored from the start, it was not the only operating system IBM introduced with the PC. Two other operating systems, each with its own base of supporters, were also introduced and given official IBM approval. These operating systems were CP/M-86 and the UCSD p-System, an operating system closely tuned to the needs of the Pascal programming language. In those days, however, nobody wanted to use more than one operating system because it was very inconvenient to switch from one to another and nearly impossible to share data or programs between them. For practical reasons, there could be only one winner in the battle for operating system supremacy, and that winner was DOS. (Modern operating systems, such as OS/2 and the UNIX-based PC systems—AIX, UNIX, and XENIX—can share files with DOS, making it feasible to use more than one operating system on a computer. With the older operating systems, such sharing was just not possible.)

Although DOS was a competitor to CP/M for the PC, the design and operation of DOS were based on the facilities that CP/M provided. DOS, as it was initially introduced, had the flavor and style of CP/M for an important and deliberate reason. DOS developers wanted to make it as convenient as possible for computer users who were familiar with CP/M to learn to use DOS and to make it easy for existing 8-bit CP/M programs to be adapted for the PC.

The influence of CP/M appears in the very first thing you see when you use DOS: the command prompt. In addition, DOS shows the design influence of CP/M in many of the ways in which it works with you and your programs.

Although experienced eyes can see the similarities between DOS and CP/M, the most important ways that CP/M set the style for DOS aren't visible because they are ideas. Foremost among them was the scope and use that was intended for DOS from the beginning. DOS was built with the most primitive concepts of personal computing in mind. This included the assumption that only one person would be using the computer and that the one user would ask the computer to do only one thing at a time (not, for example, printing out one document while computing on something else, which would be performing two tasks at the same time). DOS was designed to be a single-user, single-tasking system. This was natural because its roots came from an operating system and a family of 8-bit machines that weren't suited to anything more ambitious.

413

The PC family, however, had more ambitious goals, and the limitations of the CP/M heritage would have severely restricted DOS's capability to grow with the PC. On the other hand, the UNIX operating system was widely admired for its broad features, and Microsoft had extensive experience with the UNIX style based on its work with XENIX, a variation of UNIX. So, when the time came to make a major revision of the features and internal structure of DOS, many of the concepts used in UNIX/XENIX were stirred into the DOS recipe. The result was DOS version 2.0 and all the subsequent versions.

The influence of UNIX is visible in the subdirectories that you use to organize and subdivide disks. It is even more apparent in the internal structure of DOS and the services that DOS provides for programs. Chapter 21 shows an important example of that when I discuss the two ways DOS provides for programs to work with files: an old CP/M method and a new UNIX-inspired method.

The DOS that you know and use today is a blend of the styles and design features of CP/M and UNIX. Although DOS contains many of the expansive and forward-looking features of UNIX, it still suffers from many of the limitations of CP/M. Because DOS originally gave every program total control over the computer and all its memory, it is difficult for more advanced versions of DOS to impose the limitations that are required to have two programs running at the same time. Like so many other things, DOS has been able to grow and develop far beyond what it was in its earliest days, yet it still feels the restrictive tug of its predecessor. Later in this chapter, I discuss some of the attempts that are being made to transcend those limitations. First, though, you learn how DOS has become a flexible tool.

Installable Drivers and Flexible Facilities

In its earliest form, DOS was a rigid creation that had predefined into it all the devices, disk formats, and such with which it could work. This was DOS version 1, the release based solely on the model of CP/M. That version of DOS was unable to adjust itself to changing circumstances or to incorporate new devices, such as new disk formats.

But, as the PC family grew, it became important to be able to adjust DOS to the special needs of each computer and computer user and to be able to make DOS accept and accommodate new peripheral devices, particularly the many kinds of disks that were being used with PCs. So, with DOS 2.0, which included many new UNIX concepts, DOS was made adaptable through a facility known as a configuration file.

The configuration file is the key to DOS's flexibility and adaptability. When DOS first begins operation, it looks on the start-up disk for a file with the name CONFIG.SYS. If it finds that file, DOS reads it and follows the commands that define how DOS is to be configured and adapted. Following is an example of a configuration file:

```
rem * ===================================
rem * CONFIG.SYS (July 26)
rem *  -- DOS version: 6.0
rem * ===================================
rem -- Load memory management programs
device = c:\dos\himem.sys
device = c:\dos\emm386.exe NOEMS HIGHSCAN
dos = high,umb

rem -- Set options

break = on
buffers = 30,8
files = 41
lastdrive = f

rem -- Install device drivers

devicehigh = c:\dos\ansi.sys /x /l
device = c:\dos\smartdrv.sys 4716
devicehigh = c:\dos\ramdrive.sys 4096 /e
device = c:\dos\$fdd5.sys

rem -- Install memory resident programs

install = c:\dos\fastopen.exe c: d: /x
install = c:\dos\doskey.com
```

```
rem -- Set up the command processor: 400 byte environment

shell = c:\dos\command.com /e:400 /p
```

DOS can be customized, modified, and configured in five important ways. As you can see, the CONFIG.SYS file is divided into five parts. If you want to learn more about CONFIG.SYS, you can look at my DOS book, *Peter Norton's DOS 6 Guide*, published by Brady Books.

The first part of the sample CONFIG.SYS file sets up the programs that manage extended and expanded memory. In this example, HIMEM.SYS is the extended memory manager, and EMM386.EXE is the expanded memory manager. These DOS commands control the loading of part of DOS into upper memory.

The next part tells DOS how to set up certain options and system values. The BUFF-ERS setting, for example, tells DOS how many disk buffers (temporary read/write areas) to use. Choosing the number of disk buffers involves a simple trade-off: the more buffers, the less often DOS has to wait for information to be read from the disk but the less memory there is for programs to use.

The third part of the CONFIG.SYS file involves programs called device drivers that can be integrated into DOS. Naturally enough, DOS has built-in support for all the standard types of peripheral devices. However, you may want to add other compo-nents to DOS, and that's what the DEVICE and DEVICEHIGH commands enable you to do. DEVICEHIGH installs the driver in upper memory to leave more regular memory for programs.

The device drivers are written following a strict set of guidelines that enable them to work in close cooperation with DOS without disrupting any of DOS's other work-ings. The sample CONFIG.SYS file shows five examples of device drivers.

The first two device drivers, HIMEM.SYS and EMM386.EXE, are the memory man-agers already discussed. The next device driver is ANSI.SYS, which provides extended keyboard and screen control. The rest of the device drivers have to do with disks. SMARTDRV.SYS sets up a disk cache, RAMDRIVE.SYS creates a virtual disk (a RAM disk), and $FDD5.SYS provides support for an external 5.25-inch disk drive.

The fourth section of the CONFIG.SYS file installs memory-resident programs. In this case, FASTOPEN provides a facility to help DOS access disk directory information quickly. DOSKEY is used to recall and edit previous DOS commands and to create macros (abbreviations for lists of commands).

The final configuration task uses the SHELL command to set up the command processor. In this case, you are using the default command processor, COMMAND.COM, that comes with DOS. It is also possible to specify an alternative program, such as the NDOS.COM command processor that comes with the Norton Utilities (version 6.0 and later).

Whatever purpose installable device drivers and programs serve, they provide a way for you to modify, extend, and expand the capabilities of DOS within the basic design of the operating system. There are other ways to expand and change DOS, though, that don't work from within DOS. This is the subject of the next section.

Shells: The Norton Commander and Microsoft Windows

Certain inherent characteristics of DOS define how DOS appears to you (the face it presents to the user) and what DOS is and isn't capable of doing. As you know from experience, DOS's user interface is based on a simple command prompt and commands that must be typed from the keyboard. You also know that DOS can run only one program at a time. DOS doesn't give you any way of having more than one thing going at a time (except for things such as the PRINT command, which can print while you run other programs). You also cannot suspend a program during operation (put it on hold) while you run another program and then return to the first program.

Just because DOS doesn't provide a way of doing these things, however, doesn't mean that they aren't desirable or can't be done. In fact, many of the most talented minds in the PC community have been working hard to provide you with programs that can add fancy facilities to DOS.

You can transform the operation of DOS by using any of a class of programs commonly called visual shells (although that name describes only part of what this class

417

of program can do). Shells are programs that essentially wrap themselves around DOS and provide facilities that DOS does not have.

There are any number of things that such a program might undertake, but of the ones that have received the most attention from the PC community, two stand out. One is providing a more appealing and useful "face," that is, a nicer way to enter commands. The other is some kind of multitasking that enables you to use more than one program at a time. When a shell uses graphics, it often is called a graphical user interface, or GUI.

The best publicized program of this type is Microsoft Windows. I briefly discuss Windows to give you an idea of why this sort of program has been discussed and energetically worked on. This program stands as a representative of the broad class of shell programs that have appeared, and which you can expect to see more of. (For more information on Microsoft Windows, see Chapter 23.)

One of the reasons that there has been so much interest in the idea of shells is that DOS's command interface provides you with so little help in entering commands. To run a program with DOS, you must remember the name of the program and type it in along with any parameters that are needed. Until you figure out what command to enter, the computer sits dumbly, waiting, doing nothing.

Shell programs, like Microsoft Windows, on the other hand, show you a list of all the commands that you might want to use. You simply can select a command and execute it without having to type the command name. Using cursor keys or a mouse, you can point to the command that you want performed and send it into action with a single press of the Enter key or click of the mouse button.

The command interface can be enriched even beyond that, from the verbal to the visual, by replacing the names of commands on the screen with drawings called icons, which represent the function that the command performs. Some of the most advanced visual shell programs work in this way.

But, easier or more attractive command entry is not the main reason for the interest in visual shells. Equally important is the capability of some shells to work with more than one program at a time. This can be done in a variety of ways, each of which has its own unique technical challenges. Some shells actually have several programs in active operation at the same time, as Microsoft Windows does; others put programs on hold while other tasks are performed and then return to the suspended program without starting it from scratch. The DOSSHELL application, supplied as part of

DOS versions 5.0 and later, is one of these. (Yes, DOS 4.0 also has a shell program, but it doesn't compare with the functionality of later versions or Microsoft Windows. Most users agree with me on this!)

Shells are found in other PC operating systems besides DOS. OS/2, IBM's multitasking and multiuser operating system that competes directly with Microsoft Windows and Windows NT, uses an icon- and window-based GUI called the Presentation Manager. UNIX systems also have shells. Two examples are Motif and Open Look, both of which are based on the X-Window System developed at MIT.

Another approach to DOS shells is to forgo the icons and other pictures and to provide a simple, straightforward DOS interface. These types of shells (my Norton Commander and the integral DOSSHELL are examples), enable both experienced and novice users to navigate the world of DOS without having to deal directly with DOS commands or the DOS prompt. (The DOS 5.0 and later shell also works in "graphics" mode, but it still doesn't offer anything like the icon support of Windows.)

These simpler shells have two advantages over the more elaborate shells. First, they operate in text mode rather than graphics mode. Text mode requires less overhead and works with older text-based displays. Second, theses shells work just as well on older PCs.

Each type of shell has its advantages. Microsoft Windows is actually a whole operating environment; the Norton Commander is a new face for DOS.

DR DOS

Earlier in this chapter, I said that, in the beginning, DOS wasn't the only operating system offered for the IBM PC. Today, by far the vast majority of PCs run MS-DOS or IBM's version, PC DOS. A few run UNIX or a UNIX derivative, and maybe 10 percent or less use Digital Research's DR DOS, now owned by Novell, the networking company.

DR DOS so far hasn't proved to be a strong competitor for MS-DOS, but for its dedicated users, DR DOS has repeatedly beat Microsoft to the market with upgrades and new features and now, under Novell's guidance, promises to become an even stronger contender.

The latest version of DR DOS, 7.0, which wasn't released when this book was written but was on its way, promises to add some significant features that may woo Microsoft users away. DR DOS has kept up with Microsoft and now offers, in addition to the features included in MS-DOS 6.0, full peer-to-peer networking. If the rumored plans come to pass, two machines running Novell DOS 7.0 (as the new product will be named) can share printers, disk drives, and other facilities without additional networking software. This is akin to Microsoft's Windows for Workgroups, the GUI environment based on Windows 3.1 that also includes peer-to-peer networking.

In addition, the rumors for Novell DOS 7.0 say that it will include support for protected mode operation, opening the door to multitasking inside DOS, the same sort of multiple program execution now available in Windows. And, of course, with networking included, the logical assumption is that some form of scheduling and mail services—joint software to be shared among networked users—will be included as part of the intrinsic DOS utilities.

All this still doesn't mean that the majority of users will switch to Novell DOS 7.0, but these features doubtless will swell the ranks of alternative DOS users. And, with features such as these and the backing of a big company like Novell, that could mean that a growing number of computer manufacturers and OEMs will bundle Novell DOS with their machines, further broadening the market.

Luckily, even with its extended features, DR DOS has traditionally mirrored MS-DOS closely. Some of the utility names are different, and there are some new features, but in general, after you get DOS running (MS-DOS or DR DOS), you aren't particularly aware of where the system software came from.

Some Things To Try

1. Why is it that the PC's original processor, the 8088, can't safely run many programs at the same time? How can a program like Microsoft Windows try to overcome some of these problems? What advantages does Microsoft Windows have when it is running on a 386-, 486-, or Pentium-based PC?

2. If you were designing a shell for DOS, a new way of making it easier for the PC user to give commands, how would you design it? Work out the best approach that you can think of and consider what compromises you might have to make to balance different needs.

DOS Serving Us

N ow you're ready to see what DOS does. In this chapter, I look at what DOS does for you, the user. In Chapter 22, l see what DOS does for software, that is, providing services that programs can use.

First, you learn how the DOS command processor works. Then you see how command processing is enriched and made more complex by batch file processing.

Command Processing

Of all the things that DOS does in supervising a computer, the one that you're most directly aware of is command processing, which is DOS's capability to accept and act on commands. The job of command processing falls to the one visible component of DOS's three key parts, the program known as COMMAND.COM.

COMMAND.COM issues the terse command prompt that you're used to seeing, which usually looks something like this:

```
C:\>
```

When you see the command prompt, it means that DOS (or more particularly, the COMMAND.COM command processor) is waiting for you to enter a command for it to carry out.

Just what is a command? It's really nothing more than a request to run a program. The command you issue—the first word you type on the command line—is simply the name of a program you're asking DOS to run. After the program name may come one or more command parameters or switches that control how the program operates. If, for example, you issue the following command, you're doing nothing but asking DOS to find a program named FORMAT and run it for you:

```
FORMAT A: /S /V
```

Everything else in the command line (in this case, A: /S /V is simply further instructions to the program, telling it what to do. You're giving parameters to the program, and DOS passes them on; to DOS they mean nothing, and the command processor pays no attention to them.

The programs that the command processor can carry out for you fall into four categories, and it's important that you understand what they are and how they work because your effective use of the computer is based largely on how well these commands are put at your disposal. The four categories of commands are internal commands and three types of external commands: COM programs, EXE programs, and BAT (batch) commands. I start by looking at the division between the internal commands and the three types of external commands.

Most programs (that is, the commands that DOS can perform for you) are separate entities that are stored in files on disks. Not all of the commands that DOS can perform work that way, however; not all of them are kept in their own disk files. The COMMAND.COM command processor includes some of the most important and frequently used command programs, so it isn't necessary to fetch a program file from disk to carry out these commands. These are called internal commands because the programs that perform the command work are inside COMMAND.COM. These commands load when DOS boots and are resident in memory and ready to run at all times. External commands, on the other hand, stay on disk until you call for them by entering the name of the file on the DOS command line.

The list of internal commands varies from version to version of DOS. Table 21.1 shows DOS 6.0 internal commands. Note that regular commands also can be used in batch files, but you normally can't use the commands specifically designed for batch programs at the DOS command prompt. In addition, some of the regular commands in table 21.1—SET, PATH, DATE, TIME, LOADHIGH—most often are used in batch files. (Although you can use them at the command line, normally you use them as part of the configuration process in a batch file.) The commands listed in the CONFIG.SYS column are designed for system configuration and can be used only in the CONFIG.SYS file, with the exception of the ones marked with an asterisk, which also can be used at the DOS command prompt. (Note that I have included one external command in table 21.1 just to make the list complete. COUNTRY is an external command that only can be used in the CONFIG.SYS configuration file.)

Table 21.1. *DOS 6.0 Internal Commands*

Regular Commands	Batch Commands	CONFIG.SYS Commands
BREAK	CALL	BREAK*
CHCP	CHOICE	BUFFERS
CHDIR(CD)	ECHO	COUNTRY

continues

Table 21.1. *continued*

Regular Commands	Batch Commands	CONFIG.SYS Commands
CLS	FOR	DEVICE
COPY	GOTO	DEVICEHIGH
CTTY	IF	DOS
DATE	PAUSE	DRIVPARM
DEL(ERASE)	REM	FCBS
DELTREE	SHIFT	FILES
DIR		INCLUDE
EXIT		INSTALL
LOADHIGH(LH)		LASTDRIVE
MKDIR		MENUCOLOR
PATH		MENUDEFAULT
PROMPT		MENUITEM
RENAME(REN)		NUMLOCK
RMDIR(RD)		REM*
SET		SET*
TIME		SHELL
TYPE		STACKS
VER		SUBMENU
VERIFY		SWITCHES
VOL		

The command processor holds a table of these internal commands and the program code to carry them out. When you give DOS a command, COMMAND.COM first looks up the command name in its table to see whether you're asking for an internal command. If so, COMMAND.COM can carry out the command immediately. If not, COMMAND.COM must look on a disk for the file that holds the external command program.

The command processor identifies the files that hold external commands by two things. First, the filename of the disk file is the name of the command; second, the extension to the filename identifies the file as one of the three types of external commands: a COM file, an EXE file, or a BAT batch command file.

Because the filename of the program file defines the name of the command the program file will carry out, you have a great deal of freedom to change the names of your commands. You can do it simply by renaming the files (but keeping the extension the same) or by making a copy of the command file under another name so that the command is available under its original command name and under any other name you want to give it. I do this all the time and find it one of the handiest DOS tricks there is. I use it primarily to abbreviate the names of the commands I use most.

You can give your commands any name that's allowed under the DOS filename conventions, and you can give them alias names simply by duplicating the files under different names. For internal commands, you can use the new macro facility offered in the DOSKEY command (with DOS version 5.0 and later). DOSKEY enables you to define any name as an abbreviation for a list of commands. So, for example, you could define the one-letter name T to stand for the TIME command as follows:

```
DOSKEY TIME = T
```

I use DOSKEY to add switches and optional features to DOS commands, too. For example, I like the DIR command always to sort the files by name order and pause when the screen is full. I do that with this DOSKEY command:

```
DOSKEY DIR=DIR $1 /on /p
```

The /on parameter tells the DIR command to order the file list by name, and the /p parameter tells DIR to pause when the screen is full. Note that I also add the variable support $1 to enable me to specify file characteristics for any directory list. Without the $1 variable support, every DIR command would produce a full directory listing of the current directory only. By adding $1, I can issue commands, such as the following (which displays a list of all files with names beginning with PROG that have the TXT extension), and still get a sort by name and a pause when the screen is full:

```
DIR PROG*.TXT
```

Of the three kinds of external commands, two (COM and EXE files) are variations on the same principle. The BAT file is something else entirely. Both COM and EXE are proper program files that the command processor loads and executes for you.

From the point of view of the user who fires up programs through the command processor, the differences between COM and EXE program files have no practical importance, but it's interesting to know the difference. COM files have a simple, quick-loading format, and EXE files are more complex. A COM file is sometimes called an image file, which means that what's stored on disk is an exact image of the program as loaded and run in the computer's memory. A COM file needs no further processing or conversion by DOS to run; it's just copied into memory and away it goes.

You may think that all program files are like that, but many programs require a small amount of last-minute preparation before they can run. The crux of this load-time preparation is the one thing that can't be known in advance when a program is created, and that is the memory address to which the program will be copied. In general, the various parts of a program are closely linked. All sections of the executable code know where the other sections are (so that they can call each other), and the program code knows the memory locations of all the bits of data that come with the program. Although any program can know the relative location of its parts, no program can know in advance the absolute memory addresses of those parts. After all, where a program is loaded into memory depends on how much memory is being used by DOS and memory-resident programs, and that can change.

It is possible for a program to adapt itself automatically to wherever it happens to be placed in memory. That's exactly what COM-type programs do. Because they take advantage of segment registers and careful programming conventions, COM programs don't have to be adjusted depending on where they are located in memory. However, not all programs can work that way because the COM format is rather restrictive. Under normal circumstances, COM programs can't be any larger than 64KB, and that's not enough to accommodate more sophisticated programs. Thus, the EXE format exists to handle programs that can't be loaded as a pure memory image.

When DOS loads an EXE program into memory, it performs any last-minute processing needed to ready the program for execution. One main part of that preparation is to plug into as many parts of the program as need it the memory address at which the program is loaded. To do that, the EXE file format includes a table that shows which parts of the program need to be modified and how it should be done. That's not the only special work that has to be done for EXE programs, though. Other things, such as setting up the program's working stack also must be done (COM programs take care of that for themselves).

Also, COM programs and EXE programs are loaded differently, and there also are differences in the ways they are written. Slightly different programming conventions are used to accommodate the different ways they are loaded and run. Also, somewhat different steps are used by programmers to prepare these programs (as you learn in Chapter 24). All in all, though, this is just a technical matter that concerns program developers. From the point of view of the computer user, there is no difference between COM and EXE programs.

When DOS runs a program, either COM or EXE, the command interpreter finds the program on disk, loads it into memory (processing EXE as needed), and then turns control of the computer over to the program. When the program is finished, it passes control back to the heart of DOS, and DOS reactivates the COMMAND.COM command processor. Although the core parts of DOS are held permanently in low memory locations, most of the command interpreter is kept in high memory, the area that programs can use for their data. This is done to avoid permanently tying up much memory for the command interpreter. If a program needs to use the memory in which the command interpreter is located, it simply does so (without even being aware that it is overwriting the command interpreter). When a program finishes and hands control back to DOS, DOS checks to see whether the command interpreter has been disturbed. If it hasn't, DOS simply starts using it again; if it has, DOS loads a fresh copy from disk. That's why, with old PCs that did not have a hard disk, you sometimes had to have a copy of COMMAND.COM on your working disk even though COMMAND.COM was on the DOS system disk you used to start the computer.

That's the essence of the way DOS runs programs, DOS's own internal command programs, and the command programs (COM and EXE type) that are stored on disk. However, there is one more type of command that DOS can carry out for you, the batch file command.

Batch Processing

Batch files represent a powerful expansion of DOS's capability to carry out commands for you. Properly speaking, however, batch files are not a fourth kind of program in the sense that DOS's internal commands and COM and EXE files are programs. Instead, batch command files are scripts of conventional program commands that DOS can carry out, by treating all the steps in the script as a single unit, when you enter a single command.

Batch files are identified by the BAT filename extension. Inside a batch file is simply data in the format of an ASCII text file. Each line of the text file is a command that the command interpreter will carry out.

The simplest kind of batch file is a series of conventional program commands that have been gathered into a batch file so that you can conveniently run them in sequence as a single unit. However, there is much more to batch file processing.

For one thing, parameters can be used with batch files just as they can with ordinary programs, and the command interpreter can take the parameters you give with the batch command and pass them on to the programs inside the batch file. And, even more sophisticated than that, is a whole batch command language, which enables the command interpreter to carry out logical steps to repeat the execution of programs or to skip steps depending on errors that occur, parameters you give, or whether the files you need actually exist.

If you have the Norton Utilities, you can use the Batch Enhancer facility to supercharge your batch files. The Batch Enhancer offers an array of features to augment the standard DOS batch commands.

Although this isn't the place to go into the complexities of DOS's batch processing command language, it's worthwhile to note that it exists and that it's one of the most powerful tools you have to help you make effective use of DOS. Experienced users of DOS tend to do practically everything in their computers through the batch processing facility because it enables them to avoid the work of entering a series of commands repeatedly. To give you an idea of how much I use batch files, I just counted the number of batch files I've built for myself. They total an amazing 145! That might be a lot more than you need (I suspect it's more than I really need, too), but it gives you an idea of just how important batch files can be.

If you haven't already mastered the uses of the batch file, I highly recommend that you take the time to do so. Be aware, though, that there are advanced parts of the batch command language that can be quite confusing when you first try to use them. I recommend that you try to learn about and take advantage of batch files in an incremental way, first using the simplest features and then, when you're comfortable with them, moving on to see whether you have any use for the more advanced ones. If you need some help, my book, *Peter Norton's DOS 6 Guide*, published by Brady Books, covers batch files in depth.

Some Things To Try

1. Using any snooping tool available to you (such as DEBUG or my Norton Utilities), browse around inside your computer's COMMAND.COM and find the names of the internal commands. Do you find anything unusual? What else, besides the command names, does COMMAND.COM need to hold? (For information on how to use DEBUG or the Norton Utilities, see Chapter 26.)

2. How do you think a COM-type program can adjust itself to wherever DOS loads it into memory? What are some of the problems that might have to be solved, and how can a program overcome them?

3. If you're familiar with the ins and outs of DOS's batch command language, analyze it to see what you think are its strong and weak points. Particularly look for the parts that are awkward to use. Try inventing your own batch language. What features do you think would be the most useful or powerful?

How DOS Serves Programs

22

N ow that you understand some of the basic ideas behind DOS and how DOS works for you, it's time to see how DOS works for programs. This chapter is a parallel to Chapter 19, which covered the services that the ROM-BIOS provides for programs; this chapter does the same for DOS. The similarity is strong, of course, but there are two important differences. As you learned in Chapter 21, one difference is that DOS does much to serve the computer's users directly, which the ROM-BIOS does not. The other difference is that the ROM-BIOS provides services for programs on a very low level; many of the services that DOS provides for programs are complex and on quite a high level. That's one of the themes that should emerge as you tour the DOS services.

DOS Services and Philosophy

The services that DOS provides for programs are subject to several conflicting tugs that have pulled them in several directions and which account for some of the contradictory nature that you see in them. Although the ROM-BIOS services that you studied in Chapter 19 were designed as a whole and created afresh in the best way their designers could manage, the DOS services have had the benefit neither of a single underlying purpose nor of being built in one integrated effort.

Four main influences have shaped the DOS services into what they are today. Two of the four are other operating systems that served as the foundation of DOS.

The first influence, as you learned in Chapter 21, was CP/M. Because CP/M was the dominant operating system for the eight-bit generation of computers that was the predecessor of the PC family and because there was so much CP/M-based software available, DOS was carefully designed to be enough like CP/M to make it relatively easy to adapt CP/M programs to the PC and DOS as well as to make it easier for experienced CP/M users to use DOS. The key to this was having DOS present to programs an appearance very much like that of CP/M. The appearance had to include identical or nearly identical operating system services and a similar philosophy in the design of the disk architecture so that CP/M programs would not have to be redesigned from scratch. Thus, DOS's first big influence was the imitation of CP/M.

The second major influence, which came later, was UNIX. Not long after the appearance of DOS and the PC, it became clear that the CP/M framework had too limited a horizon to accommodate the PC's future. The UNIX operating system, on the other hand was highly regarded, and Microsoft (DOS's creator) had extensive experience developing its variation of UNIX, called XENIX. When it came time to revamp DOS into something more forward looking, much of the style and many of the features of UNIX were stirred into DOS. This became DOS's second big influence.

Two other factors have played a big part in the character and evolution of DOS. One was the desire to make and keep DOS as hardware nonspecific as possible, that is, to have it be computer and peripheral independent. Some of the working parts of DOS must be specifically adjusted to the hardware features of the machines on which it is working, but this is limited to a specific machine-dependent part, called the DOS-BIOS (and distinct from the machine's own ROM-BIOS). Outside of the DOS-BIOS, DOS basically is unaware of the characteristics of the computer with which it is working. This is beneficial because it makes DOS and, particularly, the programs that are designed to use DOS services machine independent. It also has some important drawbacks, however, because it tends to remove many of the most useful machine features from the realm of DOS services.

The most painful example is the use of the display screen. The services provided by DOS do not give programs a way to position information on the display screen. Software is faced with a choice of either using the screen in a crude Teletype-fashion or giving up the machine independence that using only DOS services provides. That has prevented users from having a wide range of powerful programs that automatically work on any computer that uses DOS, even computers that aren't fully PC-compatible. In any event, the reluctance to give DOS features like full-screen display output has been an important influence in DOS's evolution.

The final major influence that has shaped DOS has been the relatively ad hoc addition of features needed to support the new directions in which IBM has taken the PC family. In general, you can say that, rather than being designed in a unified way, features have been added to DOS on an as-needed basis. Thus, the various parts have not fit together quite as smoothly as they might have otherwise. This ad hoc approach has resulted in versions of DOS that, for example, had no memory management services. Then designers attempted to add memory management to what had been an unruly every-man-for-himself approach to the use of memory. The same has been true of the services necessary for shared resources and networking and for multiprogramming and multitasking of programs.

When you stir together these four main influences, out comes the DOS that you know and use. Emerging from this DOS stew is the collection of services that DOS provides for programs.

All the DOS Services

Now you're ready to work your way through the main list of services that DOS provides for programs. Read on if you want to get a good idea of what DOS can do for programs and, thus, for you. Some of them are remarkably interesting. I don't elaborate on each one individually because that would make this chapter impossibly long and test your stamina. Instead, I present an overview that hits the essence of the services DOS provides.

The DOS service routines are all invoked by a common interrupt instruction, interrupt 21 (hex), which is used as a master way of requesting the services. The specific services are requested by their service ID number through the simple process of loading the service number in one of the processor's registers, the same way they are used to request ROM-BIOS services in each service group (such as the video group).

The DOS services also are organized into groups of related services, but in a more informal and less tightly defined way. I cover the services in terms of these groups, roughly in numeric order. One thing to bear in mind is that, unlike the ROM-BIOS services, which are relatively static, the list of DOS services continues to grow, with new ones being added with each release of DOS. This is both good and bad. Although new features are constantly being added, this can create problems when program designers want to take advantage of the latest DOS features. Because many PCs continue to use older versions of DOS, programs that incorporate newer features can't run on machines that use early versions of DOS. In this discussion, I point out which services are included with particular versions of DOS.

I begin with the most elementary group of DOS services, the ones designed for console I/O (interaction with the user). The input services read from the keyboard, and the output services display information on the screen in the simplest and crudest way, treating the screen like a printer and placing information on the screen without any sense of position. These services are a carry over from CP/M and are crude because they are intended to be completely machine blind; that is, they are designed to work uniformly without any awareness of the features of a particular display screen. (This is why the screen output services cannot position information in particular locations on the screen.)

As part of the CP/M heritage, these services are a screwy hodgepodge. There is, for example, a simple keyboard input service and a simple screen output service. In addition, there is another service that acts as input or output or combines both depending on which way you use it. All these CP/M-style services were provided to make it relatively easy to translate CP/M programs to DOS. That was part of an effort to help the PC in its early days when there was a lot of CP/M software and very little PC software. That thinking has long been obsolete, but these services remain.

Part of the same group of elementary DOS services are services that send output to the printer and read and write data to the communications line (the serial port).

All the DOS services that fall into this group are matched by similar or, in some cases, even identical ROM-BIOS services. Why would DOS duplicate services that the BIOS provides? The answer lies in the theory that programs should turn to DOS for all their services so that they are not tied to the features of one machine. Using DOS services is, in principle, more adaptable and makes it possible for programs to run on other machines. DOS services also enable far more flexible handling of I/O, for example, by rerouting data. That's one of the functions the DOS MODE command provides: it enables you to direct printer output to the serial port. If a program used the ROM-BIOS printer services, that function would be impossible.

Unfortunately, that principle works well for only very simple input and output operations with the printer, serial port, keyboard, and the screen. Most programs have much more sophisticated needs, though, particularly for screen output. DOS lets you down in that regard because there are no screen-positioning services in DOS's basic complement of services. Using the internal driver, ANSI.SYS and some careful programming, however, you can position individual characters anywhere you want on the screen. This is another example of how DOS has expanded through add-on facilities that probably now should be part of DOS proper.

Although the first group of DOS services provides essentially nothing more than you already have available in the ROM-BIOS, the next group ventures into realms that naturally belong to DOS: high-level disk services, particularly file input and output.

This group of services also is related to old design features of CP/M and is based around an approach that has been made obsolete by new developments in DOS. These older file services are called, in DOS's terminology, the traditional file services, and they are based on the use of a file control block, or FCB. FCBs are used by programs to provide the names and identification of the files with which programs work. The FCB also holds status information while a file is in use. When programs use these traditional file services, DOS keeps records of what's what in the FCB, making these services vulnerable to tinkering by the programs you run. (Newer file services hold DOS's control information apart from the programs, ensuring safer and more reliable operation.)

These FCB-oriented traditional file services can do a variety of things. First, to track down files, a pair of services can locate files matching wild-card filenames that include the characters ? and *. Programs can use the wild-cards either to find the first matching filename or to find the full list of files that match the specification.

Other traditional file services open a file (prepare for reading or writing data) and later close it. Then there are services that enable the computer to read or write a file sequentially from beginning to end or to read and write randomly, skipping to any position in the file.

The console services and the traditional file services make up the majority of the universal DOS services, the services that were available in the long-forgotten DOS 1.0. A handful of additional services exist in this universal group. These are services that read or set DOS's record of the date and time, end a program, turn disk verification on and off, and perform other technical services.

Because these universal services were available from the very beginning, they can be used with every version of DOS. The DOS services I discuss from this point on have been added in later releases of DOS, mostly beginning with version 2.0. Thus, programs that use these services must run on machines that use a version of DOS that supports these features.

The first of these services, which is now obviously an essential service, reports which version of DOS a program is running under. This service enables the program to find out whether the services it needs are there. If not, the program can adjust itself to what's available or at least exit gracefully, reporting that it needs a different version of DOS. Because this service was introduced in DOS 2.0, it would appear to have come too late. Fortunately, thanks to the way earlier versions of DOS work, if a program uses this service, these early DOS versions report themselves as version 0; that's not exactly correct, but at least it properly indicates a pre-2.0 version.

Beginning with DOS 5.0, an external utility, SETVER, enables you to fool an application expecting a certain version of DOS into thinking it is running with the correct version. An internal version table holds information about popular applications so that when one of these applications runs, DOS can scan the version table and tell the application what it wants to hear. If an application you want to run isn't already in the version table, you can add new programs to the list.

For file operations, DOS 2.0 and all later versions provide an alternative to the FCB-oriented traditional file services. These new file services work with a handle, which is simply a two-byte number that uniquely identifies each file in use by a program.

When a program opens a file using these new file services, DOS gives the program a handle that identifies it for all subsequent file operations until it is closed. This use of handles enables DOS to keep all critical file-control information safely apart from the program, protecting it from damage or tinkering. These handle-oriented services provide all the facilities that the FCB-oriented traditional services provide, but they do it in a cleaner fashion. Programs are provided with several standard handles, one for writing ordinary information on the display screen, another for error messages (which appear on the screen even if the user tells DOS to reroute screen output), and so forth.

In addition, all versions of DOS from 2.0 on provide services that are closely related to the extra structure that has been added to DOS disks. These include services to create and remove directories, change the subdirectory, move a file's directory entry from one directory to another, and so forth.

There are also services that enable programs to work more intimately with the hardware, without having to break out of the DOS framework. Previously, programs could either look at devices, such as disks, in a dumb way through DOS or in a smart way on their own. These new device-control services bridge the gap. As an example, with these device services, a program can determine whether a particular disk drive is fixed (a hard disk or RAM disk) or removable (a floppy disk) and, for removable media, whether the drive can sense when you switched disks. (Most drives include a signal line that changes state when the drive door has been opened. This enables DOS or other applications to be aware that the same disk as before may not be in the drive.) All these services enable programs to use the computer in a more sophisticated way.

There are also memory services, which enable programs to work together with DOS in grabbing and releasing memory. Normally, each program that runs under DOS has the exclusive use of all of the computer's memory, but these memory services enable a broader sharing of memory.

Some of the services provided by DOS 2.0 and later versions enable a program to load and run subprograms and program overlays and give them a degree of independence from the program that started them.

Many of the significant additions to DOS appeared with version 2.0, but other features have been added in later versions. Version 3.0 added extended error codes, which enable a program to get a much more detailed explanation of what has gone wrong when an error is reported. The main additions that appeared in DOS 3.0 and 3.1 concerned the special problems of using networks. These new services provide the locking and unlocking of access to all or parts of a file, making it safe and practical for several computers to share access to the same file through a network without interfering with one another. Similar network-related services deal with the control and redirection of printer output.

DOS 3.2 added a new facility for the use of languages other than American English and support for IBM Token-Ring networks, 3.5-inch disk drives, and the PC Convertible. DOS 3.3 enhanced the language support (with code pages) and added the capability to partition large hard disks (greater than 32MB) and to support up to four serial ports. DOS 4.0 added more language support, the capability to use large hard disks without making partitions, and a built-in extended memory facility.

DOS 5.0 added new services and features in several different areas. First, DOS's memory management capabilities were greatly enhanced, and new extended memory and expanded memory managers were added. In addition, DOS 5.0 could make use of unused memory addresses above 640KB to load device drivers, memory-resident programs, and even part of DOS itself. Programs can explicitly ask for and use this extra memory (called upper memory blocks).

Second, DOS provides a way for programs to indicate that they are waiting for some event, such as for the user to press a key. This enables multitasking systems, such as Windows, to take advantage of the waiting time.

Third, DOS 5.0 has built-in help. Programs can be designed to make use of this system so that the HELP command can provide help on any program, not just DOS commands.

Fourth, there are some programs that work with only specific versions of DOS. DOS version 5.0 uses the SETVER utility to tell these programs that they are running under the version of DOS that they expect.

Fifth, DOS 5.0 provides an easy way for programs to examine the volume identification information associated with a disk, such as the volume serial number. (This is a unique identifier assigned by DOS when the disk is formatted.) Checking this information enables a program to determine categorically which disks are present. Before a program updates a file on a floppy disk, for example, it can make sure that the disk has not been changed.

Finally, DOS 5.0 provides ways for programmers to ensure that their programs will work safely in multitasking (Windows) and task-switching (the DOS Shell) environments.

With the release of DOS 6.0, the PC operating system began moving toward providing the type of operating system services large machine users have had for years. It's not there by a long shot, but it's moving in the right direction.

This latest version of DOS, for example, includes DOUBLESPACE, a utility that compresses information as it is written to disk and decompresses it on the fly when it is loaded into memory. This feature essentially can double the amount of disk space available on each physical drive. A 100MB drive becomes a nearly 200MB drive. Just how much compression is possible depends on the type of data and programs you use, but a doubling of space is close to what most users get. There has been much written about problems with the first releases of this integrated utility, but those problems were mainly from the upgrade process. Users who installed DOS 6 with DOUBLESPACE on a new drive didn't have so many problems.

There are other new features in DOS 6 as well. The help facility has been much improved, making it an interactive, full-screen facility that you can read, search, and study, more like a Windows help system. And, memory management is the best yet provided with DOS. Using technology licensed from Helix software's Netroom memory manager, DOS now automatically figures out the best use of your memory and installs the proper program calls in your CONFIG.SYS file to make it happen.

The backup and restore facilities have been greatly enhanced by using technology licensed from the Peter Norton Backup utilities. Now, instead of having to purchase third-party software to do something that should have been part of DOS in the first place (because the original backup and restore utilities were balky, hard to use, and didn't always work properly), you can depend on intrinsic DOS services.

Additional utilities, including a CD-ROM support driver, facilities for building multiple configurations right into CONFIG.SYS, a CHOICE program to prompt a user for input from a batch file, a DEFRAG utility to eliminate disk fragmentation, and DELTREE, a command that enables you to delete an entire disk subdirectory and the directories it holds, have been added to DOS 6.

There also is INTERLNK, a utility that links two computers through serial or parallel ports so that they can share disks and printer ports. This isn't really networking, but it is a way to reduce the need for "sneakernet" between two machines in the same office or workgroup. You also can use INTERLNK to transfer information quickly from your desktop computer to your laptop and back again.

The MSAV command scans the computer for viruses and removes them if you tell it to. A companion utility, VSAFE, installs itself as a RAM-resident scanner that continuously monitors for viruses.

In addition, some of these services are installed in a Microsoft Windows application window so that you can call them up easily from inside Windows.

There's another interesting addition to DOS 6, the MSD utility that scans your computer's hardware and memory and reports on what it finds. This program was first included with very early versions of Windows 3.0 and was used primarily to report hardware configurations of beta sites to Microsoft. MSD is a useful utility when you are installing new software or hardware or when you simply want to know something about how your computer is configured.

As a preliminary move to support green PCs and the growing laptop generation, DOS version 6 includes a POWER utility that reduces power consumption when applications and the computer itself are idle. The POWER.EXE file is loaded as a device in the CONFIG.SYS file.

So far, I've discussed only the mainstream DOS services, but there are others that are quite interesting and useful. Probably the most fascinating of all are the terminate-and-stay-resident services that enable programs to embed themselves into the computer's memory and remain there while DOS continues to run other programs.

These are the resident programs that PC users have become so familiar with—programs such as Prokey and Sidekick and resident parts of DOS like the MODE and PRINT commands. There are two stay-resident services that these types of programs use: an old one that's part of the universal DOS services and a more advanced one that's part of the services introduced with DOS 2.0. Both services enable programs to become resident in a part of the computer's memory that is not used by subsequent programs that DOS runs.

Related to the operation of these programs is a DOS service that helps a resident program tell whether it is safe to swing into operation. In Chapter 19, I discussed the fact that the ROM-BIOS programs must be reentrant, so that they can be suspended or doubly active without difficulty. DOS, however, does not work in a completely reentrant way, which means that, at certain times, if DOS is in the middle of one operation, it is unsafe for a program to request another DOS service. A special DOS service is used to report whether DOS is in that dangerous state. Some memory-resident programs use this interrupt to see whether DOS is in the middle of doing something before they pop up. If DOS is not to be bothered, the memory-resident program alerts you (by making a beep, for example).

Another interesting DOS service is the one used for country-dependent information, such as the currency symbol (dollar sign, pound sign, and so on) that should be used and the way numbers are punctuated (12,345.67, 12.345,67, and so on). DOS is designed to adjust to different national conventions and can report the country-specific information to your programs so that they can adjust. Not only can your programs learn the country information from DOS, they also can instruct DOS to change the country code with which it is working.

There are more DOS services, but what you've seen should give you a sound feeling for the main range of DOS services as well as a peek at some of the unusual curiosities. Now you're ready to move on to your next adventure, learning how programs are constructed.

How Programs Are Built

23

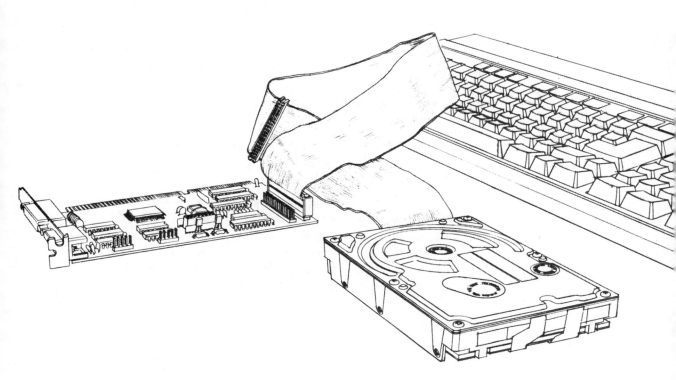

Among the most fascinating topics regarding the PC family is how programs are built. Whether you plan to create programs for the PC or just use PC programs and want to have the intellectual satisfaction of knowing what lies behind them, it's wonderful to understand the mechanics of creating a program. That's what I cover in this chapter.

I present a brief survey of how programs are constructed so that you get a feel for what's involved. For a deeper understanding of the steps involved in program building, you can turn to any number of specialty books on programming for the PC family, including *The Peter Norton Programmer's Guide to the IBM PC and PS/2*.

Programming Language Overview

In the end, a computer carries out only the instructions it is given in machine language. However, most programmers don't write programs in machine language. They write programs in programming languages. Programming languages are the tools programmers use to create programs, just as English and other spoken languages are the tools writers use to create books.

If you want to understand programming languages, you need to know what they are like and how they are turned into machine language. In this section, I focus on the nature and characteristics of the programming languages. Later, I describe how the programming languages that humans use are translated into the machine language that the computer uses.

Perhaps the first thing you need to know about programming languages is the distinction between assembly language and all other programming languages, which are collectively called high-level languages.

Assembly language is essentially the same as the computer's own machine language, only it's expressed in a form that's easier for people to work with. The key thing about assembly language is that a programmer who writes in assembly language is writing out, one by one, the detailed instructions for the computer to follow when carrying out the program. You've had a few glimpses of assembly language before (for example, in the "Looking at an Interrupt Handler" section in Chapter 4).

The listing below is an assembly language subroutine that I use in my programs. It flushes the keyboard buffer. This is an important operation that must be done before a program asks a question such as, "OK to delete this file?" Flushing the keyboard buffer protects against a reply being typed in before the question is asked. If you want to know what an assembly language subroutine looks like, complete with all its window dressing, you can learn a lot just by studying the routine below:

```
; FLUSHKEY - clears DOS keyboard input buffer
; DOS generic
          PGROUP  GROUP PROG
          PUBLIC  FLUSHKEY
PROG      SEGMENT BYTE PUBLIC 'PROG'
          ASSUME  CS:PROG
FLUSHKEY  PROC    NEAR
TEST:

          MOV     AH,11    ; check keyboard status
          INT     33       ; function call
          OR      AL,AL    ; if zero
          JZ      RETURN   ;   then done
          MOV     AH,7     ; read one byte
          INT     33       ; function call
          JMP     TEST
RETURN:

          RET
FLUSHKEY  ENDP
PROG      ENDS
          END
```

While machine language instructions appear in almost incomprehensible hexadecimal codes, assembly language codes are easily intelligible to experienced programmers. With just a little practice, you also can make sense of at least some of what's written in an assembly language program. For example, the first active instruction in the listing above is MOV AH,11, which tells the computer to move the number 11 into the register called AH. I don't claim that the meaning of MOV AH,11 should be obvious to anyone, but you can see how it shouldn't be too hard to get the hang of reading and even writing this kind of stuff.

To understand what assembly language programming is all about, you need to understand that there are essentially three parts to it. The first part is what people think of assembly language as being—individual machine language instructions written in a form that programmers can understand (like MOV AH,11). In this part of assembly language, each line of program code is translated directly into a single machine language instruction.

The second part of assembly language programming consists of commands that control what's going on, essentially setting the stage for the working part of the program. In this example, everything before MOV AH,11—for example, the line that reads ASSUME CS:PROG—is part of this stage-setting overhead. ASSUME CS:PROG indicates what's happening with the code segment (CS) register (for information on registers, see Chapter 4).

The third part of assembly language programming is a labor-saving device. Whenever a series of instructions is repeated, assembly language enables the programmer to abbreviate many instructions in a macro instruction, or macro for short. (Note that, when I use "macro" here, I use it in a different sense than when I refer to spreadsheet macros or macros defined by DOS's DOSKEY command.)

This assembly language example doesn't include any macros, but it could. Notice that a pair of instructions (MOV AH,X and INT 33) appears twice with only a slight difference between them—the MOV has a different number in it. These instructions can be replaced with a single line of code, the macro, representing the pair of instructions. (The macro facility in assembly language can accommodate the difference between the two pairs of instructions by substituting a parameter that contains the appropriate number; macros can handle this trick and others that are much more elaborate.)

In a nutshell, these three elements—program instructions that are turned into machine language code, overhead commands, and macro abbreviations—are the heart of assembly language.

Writing a program in assembly language is an exceedingly long and tedious process. To give you an idea of just how many instructions are involved in a program (not just a brief subroutine, like the one listed above), a very early version of the main Norton Utilities program—a medium-sized program—contained about 20,000 machine language instructions. A large and complex program easily can consist of hundreds of thousands of separate machine language instructions. If such a program is written in assembly language, the programmer must write out all those separate commands, each of them intricate and each of them a potential bug. Think of it: if any of the words in this book are speled rwong, it doesn't necessarily destroy its usefulness, but any tiny mistake in a program can potentially render it useless. And, when a program written in assembly language has 500,000 or even 5,000 instructions (also called lines of code) in it, the possibilities for errors are enormous.

High-level languages—every computer language other than assembly language—are designed to eliminate the tedium and error-prone nature of assembly language by enabling the computer to do much of the work of generating the detailed machine language instructions. High-level languages rely on two ideas to make this possible. One is the idea of summarizing many machine language instructions into a single program command. This is the same idea as assembly language macros but applied in a broader way. The other idea is to remove from sight details that have to do with how the computer operates but that have nothing to do with the work you want to accomplish—for example, which registers are used for what.

If you ask a program to add three numbers, the program uses one of the computer's general-purpose registers, such as AX, BX, CX, or DX, but this information is not important to you. Assembly language programmers have to concern themselves with such details as which register to use for what (and using it consistently). High-level language programmers are spared that effort. High-level languages are characterized by the fact that they generate a lot of machine language code for each program command (a many-for-one saving of human effort that gives high-level languages their name) and by their avoidance of unnecessary detail (such as specifying which registers and memory addresses are used).

Assembly language and high-level languages have their benefits and drawbacks. I've focused on some of the drawbacks of assembly language—mainly that it requires more work to write because it requires more lines of program code and is more error-prone because it involves many details—but there are others. One important one is that assembly language requires more expertise to write than most high-level languages. However, it has important advantages as well. Assembly language programs are usually smaller and run faster because assembly language programmers use their skills to find efficient ways to perform each step. Also, using assembly language, programmers can tell the computer to do anything it's capable of doing, while high-level languages normally don't give people a way to use all the tricks the computer can do. Broadly speaking, you can say that high-level languages enable programmers to tap into 90 percent of the computer's skills, while assembly language enables them to use 100 percent, if they're clever enough.

So far, I've talked about high-level languages as a category, as if they were all alike. They do have a lot in common, particularly in contrast with assembly language, but there are many important differences among them. The next step is to look at the varieties of high-level languages, which can best be done by talking about the most important and widely used PC programming languages. There are literally hundreds of programming languages, and easily dozens that are used on the PC, but I only talk about an important few—BASIC, Pascal, C, and dBASE—and use them to paint a representative picture of all high-level languages.

BASIC is the closest thing to a universal language for personal computers. Essentially, every DOS user has access to BASIC in one form or another. With IBM PC DOS before version 5.0, the program is BASICA.COM. With MS-DOS, the program is GWBASIC.EXE.

The old forms of BASIC—BASICA and GWBASIC—have some major limitations. They run more slowly than other high-level languages and are severely limited in the size of programs and the amount of data they can handle. Also, from the point of view of professional craftsmanship, these forms of BASIC provide a clumsy set of tools. There are newer forms of BASIC that incorporate the features that programmers need to write well, but these features aren't available in the BASIC that comes free with DOS.

Fortunately, starting with version 5.0, DOS includes QBasic, a new form of BASIC similar to Microsoft's QuickBASIC. QBasic comes with an online help system and an easy-to-use programming system. Its major limitation is that it cannot produce stand-alone executable programs. An optional compiler for QBasic programs is available for an additional price from Microsoft.

BASIC's strength is that it is easy to fiddle with and includes features that give users easy access to most of the PC family's special features, such as the capability to play music on the computer's speaker. (Most other high-level languages have only general features that can be used on any computer. To use the PC's unique characteristics, programmers using those languages have to use special methods, which usually means tapping into some assembly language. I discuss that later in this chapter.)

Two other well-known languages ideally suited for professional programming are Pascal and C. Both have the features considered most useful in helping programmers create well-crafted programs that are reliable and easy to update. To see what each language is like, I've included two fragments of Pascal and C from my working programs. They give you a quick way to get a feel for what Pascal and C programs look like and how they are built. The fragment below is from a Pascal program:

```
{A Pascal Program to Count Words}
program count (output,input_file);
var
  input_file : text;
  i          : word;
  thousands  : word;
  units      : word;
  line       : lstring (255);
  alpha      : boolean;
  active     : boolean;
procedure report;
  var
      i, x : word;
  begin
    write (chr(13));
    if thousands = 0 then
      write (units:7)
    else
      begin
        write (thousands:3);
        write (',');
        x := units;
        for i := 1 to 3 do
          begin
            write (x div 100 : 1);
            x := (x mod 100) * 10;
          end;
      end;
  end;
procedure add_to_count;
  begin
    units := units + 1;
    if units >= 1000 then
      begin
        units := units - 1000;
        thousands := thousands + 1;
      end;
    if (units mod 100) = 0 then
```

```
                report;
          end;
      begin
        thousands := 0;
        units     := 0;
        reset (input_file);
        while not eof (input_file) do
          begin
            active := false;
            readln (input_file,line);
            for i  := 1 to line.len do
              begin
                if active then
                  begin
                    if line 9i: = ' ' then
                    active := false;
                  end
                else
                if line 9i: in 9'a'..'z','A'..'Z': then
                  begin
                    active := true;
                    add_to_count;
                  end;
              end;
          end;
        report;
        write (' words.');
      end.
```

The fragment below is from a C program:

```
/* A 'C' Program to Draw a Double-Line Box Outline */
box ()
  {
    drow =  0; dcol = 1; vdup (205,78);
    drow = 24; dcol = 1; vdup (205,78);
for (drow = 1; drow < 24; drow++)
  {
    dcol =  0; vdup (186,1);
```

```
      dcol = 79; vdup (186,1);
   }
drow =  0; dcol = 0; vdup (201,1);
    dcol = 79; vdup (187,1);
drow = 24; dcol = 0; vdup (200,1);
    dcol = 79; vdup (188,1);
if (TEST)
  {
    if (swtchset ("X"))
      {
        int       i;
        unsigned x;
        char      s 940:;
        int       sl;
      for (i = 1; i <24; i++)
        {
          sl =    0;
          decint (s,&sl,i,3);
          drow = i;
          dcol = 77;
          vstr   (s);
        }
      drow = 24; dcol = 3;
      x = spstart - splowest;
        decint0 (s,x);
        vstr    (" ");
        vstr    (s);
        vstr    (" stack used ");
      dcol += 2;
        decint0 (s,poolleft);
        vstr    (" ");
        vstr    (s);
        vstr    (" pool left ");
      dcol += 2;
        x = pool - poolsave;
        decint0 (s,x);
        vstr    (" ");
        vstr    (s);
```

```
    vstr    (" pool used ");
  dcol += 2;
    x = poolends - poolend;
    decint0 (s,x);
    vstr    (" ");
    vstr    (s);
    vstr    (" heap used ");
  }
 }
}
```

Pascal and C have many similarities, including structural features that promote good programming practices. Both are very suitable for professional use in the building of large and demanding programs. Pascal finds its champions among those who have studied it in school (it is the language most favored for teaching computer science and, in fact, was originally created as a language for teaching rather than professional use) and those who have the inexpensive and extremely popular Turbo Pascal compiler. C is favored by programmers who are looking for the utmost efficiency in a high-level language and who want their programs to be in tune with one of the directions in which personal computers are evolving. Later versions of the C language, including C++ , for example, offer enhanced programmer tools, expanded features, and more efficiency.

I have used both Pascal and C in my own programming for the PC family. My Norton Utilities programs were first written in Pascal and later converted to C. I am fond of both languages. By itself I consider Pascal to be the better language—cleaner and less error-prone. On the other hand, C is particularly good for writing programs that need to be tight and efficient and that work closely with the computer's BIOS and DOS. It's also worth noting that, for both the Pascal and C versions of my programs, I had to use assembly language subroutines to perform tasks that couldn't be done in the high-level languages. The assembly language subroutine shown in the beginning of this chapter is one of those. This illustrates an important point regarding the creation of professional-quality programs: often the best programming is done primarily in a high-level language (such as Pascal or C) with assembly language used as a simple and expedient way to go beyond the limits of the high-level language.

My experience points up some of the most important factors to be considered in the choice of a programming language. Usually a programming language is chosen on very pragmatic grounds: which languages the programmer already knows (or can easily learn) and how well suited the programming language is to the work that the program has to accomplish. Personal taste and convenience also play a major part in the selection of a programming language—and why shouldn't they?

The last group of programming languages to consider are what I call application languages. These are programming languages that are an integral part of major application programs, such as dBASE IV and Framework (with its Fred programming language). This sort of programming language also sometimes is called a very high-level language because it involves a step up in the power of the features that the language provides, thanks to the application (database system or whatever) of which it is a part. Individually, each of these application languages is a whole world unto itself, and there is very little similarity between its features and programming characteristics and those of other languages. This is very different from the group of high-level languages that as a whole tend to be quite similar in what they can do and even how they do it.

Probably the most widely known and used kind of application language is the spreadsheet. Spreadsheets are programming languages because they enable users to set up and store commands that can be used over and over again, which is the essence of what a programming language is. A spreadsheet programming language is much more specialized than most programming languages. It's more powerful in some ways because it contains some built-in features and much more limited in other ways because it has to work within its own spreadsheet context.

In a broad, general way, application programming languages are divided into two groups. One group, typified by the spreadsheets, has a narrow range of uses restricted to the basic purpose of the application. The members of this group are essentially application programs that have been made partly programmable. The other group, represented by dBASE IV and Framework's Fred language, has broader powers, powers that are nearly as general and flexible as those of traditional programming languages like BASIC. The members of this group are essentially full-fledged programming languages that can take advantage of special application features (such as accessing a database).

In addition to these fairly standard programming tools, there is a new class of language evolving that is used increasingly for system development as well as end-user applications. This is object programming. Object-oriented tools are very high-level languages designed around intelligent modules. An intelligent module may be one designed to handle screen services, draw a menu, set up the answers, conduct error

453

checking of user entered data, and the like. In addition, user- and programmer-generated objects (such as data or graphics) can be incorporated into intelligent objects for further manipulation and presentation.

Object-oriented languages (sometimes called OOPS products for object-oriented programming system) were once thought to be cult-type products with limited applications. That's not true of course and they now are moving into the mainstream. In fact, nearly every conventional programming language is developing a subset or superset of features to support object programming. Microsoft's new Visual Basic, for example, is much easier to use for programming Windows-like applications because it includes built-in routines and intelligent modules for drawing windows, dialog boxes, producing sound, manipulating images, and the like. As this book goes to press, Microsoft is talking about including Visual Basic, or elements of it, as the basis for macro languages in its mainline products. So, you can see that the object programming concept is not that foreign or difficult to learn. Application macro languages are something that need to become more user friendly to open up the world of macro design and writing to a broader range of application user.

So far, I have given you a short look at programming languages. What I look at next is how they are implemented—what turns them into usable machine language instructions that computers can carry out.

Translating Programs

Before any program, regardless of what programming language it is written in, can come alive, it must be translated into the only thing a computer actually can execute—machine language instructions. There are three main ways for this translation to be done: interpreting, assembling, and compiling. Understanding each of these three ways of translating programs is important because it helps you comprehend what is going on in the computer as well as some of the important limitations of software and why some programs run fast and others quite slow.

Interpreting is a special kind of translation, in which the program essentially is translated into machine language on the fly, that is, as the program is being carried out. Interpreting on the computer is quite a bit like what's done at international conferences when the words of the person speaking are simultaneously translated into other languages.

The program to be interpreted (program P) is worked over by an interpreter program (interpreter I). When you use program P, the computer actually is running interpreter I, and interpreter I carries out the steps of program P. Interpreter I scans the text of program P and, step by step, performs the work of program P. In effect, interpreter I is translating program P word by word and step by step and carrying out (executing) the instructions on the fly.

Interpreting is inherently slow and inefficient, but flexible. It's slow because the translation is being done at the same time the work of the program is being carried out, so time is being taken up performing two tasks (translating the program and doing the program's work) instead of just one (carrying out the work). It's inefficient because the translation is done over and over again—not just each time the program is run but each time a step of the program is repeated. Because much of the power of programs comes from repeated steps (program looping, as it's called), plenty of instructions are repeatedly translated when a program is interpreted.

On the other hand, interpreting is flexible because an interpreted program can be adjusted, changed, or revised on the fly. Because the translation of an interpreted program is done continually, changes can be made on the spot and accommodated immediately.

I have plenty of experience with interpreted programs. The BASIC that comes with DOS and many programming applications, like spreadsheets and databases, is interpreted.

There is an important technical issue concerning interpreted programs. When you run an interpreted program, such as any of the QBasic programs shown in Appendix C, you think of that program as what's running in the computer. In a strict sense that's not true. From the computer's and the operating system's viewpoint, the program being executed is the interpreter, and what you think of as the program is just the data that the interpreter is working with. For a BASIC program, the actual program that's running is BASIC.COM, and the "program" is just data for the program. Of course, this is a very special kind of data, it's data that describes the steps that you want the computer to perform, which is exactly what a program is to users. Under most circumstances, this technical distinction is of no importance, but at times you may bump into some of its ramifications. For example, because the BASIC interpreter is designed to work with only a single 64KB data segment (recall the discussions of memory and data addressing in Chapter 17), interpreted BASIC programs can't exceed a total of 64KB for both the "program" (which is technically data to the interpreter) and the program data.

With the newer QBasic, the same considerations hold, but the size limit for the program plus its data is extended to 160KB. The interpreter uses separate segments for each subprogram, the main data area, and certain types of arrays (lists of data elements). Thus, within the 160KB limit, each of these components can be up to 64KB long.

Although BASIC, spreadsheet programs, and database programs often are interpreted, they don't have to be. While the normal form of these languages is interpreted, there are some compiled forms as well, and I come back to this later.

Interpreted programs, as I've said, are translated on the fly as the program is being run. The other two types of program translation—assembly and compiling—aren't done that way. Instead, they are translated in advance and permanently converted into the machine language. Assembly and compiling have more in common than they have differences, so I cover the similarities first.

Assembled and compiled programs are translated into machine language by the program developer before the program is used. For these programs, translation is part of the program development process. This means that the user of the program doesn't have to waste time translating the program and that translating software does not need to be available. Programs prepared in this way are complete in themselves. In contrast, interpreted programs only can be used if you have the interpreter as well. You only can run BASIC programs if you have the BASIC interpreter. (With the old versions of DOS, the interpreter is BASICA.COM [PC DOS] or GWBASIC.EXE [MS-DOS]. With DOS 5.0 and later, the interpreter is QBASIC.EXE.)

The people who design an assembler or compiler for any programming language must make many decisions about how the translator will work, including the exact details of what features the programming language will have. You may think of a programming language—say, Pascal—as being just one thing, but that's really not true. To anyone writing programs, a programming language like Pascal is the child of the marriage of two elements—the general form of the programming language (which defines the language's main form, its syntax, and principle features) and the specific implementation (which defines the specific features and the way they're used).

For these reasons, programmers don't really write programs in a general programming language. They write them using the characteristics of a specific implementation of a general programming language. Programs aren't written in Pascal or C; they are written in Turbo Pascal or Lightspeed C. Whether you are setting out to write your own programs or just want to understand how the choice of a programming language affects the programs you use, this is an important thing to know.

Most compilers and assemblers for the PC family follow a standard mode of operation that was created as part of the overall organization of DOS. In this standard operating mode, the translator converts a program from the language in which the programmer wrote it into the computer's machine language instructions. However, that doesn't mean the translated version is ready to use. Normally, it's not. Although a program has been converted into executable machine language instructions, the instructions aren't yet ready for action. (You see the reason for this and look at the additional steps that are needed to get programs ready in the next section.) Not all program language translators work that way, however. Some follow their own rules and have their own conventions for getting a program ready for work. The best-known examples of this are Borland's Turbo Pascal and Microsoft's QuickBASIC and Quick C. With these compilers, a program can be executed immediately after it's translated. The advantage of this is obvious, but there are real disadvantages as well. Translators like these go their own way and don't fit into the DOS world as comfortably as conventional ones do.

In the first section, of this chapter I noted the distinction between low-level assembly language and the high-level languages (Pascal, C, BASIC, and so on). In assembly language, a programmer must write out the equivalent of every machine language instruction that the finished program will perform. In a high-level language, the programmer can write a program in terms of larger steps, steps that will be translated into many individual machine language instructions. In keeping with this distinction, the translators for assembly language are called assemblers, and the translators for high-level languages are called compilers. Depending on your focus, the distinction is either important or inconsequential. From one viewpoint, both are the same; they convert the programmer's high-level language program (the source code) into machine language instructions (the object code).

From another viewpoint, a compiler is given the very creative and demanding task of deciding what kind of machine language instructions will be used and making strategic decisions about how the computer's resources are to be used, for example, what the registers will be used for. On the other hand, an assembler performs a very mechanical and uncreative conversion of the programmer's instructions into the equivalent machine instructions. From this perspective, a compiler is a very complex beast, and there is enormous potential for differences in the quality of compilers (one compiler might generate very efficient code, while another could produce lousy code). These differences don't apply to assemblers.

When a programmer works with a compiler or an assembler, his or her source code is fed into the translator and checked for errors. If it's in workable shape, machine language object code is the result. You can identify any object code files that you might come across by their filename extension, OBJ. The object code is ultimately for use by the computer as a finished, executable program. For the programmer's use, the compiler or assembler displays error messages indicating flaws in the program (not logical flaws, or bugs, which are the responsibility of the programmer, but syntactic flaws, such as misspelled keywords and missing punctuation).

Because an assembly language programmer is working very closely with the computer's basic skills (its machine language instructions), an assembler gives the programmer lots of technical information about the results of the assembly. To give you an idea of what it looks like, the assembler listing for the assembly language program shown earlier is listed below:

```
                              ; FLUSHKEY - clears DOS keyboard input buffer
                              ; DOS generic
                              PGROUP   GROUP PROG
                              PUBLIC   FLUSHKEY
0000                 PROG     SEGMENT BYTE PUBLIC 'PROG'
                              ASSUME   CS:PROG
0000                 FLUSHKEY PROC   NEAR
0000                 TEST:
0000    B4 0B                 MOV      AH,11    ; check keyboard status
0002    CD 21                 INT      33       ; function call
0004    0A C0                 OR       AL,AL    ; if zero
0006    74 06                 JZ       RETURN   ;   then done
0008    B4 07                 MOV      AH,7     ; read one byte
000A    CD 21                 INT      33       ; function call
000C    EB F2                 JMP      TEST
000E                 RETURN:
000E    C3                    RET
000F                 FLUSHKEY ENDP
000F                 PROG     ENDS
                              END
```

One of the things an assembly listing shows is the exact machine language instructions in hexadecimal. Normally, a compiler does not give a programmer so much technical information; after all, one of the main purposes of using a high-level language is to avoid working with technical details. However, if a programmer wants to know more about the machine language code that a compiler is generating, most compilers can print out an assembly language equivalent of the object code that has been created. The object code listing enables an experienced programmer to evaluate the quality of the code the compiler generates and can be helpful in deciding which way of writing a program is most efficient.

Depending on how you look at the process of translating a program from source code to object code, you can think of compilers and assemblers as very different creatures or as minor variations on the same theme. Either way, compilers and assemblers are charged with the task of converting what programmers write into what computers can do. After that comes the final steps of putting a program together into a working whole, and that's what I cover next.

Putting Programs Together

One of the key elements in practical programming is the old principle of divide and conquer; any task becomes more manageable when it is broken down into smaller parts. Programming also works that way, so the process of program development has been set up in a way that makes it practical to break a program into functional, modular parts and then piece together the whole program from its parts. In this section, I cover the mechanisms that make it possible to put programs together from parts and how those mechanisms work.

Three things enable programmers to divide and conquer: subroutines, linking, and libraries. Subroutines, as you know, are relatively self-contained fragments of a program. In different languages they are known by different names. For example, in C they are called functions; in Pascal they are called procedures. They perform a particular part of the program's work, acting as a building block for the program. One of the key reasons for creating subroutines is to subdivide and therefore simplify the task of creating a program.

After a program is divided into logical parts, and those parts are made into subroutines, the next logical step is to remove the subroutines from the main program. After all, the point of subroutines is to reduce the logical clutter in a program by isolating work into discrete components. If you're going to sweep the subroutines off into a logical corner to tidy up the design and organization of the program, you may as well move them out of the way entirely. Programmers take the subroutines out of the program and treat them separately, including compiling or assembling them separately. This idea of separate compilation is a key adjunct to the idea of creating subroutines in the first place. Because the program is divided into logical modules, you may as well make them completely separate by putting the source code (what the programmer writes) into separate disk files for each module and compiling (or, in the case of assembly language, assembling) these files as separate items.

There are two main advantages to separating the subroutines from the main program. One is that it shortens and simplifies the source code of the main program. The other is that it makes the subroutines available for use by any program. If you had to keep your subroutines inside each program, then when you create a new program that could use some of the old subroutines, you'd have to copy the source code for the subroutines into the new program. By separating subroutines and compiling them separately, you keep them available for any program to use. You also save time and trouble by having to compile a subroutine only once.

The whole idea of separately compiled subroutines requires that you have a way of combining the different parts of a program into one piece. This is done in a process called linking and is performed by a program called LINK, which comes as a part of DOS. The process of linking is something like building models. In effect, a program that needs a subroutine named X has an empty slot marked X, and a separately compiled subroutine has the computer equivalent of a tab marked X. The job of the LINK program is to fit the two together.

Linking involves making all the connections between the pieces of a program to make them work as a whole. In the last section, I mentioned that compilers and assemblers generate their machine language instructions in a form called object code, which isn't completely ready to be run as a program. The reason for this is that object code is set up in the form that's needed for linking, with all the "tab" and "slot" markings. The job of LINK is to gather all the parts of object code, make the connections between them, and then output the results in a form that is ready to be run by the computer. Even when a program doesn't need any subroutine connections, standard DOS compilers and assemblers still translate their programs in the object code format.

You can see that creating a program involves two basic steps beyond writing the program in the first place: translating the program's source code into object code with a compiler or assembler and then converting the object code into a finished program with the linker.

It's worth pausing here to note that I'm talking about the standard DOS way of creating programs, which is used by most programming language versions. However, not every one follows the DOS standard. For example, the extremely popular Turbo Pascal and Quick C compilers go their own ways and avoid the use of object code and linking. Instead, this type of compiler creates executable programs, effectively combining compiling and linking into one step. This has the advantage of simplifying and speeding up the process of developing a program, but also eliminates much of the flexibility that comes with separate compilation and linking.

Another important example is the QBasic interpreter that comes with DOS (versions 5.0 and later). QBasic combines the speed of compiled programs with the flexibility of interpreting.

When you first load a program, QBasic immediately converts it into an intermediate, partially compiled, form. When you run the program, QBasic completes what is left of the compilation. Because a lot of the work has been done already, your program starts to execute almost immediately. When you make a change, QBasic reprocesses just the part of the program affected by the change—usually a single subroutine or less. All of this makes for an extremely fast program development environment.

However, QBasic has a significant limitation: it cannot create separate executable programs. You can run QBasic programs only within the QBasic environment.

Microsoft's QuickBASIC product is a combination. It uses a high-speed interpreter as well as a compiler. You use the interpreter for development. After you are finished, you can use the compiler to create an executable program.

If you create lots and lots of subroutines, you will be faced with the problem of having lots and lots of object code files cluttering up your disks. There is nothing uncommon about a programmer developing dozens of subroutines, and for a large programming project or for a programming language that makes liberal use of built-in subroutines, the number easily can grow into the hundreds. For example, an early version of my Norton Utilities included approximately 175 subroutines and program modules, which is just too many to conveniently keep track of.

The solution to that practical problem is libraries of object modules. An object library is a file that can contain the object code for any number of program subroutines. After a subroutine is written, the programmer compiles (or assembles) the subroutine into object code and then uses a special DOS program called LIB, which takes the object code and stuffs it into a library with other subroutines. LIB makes it possible to gather the clutter of many subroutine object files into one tidy package—an object library file. You can identify any object libraries that you come across by their filename extension, LIB.

So far you've seen all the pieces of the programming puzzle. Now I put the pieces together so that you can see them in action. I run through a little example from my programming work to illustrate the main steps of the process.

I begin with the assembly language subroutine that you saw at the beginning of this chapter, FLUSHKEY. After FLUSHKEY has been written by the programmer (me), the programmer's source code is stored in a file named FLUSHKEY.ASM. Each programming language has its own standard filename extension for source code; for assembly language, it's ASM. To assemble FLUSHKEY, I use the assembler program named MASM (which is short for macro assembler) with a command like this:

```
MASM FLUSHKEY
```

This gives me an object file named FLUSHKEY.OBJ. Next, I can add FLUSHKEY to my object library, which I call OURLIB:

```
LIB OURLIB+FLUSHKEY
DEL FLUSHKEY.OBJ
```

Notice that the command line for LIB has a plus sign (+) in it. That's my way of telling LIB to add FLUSHKEY to the library. There are other operations that LIB can perform as well. You also see that, after adding FLUSHKEY to the library, I delete the object file because I no longer need it.

That takes care of subroutines. The next step is to compile and link a main program. For this example, I consider a program, called NU, written in the C programming language. The source code file for that program is called NU.C, and C is the standard filename extension for a C program. I have two choices for the C (I'm using Microsoft C) compiler. I can use one command to ask the compiler to call the linker automatically after compiling:

```
LINK C+NU,NU,,OURLIB
```

Or, I can use a separate command for each step:

```
CL -C NU.C
LINK NU.OBJ,,,OURLIB.LIB
```

To fully understand what's going on here, you have to know more about program building. However, even in this simple outline, you've seen the essence and all the key parts of how programs are built and put together.

In Chapter 26, I get into the business of snooping, tinkering, and exploring, and that includes snooping inside some of the programs that you use. It's another way of gaining insight into how programs are built. In the next chapter, I talk about one of the most important changes in the PC world ever, Microsoft Windows. Don't get me wrong. Windows certainly is not the best program around, but it solves many problems that have plagued PC users for years and is setting a new, widely accepted and much needed set of standards. It probably is as important to you as DOS, so give the next chapter some time.

Some Things To Try

1. In this chapter, I briefly mentioned the function of the LIB program. To manage a library well, LIB has to have a variety of skills. What are they? Work up a list of the separate functions that you think LIB needs to perform.

2. Batch command files are the key to combining program steps like the ones I've mentioned for building programs. Try your hand at writing a batch file to assemble a program and add it to an object library. Write another to compile and link a program. If you know how to use batch file logic, make your batch files adjust to any errors that occur.

3. As I explained earlier, the QBasic interpreter partially compiles your program before you start work. When you make changes, only small parts of your program have to be reprocessed. This makes for an especially fast and flexible working environment. Are there disadvantages to this system? Why do you think all language processors do not use these same techniques?

Microsoft Windows: Role and Function

24

A cleaning product commercial of a few years ago coined a phrase that remains in one form or another as part of our ongoing social chat: "I don't do windows."

Many personal computer users still "don't do Windows" because either the right applications aren't available or users perceive the environment as too restrictive or unfamiliar. Those who cut their computer teeth on DOS—or CP/M, UNIX, or other command-oriented operating systems—were slow to embrace Windows. I have to say that I still lean toward DOS as my favored operating environment, but I also use Windows. Not necessarily because I want to, but because it doesn't make sense not to.

Since Microsoft Windows 3.0 hit the street in the early summer of 1990, many software vendors have announced products to support this graphical user interface. The release of Windows version 3.1, which includes many enhancements, has further fueled the growth of Windows-based applications. Now, with Windows for Workgroups, which includes a pretty capable networking scheme, and Windows NT, there are windowing environments for beginning, intermediate, and advanced users from the same source and with much the same user interface.

And, Windows may be even more popular than users, buyers, and industry watchers predicted when it was first released. When Windows was first developed, it was competing with an entrenched GUI environment, the Macintosh, and the first few releases of Windows simply weren't as well done as the Apple product. Besides, there weren't many applications that made use of the Windows interface. You could run programs in Windows, but there was little benefit.

Why has Windows become so popular? Windows-based programs simply are easier—many times easier—to learn and use than conventional DOS applications. And, as more and more mainstream products—the ones most PC users already have and love—have joined the Windows ranks, the real power of computing is being made available to people who couldn't use it before.

I've saved the discussion of Windows to near the end of this book because this is primarily a book about PC hardware and how it works. I talked about DOS earlier because the operating system works so closely with the hardware as to be almost a part of it. But Microsoft Windows also is an important part of the changing PC world, and I feel any reader of this book needs to be comfortably familiar with Windows as well as with DOS and the PC hardware.

In this chapter, I cover what Microsoft Windows is, how it works, how you use it, and what it means to you, the user of computer software. Toward the end of this chapter, I look a little deeper into the Windows environment. Overall, this chapter is really an introduction to this GUI interface and how it is changing the face of PC computing.

What Is Windows?

Even if you have been using a PC with Microsoft Windows for a while, a clear definition of Microsoft Windows may be difficult. Certainly, if your only experience with a PC is a DOS-level interface, understanding what the hullabaloo over Windows is all about is difficult or impossible. Whether you already have installed Windows and are using it daily or merely contemplating moving to the Windows environment, it is helpful to know a little bit more about this trend-setting software.

The earliest computer users were technical types who understood the hardware and software design. They took to cryptic procedures and arcane commands easily. As computer power became available to a wider audience, however, users struggled with "computerese" and sought ways to ease access to applications. The Apple Macintosh was the first consumer-oriented product to provide a natural, picture-oriented interface for the computer. The Macintosh operating system and other features were designed from the beginning with this graphical user interface (GUI) in mind.

A GUI is simply computer software, such as Microsoft Windows, that represents programs and procedures as graphics symbols. Users interact with the computer by manipulating these symbols instead of by issuing discrete commands.

DOS and Windows Screens

The more popular, more available, less expensive PCs remain command-oriented, requiring English-like—but certainly not English—commands to load and run applications and conduct system-level operations. This is due in part to the heritage of the operating system. You easily can see the difference between the PC's command-line design and a GUI by comparing the screen in figure 24.1 with the one in figure 24.2.

Figure 24.1. A typical PC command-line screen.

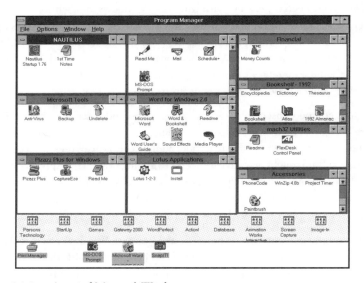

Figure 24.2. A typical Microsoft Windows screen.

To maintain compatibility with the earliest PCs, IBM and its imitators improved the existing DOS, but kept its memory and command constraints.

By the time Microsoft released the first Windows offering, millions of PC users had gained experience with the command interface, and thousands of software packages already existed that ran under DOS alone. And, because the first releases of Windows were decidedly limited compared with today's version, acceptance was not rapid or widespread.

With Windows 3.0, released in mid-1990, however, developers and users alike began to take to this new way of running PC software. Subsequent improvements with later versions have made Windows an even better product, and most major software producers now have Windows-based versions of their most popular packages.

Today, millions of PC users have switched to the Windows environment and are running their applications from screens that look like the typical sample in figure 24.2.

DOS and Windows: What's the Difference?

The screen samples in the previous illustrations should point out quickly the basic differences between DOS-only and Windows environments. A DOS-based computer uses a text screen; a Windows-based computer uses a screen full of colorful pictures.

Executing Commands

To make this difference even clearer, consider a typical program example. Suppose that you are using Money Counts, an accounting software package from Parsons Technology. Unless you have done a fair amount of advance work—writing macros, setting a PATH for DOS to use when loading the application, and that sort of thing—the DOS command to start this program looks something like this:

```
C:\MC\MC  C:\MC\PERS1993
```

To do the same thing in Windows, on the other hand, you use a hand-held mouse to move an electronic arrow to a picture of money bags (fig. 24.3) on the screen and press a switch on the mouse twice.

Money Counts

Figure 24.3. *The Money Counts icon.*

Why Use Windows?

There are some strong and obvious reasons for using Windows, and one of the best is the GUI, which makes the process of using your computer and its programs a lot easier.

In addition, as Windows has evolved it has provided a higher level of compatibility among various applications for easy operation and interchange of data. With Windows-compliant programs, for example, you easily can grab data or images from the screen of one program and drop them into another application. You can set up links between applications so that, if you change data in one program, the changed information shows up immediately in a linked application.

This capability is possible because of an application interface standard that Microsoft calls DDE for dynamic data exchange. DDE is a programmer-level interface that enables one Windows application to access the data files from another Windows application. You can include data, or even a graphics chart, from an Excel spreadsheet in a Write document, for example. If you change the source data in Excel, the result in the Write document also changes.

Whether or not you benefit from DDE depends on which applications you run. DDE is not something a user accesses; instead, it is something a program supplies. While more and more Windows applications support DDE, currently not all Windows-based programs can use it.

Obviously, this type of information linking can be very useful in maintaining current reports when you are working with dynamic data such as regional sales information. In such a case, you might want to print regular memos about sales performance. You could use Write to create the memo and Excel to maintain the sales data. After a DDE link is established, you could print an updated memo at any time simply by keeping the Excel spreadsheet information up to date.

A DDE link is created in Write, Microsoft Word for Windows, or other compliant software with the Paste Link selection from the Edit menu. To do this, open a source application—such as PaintBrush—and load the file that contains an object you want to link. Select the data you want to link to a destination program, such as Write. Use Edit Copy to place a copy of this object on the Clipboard. Finally, switch to the destination application and use Edit Paste Link to bring the object in. Objects merged into a document from the Clipboard using the Paste Link command bring with them information about the application that created them, enabling the dynamic data sharing.

Another form of data exchange also exists in Windows 3.1; it is called OLE, for object linking and embedding. This also is a dynamic link, but the embedded object—an Excel graph or Paintbrush image, for example—carries even more information about itself. After you have inserted an object into a destination file or document, you can launch the application that created it in the first place and manipulate the data by simply double-clicking on the object.

Like DDE, OLE technology isn't universally supported among Windows applications. However, it is destined to become increasingly popular.

In addition to good information linking, Windows provides its own memory management, giving you a reason for having all that RAM on your 386-, 486- or Pentium-based computer. In general, the more memory you have, the better Windows and its applications like it. (At least up to 64MB, which is about all Windows can use right now. In fact, after 16MB or so, I doubt that you get much improvement in Windows operation, at least not at this time.)

In short, the Windows environment is bringing a new ease of use as well as level of standardization and compatibility to PC computing.

Why Use DOS?

As good as it is, Windows doesn't necessarily do everything for everybody. Sometimes there really is no substitute for DOS. Particularly if you already have DOS experience, a simple operation such as formatting a floppy diskette or copying over a subdirectory to another drive or directory can be done quicker and easier in DOS than in Windows.

In addition, you still may have to install some DOS-based applications from the DOS command line rather than from Windows simply because some programs aren't designed for Windows. And, if you are using a low-end PC with limited memory and a small disk drive, Windows may operate too slowly (or not at all, in some cases). Thus, people use Windows for applications that require Windows and switch to DOS for programs that run only with DOS.

Whatever your needs, however, you should seriously consider upgrading from DOS to Windows. When you install Windows on your machine, you don't do away with DOS, of course. You must have DOS to run Windows. However, the Windows environment will enhance your computer, make applications easier to learn and use, and provide a very desirable level of compatibility with other software now coming on the market. The upgrade process is relatively easy, and the cost is quite modest.

First, however, to run the latest version of Windows you must have a 386-, 486-, or Pentium-based machine with at least 2MB of RAM. That's the minimum configuration that runs Windows. However, to use Windows effectively, you need at least 4–8MB of RAM.

In fact, the most difficult part of upgrading from DOS to Windows could be adding more memory to help Windows run better. Also, the most basic Windows installation requires around 4MB of disk storage, with about 10MB as a more desirable amount. That means you must have 4–10MB of free space before you start installing Windows. Obviously, more space is desirable because, if you are just adding Windows to your system, undoubtedly you will add Windows-based programs, which will require more room on your hard disk.

After you decide to upgrade to Windows from DOS, all you need do is insert the first diskette in the Windows package and type **setup**. You then answer a few simple questions, and the Setup utility installs Windows for you more or less automatically.

Windows Features

Perhaps more important than the ease of use offered by Windows-based software is its standardized interface. After you learn a few Windows conventions—menus, what icons mean, how to navigate the Windows screen, where to find help, and so on— the basic operation of one software package is pretty much like another.

In figure 24.4, you can see a typical Windows screen with some open group windows. Even a cursory look at this screen shows quickly what applications are available. The combination of icons and short descriptions enables even a novice to access almost any application.

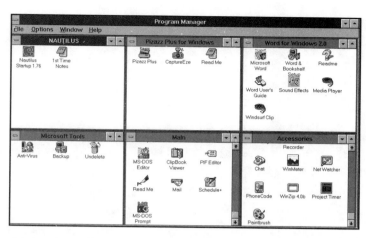

Figure 24.4. *A typical Windows 3.1 Program Manager screen.*

This view of Windows shows you several important basic Windows components. I look at those components in the next section of this chapter.

The Windows environment consists of several easily identified components, all represented by symbols that have consistent meaning throughout Windows. When you load Windows, the first thing you see is the Program Manager screen. The Program Manager is a Windows facility that manages program groups and items. The Program Manager is the actual user interface for Windows and is used to install and run applications.

Unless you have modified your system, the Program Manager is a large window with a title at the top, a menu bar on the next line, and several group icons and/or windows. Figure 24.5 shows a typical Program Manager screen with the major components labeled.

Title bar ——

Application or —
group windows

Application or
group icons ——

Running
programs ——

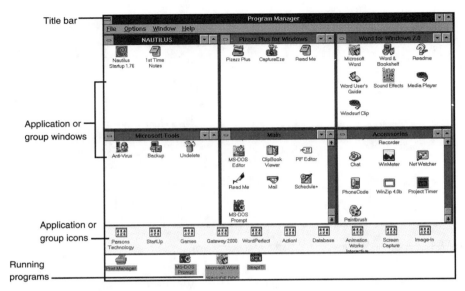

Figure 24.5. *A typical Program Manager screen.*

The Program Manager is what you see when you work with Windows. It is the visual part of the Windows environment that holds group icons as well as open group windows.

A group is an association of program files displayed in the Program Manager as a single named icon. Individual program item icons are stored inside groups to help with application management. A group window, on the other hand, is a window that contains individual program item icons that are part of a given group. The group window is displayed within the Program Manager.

Additional icons—program item icons—are contained inside an open group window. As you can see from figure 24.5, it is easy to see which general classes of applications are available (group icons) and which specific programs you can run (program item icons).

A running program occupies an application window, which is an open window within the Program Manager that holds the screens associated with a running program or application. WordPerfect runs in an application window, for example, as do Lotus 1-2-3, Paradox3, and other programs.

You can run DOS-based and Windows applications in a window smaller than full screen size if you are running in enhanced 386 mode. See the hardware discussion later in this chapter for more information on Windows modes.

In Windows terminology, the Program Manger, group icons, group windows, and application windows constitute the Windows desktop, a collection of numerous screen objects that help you use the computer and its applications. In the Windows environment, an object is any on-screen symbol that can be manipulated. Most Windows objects are represented by icons, or small drawings.

When you first look at a Windows screen, you may have mixed emotions. On the one hand, it appears easy to see what is available on the disk, but at the same time, you may wonder how you can get to everything. By keeping a few basic principals in mind, however, navigating through Windows screens is relatively easy.

First you should familiarize yourself with basic Windows components. Look again at figure 24.5. This shows you the most obvious Windows features and the proper names for them.

Windows applications, including the Program Manager, have some features and components in common. At the top of an open window is the window title, called the title bar. To the right of the title bar are two icons shaped like arrowheads. The first of these is the Minimize button, which reduces the window to a small on-screen icon; the second is the Maximize button, which switches the application from a small window to full screen. After an application is running full screen, the Maximize button changes to a double-pointed arrow, indicating that you can shrink the window to less than full screen and bring it back again to full screen with this same button. The Minimize button changes an application to an icon whether it is running in a full or partial screen window.

One example of the standardization of this user interface is the menu bar at the top of the Program Manager screen. Each Windows-based product has its own menu structure, but you are likely to find certain things in all Windows-compliant programs. You are sure to find File, Edit, and Help selections, for example. And, while each File, Edit, and Help submenu may have choices unique to each application, there are some choices within each of these menus that are the same.

Under File, almost certainly, are New, Close, Open, and Exit options. What other choices appear under File depends on the specific application you are running, but you can be fairly sure that these basic choices will be available and will perform the same task in all applications.

Under Edit look for Cut, Copy, and Paste selections as well as any other necessary application-specific choices. And, the Help menu should include Index and About selections as well as application-specific choices.

The more you use Windows applications, the easier it is to run any new application. This is because of the similarities among different programs designed to run with Windows.

The easiest way to get to any Windows programs and components is with the mouse. Simply move the mouse along the desktop, or across its dedicated pad if you have one, until the arrow pointer rests over what you want to select. In Windows, when you select an object, you mark or activate it. In most cases, you select an object by clicking on it.

When you select an item, it becomes ready for some action. When you select a menu entry, for example, a pull-down list of options or a dialog box usually is presented. When you select a group icon, that group's control menu is displayed. A dialog box is simply a pop-up box or window that asks for additional information before conducting a chosen operation. When you issue the File Save As command in Windows, for example, a dialog box pops up to ask for the name of the file.

If you have used only the DOS command line and programs with menus, getting used to selecting items with the mouse takes a little adjustment—but only a little.

When you first load Windows, somewhere on your screen within the Program Manager, appears a small arrow. This is the mouse pointer. If you move the mouse around on its pad or the desktop, this pointer moves around on the screen. You can point to any object on the screen—an icon, an open window, or a menu item—and click once to select it.

So far, I've described how to use Windows with a mouse. In general, however, you can do almost everything in Windows from the keyboard as well. The list in table 24.1 shows you how special keyboard keys are used to navigate the Windows screens.

Whenever possible, use the mouse. That is the way Windows was designed to be used. At times, however, you may find it more convenient to use the keyboard.

Table 24.1. *Windows Keyboard Features*

Keys	Result
Ctrl-Tab	Select next window or group icon
Arrow keys	Select next program item
Enter	Choose selected item

Keys	Result
Esc	Cancel (close current dialog box)
Alt	Activate menu bar
Alt-Enter	Edit properties for selected item
Del	Delete selected item
F1	Help
F7	Move selected item
F8	Copy selected Item
Shift-F4	Tile windows on screen (i.e., place them side by side)
Shift-F5	Cascade windows on screen (i.e., randomly overlap them)

Using Windows

To run an application from a Windows icon, you must install the application into a group on the desktop. A group is a collection of filenames displayed as a single icon on the screen. When you expand or maximize a group icon, the individual applications it contains are displayed as separate icons.

Groups combine related applications so they appear together in a window. These applications can reside anywhere on the disk or on different disks. Combining related applications within a group helps you find and execute these applications as necessary. You can install a new application into an existing group or create a new group for it.

If no group file already exists to hold the application you want to install into Windows, create a new group file for it. This is a simple process that uses easy-to-understand dialog boxes to prompt you along the way. Access this dialog box with the File selection from the Program Manager menu to create a new group icon and window. Group files appear in the Program Manager.

A program item is an icon and program name that helps you start up a program (application) from within Windows. A basic program item definition consists of the following:

- A description

- An icon

- A program name that includes a path

In addition, you optionally can specify a working subdirectory and a shortcut key combination. A working directory is the disk directory you want the program to use automatically when it runs.

To have the same application appear in multiple groups, create a separate program item for the application in each group where you want it to appear. The path and program information are the same, but you can select different icons for each instance of the same program if you want.

Windows supports DOS-based applications as well as programs designed for Windows. The program item installation is the same for either type of program.

Program items appear within specific group windows. When you double-click on a group icon, a window is opened, and all of the program items within that group are shown as icons with short descriptions.

If you don't see the group you want on the Program Manager screen, that group already may be open and hidden by other windows or it may be minimized but hidden by other open windows or because the Program Manager window is too small. In any case, press Ctrl-Tab to step through available groups until the group you want to access is highlighted and brought to the foreground of the display.

Windows and DOS

If you're like me, you can't help but be impressed with the features of Windows and maybe a little excited about the potential. But (like me) you also probably are saying, "I'm a DOS user, and most of my applications are written for DOS."

Don't worry. Although programs designed for Windows provide a more flexible user interface and integrate better into the GUI environment, you should be able to run all of your existing DOS applications under Windows, including older programs that have been around since before Windows existed.

The Program Manager handles the basic program item installation for DOS programs just as it does for Windows programs. If you accept the suggested defaults when you

478

install a DOS application, your application should operate satisfactorily. However, you can—and perhaps must—make some changes that affect how DOS programs operate.

For example, you can set up a DOS application to run in a window instead of taking the full screen or you can have a file loaded with the program. In addition, you can set the minimum amount of memory each application needs, how video memory is used, and more.

These specifications for DOS-based programs are contained in a program information file (PIF) associated with the application. Some DOS applications are supplied with a PIF. If your application doesn't have a PIF, you can create one by using Setup to install the application or using the PIF Editor that is part of the Accessories group in Windows. The PIF is a data file that feeds information about an associated DOS application to Windows so that Windows knows how to run the program when it is loaded. Each DOS application has its own PIF data file or uses a generic data file that is part of Windows. Windows-based programs don't need PIF data because they know how to talk to Windows to provide this information automatically.

Viewing and Editing PIF Information

Only DOS applications have PIF files; Windows programs handle PIF-type data internally. PIF data must be available to run a DOS program under Windows. An application's PIF file is named the same as the executable file: WP.PIF for WordPerfect's WP.EXE program, for example.

However, there may not be PIF data specifically tied to all applications. If the manufacturer didn't supply a PIF file with the program, and your application is one Windows doesn't already know about, then the program uses generic PIF data supplied with Windows. This default PIF data is stored in the file _DEFAULT.PIF and is in the same directory as your Windows program and support files. Windows automatically uses this data if the DOS application you are running has no PIF.

A PIF is created automatically, using _DEFAULT.PIF for DOS applications when you install them with Setup unless a PIF is supplied with the application. You can edit this default PIF or the PIF Windows created using the default. And, while there are numerous data fields in each PIF file, as a practical matter, there are only three common reasons to edit a program's PIF data:

- To change from full-screen to windowed operation

- To set or correct the working directory information

- To change operation from exclusive to background so that you can have more than one program operating at a same time

Particularly when a software manufacturer includes PIF data with the application, you probably will find that most preset parameters are correct. These include the amount of conventional and high memory the program requires, the program name, and the like.

However, it seems that most PIF files provided by applications specify exclusive operation in a full-screen mode. So, when you load the application, it requires the full computer screen, and no other process can go on in the background while you are using it. You may want to change the two operational parameters so that you can run the application in a window and have it operate in the background while other foreground processes continue at the same time.

You do this with the PIF Editor utility provided as part of Windows. If you need to change the PIF data for an application, simply open the Main group window, click on the PIF Editor icon, and use the File Open command. Then, select the file you want from the list, or specify another directory and choose a file from the resulting list, or type in the path and filename in the File Name field.

From there, you can review existing settings, create new ones, or change the current ones. Use the mouse, Tab/Shift-Tab, or the Alt-key combinations to jump directly to a field for editing. Issue the File Save command from the PIF Editor menu bar to save the edited file.

There are a few advanced settings on the second PIF editor screen that may require changes for a few applications. In general, however, you can leave these settings at the default and achieve acceptable operation. To display these options, click on the Advanced button at the bottom of the first PIF Editor screen. You get the display shown in figure 24.6.

Although most of these settings are best left to Windows to select, you may want to change the amount of CPU time allocated to a program when it runs in the background and when it runs in the foreground.

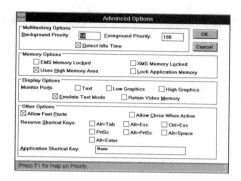

Figure 24.6. *The PIF Editor Advanced Options dialog box.*

Windows is a multitasking environment, which means that multiple applications (programs) can run at the same time. Because there is only a single CPU in today's PCs, its processing power must be shared among all active processes. By adjusting the amount of CPU time allocated to background and foreground programs, you can adjust the speed of these processes. When more time is allocated to the background program, the background process runs faster; when more CPU time is given to the foreground process, the foreground process runs faster.

Use the background/foreground priority settings to control how each DOS application performs when it is running in a window. Enter numbers between 1 and 10,000 in each field. The ratio between the background and foreground numbers determines how much relative CPU time is given to an application. Again, the default setting probably is adequate for most programs, but if a particular combination of programs seems to cause problems when using the default settings, experiment with the background/foreground settings to improve things.

Here's a quick trick to help standardize your DOS programs in Windows. Use the PIF Editor to modify the _DEFAULT.PIF file in the Windows directory so that all programs that don't have their own PIF file load and run in a partial screen window. Do this by loading the _DEFAULT.PIF file with the File Open command in the PIF Editor, changing the Full Screen default to Windowed, and then saving the file with the File Save command.

I prefer that all applications start this way because I can interface with more than one program at a time. If I spend a lot of time in one application or another—such as a word processor—I use the Maximize button to expand the window.

Multitasking in Windows

You can run multiple applications at the same time in Windows if you are running in enhanced mode with a 386-, 486-, or Pentium-based computer. You can start a process in one window—a database sort or lengthy report, for example—and switch back to your word processor. Both programs run at the same time.

Or, suppose that you are working on a document in your word processor and decide to log on to a remote computer to download a large file. Simply launch the communications program in a window, complete the log-on process, and start the file transfer. Now, while this process works in the background, switch back to your word processor and keep working. The file transfer takes place in the background.

Of course, both processes run slower than they would if each were running alone, but the overall effect is to get more work done quicker. As with many word processing operations, speed is not really a factor anyway (unless you are using a highly graphic-oriented product such as WordPerfect for Windows or Word for Windows) because most people don't type or write that quickly.

To launch a second (or subsequent) application, simply double-click on the appropriate program item icon. In quick succession, the group window that contains the application you selected becomes the current window, and then the second application starts. The program you were running previously continues to execute, conducting its duties in the background.

If you already have more than one application running, you can switch among them by clicking on the window you want or by selecting the application from the Task List. The Task List is a pop-up window that shows which applications have been launched since you started the current Windows session. Display the Task List by pressing Ctrl-Esc or by double-clicking with the mouse outside the Program Manager main window.

Programs designed for Windows pretty much take care of their multitasking requirements automatically, but you may have to do some tweaking to get a DOS application to share the processor. One way to do this, as I have mentioned, is through the PIF Editor. There's another way that can be done on the fly. Click on the Control Menu button in the upper-left of the screen (see fig. 24.7) to display the Control menu (see fig. 24.8).

Figure 24.7. *A DOS application Control Menu button.*

Figure 24.8. *The Control menu for a running application.*

Select Settings from this menu to display a configuration dialog box like the one in figure 24.9.

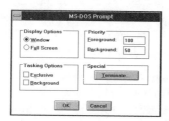

Figure 24.9. *The Settings dialog box from the Control menu.*

If you don't see a Control Menu button for a DOS application, it is running in full-screen mode (no other windows are visible on the screen). To change to windowed execution, press Alt-Enter. The application should shrink, showing other windows and presenting the Control Menu button in the upper-left portion of the screen. To return to full-screen mode, press Alt-Enter again.

The Settings dialog box contains four separate windows for different procedures: Display Options, Priority, Tasking Options, and Special.

Click on Window or Full Screen in the Display Options window of this dialog box to set how this DOS application will run. If you select Window, the application executes within a window that is a small portion of the entire screen. Select Full

Screen to cause the application to operate as it would in DOS, taking over the entire display.

If you use these selections to change the current mode of operation, the DOS application changes immediately when you click on OK. If you select Full Screen when the program is running in a window, the program runs in full screen mode when you close the dialog box.

The settings in the Priority window determine how much of the available CPU time is given to the background and foreground processes. You can enter numbers between 1 and 10,000 in each field of this window. The ratio between these numbers determines how much processing power the application gets when it is running in each mode.

To make the foreground mode run faster, place a higher number in the foreground field; to devote more CPU time to the background process, and slow down any foreground process, make the background number larger. By default, most applications have 100 in the foreground field and 50 in the background field, which gives the foreground application twice as much CPU time as the background process (a ratio of 100:50 or 2:1). When one program is running in the background and one in the foreground, this is a pretty good choice.

Precisely how this functions depends on how many background applications are active, however. Obviously, if more than one background process is operational, all of them can't have 50 percent of the CPU time. Instead, all of the background applications share the available background CPU time.

If you want to further adjust the weight or priority given to one or more of the background processes, you can change the background number from the default. For example, assume that three programs are running in the background. Program 1 has a background setting of 25, program 2 has a background setting of 50, and program 3 has a background setting of 100. In this scenario, program 1 gets half as much background processing time as program 2; program 3 gets twice as much background CPU time as program 2 and four times as much as program 1.

How much CPU time does the foreground process get? That depends on the foreground/background settings of the foreground program. If you are using the default of 100 for foreground, then this foreground program gets just over one-third as much CPU time as the combined background processes. This is because the combined background and foreground settings are 275 (25+50+100+100). The foreground setting is 100, for a background-to-foreground ratio of 275:100.

As a general rule, to compute the weighting of background and foreground times, add all of the background times to the foreground time and compare the foreground setting to the total of the background and foreground times. Note that the you should not include the background time that you set in the foreground-to-background weighting option. You may have to experiment with several settings on programs you run frequently in multitasking mode to get the best results.

Unless you have checked one of the options in the Tasking window, DOS applications operate in exclusive mode. That means that while they are operating they receive full CPU power and other running applications are suspended. If you click on Background in this box, however, you can leave a DOS process operational and start up another program so the two (or more than two) applications can operate at the same time. Use the mouse to click on the option you want or issue the Alt-X or Alt-B commands to select the proper tasking option.

The Special window provides a way to terminate a running DOS program that couldn't be ended normally. This exit routine is provided for times when incompatibilities between an application and Windows makes it impossible to close an application in the normal way. If, for example, an application doesn't handle memory correctly, it may hang, preventing you from using the normal menu routines for quitting the program. If the application's menu procedure doesn't work properly, you may be able to access the Control menu and use Special to close the window.

Sometimes, however, you can't even get the Control menu for a malfunctioning application to display. In this case, press Ctrl-Alt-Del and follow the instructions on the screen.

Notice that when you open the Control menu of a DOS application there are some additional choices. One of the most important ones is the Edit selection, which enables you to mark a section of the DOS application screen and copy it to the Clipboard. You also can use this menu selection to paste information from the Clipboard into a DOS application. Cut and Paste don't work exactly the same with DOS applications as with Windows programs, but you can use these features by going through the Control Panel and choosing Edit from the menu.

The Microsoft Windows environment is extremely rich. I could write an entire book (or two or three) on how Windows works and what you can do as a user to customize it for your preferences. That's enough for now, however. From the information in this chapter, I think you can get a good idea of what Windows is and what it does. Moreover, you can learn how to integrate your DOS programs into Windows if you decide to make the transition, which is something I think PC users should do.

Windows still may not be for everyone, but the standards it brings to the computer, the picture-oriented screen, and pointer access with the mouse make Windows a logical choice for at least part of the computer work done by just about everyone.

Some Things To Try

1. Install multiple versions of your word processor in a group window. Specify a different working directory for each one. To work on specific documents, also include a command to load a document file as part of the command line. If you have several different start-up parameters for the same program, you might want to create a separate group for them.

2. Move a program item from one group to another by dragging its icon out of its current window and dropping it on another group icon or into an open group window. The program should show up in the new location.

3. Launch a DOS application from inside Windows. Does it take over the whole screen or does it run in a smaller window? Can you change how it works, making a full-screen program run in a partial-screen window and vice versa?

4. I mentioned the Control menu that is a part of every Windows application when it runs. Can you find the Control Panel, a separate application that helps you configure the Windows environment? Launch the Control Panel and poke around in its many sections to discover some interesting facts about Windows and how it works.

Printers, Communication, and Sound

25

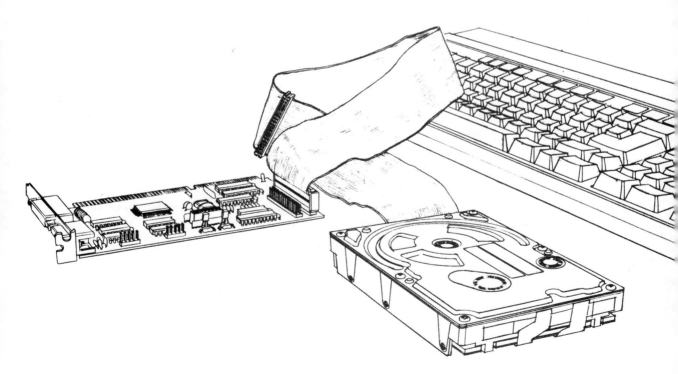

I n other parts of this book, I've talked about the core hardware that makes up a PC and the software—DOS and Windows—that make it run. In this chapter, I give you a quick look at some of the external components that help enhance and expand your computer. In fact, a printer is such a necessary part of the computer for most users that it almost could be considered part of the computer. I talk about printers first and then move on to communications and sound.

Printers: The Parallel Port

Beginning with the first PCs, computers have included a port through which you could attach a printer. The earliest computers I used had a current loop port to connect to a teletype machine. Then manufacturers began adding serial ports (see the next section), and today the parallel port is the most common printer connection.

You sometimes hear the parallel printer port on a PC referred to as a Centronics port, after the company that popularized it. The technology of that port has changed very little over the years, except that the original interface used a 36-pin connector, and today's version generally uses a 25-pin D-shell connector (DB25). That reduces the real estate requirements for the connector and doesn't really compromise operation of the interface. About all that is dropped in the newer connector are a few ground leads. The original connector required multiple, redundant signal grounds. The new connectors simply use fewer of them.

This printer interface is called a parallel interface because data moves from the computer to the printer along parallel wires, that is, all eight data bits travel together. In a serial interface (see the next section), each data bit as well as control information is sent along the wire in a train-like fashion, that is, one bit at a time sent one behind the other.

Figure 25.1 shows a drawing of a typical parallel port connector, and table 25.1 shows the electrical connections for the computer side of the cable.

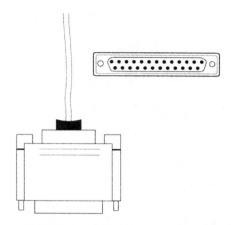

Figure 25.1. *A typical DB25 printer cable connector. (Drawing courtesy of Gateway 2000.)*

Table 25.1. *Parallel Port Pinout Connections*

Signal Name	Pin
-STROBE	1
Data 0	2
Data 1	3
Data 2	4
Data 3	5
Data 4	6
Data 5	7
Data 6	8
Data 7	9
-ACK (Acknowledge)	10
Busy	11

continues

Table 25.1. *continued*

Signal Name	Pin
Paper Empty	12
+Select	13
-Auto FDXT	14
-Error	15
-Init	16
-Slctin	17
Ground	18
Ground	19
Ground	20
Ground	21
Ground	22
Ground	23
Ground	24
Ground	25

As you can see from table 25.1, there still are a fair number of ground connections—eight to be exact. Why eight? These ground connections correspond to the eight data lines; there is one separate ground wire for each data line.

The -STROBE line on pin 1 is used to tell the printer when the current data stream is complete and that it is okay to print a character. Notice that the strobe line is identified by a negative sign in front of it. That means that the strobe pulse is a negative pulse. When the computer has finished sending a byte of data to be printed, the strobe line is pulled low.

The eight data lines carry the eight bits of a byte of information. This is accomplished digitally, with a high voltage on a line meaning a set bit, and a low voltage or no voltage meaning a clear bit. As I showed in Chapter 16, information can be stored within a computer using binary digits of this nature.

The Acknowledge line, pin 10, is a signal from the printer back to the computer that says, in effect, "I am ready to receive more information." As long as this line is high, the computer doesn't send any new data. When the line goes low (notice the negative sign in front of it in table 25.1), the computer knows the printer is ready for more information.

The Busy line signals the computer when the printer is busy. The computer waits until the printer buffer is emptied to send more information. Obviously, with parallel data lines the computer could outdistance the printer rather quickly if there weren't some way to tell the computer to wait before sending more information.

Like the Busy line, the Paper Out line tells the computer to stop sending information because the printer isn't ready to receive it. The printer could simply send a Busy signal, but then the computer has no way of knowing why the printer stopped. Some applications use the Paper Out line to report to the user that paper is needed.

The Select line shows that the printer is selected, meaning that the printer is online. (The front of your printer probably has an online switch and light.) When the printer is offline, it cannot receive characters from the computer.

The -AUTO FDXT (Auto Feed) line controls how the printer handles a new line. The printer either can advance the print head to the next line when a Carriage Return is received (the usual action) or can merely interpret the Carriage Return literally and move the print head back to the beginning of the line. When the computer holds this line low, the printer adds a Line Feed to the Carriage Return character. With -AUTO FDXT high, a Carriage Return means just that and nothing more.

The -ERROR (or Fault) line is a general-purpose line to signal any other printer errors. The computer may not be able to determine precisely what is wrong, but it knows that the printer probably is not out of paper and that some other unusual condition is preventing the printer from processing data.

The -INIT line is a way for the computer to control the printer. By signaling the printer on this line, the computer essentially resets the printer to its power on defaults. That prevents the printer configuration from the last program—a special graphics mode, for example—from being carried over to the next print job. With the -INIT line, an application can reset the printer to a known state before trying to send anything down the wire.

The -SLCTIN (Select Input) line is a way for the computer to control whether the printer is ready to accept data (online or offline). When this signal is low, the printer can accept data; when it goes high, the printer is offline and cannot accept data.

The good news about parallel connections is that with eight wires to carry data simultaneously, information can flow from the computer to the printer quickly compared with most serial connections. In fact, the parallel port is theoretically capable of sending around half a million characters per second down the line. A printer may be able to take this for a while, but eventually would fall behind, so the Busy line stops the computer while the printer catches up.

And, while you most often use your printer port to send information from the computer to the printer, you also can use it to accept data from an external device (this wasn't true with early PCs, which had an output-only design on the parallel port). There are software/hardware packages available today to do just that. By connecting two computers together through a null cable (one with the wires crossed so that the output wires of one machine are connected to the input wires of another) and installing some software, you can share data, transfer files, and the like.

You may wonder why, if the parallel port is so fast, that parallel links aren't used for everything. One of the main reasons is the distance limitations of parallel lines. Because the data lines are parallel, there is more chance for interference—resulting in data errors—as the line length increases. Parallel communication is good for distances of 12 feet or less. For longer lines, use your serial port.

Communication Lines: The Serial Port

The other standard communications port you can find on your PC is the serial port. In fact, today's PCs generally have at least two serial ports.

As the name implies, the serial port differs from the parallel port in that the data is sent down the line in a serial stream instead of in parallel. This slows down data transfer, to some extent, but enables you to communicate over long distances. Instead of the parallel port's maximum 10–12-foot range, you can use a serial line for 50 or more feet and still get reliable communications. In fact, back in the days of minicomputers, I have run shielded serial cable through metal conduit inside walls and ceilings for 150 feet or more. That much distance isn't recommended, but with quality wire, conduit, and careful grounding, you can (sometimes) get away with it.

The RS-232 serial standard calls for 25 lines, but as a practical matter, you can get by with a lot less. Figure 25.2 shows the type of 9-pin D-shell connector commonly used for the COMM 1 port on most PCs today. The COMM 2 serial port uses the older DB25 connector. However, even the larger connector usually doesn't have all 25 pins connected to anything.

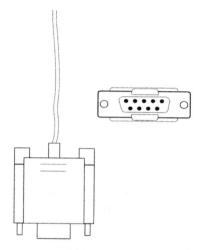

Figure 25.2. *A typical 9-pin serial connector. (Drawing courtesy of Gateway 2000.)*

When you purchase a commercial serial cable, it rarely has all 25 lines connected. And, when you wire one yourself, you probably aren't going to string all 25 wires between connectors. In fact, the most common connections are those shown in table 25.2.

Table 25.2. *Common Serial Connections*

Signal	Name	DB9 Pin	DB25 Pin
DCD	Data Carrier Detect	1	8
RX	Receive Data	2	3
TX	Transmit Data	3	2
DTR	Data Terminal Ready	4	20

continues

493

Table 25.2. *continued*

Signal	Name	DB9 Pin	DB25 Pin
GND	Signal Ground	5	7
DSR	Data Set Ready	6	6
RTS	Request to Send	7	4
CTS	Clear to Send	8	5
RI	Ring Indicator	9	22

The pin assignments shown in table 25.2 are for the cable that attaches to your PC because PCs are considered DTE (Data Terminal Equipment) devices. Normally, when you purchase or build your own serial cable, the connections on the other end are the same. You connect wires straight through from DCD to DCD, for example, from RX to RX, from TX to TX, and so on. You can do this because normally two DTE devices don't connect to each other in the serial world.

When you plug a cable into a DTE device (your computer), the assumption is that you will plug the other end of the cable into a DCE (Data Communications Equipment) device, such as a modem. A DCE device has different serial pin assignments so that the TX line from a DTE device attaches automatically to the RX pin of a DCE device. Similarly, the TX line from the DCE unit hooks up to the RX pin of the DTE device.

Other lines require reverse connections as well. For example, the RTS line from one device must connect to the CTS line of another. That makes sense, when you think about it. The Request to Send line (RTS) is a query that must be answered by the Clear to Send (CTS). The DTR/DSR lines also must connect to each other, and the DCD line from one device usually connects to the DTR line of another.

Again, this kind of cross-connection takes place automatically when you are using one DTE and one DCE device. If you want to connect two DTR devices, as you would do if you wanted to hook up two computers via the serial line to exchange files, the cable itself must make the swap. Such a cable is called a null modem cable. You can see how this cable is wired by studying the drawing in figure 25.3.

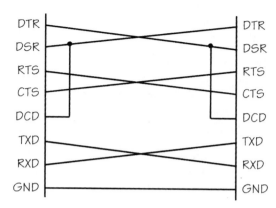

Figure 25.3. *Null modem serial cable wiring. (Drawing courtesy of Gateway 2000.)*

Depending on what you're using the serial line for, you might actually be able to get by with even fewer connections. In the minicomputer days when serial terminals were used extensively, I frequently ran serial lines with only three or four wires, the RX, TX, ground, and maybe one other line such as the DCD or DSR line.

Today, one of the main reasons for having a serial port in the first place is to connect your computer to a modem or other external device. And, because you don't always know what that device will be, it is best to have at least the lines shown in table 25.2 connected. With that set of nine lines, you can support a modem, serial printer, plotter, and other common serial devices.

Now I look briefly at each of these serial signals so you can understand what each one does. This level of technical discussion also should help you understand the status lights on your modem and how to configure your communications software. I look at those topics in the next section.

The Data Carrier Detect (DCD) line (or simply Carrier Detect; CD) is used by modems to indicate they are talking to each other at some level. When your local modem links with the remote modem and gets a good carrier signal, the local modem places a positive signal on the DCD line. This tells your computer and its communications software that a modem-to-modem link has been established.

The Receive Data (RX) line is obvious. It is through this connection that your computer or the DCE device receives information transmitted to it from a remote device.

The Transmit Data (TX) is the channel over which your computer or the remote DCE unit transmits information. Notice that there are two data lines, one for send (transmit) and one for receive. That means that, with the proper software, two serial devices can send data at the same time.

The Data Terminal Ready (DTR) line carries a positive signal from the DTE device (normally, your computer) to the remote device to indicate that a DTE device is connected to the serial cable. The companion to this line is the Data Set Ready (DSR) line. For two devices to communicate, these two lines usually must be high, each telling the other it is there and ready for communications.

The Ground (GND) pin is a signal ground, or the other side of the transmit and receive signals. In most serial installations, this connection actually is not at ground potential. That is, it is not attached to the computer or DCE chassis.

The Data Set Ready (DSR) is the other half of the DTR/DSR pair I talked about earlier. DSR is a positive signal from a DCE unit that tells a DTR device it is online and ready to communicate.

The Request to Send (RTS) line also is part of a signal pair (the other half is the CTS line) that enables two connected units to tell each other when they are ready to receive data. The RTS line is controlled by the DTR device, while the CTS line is controlled by the DCE unit.

The Clear to Send (CTS) line is the other half of the RTS/CTS pair. Unless a positive signal is present on both the CTS and RTS lines, no data can flow across the serial connection in many communications links. There are exceptions, of course. The most common is the serial terminal attached to a remote computer. This link may or may not use the CTS/RTS lines. And, it is fairly common practice to hardwire these signals inside the local connector so that you don't have to run as many wires. So, for example, you can connect pins 4 and 7 as well as 8 and 6 inside the 9-pin connector that attaches to the PC. Then you only need to connect a lead from pin 3, Transmit Data, on the PC to pin 3, Receive Data, on the printer or other DB25-type device; connect a ground between pin 5 on the PC and pin 7 on the remote device; and connect a handshake wire from pin 6 on the PC to pin 19 on the printer or other device. Now you have a one-way PC-to-printer cable with only three wires.

The Ring Indicator (RI) is a way for the local modem to tell the computer to which it is attached that a call just came in. This enables the communications software to know that an impending modem connection is coming.

Modems: Reaching Out

The word modem stands for modulator/demodulator, which is what it does. Modulation is a technique for exchanging information by superimposing a varying signal wave on top of another, more stable, carrier wave. The modem at the sending end of the connection modulates the signal to transmit data across the telephone line or serial connection; the receiving modem demodulates the signal to convert it back into digital information to send to the computer.

Although modems can be used to send computer information along dedicated wires between computers, by far the majority of modem hardware is used to connect computers to voice-grade telephone lines for dial-up communications. Reasonably priced and full-featured modem hardware coupled with communications software are opening up desktop computing to worldwide communications.

When PC users first started using modems for online communications, modems were slow and relatively expensive devices. The first modem I used was capable of a snail's pace of 110 bps (bits per second), was the size of a bread box, and was relatively expensive. Today, I have most of my computers equipped with 14,400-bps modems that fit in the palm of your hand and cost less than $200. Like everything else in the personal computing world, prices are going down, while features and functions are going up.

One reason early modems were so slow is the inherent limitations of voice telephone lines. Because only a limited bandwidth is needed to transmit voice data, telephone lines carry audio signals only between 300 and 3,000Hz. This narrow bandwidth places severe limitations on modem communications, which depend on rising and falling audio signals to carry data.

The newest modem technology is breaking this barrier, however. As I mentioned, current modems transmit and receive data at a minimum of 14,400 bits per second, or about 1,440 bytes per second. This is accomplished through a complex series of coding and decoding steps. Suffice it to say that today's data communications rates over standard telephone lines are several times what was thought possible ten years ago.

Sound

The earliest PCs included a little support for sound through the built-in speaker. About all those first PCs did was beep and blip when the user made a mistake.

Then came the PCjr, which had an internal speaker and some additional sound hardware that programmers could use for more serious sound output. For a short while there, users heard unusual sound effects and music coming out of their PCs.

At about the same time, I remember seeing several software packages that included some pretty sophisticated support for PC speaker sound. Some programs, especially educational software and game programs, could play tunes and produce some interesting sound effects.

Still, there wasn't a lot you could do with sound on the PC until years later. As the 90s began, an increasing number of off-the-shelf PCs were equipped with a dedicated sound card designed to produce stereo sound and music of very good quality. Although there isn't universal support for internal PC sound cards, multimedia software applications are fueling better sound support for more and more PCs.

When you load an MPC application or sophisticated game, you can hear narration, synchronized sound with motion video, music, and sound effects, in stereo and at levels that really can be heard. Most sound cards have a stereo line out that you can connect to any standard stereo line input. With this connection, if you want 100-watt-per-channel car horns, music, or screeching tires, you've got it.

But there's more. This 8- or 16-bit expansion card also has a microphone and line input, which means you can attach a CD-ROM player so that the sound from game and multimedia disks plays back through the sound card and so that you can speak into the microphone to record sound directly. This recorded sound can be saved in disk files and used in multimedia presentations or in databases or word processors to help with presentations, training, and the like.

All of this sound in and sound out processing takes place inside hardware that is part of the plug-in sound card. When software generates sound, it is in digital form like all other computer data.

This digital audio—like any other computer data—can be sent along the computer's bus to the sound card. However, audio amplifiers and speakers handle information in an analog format, that is, a direct representation of the physical sound waves. This means some conversion must take place inside the card.

The analog-to-digital and digital-to-analog conversion takes place in dedicated hardware that is part of the sound board. A digital-to-analog converter transforms sound from the computer format to standard format, while an analog-to-digital converter transforms sound from the outside world into digital format for the computer to use.

Current multimedia standards require that standards-compatible sound devices convert sound at a sampling rate of 22.05KHz or higher. That means the converter hardware and software capture 22,050 samples of sound every second. That is the minimum for MPC compliance. Microsoft Windows supports sampling rates at half (11.025KHz) and twice (44.1KHz) the minimum.

The higher the sampling rate, the better the audio quality you can achieve. However, large sampling rates also require more storage. You may find that for some applications the lower sampling rate is sufficient to produce the quality required. Many voice-only applications such as narration, for example, may not suffer with the lower sample rates. On the other hand, if you mix audio with different sampling rates, the viewer of the program may notice a difference in the sound quality of the different segments.

In addition to the sampling rate, digitized sound quality is affected by the number of bits used to store the samples. Each sample in an 8-bit card is only 8-bits wide. That means that all of the components of the digitized sound wave must be represented by a maximum of 256 values ($2^8 = 256$). A 16-bit card, on the other hand, captures and digitizes sounds with 16 bits of resolution, giving up to 65,536 possible values to describe the digitized sound ($2^{16} = 65,536$). Obviously, a 16-bit-wide sample can produce truer, better quality sound than an 8-bit-wide sample.

You pay for the better quality derived from 16-bit samples in the form of more storage requirements, however. One minute of 16-bit, 44.1KHz sound, for example, requires about 10.5MB of hard disk space. One minute of sound sampled with 8 bits at an 11.025KHz rate requires about 6,355KB of storage.

Today's full-featured sound cards have a way around the high storage requirements of quality, digitized sound: MIDI (musical instrument digital interface). MIDI is a form of synthesized sound that can be produced by software on the fly. That way you don't have to store the sound on disk to play it.

MIDI hardware synthesizes audio by generating electronically the sound wave combinations required for a specific sound. The computer MIDI sound port captures the instructions for recreating the sound on the synthesizer rather than recording the actual sound in digital format. By the same token, computer software can generate MIDI sounds by sending instructions for producing specific frequency combinations to a MIDI device.

By using a separate synthesizer for sound input and output, storage requirements are reduced drastically from digitized audio. An hour of stereo MIDI sound can be represented in the computer with about 500KB of storage, for example.

The future of computer-based audio may be with a technology different from what is in common use today, however. Digital signal processors (DSPs), programmable chips that can handle all of the digital and synthesis audio requirements of the MPC standard, offer much broader functions than simple digital-to-analog and analog-to-digital converters.

In addition to handling standard audio functions while maintaining compatibility with existing sound card standards, DSPs are compact and can be programmed for such additional functions. For example, you can program a DSP for audio compression and decompression, video compression and decompression, speech recognition, voice mail, data and FAX modem services, telephone or answering machine duties, and speakerphone functions.

Video Capture Boards

A natural companion to an audio input/output board is a video input/output board, sometimes referred to as a video capture board. With increasing ease, popular PC software from word processors to spreadsheets to databases are including support for still pictures and motion video. One of the most common ways to get photographic information into your computer is with a board that converts the standard television signal from your VCR or video camera into digital information the computer can manage.

While the process inside the board is fairly complex, using these video boards is fairly simple. You just plug in your VCR or camera to the input port on the board, attach a TV monitor to the output of the board, and roll the tape.

Many video boards also support a cross-board attachment to your computer's VGA card through the feature connection. When you do that, you can view computer information and video data at the same time on your VGA multisynch monitor.

Either using the software that came with your video capture card or a third-party package, such as Microsoft Video for Windows, you can capture any video information that appears on the input port of the video card. Usually, you can't store and play back that data at a full 30 frames per second, the rate for full-motion, television-type video. But, you can capture and store around 15 frames per second. In addition, to keep processor and storage requirements to a minimum, most video capture software supports relatively small windows of video.

There are, of course, high-end software packages that enable support for full-motion, full-screen video. These packages, such as D/Vision from TouchVision Systems and Personal Producer from Matrox, are designed for desktop video editing. Coupled with other hardware in addition to the video capture board, these packages offer editing and production features that rival editing suites at a fraction of the cost.

In addition to motion video, video capture boards can be used to capture and store still-frame images for use in photo databases, newsletters, and multimedia presentations. Some boards can capture full 24-bit color for high-resolution, high-quality images.

Video and sound hardware, coupled with high-end software, are changing the face of desktop computing. When I wrote the first edition of this book, soon after the IBM PC was released, no one envisioned how much computers would change many people's everyday lives.

Exploring and Tinkering

On the surface of things there is only so much that you can discover, but when you dig down just a little, you can unearth wonders. That's pretty much what this chapter is about: how you can dig into the PC and explore and tinker with it. In this chapter, I cover the good reasons why it's not just interesting but truly valuable to know how to dig below the surface of the PC, and you learn about two of the tools that can be used to do this exploring.

The Point of Exploring and Tinkering

There are more reasons than you might imagine why it's beneficial to know how to explore, examine, change, and tinker with the PC. The best reason of all is one that doesn't have a direct, immediate benefit: exploring widens and deepens your knowledge of the PC family, and that makes you a more proficient PC user, better able to use the full range of the PC's powers, better able to avoid problems with your PC, and better able to deal with problems when they do occur.

Among the things that you can learn by tinkering with the PC is how data is organized on the disk, both the structure of the disk itself and the internal structure of the data files with which programs work. Similarly, you can learn a great deal about how programs work, how they manage data, and how they use memory and other parts of the computer's resources. There often are hidden wonders in programs (particularly some very interesting messages) that you can unveil.

There are direct benefits to tinkering, as well. If a disk is damaged or the data in a file is corrupted so that the program working with that data rejects it, you sometimes can use your tinkering skills to repair the damage. This isn't always possible, of course, but sometimes you can hammer things back into shape and carry on.

So whether it's to expand your knowledge, satisfy your curiosity, or attempt emergency repairs, exploring and tinkering can be quite worthwhile. You can use many program tools to do your exploring and tinkering, but this chapter focuses on the two that are most widely available and that provide a good spectrum of features: DOS's DEBUG program and the Disk Editor program from the Norton Utilities. (If you have a version of the Norton Utilities earlier than 5.0, use the NU program.)

DEBUG is in some ways the more powerful and also the more difficult to use. To a certain extent, of course, those two properties go hand in hand; powerful features are almost necessarily accompanied by complex commands. But that isn't the only reason DEBUG is more demanding.

Any program tool, from a spreadsheet to the tinkering tools discussed here, is designed to serve a particular need. In the case of DEBUG, the technical needs of advanced programmers were the target. As a free program included with every copy of DOS, DEBUG wasn't intended to be the ultimate programmer's tool, just a good basic tool for programmers. DEBUG's features are technical, and its command structure and user interface are crude, but it gets the job done.

Together, DEBUG, the Disk Editor, and NU give you a good example of the range of utility program features that enable you to tinker and explore.

Working with DEBUG

This section discusses the things you can do with DEBUG. And, because DEBUG is included with every version of DOS, everyone who has a PC has a copy.

You can find instructions for using DEBUG in your DOS manual. If you are using IBM's PC DOS version 3.3, 4.0, or 6.0 you must look in the *DOS Technical Reference Manual*, which is sold separately. However, because this manual is interesting and useful, you may want to buy it regardless of what version of DOS you are using.

Another source for DEBUG information is my book, *Peter Norton's DOS 6 Guide*, published by Brady Books. In that book, I discuss all the commands and how to use them.

As already explained, DEBUG is a technically oriented tool designed to serve the needs of programmers and others who have no difficulty working with the microprocessor and are comfortable using hexadecimal numbers and segmented addresses. Almost everything you can do with DEBUG requires that you specify your commands in hex and that you enter and interpret segmented addresses (also given in hex). If you are not familiar with these things, you may want to forget about using DEBUG. If so, skip this section, and move on to the next, where you learn about a more civilized tool, the editing functions in the Norton Utilities.

DEBUG is a powerful tool with many features, and a great deal more power than I can explore here. You already have had a taste of some of that power with the

DEBUG U (Unassemble) command, which can be used to decode the hexadecimal of absolute machine language instructions into the more intelligible assembly language format. You saw that DEBUG feature in the discussion of interrupt drivers in Chapter 4. DEBUG also has an A (Assemble) command, which acts as a crude assembler turning assembly language statements into machine language, and features that enable you to follow the steps a program takes, watching it execute and seeing the results of each step. Those commands and others like them are fascinatingly powerful, but they're more than I can deal with here. These details belong in a book on advanced programming techniques.

This chapter discusses some of the DEBUG commands that enable you to snoop and explore. I begin with some background on DEBUG. DEBUG works with a minimum of fuss (and a minimum of online help), which takes a little getting used to. You start the program with this simple command:

DEBUG

DEBUG then displays its command prompt, which is a hyphen. Whenever you see that DEBUG command prompt, DEBUG is ready to receive a command. All of DEBUG's commands (except for a few of the newer expanded memory commands added with DOS 4.0) are abbreviated as a single letter. You might as well start by learning the command to finish using DEBUG and return to DOS. It's the Q (Quit) command.

For snooping around with DEBUG, one of the main commands to use is the D (Display) command. D tells DEBUG to display some of the contents of the computer's memory in a form that combines hexadecimal and character format. Following is an example of what the D command might show you:

```
2B68:0100   66 7F 06 06 0F 00 00 00-0A 0E 00 00 7F 60 60 60   f............"""
2B68:0110   7E 03 03 63 3E 00 00 00-0A 0E 00 00 1C 30 60 60   <til>..c>....0""
2B68:0120   7E 63 63 63 3E 00 00 00-0A 0E 00 00 7F 63 03 06   <til>ccc>....c..
2B68:0130   0C 18 18 18 18 00 00 00-0A 0E 00 00 3E 63 63 63   ...........>ccc
2B68:0140   3E 63 63 63 3E 00 00 00-0A 0E 00 00 3E 63 63 63   >ccc>.......>ccc
2B68:0150   3F 03 03 06 3C 00 00 00-0A 0E 00 00 00 18 18 00   ?...<...........
2B68:0160   00 00 18 18 00 00 00 00-0A 0E 00 00 00 18 18 00   ...............
2B68:0170   00 00 18 18 30 00 00 00-0A 0E 00 00 06 0C 18 30   ....0.........0
```

This display information appears in three parts. On the left is the memory address of the data being displayed; in the middle is the data in hex format; and on the right are the characters that correspond to the hex information shown. DEBUG censors the character data, showing only ordinary text characters. This censoring has its good and bad aspects. It doesn't show all the interesting characters that lurk in the data, but it does ensure that you can copy the data to a printer without accidentally sending a control code that might make the printer act up. (By contrast, the data displays generated by the Norton Utilities show every character so that you can see it all, but you may not necessarily be able to print it.)

DEBUG displays any data it has in memory, which can be just about anything. As you saw in Chapter 4, DEBUG can look at the beginning of the computer's memory (say to look at the interrupt vectors) or at the higher reaches of memory where the ROM-BIOS routines are stored. You look at some of those shortly. From the middle part of memory, you can display DEBUG's ordinary program data area. This is where you have DEBUG load a program or data file you want to inspect.

If, for example, you want to use DEBUG to browse around in DOS's command interpreter COMMAND.COM, you can tell DEBUG to load COMMAND.COM into memory when it starts and then display the beginning of the contents of COMMAND.COM, like this:

```
DEBUG COMMAND.COM
-D
```

When you do that, you get a display like the following (I've skipped from the beginning of COMMAND.COM to a part that you can recognize):

```
1D1C:13F0   49 42 4D 20 44 4F 53 20-56 65 72 73 69 6F 6E 20   IBM DOS Version
1D1C:1400   34 2E 30 30 20 28 43 29-43 6F 70 79 72 69 67 68   4.00 (C)Copyrigh
1D1C:1410   74 20 49 42 4D 20 43 6F-72 70 20 31 39 38 31 2C   t IBM Corp 1981,
1D1C:1420   31 39 38 38 4C 69 63 65-6E 73 65 64 20 4D 61 74   1988Licensed Mat
1D1C:1430   65 72 69 61 6C 20 2D 20-50 72 6F 67 72 61 6D 20   erial - Program
1D1C:1440   50 72 6F 70 65 72 74 79-20 6F 66 20 49 42 4D FF   Property of IBM.
1D1C:1450   04 00 15 13 00 54 00 14-00 64 00 15 00 6D 00 16   .....T...d...m..
1D1C:1460   00 73 00 17 00 86 00 18-00 8D 00 19 00 AB 00 1A   .s.............
```

The DEBUG D (Display) command by itself shows just 128 bytes from its current work area. If you want the command to show another area, you can give it the address you want it to show, such as D 13F0 (which is what I used to display the part of COMMAND.COM that you see above) or D 0:0 (which is what you would do to get the very beginning of memory). To have the D command show more than 128 bytes at a time, you just add the letter L (for length) and indicate in hex the number of bytes you want shown. The command D F800:0 L 300, for example, shows hex 300 (768) bytes, starting high in memory in the ROM-BIOS area.

All by itself, the D command can be used to explore much of the PC's memory and disk data, but other DEBUG commands help you find even more.

The S (Search) command enables you to search through data, which can be very helpful in finding messages that you know are stored in a program. If you know the text of one message and use DEBUG to find it, you're likely to find the area where other messages are stored, and studying these messages can tell you a lot.

Like the D command, you enter the search command with the initial letter S followed by whatever memory address and length you want the search to act on. Following that, you tell DEBUG what you want it to search for, either as a number in hex or, if you're looking for characters, a string of characters enclosed in quotation marks. Following is an example:

```
S F000:0 L FFFF "1790"
```

I used this command once when an old PC AT that belonged to a neighbor of mine acted up. It started displaying error message number 1790, but he didn't know exactly what that meant. Because the message appeared when his machine was first turned on, I knew that the message was part of the power on self-test routines that are stored in the computer's ROM-BIOS. To find out more about this message, I used DEBUG to find this message, searching through the ROM-BIOS area (from address F000:0 for a length of hex FFFF, the full 64KB of the ROM-BIOS area) for the text 1790. (With the PS/2s, as discussed in Chapter 17, the ROM-BIOS area starts at E000:0 and is 128KB long.) DEBUG located the message and told me where it was by displaying the following message:

```
F000:E3DB
```

Then I used the D command to display the full message and anything around it. I gave DEBUG a starting address just ahead of where it found the 1790, so that I could see more of the surrounding messages. I entered D F000:E390, and DEBUG showed me the following:

```
F000:E390   72 0D 0A 31 37 38 30 2D-44 69 73 6B 20 30 20 46    r..1780-Disk 0 F
F000:E3A0   61 69 6C 75 72 65 0D 0A-31 37 38 31 2D 44 69 73    ailure..1781-Dis
F000:E3B0   6B 20 31 20 46 61 69 6C-75 72 65 0D 0A 31 37 38    k 1 Failure..178
F000:E3C0   32 2D 44 69 73 6B 20 43-6F 6E 74 72 6F 6C 6C 65    2-Disk Controlle
F000:E3D0   72 20 46 61 69 6C 75 72-65 0D 0A 31 37 39 30 2D    r Failure..1790-
F000:E3E0   44 69 73 6B 20 30 20 45-72 72 6F 72 0D 0A 31 37    Disk 0 Error..17
F000:E3F0   39 31 2D 44 69 73 6B 20-31 20 45 72 72 6F 72 0D    91-Disk 1 Error.
F000:E400   0A 32 01 04 00 00 80 00-00 00 00 00 00 31 01 11    .2...........1..
```

Given the full text of those messages, my friend was able to get a clearer idea of what had gone wrong with his machine. This is just one real-life example of the variety of things that DEBUG can do for you.

If you want to learn more about what DEBUG can do for you, you must be prepared to cope with some messy technical details, but DEBUG can reward your efforts with a wealth of information. Although I don't have space here to explain all the wonders of DEBUG, I can list the DEBUG commands that are most important for exploring and tinkering. You already have learned about the D and S commands. To make changes to data, you need to learn about the E (Enter) and F (Fill) commands. To read and write data stored on a disk, you need to learn about the L (Load) and W (Write) commands. If you learn the basics of these DEBUG commands, you can inspect and change any data in your computer.

Next, you learn about another tool, one whose powers have a different dimension than DEBUG's and one that can be quite a bit easier to learn and use.

Working with the Disk Editor

The Norton Utilities' Disk Editor, like DEBUG, is a program that can teach you many things about your PC's disks and memory. The Disk Editor cannot do everything that DEBUG can; in particular, the Disk Editor does not concern itself with the PC's machine language instruction set the way DEBUG's U (Unassemble) and A (Assemble) commands do. The Disk Editor does, however, enable you to examine and edit any floppy or hard disk, even those that for some reason cannot be read by DOS. Moreover, you can use the Disk Editor to examine any area of memory.

Using the Disk Editor is easy. All you have to do is press either the Alt or the F10 key to access the pull-down menus. Move to any menu and select your choice. If you have a mouse, you can click a menu name and then click the option of your choice.

After you choose a disk, you can use the Info menu to display information. You see an outline of all the basic information about your disk. You see absolute information, such as the size of the disk, the number of sides and tracks, the number of sectors per track, and the hexadecimal drive ID number. And, you see such DOS-related information as the size of a sector, the size of a cluster, the number of clusters, and the size of a FAT entry.

This information provides a small gold mine of information about the dimensions and setup of any disk, including virtual disks (RAM disks). By using the information in this screen, you can learn how each disk is structured.

Even more fascinating than the technical disk information is the disk space map, which provides a representative drawing of how the space on the disk is being used. Each position on the map represents a small portion of the disk storage space. You can see which areas are in use and which areas are free. If the disk has any bad track areas, they also are shown. Finally, you can see exactly which clusters are occupied by the file you have selected.

You also can select a particular file and ask to see its characteristics. You then are shown information about the file's directory entry, including the filename and extension, the size, the date and time stamp, and file attributes. You also can see information that usually is unavailable, such as the number of clusters used by the file, the starting cluster number, and how fragmented the file is. (This refers to how many contiguous sets of clusters are being used.)

In addition to finding out about a part of a disk, you can look inside it. The Disk Editor displays the information in the format that makes the most sense, in hexadecimal or as ASCII text. The Disk Editor also formats information for viewing special areas, such as directories, the file allocation table (FAT), the partition table, and the boot record.

One of the things you can do with the Disk Editor is make direct changes to the data you are displaying. To guard against catastrophes, however, the Disk Editor defaults to read-only mode, in which you cannot make changes. If you do want to modify something, you can select the Configuration option from the Tools menu and turn off the read-only setting.

To make changes, all you have to do is move to what you want to change and type right over it. You can do this not only with files but with directories, partition tables, and so on. Be careful though; unless you know exactly what you are doing, you may cause irreparable damage. Before you make changes, you might want to read the *Disk Explorer* book that comes with the Norton Utilities. The first chapter provides a basic primer on disks.

Using the features of the Disk Editor, you can get into any part of the disk, see what's there, and, if you know how, tinker with and modify the data (either change it or repair damage). The third chapter of the *Disk Explorer* book explains how you can make such repairs.

Following are some examples, from my own experience, of situations in which this capability came in handy. DOS contains two programs, BACKUP and RESTORE, that are used to back up hard disk data onto floppy disks. In an early version of DOS, the BACKUP program sometimes recorded one of the backup disks incorrectly, with a hex 0 in place of part of one of the filenames. This tiny error made it impossible to restore data that had been copied to the floppy disk—a disaster.

Fortunately, when this happened to me, I was able to use Disk Editor to browse around on the bad disk until I discovered what the problem was. After I figured it out, all I had to do was replace the erroneous hex 0 with a proper character for a filename. It was an easy repair job, which would have been impossible without an exploring and patching tool. In that case, the Disk Editor saved an entire hard disk full of data.

Another example is the time that a computer belonging to one of my associates had been used for DOS and UNIX. He decided he wanted to devote his entire hard disk to DOS, but there was still an old UNIX partition on it. The current version of DOS (before 5.0) would not delete the unwanted partition. Using the Disk Editor, he was able to modify the partition table and delete the partition. (Of course, this is not the type of thing you would do unless you knew exactly what you were doing.)

These examples offer powerful demonstrations of why it can be worthwhile to have a tool like the Disk Editor and to know how to use it.

Some Things To Try

1. Using DEBUG, search through your computer's ROM to find the copyright notice on the ROM-BIOS. Give DEBUG the command D F800:0 and then follow that with the command D until you see what you're looking for. If you don't find the message starting at F800:0, try again at F000:0. If you have a PS/2, try a search starting at E000:0. (Remember, PS/2s use both the E and F blocks for the ROM-BIOS.)

2. If you have the Norton Utilities, use the Disk Editor (or NU) to look at the dimensions of each disk you have. What do the figures tell you?

3. Again, if you have the Norton Utilities, make a copy of one of your floppy disks and experiment with making changes to it. Find the root directory and change one of the filenames by typing over the name. Test to see whether the name was properly changed.

4. Using the Disk Editor's capability to show the same data in directory and hex format, display part of your disk's directory and then try to find just where each part of the directory (name, extension, date, and size) is recorded in the hex part. Changing the hex data and seeing what changed in the directory display can help you tell what's what.

A Family
Tree

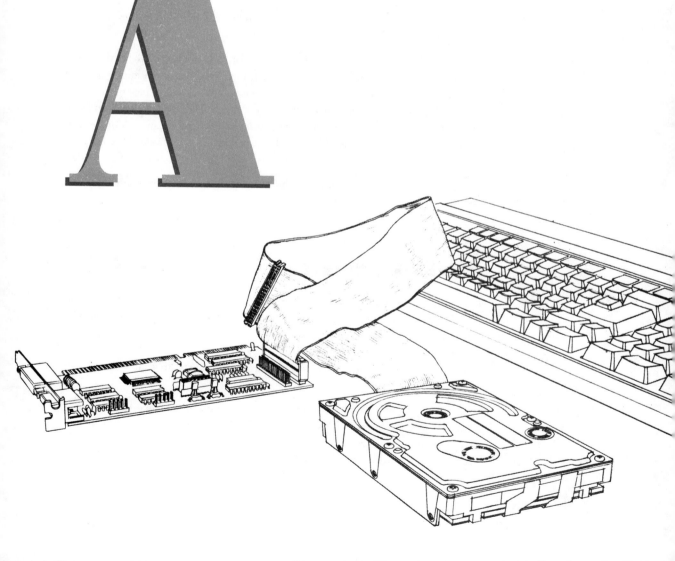

One of the most important and interesting things about the family of IBM personal computers is that it is a family of families—several groups of related computers and processors. This makes the story of the PC a rich and fascinating one and makes the PC more important and useful. Why? Because, as a family with many members, the PC gives us a wide selection of computers differing in features, price, and performance. However, because of their common bonds, all the members of the PC family have a great deal in common and work pretty much the same way. In fact, after you finish this book, you should have a good overall understanding of just about any IBM or IBM-compatible personal computer.

In this appendix, I take a look at the PC family tree. It's a multifaceted tree because there are several different ways to view it and, as I mentioned above, there are families within families.

One part of the story is historical—it covers the chronological unfolding of the original IBM PC (and its relatives) and its growth into today's modern family of PS/2 computers. Another part looks at the different models of PC. This aspect of the story, the model-by-model description, emphasizes the range of computing power and features in the PC family. Finally, the third part is the tale of the family of processors that act as the "brains" of the PC family. It is these processors that lead the PC into the future.

An important aside to these factors is the group of IBM-compatible computers, the so-called "clones," that form yet another family.

Some Family History

The public history of the PC began in August 1981, when IBM first announced the IBM Personal Computer—the original PC. The behind-the-scenes story began earlier, of course, but not as early as you might guess. It took a small group of IBM designers just about a year from the day the decision to build an IBM personal computer was made to the day the PC was announced—a remarkably short time for an institution such as IBM.

By the spring of 1982, PCs were being shipped in volume, and, to everyone's amazement, the demand far exceeded the supply. The PC was an unexpected overnight success. While this success may have caught IBM and the rest of the computer industry off guard, everyone quickly woke up to the possibilities that the PC created.

During the earliest days of the PC, a number of experienced computer executives and engineers realized that there was a real need for a version of the PC that could be carried around. That idea turned into the first product of Compaq. Compaq's first addition to the PC family—the first addition by IBM or anybody else—was the Compaq Portable. It was announced in November 1982, a little over a year after the original PC was announced.

IBM's first addition to the PC family, the PC XT, which added a hard disk storage facility, came shortly thereafter. The PC XT soon filled the role of successor to the original PC. Compaq matched the PC XT in the fall of 1983 with another portable computer—this one with a hard disk—called the Compaq Plus.

Around this time, IBM introduced its own portable, the Portable PC. However, it was not a success and had only a slight impact on the market.

In 1983, word began leaking out that IBM was planning a less expensive scaled-down PC that could be used either as a home computer or as an economical business machine. This machine was the PCjr, affectionately known as the "Peanut."

Nearly everybody expected the PCjr to be an even bigger hit than the original PC, but that was not the case. Design problems, along with a less-than-expected interest in home computers in the PCjr's price range, made the machine a disappointment. Throughout 1984, the PCjr limped along, and in 1985, despite several heroic attempts at rejuvenation, IBM discreetly discontinued the machine.

Although 1984 was disappointing for the low-end PCjr, it was exciting for the high end of the family. In August, IBM introduced the PC AT, which had a much greater computing speed than the PC and PC XT. The PC AT was a success and, over the next few years, served as IBM's flagship personal computer, inspiring a host of clones, many of which offered enhanced features and lower prices.

From 1984 to 1987, IBM made no large-scale changes in the PC line. There were new models of the PC AT, but they were all variations on the same theme. The most significant change was the introduction, with the last PC AT, of the 101-key enhanced keyboard, which became the industry standard.

However, in April 1987, IBM changed course drastically. It introduced a whole new family of personal computers, the Personal System/2, or PS/2, line. Since then, IBM has chosen to give its computers model numbers rather than abbreviated names; the first of these new computers were the PS/2 models 30, 50, 60, and 80.

IBM spent more time planning the PS/2 line than the original PC and its relatives. The new computers boasted a completely new design that incorporated modern technology and contained far fewer off-the-shelf parts. This meant that it was much harder for third-party companies to clone the new computers. Moreover, for all but the low-end PS/2s, IBM introduced a new facility called the Micro Channel Architecture, or MCA.

MCA is a very important development, which I discuss in greater depth in Chapter 2. First, MCA offers significant improvement over the system used in the PC, PC XT, and PC AT. Second, the new system changes the nature of adapter boards; the old boards don't work with MCA computers.

Unfortunately, the introduction of these new computers had a deleterious effect on the computer world which few people expected. IBM had taken great pains to make sure that the PS/2s could run all the old software. However, as I mentioned, the hardware design was much different from that of the old computers, and the rest of the industry refused to change.

Up to then, IBM had set almost all of the important hardware standards—standards that were followed by the companies manufacturing and selling IBM-compatible computers. For instance, IBM changed the layout of the keyboard twice, and the other manufacturers followed suit each time.

Of course, the most important hardware standards had to do with the design of the computer itself. Although IBM set these standards, it was lax about enforcing its rights, and thousands of companies around the world were cloning IBM computers with impunity.

With the new PS/2s and MCA, IBM chose to impose stiff licensing fees, in some cases asking companies to pay back royalties on the older computers that were copied without IBM's permission.

This time, however, other companies, led by Compaq, refused to play ball. They referred to the old IBM design as Industry Standard Architecture, or ISA, and maintained that IBM was changing unnecessarily to MCA and that they would remain committed to ISA. In other words, they ignored IBM's new architecture and kept on building computers based on the old IBM standard. These same companies later banded together to design a high-performance alternative to MCA, the Extended Industry Standard Architecture, or EISA.

This means that, with few exceptions, the current computer world is divided into two camps: IBM, with its PS/2s, most of which use the Micro Channel Architecture, and all other companies, most of which still are selling computers based on the old IBM design. Of course, in the last few years, technology has progressed considerably, and many of the new non-IBM computers are much more powerful than the PC AT on which they were based.

Fortunately, the two hardware designs run the same programs. Moreover, although IBM and non-IBM computers are built differently, they work, from the user's point of view, in much the same way.

In July 1990, IBM introduced the PS/1 (Personal System/1) family of low-cost computers aimed at the home market. For more details on the PS/1, see the "Personal System/1: IBM's Home Computer" section. For now, note that the PS/1s, like their big brothers the PS/2s, follow the PC-compatible standards and are full-fledged members of the PC family.

That's a short summary of the main points of the history of the PC family. Now I move on to discuss one of the more important branches of the family tree—the portable computers.

Portable Computers

As you know, PCs are quite small compared with their ancestors, the large mainframe and midrange computers. However, it wasn't long after the first PC was announced that the engineers were hard at work trying to make things even smaller—small enough to carry around.

These days, there are many portable PCs. Generally speaking, you can divide them into three groups. The first group is referred to simply as portables. These are full-featured computers, not too small, that must be plugged into an electrical outlet. Because these computers are more transportable than portable, they are sometimes referred to as "luggables." This was the first type of mobile machine and was very popular with people who traveled or worked out of more than one office. Business people took to these luggables straight away because they could carry them home from the office to continue work at home. This class of mobile machine is waning in popularity because smaller, lighter machines that rival desktop units in functionality have truly arrived.

This second group is called laptops because these computers are usually small and light enough to sit on your lap. In fact, the smallest of these, the notebook computers, are no bigger than a three-ring binder.

The third group comprises the very small hand-held computers. These are full-fledged PCs that are small enough to hold in your hand, like a pocket calculator.

The newest variation on small PCs is the pen-based computer. You control this type of computer not with a keyboard, but with a pen-like stylus or by touch. Instead of a display, a keyboard, and a mouse, you have a single notebook-sized tablet, the surface of which is a graphics display screen. The idea is to use the stylus like a pen, directly on the surface of the screen. You can make choices from menus, control programs, and even write directly on the screen. The computer understands and interprets your input. For example, say that you are editing a document. You can insert a new word by drawing a special symbol and printing the word, much as you would on a piece of paper.

Of course, such systems require specialized software (handwriting-recognition programs, for example) and specialized operating systems. You can expect to see two rival systems in the next few years: the PenPoint operating system, developed by Go and backed by IBM, and Pen Windows, from Microsoft.

With today's technology, the limiting factor on portability is the power supply and the input/output technology. As a general rule, laptops and hand-held computers can be either plugged into an outlet or run on batteries. Unfortunately, some of the features that most people would like, such as a bright display screen and a large hard disk, require more power than can be conveniently supplied by batteries. And, laptops that depend on batteries to power a hard disk cannot run for more than a few hours without recharging.

As for the power problem, this is getting better due to low-power designs for processors, displays, and disk drives. In addition, batteries are getting more efficient and compact, and designers are doing a better job of packaging the batteries. For example, many laptop machines today include a battery pack that can be removed easily and replaced with a fresh one, frequently without having to power down the machine. Desktop chargers that keep one or more extra batteries charged are becoming commonplace with new laptop and notebook designs.

The first important IBM-compatible portable was the Compaq Portable, introduced in November, 1982. Strictly speaking, it was portable, but not especially light, and required an electrical outlet.

Since then, many different portable, laptop, and hand-held computers have been marketed. However, until recently, except for two laptops and three portables, they all have been non-IBM computers. In 1993, IBM moved into the notebook/laptop marketplace with a highly competitive, well-engineered series called the ThinkPad.

As I mentioned earlier, IBM's first portable computer, the Portable PC, made its debut in 1983. It was essentially a portable version of the original PC and not much of a commercial success. In 1986, IBM announced the PC Convertible, its first laptop. It also was unsuccessful and later withdrawn from the market.

In May, 1989, IBM again entered this market, this time with a successful portable computer, the PS/2 model P70. Although not a laptop, the P70 offered all the features of a powerful, modern computer. In November 1990, IBM added a more powerful portable, the P75, to complement the P70.

To round out its portable offerings, IBM introduced a second laptop, the PS/2 model L40 SX, in March 1991. The L40 SX was a full-featured computer with all the power of a modern PC in a small package.

As an interesting comparison, consider that IBM's first portable, the Portable PC, offered no more functionality than the original PC and weighed about 30 pounds. The L40 SX laptop offers much more—a full-sized keyboard (with a separate numeric keypad), a floppy disk drive, a good-sized hard disk, a large amount of memory, and a fax/modem—and weighs less than 8 pounds.

The ThinkPad series is better still; it's smaller, lighter, and more powerful. The ThinkPad 720C, for example, includes removable hard disk storage up to 240MB, uses an integral mouse controller (a tiny point that looks like a pencil eraser positioned between the G and H keys), and has a floppy drive, a full complement of ports, an excellent, full-sized keyboard, and a full-color display.

You may wonder, with the constant improvement in technology, just how small computers will get? Obviously, people would like to have more and more features crammed into a smaller and lighter container. However, there are three factors that still limit the size of portable computers for most applications: the keyboard, the display screen, and the power supply.

As computers get smaller and smaller, it is difficult to maintain a full-sized keyboard that trained, or at least experienced, typists can use easily. Chip technology has reached the point where PCs too small for a keyboard and display can be built. Thus, in the interest of providing reasonable input and output, machines are built large enough to accommodate the keyboard and display requirements. In fact, a full-sized keyboard is a selling point for many portable computers.

A third factor that limits portable computers is the power supply. Computers that run on batteries are more convenient than computers that have to be plugged into the wall. However, two of the most important features, the hard disk and the display, require a relatively large amount of power.

This means that a battery-powered computer with a hard disk cannot operate for more than a few hours on a single battery. Moreover, bright, high-quality displays, especially color displays, require a relatively large amount of power. The good news is that display and battery technology are catching up. The IBM 720C, for example, has a bright, color screen that you can view from any angle. And, even with the bright display and large hard disk, a single battery charge can last nearly 5 hours, depending on how much disk drive activity you require. And, the internal battery pack is designed to slide in and out easily so you can carry an extra battery when you're using the computer away from an AC power source. After a quick and simple battery swap, you're ready for a few more hours of full-featured computing.

As an example of the popularity of this relatively new design, in mid-1993, IBM's direct marketing arm had to stop taking orders for the 720C because it ran out. Some dealers still could get the 720C during the summer, but IBM's own marketing unit couldn't. This was truly an innovative design in many ways and the careful design work became evident in the marketplace, even though the 720C was priced hundreds of dollars above other laptops at the time.

And, with the small peripherals now available with mobile computers, you may find that a laptop machine of some kind is all the computer you need. In fact, unless you need to use several kinds of peripherals that require standard expansion slots, a desktop machine adds very little to your PC experience over a quality laptop or notebook machine.

The IBM PC Family

The historical perspective should give you some sense of how the PC family has evolved. By now, you probably are getting some feeling for the irregular fits and starts that seem to mark PC family life. In this section, I help you make sense out of the way the various members of the IBM family relate to one another.

First, take a look at table A.1. It shows the most important dates in the IBM family history, starting with the announcement of the original PC. This table is just a summary because, from time to time, IBM announced variations on existing models. In fact, there are many such variations, and a full list of dates and machines would be quite long. For instance, during the life span of the PC AT, there were several different types of ATs that were offered at different times.

The dates in the table show when the computers were officially announced by IBM. Most of the time, IBM does not announce a computer until it is ready to ship. However, occasionally, for marketing reasons, IBM introduced a new product before it was generally available. The most important example of this is the PS/2 model 486 Power Platform, which was announced about half a year before it became readily available. (Strictly speaking, the 486 Power Platform is not a separate model but an upgrade of the PS/2 model 70.)

When reading this table, note that the portable computers are indicated by an asterisk; notebooks and laptops are noted after the model and name. Also, all computers dated April 7, 1987 and earlier have been discontinued (for information on other discontinued models, refer to table A.2). Finally, all PS/2 computers with model numbers of 50 and higher use the Micro Channel Architecture.

Table A.1. *A Chronological Summary of the IBM PC Family*

Date of Announcement	Computer
Aug. 12, 1981	PC
Mar. 8, 1983	PC XT
Nov. 1, 1983	PCjr
Feb. 16, 1984*	Portable PC
Aug. 14, 1984	PC AT
Apr. 2, 1986*	PC Convertible
Sep. 2, 1986	PC XT 286
Apr. 7, 1987	PS/2 model 30
Apr. 7, 1987	PS/2 model 50
Apr. 7, 1987	PS/2 model 60
Apr. 7, 1987	PS/2 model 80 386
Aug. 4, 1987	PS/2 model 25
Jun. 2, 1988	PS/2 model 50Z

continues

Table A.1. *continued*

Date of Announcement	Computer
Jun. 2, 1988	PS/2 model 70 386
Sep. 13, 1988	PS/2 model 30 286
May 9, 1989	PS/2 model 55 SX
May 9, 1989*	PS/2 model P70 386
Jun. 20, 1989	PS/2 486 Power Platform
Dec. 19, 1989	PS/2 model 70 486
Mar. 20, 1990	PS/2 model 65 SX
Mar. 20, 1990	PS/2 model 80 386
May 10, 1990	PS/2 model 25 286
Jun. 26, 1990	PS/1
Oct. 9, 1990	PS/2 model 55 LS
Oct. 30, 1990	PS/2 model 90 XP 486
Oct. 30, 1990	PS/2 model 95 XP 486
Nov. 12, 1990*	PS/2 model P75 486
Mar. 26, 1991*	PS/2 model L40 SX
Apr. 23, 1991	PS/2 model 90 SX
Apr. 23, 1991	PS/2 model 90 XP 486 SX
Apr. 23, 1991	PS/2 model 95 XP 486 SX
Jun. 11, 1991	PS/2 model 35 SX
Jun. 11, 1991	PS/2 model 35 LS
Jun. 11, 1991	PS/2 model 40 SX
Jun. 11, 1991	PS/2 model 57 SX
Summer 1992	PS/2 Server 85
Summer 1992	PS/2 Server 95
Summer 1992	PS/2 Server 295
Sep. 21, 1992	PS/2 56 486SLC
Sep. 21, 1992	PS/2 57 486SLC
Sep. 21, 1992	PS/2 M57 486SLC2 (multimedia)
Sep. 21, 1992	PS/2 DV M57 486SLC2 (multimedia)
Sep. 21, 1992	PS/2 76 486
Sep. 21, 1992	PS/2 77 486
Sep. 21, 1992	PS/2 M77 486 (multimedia)
Sep. 21, 1992	PS/2 Ultimedia 77 486DX2 (multimedia)
Sep. 21, 1992	PS/2 77 486DX2

Date of Announcement	Computer
Apr. 1, 1993	ThinkPad 710T (pen computer)
Apr. 6, 1993	PS/ValuePoint Spacesaver
Apr. 6, 1993	PS/ValuePoint Desktop
Apr. 6, 1993	PS/ValuePoint Minitower
Jun. 15, 1993	PS/2 E (low-power, flat screen)
Jun. 15, 1993	ThinkPad 300 (notebook)
Jun. 15, 1993	ThinkPad 350 & 350C (notebook)
Jun. 15, 1993	ThinkPad 500 (sub-notebook)
Jun. 15, 1993	ThinkPad 700 & 700C (notebook)
Jun. 15, 1993	ThinkPad 720 & 720C (notebook)
Jun. 15, 1993	PS/ValuePoint 325T

As you can see from table A.1, the most important dates were:

- August 12, 1981, the original IBM PC was introduced

- April 7, 1987, the PS/2's family debuted

- June 26, 1990, the PS/1 was announced

The PS/2 announcement was especially important because it set four new standards:

1. Micro Channel Architecture

2. Video Graphics Array (VGA) standard for screen displays

3. 3.5-inch disks (which replaced the older 5.25-inch floppies)

4. 101-key enhanced keyboard (although technically introduced with the last model of the PC AT, the new PS/2 computers firmly established the design as the industry standard)

Up to now, I've talked about the members of the IBM PC family in the order in which they were introduced. However, it is often more interesting and useful to rank each member according to its power.

The power of a computer depends on different factors: the processor and its speed, the disks and their speed, the type of display, and so on. However, as a rough estimate, you can rank computers by the power of their processors. Table A.2 lists the IBM family of computers from the least to the most powerful. I have included the model number of the processor for each computer. All these processors are members of the Intel 86 family. Later in this chapter, I explore this family in more detail. For now, all you really need to remember is that the members of the family, from least to most powerful, are the 8088, 8086, 286, 386SX, 386SL, 486SX, 486.

Note that the computers marked with an asterisk have been discontinued. Also, all PS/2 computers with model numbers of 50 and higher use the Micro Channel Architecture, except for laptops, notebooks, and pen computers.

Table A.2. *Members of the IBM PC Family (Least to Most Powerful)*

Processor	Computer
8088*	PCjr
8088*	PC
8088*	Portable PC
8088*	PC Convertible
8088*	PC XT
8086*	PS/2 model 25
8086*	PS/2 model 30
286*	PC XT
286*	PC AT
286*	PS/1
286*	PS/2 model 25
286*	PS/2 model 30
286*	PS/2 model 50
286*	PS/2 model 50Z
286*	PS/2 model 60
386SX*	PS/2 model 35 SX
386SX*	PS/2 model 35 SL
386SX*	PS/2 model 40 SX
386SX*	PS/2 model 55 SX
386SX*	PS/2 model 55 LS
386SX*	PS/2 model 57 SX
386SX*	PS/2 model 65 SX

Processor	Computer
386*	PS/2 model P70
386*	PS/2 model 70
386*	PS/2 model 80
386SL	ThinkPad 300 (notebook)
386SLC*	PS/ValuePoint 325T
486SX*	PS/2 model 90 SX
486SX*	PS/2 model 95 XP
486SX*	PS/ValuePoint 425SX
486SX	PS/ValuePoint 425SX/S
486SX	PS/ValuePoint 433SX/S
486SX	PS/ValuePoint 425SX/D
486SX	PS/ValuePoint 433SX/D
486SX	PS/2 76
486SX	PS/2 77
486SX	PS/2 Server 85
486	PS/ValuePoint
486*	PS/ValuePoint 433DX
486	PS/ValuePoint 433DX/S
486	PS/ValuePoint 433DX/D
486	PS/ValuePoint 433DX/T
486	PS/2 486 Power Platform
486*	PS/2 model 70
486*	PS/2 model P75
486*	PS/2 model 90
486	PS/2 model 90 XP
486	PS/2 model 95 XP
486	PS/2 76
486	PS/2 77
486SLC2	PS/2 56
486SLC2	PS/2 57
486SLC/25	ThinkPad 710T (pen computer)
486SL/25	ThinkPad 350 and 350C (notebook)
486SLC2/50	ThinkPad 500 (sub-notebook)
486SLC/25	ThinkPad 700 and 700C (notebook)

continues

525

Table A.2. *continued*

Processor	Computer
486SLC2/50	ThinkPad 720 and 720C (notebook)
486SLC2/50	PS/2 E
486DX2/50	PS/2 90 XP
486DX2/50	PS/2 Server 95
486/50	PS/2 90 XP
486/50	PS/2 95 XP
486/50	PS/2 Server 195
486/50	PS/2 Server 295
486DX2/66*	PS/ValuePoint 466DX
486DX2/66	PS/ValuePoint 466DX2/D
486DX2/66	PS/ValuePoint 466DX2/T
486DX2/66	PS/2 77 486DX2

From this table, you can make three observations which are generally true. First, PS/2 computers are more powerful than the older pre-PS/2 models. Second, the higher the PS/2 model number, the more powerful the computer. Finally, you can divide the PS/2 family into two subfamilies. The MCA computers, which are more powerful, have model numbers of 50 and above. The less powerful, non-MCA computers have model numbers below 50.

Beyond that, I have made some assumptions about relative power of different computers when the processor is the same. I ranked those with smaller cases, smaller memory, integral displays (laptops), and so on below models with the same processor that have larger cases and so on. Strictly speaking, these configuration issues don't change the power of the processor, but they frequently mean other design considerations that may affect overall computer power. Features that may affect power besides the processor include the amount of memory, whether the machine uses VESA or PCI local bus, the size of the disk drive, and so on.

Finally, any lists such as the ones in tables A.1 and A.2 are only accurate for a short time. IBM, like every other PC vendor who plans to stay in business, is updating and upgrading its product line often. As this book was being written, for example, IBM announced 40 models in the PS/ValuePoint line alone, CompuAdd announced a new line with 47 models, and every other mainline PC manufacturer announced or was preparing to announce a new product series.

Pentium-based models aren't reflected in these tables because IBM had not formally announced specific models using the Pentium processor when this book was written. However, new PS/2 machines are ready to accept the Pentium upgrade or overdrive chips, and IBM was readying Pentium-based models.

Personal System/1: IBM's Home Computer

IBM's original home computer, the PCjr, was announced in February 1983 and was not a commercial success. Users complained that the original keyboard was difficult to use and that the machine was not powerful enough for serious work.

When IBM decided to reintroduce the home computer, it wanted to avoid the problems of the PCjr. To do so, IBM broke with tradition and established a small entrepreneurial group at the IBM facility in Lexington, KY. This group took on the responsibility of designing and building the kind of computer people wanted in their homes.

The final product, the PS/1, was the result of conversations with thousands of consumers and boasted an array of built-in features oriented to the home user, including a high-quality display, a mouse, and a modem. In addition, an optional audio adapter provides a standard MIDI musical interface.

Along with the machine, IBM included a variety of free software, including the DOS operating system, a special PS/1 user interface called the PS/1 DOS Shell (not to be confused with the regular DOS Shell), and Microsoft Works (a combination word processor, spreadsheet, database, and communications package). The PS/1 design included a built-in modem, so programs to access online databases and services were also included.

Because the PS/1 originally was marketed as a home computer, many people do not realize that it also is an economical office computer. It is easy to set up and use, and IBM offers good support. However, it does have some important limitations.

First, the PS/1 is based on the old 286 processor. It cannot run any of the powerful programs and operating environments that require a 386 or 486.

Second, there are no built-in slots to add new adapters (aside from the audio card). However, it is possible to plug in an optional expansion unit that can house up to three adapter cards (which, incidentally, must be AT-style cards. The PS/1 doesn't support MCA). This is what you would have to use to, say, connect a PS/1 to a network.

Notwithstanding these limitations, the PS/1 is an interesting cousin to the mainstream PC family. And, because it is designed to be compatible, it runs the same operating system and software as the other members of the PC family. It is because of this compatibility that the principles and ideas in this book apply to all members of the PC family.

The PS/2 Family

The newer, "office" line of IBM computers includes the PS/2, which actually is split into four lines, and the new low-end (not strictly "home," but useful in the home environment), the ValuePoint line.

Perhaps the most notable part of the PS/2 line is the frequency with which IBM changes it, adding new models or packaging it differently. Basically, PS/2 computers are 486 machines with MCA. More specifically, there is a lower-end PS/2 that uses 33MHz 486 processors and a higher-end PS/2 line that uses 50MHz 486DX2 processors. In addition, there is the E line of low-power desktop models with flat screen displays and the ThinkPad line of six mobile models, each of which has multiple configurations.

Even with all of these models, IBM basically views its PC line as three different lines: the PS/2s including the E models, the ValuePoints, and the ThinkPads.

Beyond these differences, IBM in mid-1993 decided to further differentiate among PS/2 models by offering traditional and enhanced lines. According to IBM's plan, the traditional machines are for large, corporate customers who require tried and true technology, while the enhanced line is for early adopters, that is, people who want the very latest technology.

This is probably a good marketing approach that enables the company to address traditional corporate needs while appealing to users who are more technically oriented and lighter on their feet in terms of changing directions. In many corporations, for example, it can be difficult and time consuming to get approval to purchase a line of equipment. Then, when the model numbers and specifications change, the whole approval process may need to be repeated. By keeping one branch of the PS/2 line fairly stable and slower to change, IBM has addressed this sort of concern and reduced the feeling among users that technology is leaving them behind. Because some models will remain on the market relatively longer, the sharp curves and bends in the road of technological advance are smoothed out somewhat.

At the same time, by introducing a parallel line that takes advantage of new technology quickly, users who can respond—and who want to feel their computer is on the cutting edge—also can feel comfortable.

That's the basic IBM story, but if you think this tells the whole story of today's PCs, you're sadly mistaken. There are dozens of successful companies, each with its own history of models and technology and tales of business successes and failures. Unfortunately, telling the stories of all of these companies is beyond the scope of this book. Back in the days when PCs were first coming along—especially before the IBM PC was announced—people in the computer industry knew every model from every company, how much it cost, what it did, and, in many cases, who were the major users.

Today, as you can see from the previous discussion, just trying to keep up with the models of a single company is no easy task. However, by studying what one company did and is doing, you can see how fast and how far the technology has advanced and can appreciate where the industry has been and where it is going.

How IBM Developed the Personal Computer

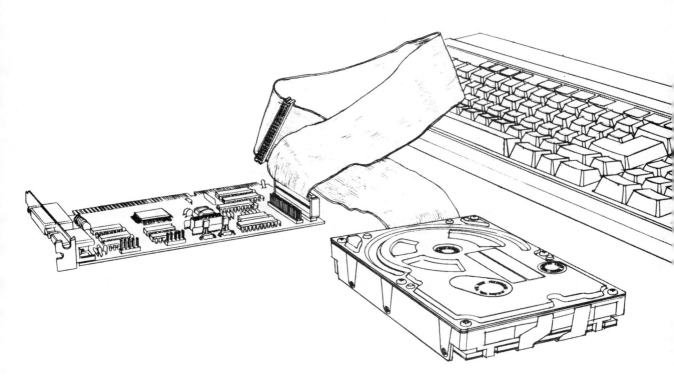

A lthough most people are not aware of it, IBM had several small computers before the first PC was ever envisioned. One of the earliest of these was the System/23 Datamaster, which was based on the Intel 8085A processor, an ancestor of the 8088 that was eventually used in the PC. Another small computer was the Displaywriter, a stand-alone, dedicated word processor based on the 8086 processor.

The next two small computers were the IBM 5100 and 5110, which were developed by engineers who had worked on the System/23. The 5100 and 5110 used an IBM microprocessor called the OP micro (OP stood for office products, the division of IBM that sold these machines). The 5100 and 5110 were small interactive computers that came in two versions. One ran BASIC, and the other ran either BASIC or APL (a mathematical programming language). In those days, disks were large, 8-inch floppies that stored only 250–500KB of data.

By 1980, a number of companies sold small computers based on processors like the Intel 8086 or 8088. The people who bought these computers were hobbyists and pioneers. At IBM, several people started wondering if the company should develop a new microcomputer for a new business market. In May of that year, IBM's top two executives, Chairman Frank Cary and President John Opel, decided that such a computer might be a valuable addition to IBM's product line. They established a task force to look into the matter.

The Group of Thirteen

At IBM, the fact that an undertaking is given a code name means that the project is going somewhere. This project was given such a name and organized into what was called the Group of Thirteen—eight engineers and five marketing people.

The members of this task force knew one another from previous work. In July of 1980, they gathered in Boca Raton, FL and began meeting formally as a committee. Their goal was to define the direction of personal computing at IBM.

When the Group of Thirteen first tackled the issue, IBM had not yet decided to make a personal computer. At the time, the microcomputer market was shared by several companies, but the two that stood out were Apple Computer, with the Apple II series, and Tandy, with the TRS-80. The IBM planners looked at the marketplace and decided there was room for IBM, but that they should market a completely new computer.

They started to build a prototype and, as they worked, searched for a name for the new machine. At the time, the Apple II was popular, so they thought they might use another "produce" name. Being in Boca Raton, the group considered every fruit that grows in Florida. Eventually, however, they decided on the pedestrian but descriptive sobriquet of Personal Computer.

On September 6, 1980, Bill Lowe, the head of the Group of Thirteen, met with Cary and Opel and demonstrated an experimental prototype. It had no formal operating system, and its microprocessor was the same 8085A that drove the System/23.

The executives liked what they saw and agreed to a project that would design and produce the IBM Personal Computer.

The Father of the PC

The person chosen to direct the project was Phillip Don Estridge. Don Estridge was a natural leader and, in many ways, an ideal person for the job. From within a mammoth company where the norm was long development cycles and proprietary technology, Estridge was able to create IBM's most open computer system in less than a year. In the words of one of the Group of Thirteen, Don Estridge was "sort of like a Steve Jobs [cofounder of Apple Computer] within IBM ... just enough of a bandit to pull it off."

What Estridge did was to lay out, step-by-step, the plans for development, manufacturing, and marketing a new type of computer. He picked up the Group of Thirteen's basic design and expanded it into a marketable machine.

Perhaps Estridge's most enduring contribution was his support of an open system. At the time, this was a concept foreign to most of the IBM decision makers. Estridge was a maverick who argued successfully for a design that would be available to the outside world. Anyone would be able to build adapters and peripherals for the new machine. As a member of the original PC design team explained, the goal was to "make the PC so acceptable that anyone who ever wanted to design hardware and software could do it on that box." In fact, the open architecture of the PC series even enabled a large number of companies to create the compatible machines which are now called clones.

533

To many people, especially those within IBM, Don Estridge is revered as the father of the PC.

The Architecture of the Personal Computer

By the time Don Estridge had taken over the project, the Group of Thirteen had defined some of the machine's specifications. Their most important decision was to use an Intel microprocessor. Other processors, both IBM and non-IBM were proposed, but in the end the Intel 8088 was chosen. This choice was made in large part because the IBM engineers had experience with Intel chips.

Most aspects of the design proved to be successful. However, there were two important limitations. The first had to do with the width of the bus (see Chapter 2 for a discussion of busses). The natural choice for a PC processor would have been the 16-bit Intel 8086. At the time, there were 16-bit adapters and peripherals available, but they were expensive. To lower the PC's cost, the designers opted for the 8088, a cousin of the 8086 that had identical functionality except that it used an 8-bit bus.

Using a narrower bus width slowed the machine down. At first, given the primitive state of personal computing, this limitation was acceptable. However, it was not long before faster processors became available, and hard disks were introduced. The 8-bit bus became a bottleneck. When IBM designed the PC AT computer (which was announced in August, 1984), it used a 16-bit bus. To this day, most adapters used in PCs and PS/2s are 16-bit cards, although the move is definitely toward 32- and even 64-bit adapters as PC busses expand.

The second limitation was far more important. The PC operating system (DOS) could use only 640KB of memory for programs and data. This limitation came about because the first PC had only 64KB of memory. The 8088 was capable of addressing up to 1,024KM, or 1MB. However, this was far more memory than anyone could ever foresee using on a small computer. In 1980, an expensive minicomputer had only 512–1,024KB of memory. And, the most powerful mainframes, costing millions of dollars had, at most, a couple of megabytes.

To allow for future growth, the PC designers multiplied the size of the PC memory, 64KB, by 10. They thought it extremely unlikely that anyone would use more memory than this and reserved the addresses from 640 to 1,024KB for special purposes.

What happened, of course, was that the cost of memory chips fell dramatically. At the same time, PCs using newer processors were able to handle many megabytes of memory, and new software was demanding larger and larger amounts of space in which to operate. However, because there were countless DOS programs that depended on the reserved addresses from 640 to 1,024KB, it was impossible to change DOS to make use of more than 640KB in a direct manner.

To be fair, it's important to remember that nobody in 1980 anticipated how popular personal computing and the IBM PC would become. The early designers expected the first PC to sell in the hundreds of thousands. Who could have predicted that, only ten years later, millions of people would have their own powerful computers, many of which would boast several megabytes of memory?

Developing the Operating System

Up to the time of the PC project, IBM always had developed the operating systems for its computers. However, as the Group of Thirteen considered alternatives, it soon became clear that IBM did not have the resources to develop an operating system for the PC quickly enough. At the time, Bill Gates and Paul Allen, partners in Microsoft, were respected veterans of the microcomputer community. They already had brought the BASIC language to 23 different machines, and IBM had hired Gates to develop BASIC and FORTRAN for the new PC. When the question of developing a new operating system came up, it was natural for IBM to ask Gates' advice. He recommended the Seattle Software Company.

The Seattle Software Company agreed to do the job and started to adapt its existing operating system QDOS (which, as the story goes, was the "quick and dirty operating system") to meet the PC's needs. However, the programmers ran into trouble. When it began to look as if they would miss their deadline, Gates lent his help, eventually taking over full responsibility for the project.

535

By August 1981, DOS was finished and became the primary operating system for the IBM Personal Computer. Although it lacked many of the features users take for granted today, such as subdirectories and support for a hard disk, PC DOS 1.0 was very successful. In many significant ways, Bill Gates' 1980 designs influence how people use their PC's today. (By the way, DOS was never the only PC operating system. By the end of 1982, there were six other systems, including CP/M, the UCSD p-System, and two forms of UNIX.)

Announcing the IBM Personal Computer

In August 1981, IBM officially announced the Personal Computer. In October, the first PC shipped with the following configuration:

- An Intel 8088 processor running at 4.77MHz

- 64KB of memory

- A 5.25-inch disk drive that used single-sided, 160KB floppy disks

- A built-in interface for a cassette tape storage device

- Either a high-quality monochrome display for text only or a color display for both low-quality text and graphics

Within a decade, this small machine of limited capabilities turned into a miniature desktop marvel that rivals—and many say, surpasses—the power and importance of the giant mainframes. The IBM PC helped set into motion a revolution unprecedented in the history of human invention, changing forever our ways of doing business and working with information. By almost any measure, the IBM PC has enjoyed success that far surpassed the hopes of its creators and has played a significant role in creating the Information Age of the late 20th Century.

QBasic
Program
Listings
C

MAZE: Start-to-Finish Maze (Introduction)

```
'Define default alphanumeric variables to be integers
DEFINT A-Z
'Declare program functions
  DECLARE FUNCTION ChooseDistance (Direction, CurrentRow, CurrentCol)
  DECLARE FUNCTION NotYetDone (CurrentRow, CurrentCol)
'Declare program subroutines
  DECLARE SUB ChooseDirection (Direction, MovingChar, CurrentRow, CurrentCol)
  DECLARE SUB DrawMessageBox (Msg$, Foreground, Background, CurrentRow, CurrentCol)
  DECLARE SUB Move (Distance, Direction, MovingChar, CurrentRow, CurrentCol)
  DECLARE SUB NextLocation (Direction, CurrentRow, CurrentCol)
  DECLARE SUB SoundTone (SoundCancel, SoundBase, SoundTime)
'Do setup work
  CLS
  RANDOMIZE TIMER
  SoundCancel = 1: SoundBase = 50: SoundTime = 100
  CurrentRow = 2: CurrentCol = 10: Direction = 1
  PLAY "MB"
  DrawMessageBox " Start ", 0, 7, 1, 1
  DrawMessageBox " Finish! ", 0, 7, 22, 68
  LOCATE 2, 9, 0: PRINT CHR$(204)
  COLOR 7, 0: MovingChar = 205
'Main program loop
  WHILE NotYetDone(CurrentRow, CurrentCol)
    SoundTone SoundCancel, SoundBase, SoundTime
    Distance = ChooseDistance(Direction, CurrentRow, CurrentCol)
    Move Distance, Direction, MovingChar, CurrentRow, CurrentCol
    ChooseDirection Direction, MovingChar, CurrentRow, CurrentCol
  WEND
'Report triumph and finish
```

538

```
      SOUND 100, 0
      FOR I = 1 TO 10
        DrawMessageBox " Finished! ", 7, 0, 22, 66
        SoundTone SoundCancel, SoundBase, SoundTime
        DrawMessageBox " Finished! ", 0, 7, 22, 66
        SoundTone SoundCancel, SoundBase, SoundTime
      NEXT I
      DrawMessageBox " Finished! ", 28, 15, 22, 66
      LOCATE 12, 25: COLOR 7, 0: SOUND 100, 0
      PRINT "Press a key to return to DOS... ";
      WHILE INKEY$ = "": WEND
   SUB ChooseDirection (Direction, MovingChar, CurrentRow, CurrentCol)
   'Subprogram to choose direction and turn corner
      RightTurn = INT(RND * 2)
      DO
        RightTurn = 1 - RightTurn
        SELECT CASE Direction
        CASE 1
          NewDirection = 3 + RightTurn
        CASE 2
          NewDirection = 4 - RightTurn
        CASE 3
          NewDirection = 2 - RightTurn
        CASE 4
          NewDirection = 1 + RightTurn
        END SELECT
        TryAgain = 0
        SELECT CASE NewDirection
        CASE 1
          IF CurrentCol > 75 THEN TryAgain = 1
        CASE 2
          IF CurrentCol < 5 THEN TryAgain = 1
        CASE 3
          IF CurrentRow < 5 THEN TryAgain = 1
        CASE 4
          IF CurrentRow > 20 THEN TryAgain = 1
        END SELECT
```

539

```
      LOOP WHILE TryAgain
      SELECT CASE Direction
        CASE 1
          IF RightTurn THEN TurnChar = 187 ELSE TurnChar = 188
        CASE 2
          IF RightTurn THEN TurnChar = 200 ELSE TurnChar = 201
        CASE 3
          IF RightTurn THEN TurnChar = 201 ELSE TurnChar = 187
        CASE 4
          IF RightTurn THEN TurnChar = 188 ELSE TurnChar = 200
      END SELECT
      PRINT CHR$(TurnChar);
      Direction = NewDirection
      IF Direction < 3 THEN MovingChar = 205
      IF Direction > 2 THEN MovingChar = 186
      NextLocation Direction, CurrentRow, CurrentCol
   END SUB
   FUNCTION ChooseDistance (Direction, CurrentRow, CurrentCol)
   ' Function to choose distance
      SELECT CASE Direction
        CASE 1
          Limit = 78 - CurrentCol
        CASE 2
          Limit = CurrentCol - 2
        CASE 3
          Limit = CurrentRow - 2
        CASE 4
          Limit = 23 - CurrentRow
      END SELECT
      IF Limit < 1 THEN Limit = 1
      ChooseDistance = INT(RND * (Limit + 1))
   END FUNCTION
   SUB DrawMessageBox (Msg$, Foreground, Background, CurrentRow, CurrentCol)
   ' Subprogram to draw a message box
      COLOR Foreground, Background
      LOCATE CurrentRow, CurrentCol
      PRINT CHR$(201); STRING$(LEN(Msg$), 205); CHR$(187)
      LOCATE CurrentRow + 1, CurrentCol
```

```
    PRINT CHR$(186); Msg$; CHR$(186)
    LOCATE CurrentRow + 2, CurrentCol
    PRINT CHR$(200); STRING$(LEN(Msg$), 205); CHR$(188);
END SUB
SUB Move (Distance, Direction, MovingChar, CurrentRow, CurrentCol)
' Subprogram to move
  LOCATE CurrentRow, CurrentCol
  FOR I = 1 TO Distance
    PRINT CHR$(MovingChar);
    NextLocation Direction, CurrentRow, CurrentCol
  NEXT I
END SUB
SUB NextLocation (Direction, CurrentRow, CurrentCol)
' Subprogram to change to next location
  SELECT CASE Direction
    CASE 1
      CurrentCol = CurrentCol + 1
    CASE 2
      CurrentCol = CurrentCol - 1
    CASE 3
      CurrentRow = CurrentRow - 1
    CASE 4
      CurrentRow = CurrentRow + 1
  END SELECT
  LOCATE CurrentRow, CurrentCol
END SUB
FUNCTION NotYetDone (CurrentRow, CurrentCol)
' Function to check for end
  IF (CurrentRow < 22) OR (CurrentCol < 68) THEN
    NotYetDone = 1
  ELSE
    NotYetDone = 0
  END IF
END FUNCTION
SUB SoundTone (SoundCancel, SoundBase, SoundTime)
' Subprogram to sound tones
  IF SoundCancel THEN SOUND 100, 0          ' cancel previous
  SOUND SoundBase + 750 * RND, SoundTime  ' generate random tone
END SUB
```

541

HEXTABLE: Generate Hex Arithmetic Tables (Chapter 16)

```
' Main Program
  DEFINT A-Z
  DECLARE SUB PressAnyKey ()
  DECLARE SUB ShowTitle (Operation)
  DECLARE SUB ShowValue (Operation, I, J)
  FOR Operation = 1 TO 2
  ShowTitle (Operation)
    FOR I = 0 TO 15
    FOR J = 0 TO 15
      ShowValue Operation, I, J
    NEXT J
    NEXT I
    PressAnyKey
  NEXT Operation
SUB PressAnyKey
' Pause
  PRINT
  PRINT "Press a key to continue... ";
  WHILE INKEY$ = "": WEND
END SUB
SUB ShowTitle (Operation)
' Titles
  SCREEN 0: WIDTH 80: CLS
  LOCATE 3, 20: COLOR 1 + 8
  PRINT "Hex ";
  IF Operation = 1 THEN PRINT "Addition";
  IF Operation = 2 THEN PRINT "Multiplication";
  PRINT " Table";
  COLOR 7 + 8
  LOCATE 5, 20
```

```
     FOR I = 0 TO 15
       PRINT HEX$(I); "  ";
     NEXT I
     FOR I = 0 TO 15
       LOCATE 7 + I, 16
       PRINT HEX$(I);
     NEXT I
     COLOR 7
   END SUB
   SUB ShowValue (Operation, I, J)
   ' Show the value
     IF Operation = 1 THEN X = I + J
     IF Operation = 2 THEN X = I * J
     Show$ = HEX$(X)
     ROW = I + 7
     COL = J * 3 + 18 + (3 - LEN(Show$))
     LOCATE ROW, COL
     PRINT Show$;
   END SUB
```

ALL-CHAR: Show All PC Characters (Chapter 13)

```
   ' Main Program
     DEFINT A-Z
     DECLARE SUB DoSetup ()
     DECLARE SUB ShowChar (CharValue)
     COMMON SHARED VideoSegment
     DoSetup
     FOR CharValue = 0 TO 255
       ShowChar (CharValue)
     NEXT CharValue
     LOCATE 23, 24: COLOR 1
   SUB DoSetup
```

```
' Subroutine to do set-up work
  SCREEN 0: WIDTH 80: CLS
  LOCATE 3, 25: COLOR 1
  PRINT "The Complete PC Character Set";
  VideoSegment = 0
  DEF SEG = &H40: VideoMode = PEEK(&H49)
  IF VideoMode = 7 THEN VideoSegment = &HB000
  IF VideoMode < 4 THEN VideoSegment = &HB800
  IF VideoSegment = 0 THEN
    LOCATE 12, 25
    PRINT "Error: unfamiliar video mode!"
    END
  END IF
END SUB
SUB ShowChar (CharValue)
  ' Subroutine to show each character
  Row = CharValue MOD 16 + 5
  Col = (CharValue \ 16) * 3 + 16
  ScreenOffset = Row * 160 + Col * 2
  DEF SEG = VideoSegment
  POKE ScreenOffset, CharValue
END SUB
```

REF-CHAR: Characters with Reference Numbers (Chapter 13)

```
' Main Program
  DEFINT A-Z
  DECLARE SUB DoSetup ()
  DECLARE SUB PressAnyKey ()
  DECLARE SUB ShowChar (CharValue)
```

```
      COMMON SHARED VideoSegment
      DoSetup
      FOR CharValue = 0 TO 255
        ShowChar (CharValue)
      NEXT CharValue
SUB DoSetup
' Subroutine to do set-up work
      DEFINT A-Z
      SCREEN 0: WIDTH 80
      VideoSegment = 0
      DEF SEG = &H40: VideoMode = PEEK(&H49)
      IF VideoMode = 7 THEN VideoSegment = &HB000
      IF VideoMode < 4 THEN VideoSegment = &HB800
      IF VideoSegment = 0 THEN
        LOCATE 12, 25
        PRINT "Error: unfamiliar video mode!"
        END
      END IF
END SUB
SUB PressAnyKey
' Pause
      PRINT
      PRINT "Press a key to continue... ";
      WHILE INKEY$ = "": WEND
END SUB
SUB ShowChar (CharValue)
' Subroutine to show each character
      DEFINT A-Z
      IF CharValue MOD 128 = 0 THEN
        COLOR 7: CLS : COLOR 1
        LOCATE 3, 25: PRINT "Reference Character Set ";
        IF CharValue = 0 THEN PRINT "1st";  ELSE PRINT "2nd";
        PRINT " Half";
      END IF
      COLOR 7
      RelativeChar = CharValue MOD 128
      Row = RelativeChar MOD 16
```

```
        Col = (RelativeChar \ 16) * 10
        ScreenOffset = Row * 160 + Col * 2 + 814
        DEF SEG = VideoSegment
        POKE ScreenOffset, CharValue
        LOCATE Row + 6, Col + 1
        PRINT USING "###"; CharValue;
        PRINT " ";
        IF CharValue < 16 THEN PRINT "0";
        PRINT HEX$(CharValue);
        IF CharValue MOD 128 = 127 THEN PressAnyKey
    END SUB
```

BOXES: Box-Drawing Characters (Chapter 13)

```
' Main Program
DEFINT A-Z
DECLARE SUB PrintTitle (BoxType, Title$, BaseRow, BaseCol)
DECLARE SUB DrawBox (Codes(), BaseRow, BaseCol)
DECLARE SUB DrawBoxExpanded (Codes(), BaseRow, BaseCol)
DIM Codes(6, 6)
CLS
FOR Expanded = 0 TO 1
  RESTORE
  FOR BoxType = 1 TO 4
    READ Title$
    FOR Row = 1 TO 5
      FOR Col = 1 TO 5
        READ Codes(Row, Col)
      NEXT Col
    NEXT Row
    PrintTitle BoxType, Title$, BaseRow, BaseCol
    IF Expanded THEN
```

```
         DrawBoxExpanded Codes(), BaseRow, BaseCol
      ELSE
         DrawBox Codes(), BaseRow, BaseCol
      END IF
   NEXT BoxType
   LOCATE 25, 1: PRINT "Press a key to continue... ";
   WHILE INKEY$ = "": WEND
  NEXT Expanded
  END
DATA "All Double Line:"
DATA 201, 205, 203, 205, 187
DATA 186,  32, 186,  32, 186
DATA 204, 205, 206, 205, 185
DATA 186,  32, 186,  32, 186
DATA 200, 205, 202, 205, 188
DATA "All Single Line:"
DATA 218, 196, 194, 196, 191
DATA 179,  32, 179,  32, 179
DATA 195, 196, 197, 196, 180
DATA 179,  32, 179,  32, 179
DATA 192, 196, 193, 196, 217
DATA "Double-Vertical:"
DATA 214, 196, 210, 196, 183
DATA 186,  32, 186,  32, 186
DATA 199, 196, 215, 196, 182
DATA 186,  32, 186,  32, 186
DATA 211, 196, 208, 196, 189
DATA "Double-Horizontal:"
DATA 213, 205, 209, 205, 184
DATA 179,  32, 179,  32, 179
DATA 198, 205, 216, 205, 181
DATA 179,  32, 179,  32, 179
DATA 212, 205, 207, 205, 190
SUB DrawBox (Codes(), BaseRow, BaseCol)
  ShowRow = BaseRow
  FOR Row = 1 TO 5
    Times = 1
    IF Row = 2 OR Row = 4 THEN Times = 3
```

```
       FOR I = 1 TO Times
       ShowRow = ShowRow + 1
       LOCATE ShowRow, BaseCol + 4
       PRINT CHR$(Codes(Row, 1));
       FOR J = 1 TO 9
         PRINT CHR$(Codes(Row, 2));
       NEXT J
       PRINT CHR$(Codes(Row, 3));
       FOR J = 1 TO 9
         PRINT CHR$(Codes(Row, 4));
       NEXT J
       PRINT CHR$(Codes(Row, 5));
       NEXT I
     NEXT Row
END SUB
SUB DrawBoxExpanded (Codes(), BaseRow, BaseCol)
   ShowRow = BaseRow
   FOR Row = 1 TO 5
      FOR Times = 1 TO 2
      ShowRow = ShowRow + 1
      LOCATE ShowRow, BaseCol + 3
      IF Times = 1 THEN
         PRINT " ";
         PRINT CHR$(Codes(Row, 1));
         PRINT "     ";
         PRINT CHR$(Codes(Row, 2));
         PRINT "     ";
         PRINT CHR$(Codes(Row, 3));
         PRINT "     ";
         PRINT CHR$(Codes(Row, 4));
         PRINT "     ";
         PRINT CHR$(Codes(Row, 5));
      END IF
      IF Times = 2 THEN
      FOR Col = 1 TO 5
      X = Codes(Row, Col)
      IF X = 32 THEN PRINT "     ";
      IF X <> 32 THEN PRINT USING "###   "; X;
```

548

```
      NEXT Col
      END IF
      NEXT Times
    NEXT Row
END SUB
SUB PrintTitle (BoxType, Title$, BaseRow, BaseCol)
  SELECT CASE BoxType
    CASE 1
    BaseRow = 1: BaseCol = 5
    CASE 2
    BaseRow = 1: BaseCol = 45
    CASE 3
    BaseRow = 13: BaseCol = 5
    CASE 4
    BaseRow = 13: BaseCol = 45
  END SELECT
  LOCATE BaseRow, BaseCol
  COLOR 9
  PRINT Title$;
  COLOR 7
END SUB
```

MSG-HUNT: Hunt for ROM-BIOS Messages (Chapter 17)

```
' Main Program
  DEFINT A-Z
  DECLARE SUB DoSetup ()
  DECLARE SUB PrintMessage (Msg$)
  DECLARE SUB TestForMessage ()
  COMMON SHARED offset&
  DoSetup
```

```
        WHILE offset& <= 65535
          TestForMessage
          offset& = offset& + 1
        WEND
      SUB DoSetup
      ' Subroutine to do set-up work
        SCREEN 0: WIDTH 80: CLS
        LOCATE 2, 1: COLOR 7
        PRINT "Searching the BIOS for apparent messages"
        PRINT
        offset& = 0
        DEF SEG = &HF000
      END SUB
      SUB PrintMessage (Msg$)
      ' Print the message found
        COLOR 7
        PRINT "At F000:";
        PRINT HEX$(offset&);
        PRINT " this was found: ";
        COLOR 1
        PRINT Msg$;
        COLOR 7
        PRINT
      END SUB
      SUB TestForMessage
      ' Subroutine to test for a message
        DEFINT A-Z
        Msg$ = ""
        COLOR 7
        PRINT "Searching at F000:";
        PRINT HEX$(offset&);
        LOCATE , 1
        Byte = PEEK(offset&)
        WHILE ((Byte >= ASC(" ")) AND (Byte <= ASC("z") AND (offset& < 65535)))
          Msg$ = Msg$ + CHR$(Byte)
          offset& = offset& + 1
          Byte = PEEK(offset&)
```

```
    IF LEN(Msg$) > 100 THEN EXIT SUB
  WEND
  IF LEN(Msg$) > 4 THEN PrintMessage (Msg$)
END SUB
```

VID-MODE: Video Mode Demonstration (Chapter 11)

```
' Main Program
  DEFINT A-Z
  DECLARE SUB CheckResults (Mode)
  DECLARE SUB DoSetup ()
  DECLARE SUB DescribeMode (Mode)
  DECLARE SUB PressAnyKey ()
  DECLARE SUB SetMode (Mode)
  ON ERROR GOTO ErrHandler
  DoSetup
  FOR Mode = 0 TO 6
  DescribeMode (Mode)
  PressAnyKey
  SetMode (Mode)
  CheckResults (Mode)
    PressAnyKey
  NEXT Mode
  FOR Mode = 13 TO 19
  DescribeMode (Mode)
  PressAnyKey
  SetMode (Mode)
  CheckResults (Mode)
  PressAnyKey
  NEXT Mode
ErrHandler:
  RESUME NEXT
```

```
SUB CheckResults (Mode)
' Check the active mode
  CurrentMode = PEEK(&H449)
  PRINT "The current mode is "; CurrentMode
  PRINT "Which is";
  IF Mode <> CurrentMode THEN PRINT " NOT";
  PRINT " the desired mode"
END SUB
SUB DescribeMode (Mode)
' Describe mode to be set
  PRINT "About to attempt to switch to mode "; Mode; " which is"
  SELECT CASE Mode
    CASE 0
    PRINT "Text mode, 40-column, no color"
    CASE 1
    PRINT "Text mode, 40-column, with color"
    CASE 2
    PRINT "Text mode, 80-column, no color"
    CASE 3
    PRINT "Text mode, 80-column, with color"
    CASE 4
    PRINT "CGA graphics, medium resolution, no color"
    CASE 5
    PRINT "CGA graphics, medium resolution, with color"
    CASE 6
    PRINT "CGA 640 x 200 graphics, two-color"
    CASE 7
    PRINT "Hercules monochrome mode"
    CASE 8
    PRINT "Olivetti, AT&T 6300 mode"
    CASE 13
    PRINT "EGA 320 x 200 graphics"
    CASE 14
    PRINT "EGA 640 x 200 graphics"
    CASE 15
    PRINT "EGA 640 x 350 graphics, monochrome monitor only"
    CASE 16
    PRINT "EGA 640 x 350 graphics"
```

```
      CASE 17
      PRINT "VGA or MCGA 640 x 480 graphics, 2 colors"
      CASE 18
      PRINT "VGA 640 x 480 graphics, 16 colors"
      CASE 19
      PRINT "VGA or MCGA 320 x 200 graphics, 256 colors"
   END SELECT
END SUB
SUB DoSetup
' Subroutine to do set-up work
   SCREEN 0: WIDTH 80: CLS
   LOCATE 2, 10: COLOR 7
   PRINT "Experimenting with Video Modes"
   PRINT
   PRINT "As we begin the video mode is ";
   DEF SEG = 0
   PRINT PEEK(&H449)
   PRINT
END SUB
SUB PressAnyKey
' Pause
   PRINT
   PRINT "Press a key to continue... ";
   WHILE INKEY$ = "": WEND
   PRINT
   PRINT
END SUB
SUB SetMode (Mode)
' Attempt to set the mode
   SELECT CASE Mode
      CASE 0
      SCREEN 0, 0: WIDTH 40     '40 column text, no color
      CASE 1
      SCREEN 0, 1: WIDTH 40     '40 column text, with color
      CASE 2
      SCREEN 0, 0: WIDTH 80     '80 column text, no color
      CASE 3
      SCREEN 0, 1: WIDTH 80     '80 column text, with color
```

```
          CASE 4
          SCREEN 1, 0              '320 x 200 CGA, no color
          CASE 5
          SCREEN 1, 1              '320 x 200 CGA, with color
          CASE 6
          SCREEN 2                 '640 x 200 CGA, two-color
          CASE 13
          SCREEN 7                 'EGA 320 x 200, 16-color
          CASE 14
          SCREEN 8                 'EGA 640 x 200, 16-color
          CASE 15
          SCREEN 10                'EGA 640 x 350, monochrome
          CASE 16
          SCREEN 9                 'EGA 640 x 350, 16-color
          CASE 17
          SCREEN 11                'VGA or MCGA 640 x 480, 2-color
          CASE 18
          SCREEN 12                'VGA 640 x 480, 16-color
          CASE 19
          SCREEN 13                'VGA or MCGA 320 x 200, 256-color
       END SELECT
    END SUB
```

COLORTXT: Show All Text Color Combinations (Chapter 12)

```
 ' Main Program
   DEFINT A-Z
   DECLARE SUB DoSetUp ()
   DECLARE SUB PressAnyKey ()
   DECLARE SUB ShowAttribute (Attribute)
   COMMON SHARED VideoSegment
```

```
    DoSetUp
    FOR Attribute = 0 TO 255
      ShowAttribute (Attribute)
    NEXT Attribute
SUB DoSetUp
' Subroutine to do set-up work
    DEFINT A-Z
    SCREEN 0, 1: WIDTH 80
    VideoSegment = 0
    DEF SEG = &H40: VideoMode = PEEK(&H49)
    IF VideoMode = 7 THEN VideoSegment = &HB000
    IF VideoMode < 4 THEN VideoSegment = &HB800
    IF VideoSegment = 0 THEN
      LOCATE 12, 25
      PRINT "Error: unfamiliar video mode!"
      PressAnyKey
      END
    END IF
END SUB
SUB PressAnyKey
' Pause
    PRINT
    PRINT "Press a key to continue... ";
    WHILE INKEY$ = "": WEND
END SUB
SUB ShowAttribute (Attribute)
' Subroutine to show each attribute
    IF Attribute MOD 128 = 0 THEN
      COLOR 7: CLS : COLOR 1
      LOCATE 3, 25: PRINT "Text Color Attribute Set ";
      IF Attribute = 0 THEN PRINT "1st";  ELSE PRINT "2nd";
      PRINT " Half";
    END IF
    COLOR 7
    RelativeChar = Attribute MOD 128
    Row = RelativeChar MOD 16
    Col = (RelativeChar \ 16) * 10
    ScreenOffset = Row * 160 + Col * 2 + 814
```

555

```
      DEF SEG = VideoSegment
      POKE ScreenOffset, 88 ' letter X
      POKE ScreenOffset + 1, Attribute
      LOCATE Row + 6, Col + 1
      PRINT USING "###"; Attribute;
      PRINT " ";
      IF Attribute < 16 THEN PRINT "0";
      PRINT HEX$(Attribute);
      IF Attribute MOD 128 = 127 THEN PressAnyKey
   END SUB
```

GRAPHTXT: Graphics Mode Text Characters (Chapter 14)

```
' Main Program
   DECLARE SUB DoSetUp ()
   DECLARE SUB ShowChar (CharCode)
   COMMON SHARED VideoSegment
   DoSetUp
   FOR CharCode = 0 TO 127
   ShowChar (CharCode)
   NEXT CharCode
SUB DoSetUp
' Subroutine to do set-up work
   DEFINT A-Z
   SCREEN 0, 1: WIDTH 80
   Pause = 0
   VideoSetment = 0
   DEF SEG = &H40: VideoMode = PEEK(&H49)
   IF VideoMode = 7 THEN VideoSegment = &HB000
   IF VideoMode < 4 THEN VideoSegment = &HB800
```

```
    IF VideoSegment = 0 THEN
      LOCATE 12, 25
      PRINT "Error: unfamiliar video mode!"
      END
    END IF
END SUB
SUB ShowChar (CharCode)
' Subroutine to show each character
  CLS
  LOCATE 2, 5
  PRINT "Displaying the Graphics Text Character Drawings"
  LOCATE 5, 5
  PRINT "For character code"; CharCode
  LOCATE 6, 5
  PRINT "Character"
  DEF SEG = VideoSegment
  POKE 828, CharCode
  DEF SEG = &HF000
  FOR ScanLine = 0 TO 7
    BitCode = PEEK(&HFA6E + ScanLine + CharCode * 8)
    LOCATE 8 + ScanLine, 5
    FOR Bits = 1 TO 8
    IF BitCode < 128 THEN Show$ = ". " ELSE Show$ = "XX"
    PRINT Show$;
    IF BitCode > 127 THEN BitCode = BitCode - 128
    BitCode = BitCode * 2
    NEXT Bits
  NEXT ScanLine
  LOCATE 18, 5
  WHILE INKEY$ <> "": WEND   ' flush key buffer
  PRINT "Press any key to stop...";
  FOR WaitASecond = 1 TO 2
    OldTime$ = TIME$
    WHILE OldTime$ = TIME$: WEND
  NEXT WaitASecond
  IF INKEY$ <> "" THEN
    LOCATE 18, 5
```

```
        PRINT "Now press any key to CONTINUE...";
        WHILE INKEY$ = "": WEND
    END IF
END SUB
```

COLOR4: Demonstrate Graphics Mode Color (Chapter 14)

```
' Main Program
  DECLARE SUB PressAnyKey ()
  DECLARE SUB DoSetUp ()
  DECLARE SUB Stage1 ()
  DECLARE SUB Stage2 ()
  DECLARE SUB Stage3 ()
  DECLARE SUB Stage4 ()
  DoSetUp
  Stage1
  Stage2
  Stage3
  Stage4
SUB DoSetUp
' Subroutine to do set-up work
  DEFINT A-Z
  SCREEN 0, 1: WIDTH 40
  DEF SEG = &H40: VIDEO.MODE = PEEK(&H49)
  IF VIDEO.MODE = 7 THEN
    PRINT "This program does not work in monochrome mode"
    PressAnyKey
    END
  END IF
  LOCATE 3
  PRINT "Color-4: demonstrate video mode 4"
```

```
      PRINT
      PRINT
      PRINT "This program works in four stages:"
      PRINT
      PRINT "Stage 1: Show pre-defined palettes"
      PRINT
      PRINT "Stage 2: Show selectable color"
      PRINT
      PRINT "Stage 3: Appear and disappear"
      PRINT
      PRINT "Stage 4: Rattling the palettes"
      PRINT
      PressAnyKey
   END SUB
   SUB PressAnyKey
   ' Pause
      PRINT
      PRINT "Press a key to continue... ";
      WHILE INKEY$ = "": WEND
   END SUB
   DEFSNG A-Z
   SUB Stage1
   ' Stage 1 - Show pre-defined palettes
      SCREEN 1, 0
      COLOR 1, 0: CLS
      FOR ColorNum = 0 TO 3
         LOCATE 5 + ColorNum * 5, 1 + ColorNum * 5
         PRINT " Color"; ColorNum
         CIRCLE (90 + 60 * ColorNum, 45 + 30 * ColorNum), 40, ColorNum
         PAINT (90 + 60 * ColorNum, 45 + 30 * ColorNum), ColorNum
      NEXT ColorNum
      FOR Times = 1 TO 10
         FOR PalNum = 0 TO 1
         COLOR , PalNum
         LOCATE 2, 10
         PRINT " Showing palette"; PalNum
         Now$ = TIME$
         WHILE TIME$ = Now$: WEND
```

559

```
      NEXT PalNum
    NEXT Times
    LOCATE 22
    PressAnyKey
END SUB
SUB Stage2
' Stage 2 - Show selectable color
    SCREEN 1, 0: CLS
    COLOR 0, 1
    FOR ColorNum = 0 TO 15
      LOCATE 3 + ColorNum, 2 + ColorNum
      COLOR ColorNum
      PRINT " Selected color "; ColorNum;
      Now$ = TIME$
      WHILE TIME$ = Now$: WEND
    NEXT ColorNum
    COLOR 0
    LOCATE 22
    PressAnyKey
END SUB
SUB Stage3
' Stage 3 - Appear and disappear
    SCREEN 1, 0
    CLS
    COLOR 4, 1
    PAINT (1, 1), 1
    CIRCLE (80, 50), 20, 0
    CIRCLE (80, 150), 20, 0
    CIRCLE (240, 50), 20, 0
    CIRCLE (240, 150), 20, 0
    PAINT (80, 50), 0
    PAINT (80, 150), 0
    PAINT (240, 50), 0
    PAINT (240, 150), 0
    LOCATE 13, 8
    PRINT " Appear and Disappear! "
    FOR I = 1 TO 50
```

```
      COLOR 3 + I MOD 2
      FOR J = 1 TO 250: NEXT J
   NEXT I
   LOCATE 22
   PressAnyKey
END SUB
SUB Stage4
' Stage 4 - Rattling the palettes
   SCREEN 1, 0: CLS
   COLOR 0, 0
   CIRCLE (160, 100), 80, 3
   PAINT (160, 100), 3
   CIRCLE (160, 100), 60, 2
   PAINT (160, 100), 2
   CIRCLE (160, 100), 40, 1
   PAINT (160, 100), 1
   CIRCLE (160, 100), 20, 0
   PAINT (160, 100), 0
   LOCATE 13, 17
   PRINT " Boom ! ";
   FOR I = 1 TO 100
      COLOR , I MOD 2
      FOR J = 1 TO 50: NEXT J
   NEXT I
   LOCATE 22
END SUB
```

KEYBITS: Display the Keyboard Control Bits (Chapter 15)

```
' Main Program
   DEFINT A-Z
   DECLARE SUB DoSetup ()
```

```
DECLARE SUB ShowData ()
DIM SHARED Msg$(16)
COMMON SHARED Continuing
DoSetup
WHILE Continuing
  ShowData
WEND
SUB DoSetup
' Subroutine to do set-up work
DEFINT A-Z
SCREEN 0, 1: WIDTH 80
Continuing = 1: LOCATE , , 0
Msg$(1) = "Insert state"
Msg$(2) = "CapsLock state"
Msg$(3) = "NumLock state"
Msg$(4) = "ScrollLock state"
Msg$(5) = "Alt pressed"
Msg$(6) = "Ctrl pressed"
Msg$(7) = "Left Shift pressed"
Msg$(8) = "Right Shift pressed"
Msg$(9) = "Ins pressed"
Msg$(10) = "CapsLock pressed"
Msg$(11) = "NumLock pressed"
Msg$(12) = "ScrollLock pressed"
Msg$(13) = "Hold state active"
Msg$(14) = "PCjr click state"
Msg$(15) = "(not used)"
Msg$(16) = "(not used)"
CLS
LOCATE 1, 5
PRINT "Displaying the keyboard control bits; press Enter to stop"
LOCATE 3, 5
PRINT "To see the changes in action, press these keys:";
LOCATE 4, 7
PRINT "Both shift keys, Ctrl, Alt, ";
PRINT "CapsLock, NumLock, ScrollLock, Ins";
FOR I = 1 TO 16
```

```
      FOR J = 1 TO I
    LOCATE 24 - I - I \ 9, 5 + J * 2 + J \ 9
    PRINT CHR$(179);
      NEXT J
    NEXT I
    FOR J = 1 TO 8
      LOCATE 15, 5 + J * 2
      PRINT CHR$(179)
    NEXT J
END SUB
SUB ShowData
' Subroutine to show the data state
  DEFINT A-Z
  DEF SEG = 0
  Bits& = PEEK(&H417) * 256& + PEEK(&H418)
  FOR Bit = 1 TO 16
    STATE$ = "0"
    IF Bits& >= 32768 THEN STATE$ = "1": Bits& = Bits& - 32768
    Bits& = Bits& * 2
    LOCATE 6, 5 + Bit * 2 + Bit \ 9
    PRINT STATE$;
    LOCATE 24 - Bit - Bit \ 9, 5 + Bit * 2 + Bit \ 9
    PRINT CHR$(192); "> "; Msg$(Bit);
    IF STATE$ = "0" THEN
  PRINT " off";
    ELSE
  PRINT " ON ";
    END IF
  NEXT Bit
  WHILE Continuing
    EndTest$ = INKEY$
    IF EndTest$ = CHR$(13) THEN END
    IF EndTest$ = "" THEN EXIT SUB
  WEND
END SUB
```

Index

Symbols

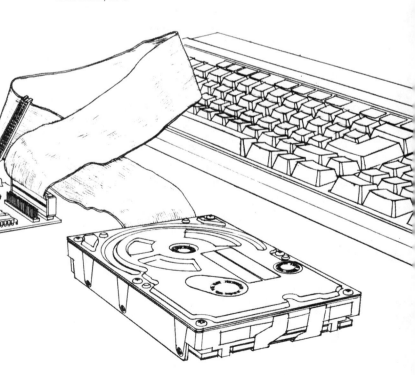

A

F

G

K

N

Q

R

W